Vegan Geographies

Vegan Geographies

Spaces Beyond Violence, Ethics Beyond Speciesism

Paul Hodge, Andrew McGregor, Simon Springer,

Ophélie Véron, and Richard J. White

Lantern Publishing & Media • Brooklyn, NY

2022
Lantern Publishing & Media
128 Second Place
Brooklyn, NY 11231
www.lanternpm.org

Printed in the United States of America

Library of Congress Cataloging-in-Publication Data

Names: Hodge, Paul B., editor.
Title: Vegan geographies : spaces beyond violence, ethics beyond speciesism / [edited by] Paul Hodge, Andrew McGregor, Simon Springer, Ophélie Véron, and Richard J. White.
Description: Brooklyn, NY : Lantern Publishing & Media, [2022]
Identifiers: LCCN 2021028342 (print) | LCCN 2021028343 (ebook) | ISBN 9781590566589 (paperback) | ISBN 9781590566596 (epub)
Subjects: LCSH: Food-supply—Moral and ethical aspects. | Veganism—Moral and ethical aspects. | Veganism—Environmental aspects. | Human geography—Social aspects. | Animal welfare. | Sustainable agriculture. | BISAC: SOCIAL SCIENCE / Human Geography | POLITICAL SCIENCE / Political Ideologies / Anarchism
Classification: LCC HD9000.5 .V39 2022 (print) | LCC HD9000.5 (ebook) | DDC 363.8—dc23
LC record available at https://lccn.loc.gov/2021028342
LC ebook record available at https://lccn.loc.gov/2021028343

CONTENTS

Introduction

ETHICAL VEGANISM FOR MORE CRITICAL GEOGRAPHIES

Richard J. White, Ophélie Véron, Simon Springer, Andrew McGregor, and Paul Hodge

Veganism as an ethic and a practice has a recorded history dating back to Antiquity. Yet it is only recently that researchers have begun the process of formalizing the study of veganism. Scholars who examine this theory and phenomenon are usually situated in sociology, history, philosophy, cultural studies, or critical animal studies. The centrality and contested nature of place in the actions and discourse of animal exploitation and liberation, however, suggest an inherently spatial praxis. As an illustration of the former, consider those billions of animals raised on factory farms and killed in slaughterhouses each year. Interrogating the geographies of these places, we can acknowledge how the animals' lives are contained within private, windowless buildings (that are, therefore, impossible to look into) and are themselves located in relatively peripheral spaces. We may equally consider the millions of animals routinely used for "scientific" experiments on university campuses. Where are these captive animals held? Where do these experiments take place? What quickly becomes clear, of course, is that the impenetrable designs and the concealed, private locations of the factory farm, the slaughterhouse, and the vivisection laboratory are not coincidental. Rather, these realities are entirely deliberate—and absolutely vital if the repertoires of violence that they conceal from public viewing and that inform the animals' experiences of life and death are to continue.

Raising consciousness towards the underexplored spatial praxis of animal liberation and trans-species social justice movements—the desire to live without places of violence (White 2015)—is both timely and important here. As scholar-activists identifying with veganism, we seek to underscore what geographers can contribute to our understanding of critical veganism and vegan praxis in this context. As underlined by Harper (2010b, pp. 5–6), "veganism is not just about the abstinence of animal consumption; it is about the ongoing struggle to produce socio-spatial epistemologies of consumption that lead to cultural and spatial change." While an interest in humanity's domination over nonhuman animals has gained momentum within critical geography circles in the last two decades (Wolch & Emel 1995; Philol & Wilbert 2000; Emel et al., 2002; Gillespie & Collard 2015; White 2015), the scarcity of available literature highlights the need for geographers to further reflect on vegan activism and the vegan practice.

Through focusing on vegan geographies, we direct attention towards the spatialization of activism—involving confrontation politics oriented to alleviating spaces of suffering, as well as more generative practices seeking to prefigure more convivial worlds.

Spaces of suffering are contested through protest, boycott, the act of bearing witness, and the politicization of consumption practices and commodity chains in order to expose and overturn human and nonhuman suffering. At the same time, new spaces are nurtured through practices of care and compassion, involving animal sanctuaries, vegan agriculture, and vegan food spaces and collectives. The spatial dimensions of veganism, though rarely considered in the literature, provide insights into how veganism is contesting and transforming urban and rural spaces. Vegan geography also looks across space and scale, exploring the appropriateness of vegan ethics in diverse social and cultural groups and within the broader neoliberal economic and political frameworks that seek to commodify and marketize the movement. Finally, vegan geographies fundamentally challenge outdated but still dominant human/nature dualisms that underpin widespread suffering and ecological degradation; they provide practical and accessible pathways for people interested in challenging contemporary systems and working collectively towards less destructive worlds. In highlighting these understudied spatial elements of veganism, this collection will considerably bolster knowledge about the practices of veganism in a time of rapidly growing public interest, while providing the foundations for a new, innovative, and much needed subfield within the discipline of geography.

Why Intersectionality?

The failure to recognize, contemplate, and respond to the position of the animal Other is the Achilles heel of the majority of the work being done under the banner of "critical" geography today. From the perspective of what we are calling *vegan geographies*, it is difficult to understand how critical geographers can speak of overwriting and erasure with regards to categories of oppression such as those based on gender, race, and ability, and then be entirely dismissive or largely unsympathetic with respect to another category, namely that based on species. Critical geographers have an excellent track record of bringing focus to racism, sexism, homophobia, transphobia, and ableism, which are all without question critically important areas deserving of our collective attention. To recognize that certain individuals are made "other" owing to their supposed underdevelopment or deviation from the normativity of white male positionality and, importantly, to organize against this and push back in ways that inspire and connect with activists have been the primary contribution that critical geographies have made over the past three decades. The imperative has been to acknowledge as fully human those who are marginalized. But what if, in the process of creating all of this positive energy and manifesting these efforts of inclusion, we had been wearing a particular set of blinders that led us in a direction decidedly premised upon exclusion? What specifically does it mean to question the category of "human" and the sanctity that is assigned to this particular mode of being? What does it mean to privilege the human—and how does such privilege make way for various forms of domination and supremacy? In light of all we know about evolution and the arbitrary nature of taxonomies, binaries, and dichotomies, why does "humanness" pervade as the measure of our ethics and empathy?

As critical geographers make the step towards greater inclusion of all members of our human family, regardless of color, religion, sexuality, ability, gender identity, geographical location, or age, there has been a peculiar reticence to take the next step, which is to acknowledge that the othering we bear witness to occurs precisely because the "Other" is in some capacity rendered bestial (Spiegel 1996; Taylor 2017; Ko & Ko 2017; Brueck 2019). This reticence is also evident within critical animal geographies. We ask, Is not all othering in this world structured upon the contestation of what it means to be human, and, thus, upon the nonhuman as an absent referent? Yet the animal Other is rarely brought into focus; instead, the discipline of geography has moved in such a direction that insists on the centering of the category of human. While we have seen the rise of animal geographies, critical animal geographies, and more-than-human geographies, it is at the species level that our "critical" capacities as geographers seemingly break down (though see Yandaarra et al. below for an example of Indigenous geographies). As the human/nonhuman binary is continually examined and called into question, geographers seem content with describing different relations and forms of agency in insightful ways, but often lack a political commitment to improving the lives of those being described. This "unpacking" is of limited value without an ethical imperative behind it. Surely, the otherness of animals intersects with other categories of alterity.

Consider, for example, how female cows are forcibly inseminated and spend their lives hooked up to machines that not only extract their milk, but also cause trauma to their udders, causing these to bleed, develop sores, and expunge puss, all to ensure that humans have the milk. If the victims in question were human, we would use a different language to describe the situation. We would immediately categorize it as torture. From a feminist perspective, why, beside as a result of Kathryn Gillespie's vital interventions with *The Cow with Ear Tag #1389*, are we not affronted by this gendered violence that is being meted out against sentient female bodies? Similarly, what about violence against nonhuman animal children, like male chicks who are fed into grinders as "externalities" of egg production, which doesn't grant them the same ostensibly "ethical" kill protocols as it does adult chickens? Here, gender, age, and species converge in such a way that unleashes some of the grisliest violence we could possibly imagine, but the intersectionality of such experiences is almost entirely ignored by some of our "critical" colleagues. One who insists upon its inclusion is met sometimes with derision, typically with apathy, or worse yet, with an uncomfortable, dismissive laughter and patronizing attitude that would surely be familiar to most feminist scholars who have made claims about gender in unwelcoming, male-dominated academic spaces.

When Worldviews Collide

Vegans are confronted with the geography of their views when they come into contact with nonvegans, which, of course, is a daily occurrence for most vegans. Things get even more complicated when those encounters are with people from different cultural backgrounds, particularly those who hold entirely different worldviews. Vegan ideals have sometimes been critiqued for not being reconcilable with the epistemologies and ontologies of many Indigenous peoples. A position that views life as integral, for example, would appreciate that all life feeds on other life, so to suggest that humans should not kill or eat other animals is to perpetuate a certain form of human exceptionalism. While life inevitably feeds on life, the question for vegans becomes how to respond to this acknowledgement in an ethical way. To determine an answer to this question requires reflection on the situatedness of the individual, which is indicative of an embodied geography. Not every individual, whether driven by ethics *or* spirituality, is necessarily going to have a range of both vegan and nonvegan choices available to them. But it is precisely the issue of suffering that becomes central to responding to such a dilemma, and for vegans, there exists an explicit desire to reduce to the greatest extent possible the felt sorrow, misery, and grief in the taking of another life. One can adhere to such principles, we argue, and still maintain respect for Indigenous peoples' food practices that embody their own ethical honoring of nonhuman kin.

The oppression of factory farming, whereby animals become cogs in a violent machine, is a far cry from the ways in which Indigenous peoples relate in and to the world. Treating them as moral equivalents only muddies the waters and ignores the ways in which knowledge is situated. Of course, some vegans are self-righteous in their outlook and even dogmatic in their attempt to enforce a single way of being. However, as geographers sensitive to Indigenous knowledges and to spatial difference, we do not adopt this universalist outlook in our approach here. Instead, we understand that there are very different sets of relations at play when it comes to large-scale, industrial factory farming on the one hand and small-scale Indigenous kin relationality on the other—space, place, scale, and temporality matter. But such a recognition is also not a repugnant "noble savage" argument that fixes Indigenous peoples in time. Indeed, it is important to recognize that there are Indigenous and other marginalized people (both scholars and activists) who support and promote veganism. The point, then, is to acknowledge that ethics is always situated in both space and time, and to focus on the particularity of circumstances, but with a relational outlook that also considers structural factors. When it comes to challenging institutions that perpetuate suffering, we need to see the micro and the macro, the near and the far, and the self and the other to chart a path towards an ethic of accountability that is itself ethical. In short, receiving our sustenance from the land as a gift from the universe is not the same as expecting and extracting it from the mechanization of animal bodies in factory farms.

Vegan practices are similarly critiqued as deriving from Western white middle-class positionalities detached from the everyday struggles of malnourished populations in the majority world. We are asked, "How can you tell someone who doesn't have enough to eat not to eat meat?" as if this exception somehow proved the rule that justified the decision of the non-malnourished person with plentiful food choices in the West to consume animal flesh. Of course, vegan geographers do not advocate that people should starve rather than eat meat; however, advocating for the closure of industrialized animal farming and a shift to vegan diets is a form of political action that, if successful, would alleviate pressure on food systems and ultimately mean more resources available to food-insecure communities. Animal farming is an incredibly resource-intensive and inefficient way of producing food. We also do not accept the claim that veganism is elitist and inaccessible for diverse social groups. It would be wrong to associate the plant-based consumerism centered on health and wellbeing that appeals to a certain middle-class demographic with the political forms of veganism we are promoting here. For us, veganism is a political commitment centered on multispecies justice and the abolition of factory farming. In this sense, it has much in common with the environmental justice principles developed by communities of color in the Americas. Indeed, it is the wealthiest countries and wealthiest groups in society, not the majority, that eat the most meat and cause the most animal suffering.

Diversions, Dilemmas, and Deceptions

In the everyday routines that shape our lives, ethical choices are usually relatively straightforward and easy to navigate. That's not to say that challenges don't arise, because they most certainly do, but on the whole, most vegans are never presented with the wild scenarios that nonvegans often subject them to. You would likely be hard-pressed to find a vegan alive today who hasn't been challenged by attempts to undermine their ethical choices in the form of questions such as, "Would you eat meat if you were trapped on a desert island?" or, "If you had to eat a squirrel or a human child, who would you eat?" Putting aside the utter preposterousness of these questions, which proceed from a logical fallacy, we may note that nonvegan people are rarely subjected to such an interrogation. That said, if we were to entertain the absurd for a moment, you also wouldn't find many people, vegan or otherwise, who would choose to spare the squirrel's life before that of the child. Ultimately, is one life more valuable than the other? In the grand scheme of things, a non-speciesist response would have to be no. So, does this make vegans hypocrites? Not at all. It merely makes us humans, who often struggle with ethics when under duress. It also reveals the paradox of ethics, which is itself geographical, as the provision of empathy almost always adheres to proximity to the notion of self. We care more about those we know and those who reflect us, which, of course, is a reflection of both privilege and prejudice. Fortunately, such difficult scenarios do not reflect the typical choices we are presented with in everyday life, wherein decisions are usually much easier to make.

The more interesting question in all of this, though, is why such do-or-die situations are always presented to people advocating for animal liberation. Would it not be offensive to pose the same questions in terms of race? With all else being equal, who would you save from drowning, the brown kid or the white kid? How about someone else's kid or your own kid? These are insensitive questions that are intended to make us uncomfortable. They force us to confront our prejudices but, thankfully, don't really reflect the reality of our everyday lives. Few of us face such dire situations, and most often, life presents us with contexts in which we have the ability to choose to empathize with and care about more than a single party. Ultimately, in the same way that we can make a choice to operate in less oppressive modes and create more egalitarian relations with other people, so, too, do we have a choice in how we engage with the animal Other. At the current moment, for many, particularly those of us living with various forms of privilege, that means we have a choice in the food we eat. We can actively refuse to consume food that is fundamentally rooted in the perpetuation of suffering. This ethic of care extends to both the nonhuman animals and the humans who are used to produce that food. So, as ethical vegans, we should think intersectionally and care as much about the cows who are killed in the slaughterhouse as we do about the workers who are being exploited by being subjected and desensitized to the horrific violence that their job entails.

Occasionally, sanctimonious nonvegans take pleasure in undermining vegans' ethical choices by raising the deceptive question of plant lives—and of vegans' supposed "callousness" towards this particular form of life. Of course, this is a red herring argument because if one really cared about plants, they would still choose veganism, inasmuch as fewer plants are killed to sustain a vegan diet than to sustain a meat-based diet. As Frances Moore Lappé (1971) argued many years ago, intensive animal farms are like protein factories in reverse, due to the massive amounts of plant material and plant protein required to produce a small quantity of meat. Animal farming also requires much more land, thus being a key driver of deforestation, land degradation, and water pollution and affecting a much wider range of animal and plant species than do more spatially constrained—albeit still problematic—forms of cropping. More importantly, though, given where our relationship with animals is thanks to factory farming, we think refusing veganism on the basis that "plant lives matter" is like saying that "all lives matter" in the face of systemic violence against people of color. Of course all lives matter, just as plants matter, but we are at a political juncture where it is imperative to shine a light on systematic, institutionalized violence and oppression. At this moment, it is Black and Brown bodies that are subjected to the worst experiences of violence within our own species, and it is enslaved animals in factory farms who are at the blunt edge of our malevolence beyond the human family. It is vital that we engage in an intersectional politics of refusal that reflects these truths.

You Can Be Lionhearted, but You'll Never Be a Lion

Of the various diversions that some nonvegans present to vegans, perhaps as a means to assuage the guilt and remorse they feel deep down, the question of what animals eat is the most interesting. People often compare themselves to lions, as opposed to gazelles, even though our evolutionary proximity to each as a species is approximately the same. It is a curious choice that reflects a politics of human supremacy. Humans tend to want to imagine themselves as exceptional and so position themselves as apex predators, rather than as prey. In these instances, people, including otherwise critical scholars, have a tendency to invoke "nature" and "instinct" that we should know well is extremely problematic. When these same cyphers are used with respect to race, gender, or age, we know that they do not constitute a valid line of argument; the same is true with respect to species. It is neither a necessity nor an instinct for humans to eat the flesh of animals. It is learned behavior and it can be unlearned. We are not lions, or gazelles, or salamanders, or bumble bees, for that matter. We don't make any other choices in our lives, certainly not ethical ones, by mirroring the patterns and behaviors of other species. Geese and dolphins regularly engage in sexual coercion and domination—what humans would call rape—but this is not a measure for how humans should negotiate sexual activity.

The bottom line is that culture and technology have moved us beyond this dichotomy of predator and prey. Whereas most animals do not have a choice in what they eat, in contrast, many humans actually do. So, for these humans, the ethical imperative comes from a personal place—we can either choose to literally have an animal suffer and die for us to satisfy our own desires or, alternatively, recognize our potential to mitigate suffering and death by making a different food choice. Human physiology allows us to be perfectly healthy when we abstain from consuming other animals, and given what we know about how industrial factory farming contributes to climate change on a monumental and devastating scale, refusing to eat the flesh of factory-farmed animals is indirectly refusing to cause the death of many more creatures, including animals, plants, and humans.

Vegans proceed from the perspective that our ethics should always be aligned with doing the least harm, whatever our positionalities or circumstances. Such an ethical situatedness is of course going to manifest in different ways, at different times and places. But right now, for those of us who live in industrialized societies and have a choice, which means most of you reading this, the systemic violence of the factory farming model, upon examination, makes clear what we ought to do. Factory farming is a unique and horrifying institution of oppression that operates on an unfathomable scale, intersecting with all of our lives in myriad ways. Over a billion unseen, uncared-for chickens are slaughtered every week. Why, then, is something so consequential to the health of our communities and our planet as a whole not a primary site of interrogation for critical geographers? Where are the outraged voices of rural geographers, food geographers, environmental geographers, and even animal geographers, calling for changes to systematic processes of violence and oppression? Just as geography was complicit in colonial expansion and the exploitation of different peoples and places, is its current silence indicative of the discipline's complicity in the ongoing exploitation of nonhuman animals and spaces?

The absence of reaction is a terrifying indication of the general apathy. If we can't get those who are trained to think and act bravely in service of social justice to care, what hope do we have? If those who pride themselves on being able to recognize othering and to contest the domination that comes with it cannot acknowledge the most fundamental form of these processes—that involving the animal Other—perhaps critical geography itself is irredeemable. While we are angered by the contemporary indifference of our discipline, we hope that this work will help spark within the field of geography the same force of change that feminists ignited four decades ago to challenge gender oppression. Fifty years from now (see Véron's afterword), we hope to be able to look back on this volume and the assembled contributions as a pivotal moment in the transformation of critical geographical scholarship, whereby the animal Other will have finally, once and for all, been placed at the center of our collective analyses.

Structure of the Book

Drawing attention to the ever-increasing number of farmed animals, as well as to human exploitation and environmental degradation, the opening chapter, by Richard White, addresses head-on the inconvenient truths that bedevil the celebrated rise of contemporary "veganism." The aim of the chapter is to find tangible ways to revive and reassert the unapologetically radical praxis that veganism stands for. To this end, five key ideas are explored. The first is to uphold the grounds upon which veganism was originally founded and defined. Plant-based consumerism—which is in the ascendency at this time—is not and never will be veganism, and this distinction must be made abundantly clear. Second is White's impassioned call for a resurgent vegan-anarchist geographical praxis, one that carries the promise of extending the geographies of nonviolence, beauty, and freedom ever further and ever deeper. The third idea focuses on vegan imaginaries and the importance of continually challenging pejorative stereotypes about who vegans are and what they eat, and other everyday excuses about the difficulty of "going vegan." Fourth is the importance of raising consciousness of the dark truths about the inherent violence of the meat and dairy industries—indeed, all forms of animal (ab)use—and contrasting these with the ethical geographies that motivate and animate veganism. Fifth, and finally, the chapter ends by arguing that veganism entails an unfolding commitment to and responsibility towards ending all forms of exploitation and aligns itself with a politics of total liberation.

The second chapter, by Alex Lockwood, focuses attention on slaughterhouses and the acts of solidarity performed by the Animal Save Movement activists towards the nonhuman animals being trucked into these facilities. Animal Save Movement activists in over twenty countries bear witness as nonhuman animals are transported into slaughterhouses; attempt to relieve their suffering momentarily (with water); and bring awareness to their plight through video footage, imagery, and testimony, with the goal of convincing others to practice veganism. Critics have suggested such activism is "useless" in that it does not "save" the particular animals in the trucks. This chapter responds by drawing attention to the effects of the heightened encounters and embodied contacts that take place in the charged spaces outside the slaughterhouse gates. While critiques of activism are necessary for an understanding of its contribution to the goal of ending nonhuman exploitation, this chapter counters that acts of bearing witness are useful practices in that they trouble the power relations that the particular spatial orientation of the slaughterhouse sets in place. The vigils politicize the logic of human domination of nonhuman others on the (often literal) verges between everyday life and industrial locations of nonhuman bodily appropriation. Employing autoethnography and the author's experience participating in vigils with Animal Save Movement activists, this chapter interrogates concepts of ethical responsibility to propose the idea of a "useful uselessness" in relation to animal activism, noting how it opens out the otherwise highly controlled and overlooked spaces of material entanglement between human and nonhuman at the intersection of slaughterhouse and public way.

In the third chapter, Mona Seymour contends that the intersections of veganism and food systems are perhaps most visible in activism against the use and treatment of animals in industrial agriculture and in the promotion of and adherence to diets that are based on plants, rather than on animal bodies and products. Yet veganism as a commitment to the rejection of violence against and exploitation of sentient beings, Seymour argues, must inform all stages, spaces, and practices of our food systems. This chapter therefore brings veganism to bear on an underexplored question on the production side of the food system: How does veganism inform agriculture beyond stipulating that it must not involve the farming of animals? What is vegan agriculture? The chapter expands on the few existing definitions of vegan agriculture by developing a set of guidelines that may characterize it. Seymour draws upon existing vegan farming standards, vegan and critical animal studies perspectives, and conversations with vegan farmers to describe how growers may practice a commitment to veganism in agricultural spaces. A case study from the U.S. veganic farming movement helps to illustrate how some of these guidelines may be enacted and what some of the ethical questions that may arise are as veganism is borne out in agricultural spaces. Ultimately, this chapter suggests what the base of a vegan food system may look like.

Reaching a similar conclusion on the question of context, though anchored around place-based knowledges, Yandaarra including Aunty Shaa Smith, Neeyan

Smith, Lara Daley, Paul Hodge, and Sarah Wright offer in Chapter Four a deeply relational account of yirraal (food). Their chapter describes the way human and more-than-human beings and co-becomings of Gumbaynggirr Country (Mid North Coast, New South Wales, Australia) are in relationships of care and responsibility, as well as the way food knowledges and practices embody an ethic of continual giving and relationality. From their different positionalities, the authors reflect on their relationships—as Gumbaynggirr and non-Gumbaynggirr people, vegans and nonvegans—through food, attending to the way food emerges as ceremony and connection, imbricated in both colonization and survivance. Sharing their collective and individual stories of coming into relationship with garlaany (pippies, or clams), the Golden Hole, and guuna (shit), the authors offer place-based examples of what it means to persist, continue, and create in colonizing and decolonizing times through yirraal. Practices of ngurrajili ("continued giving") around yirraal honor more-than-human co-becomings and, for the non-Gumbaynggirr vegan authors, involve coming into relationship with garlaany, fish, or hunted animals as ceremony. For Aunty Shaa, to center relationships and honor protocols is to embody the "practical work" of knowing one's place while refusing separation and ongoing colonial violence.

In Chapter Five, Catherine Oliver redefines the animal Other of the archive, posing confronting questions about the failure of animal geographies and other activisms to address the Being/Thing distinction in our relationships with and representations of animals. Advocating a rejection of the animal-Beings/animal-Things binary, Oliver instead looks to a spectral "in-between" in order to reposition anti-speciesist veganism as deeply political, ethical, and social. Drawing on archival material, the chapter operates in the speculative mode of "as if" and "beyond"—the latter used as a way of imagining past archives and animals themselves, the former mobilized to breach spatial, temporal, and species differences to renegotiate our shared futures. For Oliver, archival encounters and relational histories open up new imaginings of the spaces and beings/things existing beyond them, thereby challenging anthropocentrism. In these discussions, veganism is thus situated in relation to animal rights movements, to their failures and their histories; it is argued that vegan scholarship must necessarily construct animals as between animal-Being and animal-Thing, as a political and ethical impetus for us to imagine and, thus, enact vegan futures. Oliver argues that veganism may be the first means by which we enact our as-if, but it cannot be the only one. There has to be thoughtful and careful consideration in, between, and beyond our present, human entanglements with animals.

The sixth chapter, by Simon Springer, addresses the challenges of what he calls *anthroprivilege*, which is positioned as overwhelmingly pervasive in our contemporary world. What Springer means by anthroprivilege are the social norms that reinforce anthropocentrism and confer automatic, unearned benefits upon human individuals. For Springer, anthroprivilege is encapsulated in the dismissal of the animal Other as "other" and the implications this has for questions of race, gender, sexuality, or other positionalities for which privilege and normativity are key spheres of struggle. Anthroprivilege is fundamentally made possible by such an aversion to reflecting critically on human positionality and the intersectionality of the category of species within frames of understanding of social justice. Springer argues that anthroprivilege, as with all forms of privilege, is undergirded and enabled by a deep cognitive dissonance, even outright denial. Yet the implications of anthroprivilege are no mere thought experiment. Instead, he argues that anthroprivilege is a tangible and demonstrable planetary scourge, for it forms the foundations of human supremacy. For Springer, it is only through anthroprivilege that processes like extractivism, climate destruction, and factory farming become possible. The consequence of such hubris is simple. If we don't begin to get this profound sense of human entitlement in check, it will ultimately undo us as a species.

Chapter Seven advances a more empirical application of Springer's notion of anthroprivilege. Here, Hannah C. Gunderman looks at vegan landscapes within the urban environment as standing in stark contrast to an exponentially growing foodie trend, a fine-dining subculture that transforms the consumption of food from a necessity to a hobby. Characterized by foods that are high-priced, garnished with supplementary animal products, and accessible mainly within whitewashed landscapes, the foodie movement, Gunderman argues, supports spatially exclusive divisions within a city. Foodie landscapes are consequently ones of gross anthroprivilege in that the culture, which highlights the excessive use of bacon, animal fats, and dairy products, translates to intersecting layers of violence and exploitation. This creates a food landscape built upon the suffering of both humans (slaughterhouse workers, farm workers, and consumers who suffer the negative health consequences of many foodie dishes) and nonhuman animals. With this in mind, Gunderman conducts an analysis of foodie culture in three cities across the world, highlighting how each city's vegan landscape provides a more ethical consumption option. For each city, there exists a vibrant vegan culture that stands in ethical and moral contestation to the landscapes of foodie exclusion present in the city's foodscape. Gunderman's analysis sets the stage for recommendations of practical actions that intersectional vegan activists can use to combat this foodie movement, which turns violence into landscapes of luxury.

Chapter Eight is co-authored by Zoei Sutton and Nik Taylor. Their chapter considers how critical vegan analyses of the spatial practices of companion-animal "ownership" can expose, problematize, and seek to change hierarchical relationships between humans and the companion species they purport to love and care for. Sutton and Taylor draw attention to how animals-as-pet-commodities, prized for their "liveliness" yet often denied the agency to truly "live" (Collard 2014), occupy a subordinate position in the home and how this reflects the subordinate position of nonhuman species in society more generally. In this context, the authors show how an affective framing of human–companion animal relationships enabled by an anthropocentric focus poses a challenge to any critical questioning of pet commodities and human entanglements with them. In response to this, they posit that critical animal geographies, by examining the spaces and places in which human–animal entanglements occur, are well positioned to identify taken-for-granted "spatial imaginaries" that contribute to the continued oppression of animals (Gillespie & Collard 2015). The chapter makes visible the asymmetrical power dynamics in human–companion-animal relationships through an examination of the spatial orderings of the home with respect to the "inside" and "outside." Here, Sutton and Taylor argue that the spatial praxis of human–companion animal relations presents an impediment to animal agency through the prevention of motion and the "potential presence of force." In doing so, the authors persuasively capture the complex dynamic between place, space, and power as it emerges in relationships wherein power dynamics between species are assumed to be minimal.

In Chapter Nine, Andrew McGregor focuses attention on the environmental impacts of animal agriculture and calls for a reorientation of environmentalism to be in line with vegan principles. The chapter argues that Western environmentalism is facing an existential crisis associated with the loss of nature, both biophysically and conceptually, in a world that is undergoing intense planetary upheaval. A core driver of this change is the industries linked to animal agriculture, but they have rarely been the focus of environmental action, which is in many places still rooted in romantic but outdated concepts of the wilderness. McGregor draws on a case study of Australian animal agriculture to expose the violence inflicted on human and nonhuman animals and environments, as well as the urgent need for environmental groups to engage with these industries. The chapter cautions against the uptick of high-profile, ecomodernist responses that reinstate human/nature dualisms and can result in an intensification of pain and suffering for more-than-human communities; instead, it advocates a more caring, ecofeminist-inspired environmentalism. The chapter concludes by promoting contextual veganism as the most caring and effective way to reinvigorate and reorient Western environmentalism in the context of Anthropocene change.

The tenth chapter is by Darren Chang, who identifies some limitations of traditional farmed animal sanctuaries (FASes) in moving us towards animal liberation. Specifically, he argues, most FASes are currently forced to exist in rural areas or "agricultural zones" and therefore do not challenge the speciesist segregation laws that ban terrestrial farmed animals from living in urban spaces. The non-presence of farmed animals in urban environments, therefore, not only makes them invisible to most of the humans who consume them and reinforces their status as lower-class animals, but it also forecloses opportunities for them to radically alter their relations with human urbanites. Drawing on lessons from the human sanctuary city movements that seek to offer refuge to asylum seekers, on theories of nonhuman animal resistance, as well as on stories of farmed animals living in cities against bylaws that prohibit their residence, Chang explores and imagines how farmed animals and their human accomplices could dismantle speciesist segregation through direct action and civil disobedience. He argues that to successfully bring farmed animals into urban spaces, human activists could dwell and organize together, prefigure just relationships, and build solidarity networks between urban farmed animals and traditional FASes. Finally, Chang makes the suggestion that establishing a farmed animal presence could be a crucial step in the struggle to create animal-friendly, anti-speciesist cities.

In Chapter Eleven, Marco Reggio asks, Do nonhuman animals resist? In addressing this question, Reggio argues two related points: first, that nonhuman animals do indeed resist, that their resistance opens up new ways of thinking about configurations of space and what constitutes "language" and "politics"; and secondly, that forms of veganism that refuse species privilege, and in so doing recognize nonhuman animals as active subjects, embody a "multispecies solidarity"—not by speaking for animals, but by speaking with and as them. Describing nonhuman animal escape and rebellion as examples of active subjectivity, Reggio confronts human-centered ideas of what defines "resistance," making important interventions on issues of animal agency and power, of animal space and its performativity. To explore these themes, the chapter draws on critical geographies and decolonial scholarship highlighting that one of the most important challenges for a liberatory movement for animals is to imagine communities of resistance in which human solidarity expresses itself concretely, starting from a deep questioning of species privilege. Veganism as a "decolonizing of diet," Reggio suggests, provides the solidaristic link with nonhuman resistance as multispecies solidarity is manifested as criticism of the modern production system, a criticism that underlines the articulation of social inequalities, human exploitation, and environmental destruction along neocolonial lines.

David Fazzino emphasizes—in Chapter Twelve—the importance of looking beyond vegan labeling to eat ethically, as human and nonhuman suffering can be hidden in all sorts of food commodities. While the suffering is readily apparent when animal flesh is front and center on the plate, knowledge of the production processes of other commodities is becoming essential to avoiding animal suffering for ethical vegans. This chapter expands the existing ethical sphere of vegan diets by considering the processes of grain, fruit, and vegetable production. The ultimate question is, What does it mean to produce vegan food and to be a vegan farmer? Specifically, Fazzino explores the ethics of creating compassionate cuisine by considering the ecological, economic, and ethical aspects of cultivating vegan foods in the context of a continuum from industrial to artisanal production. To make his argument, Fazzino reflects on his own experiences as a farmer and educator, reviews existing farming literature, and observes trends in agricultural production and marketing.

In Chapter Thirteen, Jennifer Mateer argues that vegan geographies demand the decentering of anthropocentric ideas and practices, as well as a refocus on the agency and affect of more-than-human beings. To fit with the goals of vegan geographies, the author explores the political lives of animals as a method of decentering human political activities, examining animal life through the concepts of *Bios*, *Zoe*, and *Homo Sacer*. *Zoe* is often defined as "animal life" or "bare life," meaning that a human individual is alive (sleeping, eating, performing essential functions, etc.) but lacks the ability to remake society. *Bios* refers to political life—how humans can participate in and restructure society. For example, in our current era, citizenship is a necessary pillar of *Bios*, since it allows one to vote and actively reshape society. The *Homo Sacer* is an individual who at one time held *Bios* but has now been punished by having said *Bios* removed. Mateer discusses how the political agency of animals can disrupt the anthropocentric *Bios*, *Zoe*, and *Homo Sacer* categories, refocusing on the ways in which nonhumans can and do reshape society and, therefore, often are more closely aligned with the *Homo Sacer* rather than the *Zoe*. This discussion is one avenue for Mateer's argument that we can reconnect more-than-human actors to political subjectivities in the hopes of undoing the violence that often befalls them with impunity. More broadly, then, for Mateer, vegan geographies provide the opportunity for animals to regain their *Bios* by reconnecting these actors to non-stigmatized narratives and recognizing their political activities.

In the last full chapter, Chapter Fourteen, Jérôme Lafitte and Nicolas Maestripieri argue in favor of a vegan geography. Here, veganism is treated as a protean movement with a certain radicality, one that questions the relationship between humans and nonhumans. This, Lafitte and Maestripieri contend, reinforces the hypercomplexity of the social sphere, especially with regards to environmental and climate changes in the Anthropocene era. Crucially, this chapter asks how, under conditions of monumental flux, a humanimal geography that takes into account a vegan perspective is able to shed light on the relational issues between the carnist system and environmental changes in a heuristic manner. For Lafitte and Maestripieri, an anarchist perspective highlights the system of anthroparchal or human-determined domination to produce a critical reading of our relationship with animals, who are typically considered, through a consumerist lens, as domestic "products." The authors aim to link the extreme ontological scales of the human and nonhuman animals to the world and propose a synthesis on a planetary and continental scale. Lafitte and Maestripieri then focus on the anthroparchal system by examining the emblematic spaces and the spatialities attached to it, such as farms and the inside of slaughterhouses. Finally, they highlight the spatial and discursive practices that are part of the horizon of resistance to the anthroparchy.

The collection is completed by an afterword in which Ophélie Véron imagines what the world would look like fifty years from now if the new spaces, places, and practices advocated in this book were to be realized. Writing from a world where animal exploitation is on the verge of being totally abolished and where veganism is becoming the norm, she traces the history of events that led to such an evolution. She explains the reasons the world went meat-free, from climate change and zoonotic pandemics to autonomous politics, and the challenges that still lie ahead in the struggle to dismantle the legacy of speciesism. An attempt to provide a ray of hope and inspiration based on critical thought, this creative piece highlights the need for efforts towards animal liberation, and towards environmental and social justice to be made outside the parameters of contemporary neoliberal, statist politics. Half measures and cosmetic changes won't help build a more socially just and environmentally sustainable society, Véron argues; only structural changes will.

Conclusion: Towards Geography's Ethical Horizon

Well-trodden paths of human behavior should not be the measure of the ethical horizons we, as geographers, operate by. For example, humans have practiced slavery at many times, in many places throughout history, but no serious geographer would advocate its practice today. We acknowledge the violence, the exploitation, and the devaluation of sentient life. It seems utterly bizarre, then, that our food choices obscure similar ethical considerations. If sustenance is merely considered sustenance, as a "natural" fact with no ethical choices behind it and no consequences, it opens up a whole host of difficult problems, not least of which is the question of capitalist consumption and how "other" humans entrapped in exploitative labor relations produce the food we eat. Critical geographical scholarship implores us to care about these others and their corporeal wellbeing; but caring about nonhuman animals, unless we are talking about "pets" (but not pet food), is often a bridge too far. Some may contend that the privileging of the human capacity for choice is a problem in itself and that this creates a certain kind of exceptionalism. But this is a strange way to frame the question of ethics when in other contexts we take ethical choices, like the choice not to keep enslaved people, for granted.

Historically, in various times and places, humans have chosen to practice cannibalism, which is arguably even more taboo than slavery; however, this is not an eating habit that many geographers would condone, precisely owing to the ethical implications. Given the number of humans in the world, we would seem like a pretty reliable and easy food source, if we were to choose to take that route. Of course, this suggestion should offend everyone reading. It opens a proverbial can of worms that brings all the hierarchies and divisions among humans into sharp relief. Whom would we eat? How would we decide who lives and who dies? On what basis would some groups be spared and others not? We would have to enslave certain people and establish something like factory farms to produce and process them on a mass scale. We would have to rebrand their dismembered and mutilated body parts in clever ways—as with "pork chops" or "ground beef"—so that we don't have to think too much about what it actually is that we are consuming. Of course, the hierarchies in our thinking with respect to other species are pervasive, though our understandings are geographically and temporally disparate and diffuse. Some of us will eat cows, while others will not. Or how about dogs? There're lots of them around. Why is it that we don't eat them in the so-called "West" but employ xenophobic narratives of savagery to talk about those in the "East" who do? The answer is found not in "nature" but in culture, something that is infinitely malleable and influenced by societal values, preferences, and choices.

Without question, we do actually use the human capacity for choice all the time as reliable grounds for an ethic of reducing harm. Extending the principle of harm reduction to the lives of others is what ethics is all about, whether that "other" is a child, a person of a different ethnic background or a different gender, or a nonhuman animal. Such an extension of our ethics should be made even if our empathy runs counter to the prevailing normative trend. After all, isn't intersectionality fundamentally a recognition of the ways in which all forms of oppression and exclusion of the "other" converge under identical—or at least very similar—sets of justifications, rationalizations, and apologia? If so, in an effort to realize a more complete version of intersectionality, we should care about the overwriting, subordination, and/or erasure of the oppression of nonhuman animals. But we also need to start thinking through the culminating impact of multiple categories of oppression by considering what it means to be a human in concert with what it means to be a nonhuman animal.

Acknowledgment of the animal Other is presently on the horizon of geography's ethical vista. Most geographers know it is there, and some can even see it far off in the distance. What we need to do now is start preparing ourselves for the journey towards it—not merely a brief sojourn in the form of a single volume, but a long-term disciplinary commitment to appreciating, understanding, and exploring the implications of vegan geographies. Different, much better worlds are possible, worlds that don't involve the mass slaughter of nonhuman animals and the dismal working conditions of abattoirs and factory farms. We strongly believe that geography has something important to offer, if the discipline can grapple with the multiple ethical, political, and social challenges posed by veganism. What could be more worthwhile than working on opposing all forms of oppression, whether against humans or nonhumans? As geographers, we can work towards the realization of new spaces, places, and practices that do not rely on the systematic oppression of Earth others, and we can advocate just transitions for those whose livelihoods are currently entwined with animal exploitation. The difficulty with horizons is that they are always shifting. This realization forever gives geographers something to strive for and write about, so it should not discourage us. If we move towards the current horizon, we can at least be confident in the fact that there will be good friends—who experience the world in profoundly different ways—there to greet us as equals. When we finally come to embrace the animal Other on their terms, we may finally begin to understand that a more egalitarian, empathetic, and emancipatory world can only ever be established by all of us Earthlings, acting together.

1

A CALL FOR VEGAN ANARCHIST GEOGRAPHIES

AND FOUR OTHER WAYS TO REASSERT THE RADICAL PRAXIS OF VEGANISM

Richard J. White

> Veganism can indeed be revolutionary, and we must make it so if we are serious about social change, food sovereignty, earth and nonhuman justice, and human freedom and equity. (Konju 2010)

> Most vegans are not revolutionary in the first place. They simply want to do their part. (Dominick 2015, p. 31)

INTRODUCTION

Tara Sophia Bahna-James (2011, p. 117), in a profound reflection on how art and artists have influenced her "truth-telling" writings about nonhuman animals, observes that:

> Initially of course, it was not the artists who were my teachers, but rather nonhuman animals themselves. These animals did not instruct me on what was amiss in society. Nor did they offer me a solution to the problem that I could understand. What they did was bear witness to their soulfulness and intelligence and to the supreme richness and breadth of their own emotional lives. Since birth, I have watched individuals we call "pets" come into my life and love, smile, play, triumph, ail, grow old, and die. And they taught me the only truth I have ever known—the Oneness of all beings: The certainty of death and the beauty, sanctity, and interconnectedness of life.

In a speciesist society, the desire to teach others the many deep lessons that our fellow *Earthlings* teach us *and* to do so in ways that may effectively transgress speciesist attitudes and their inevitable, catastrophic consequences is a heavy burden to bear. It is a burden, though, that is shared—carried on the shoulders of critical vegan activist-scholars and all those who believe that truth-telling has a unique and important part to play in expressions of interspecies social and spatial justice activism. A firm belief that the pen can be mightier than the sword undoubtedly motivates the hundreds of thousands of words that are spilt in an attempt to catalyze a shamefully indifferent human world into recognizing (and taking positive action to address) "the animal condition." The *animal condition*, understood in the context of the chapter, refers to:

> The actual life situation of most nonhuman animals in human society and culture, as physically and emotionally experienced with its routine repertoire of violence, deprivation, desperation, agony, apathy, suffering, and death. (Quoted in Gillespie & Collard, 2015, p. 20)

Undoubtedly, the last two decades and more of radical literature that has emerged to define and animate the ever-expansive grounds of critical animal studies, and critical animal geographies, stand as a faithful testament to this (Adams 2010, 2015; Best 2009; Donovan & Adams 2007; Gillespie & Collard 2015; Kemmerer 2011; Matsuoka & Sorenson 2018). Such interventions have collectively sought to deepen public awareness and influence hearts and minds in the hope that society evolves more fully and acts in the name of social and spatial justice *for all*. But what difference have they made? Attempts to answer this question invite a growing anxiety and dread to loom large: What if all of the writings dedicated to advancing animal liberation and/or an interspecies ethic of care—however beautiful and eloquent the prose may be—have counted for nothing?

This pensive feeling is exacerbated when we remember that almost twenty-five years have passed since two animal geographers, Wolch and Emel, argued, "the plight of animals worldwide has never been more serious than it is today" (1998, p. xi). That assertion remains as self-evident and true now as it was then, for we—*the human apes*—are capturing, oppressing, degrading, exploiting, and destroying fellow sentient beings more extensively and more violently than we have ever done before (Thibodeau 2019; Wadiwell 2015). This is particularly the case with "farmed animals," who are more numerous than at any other time in human history. The numbers are both staggering and stupefying:

> Globally, more than 65 billion land-based beings are killed to be consumed as food every year, while the water-based other animals killed for food number in the hundreds of billions. The physical and emotional suffering from such horrific treatment experienced by each

> individual being, multiplied by the billions of individual animals who undergo it, results in a degree of severe distress and pain—every second—that defies comprehension. (Nibert 2017, p. xi)

Fueled by a toxic combination of speciesism and capitalism, it would appear that our capacity for—and capability of—wretched cruelty and violence are perhaps the only human traits we can safely claim set us apart from our fellow Earthlings. Yet paradoxically, while other animals continue to be murdered in the millions purely for our gustatory pleasure, it is also true that veganism is enjoying a remarkable surge in popularity and influence in mainstream *Western* cultures and public consciousness. For example, more countries across North America and Western Europe, where "meat" and "dairy" foods have cast a long shadow over diet, are witnessing a rise in the number of people who are consciously choosing to reduce or completely eliminate consumption of animal flesh or animal fluids and other secretions (e.g., eggs). In the United States, for example, people identifying as vegan "grew from 1 percent to 6 percent between 2014 and 2017, a 600-percent increase . . ." (Forgrieve 2018). In Britain, a 350-percent rise in the number of vegans was recorded between 2006 and 2016. This translated to 542,000 people saying they were vegan in 2016 (Hancox 2018). The trend shows no sign of peaking either: by 2018, this number had increased to 600,000, or 1.16 percent of the population (The Vegan Society, n.d.).

The aim of this chapter is to begin to critically address this troubling paradox, one that bedevils the contemporary mainstreaming of veganism in Western society, and to identify tangible ways in which the radical promise of veganism can be reasserted. While far from exhaustive, the chapter proposes five key areas for us to focus on and think through. The starting place is one that follows in the footsteps of Leslie Cross (a key figure in the formation of The Vegan Society, U.K.) over fifty years ago in seeking out an answer to the question, "What is veganism?" (1949, p. 13). In the process, a number of important truths emerge about *why* veganism continues to fall short of its potential to (1) bring new and important forms of interspecies liberation into being and (2) contribute fully to a broader intersectional framework of social and spatial justice activism. Clearing the grounds around veganism in this way is a vital step to take if we were to constructively consider ways in which the radical intent and promise of veganism can yet be reasserted. Invoking a "spirit of revolt" (White et al., 2016), the second key argument makes the case, through vegan-anarchist geographies, for a resurgent veganism as a way to better envisage and enact a both "post-capitalist" and "post-speciesist" future. The third idea is to continue, from where we are now, to increase public awareness about who vegans are, what they eat, and why, in order to create new vegan imaginaries. Fourth, efforts to raise consciousness of the ethics that underpin veganism and of the violence of the meat and dairy industries must continue, particularly at a time when the immense anti-vegan propaganda from these industries is still alive and well. Fifth, and finally, the chapter argues that veganism must not lose sight of "the animal plight" in all its manifestations and that we must continue to embrace and enact a politics of total liberation.

Searching for Veganism in 2022

Whenever the question "What is veganism?" is posed, it is important to remember that countless, anonymous individuals, groups, and communities could be seen as "being vegan" long before the term itself was conceived. Indeed, the word *vegan* was coined only recently, during World War II, in 1944, in Leicester (England) by Donald Watson and his future wife Dorothy Morgan (Stewart & Cole 2020). The Vegan Society was founded in that year, and its first newsletter, *The Vegan News*, was circulated in November. Within five years, a notable (in the context of this chapter) revision of the newsletter's title led to its being known as *The Vegan: Advocating Living without Exploitation* (*The Vegan* 1949). It is this assertion of living in freedom, "without exploitation," that defines the spirit of veganism (and as we will argue later, *anarchism*). As Leslie Cross, a prominent member of the society, observed:

> The word "veganism" is a symbol that stands for a major change, a new mutation comparable to the freeing of the serfs and the freeing of the slaves. Its official definition—"the doctrine that man [sic] should live without exploiting animals"—is accurate, precise and comprehensive, but not always fully understood. This is not as surprising as it might seem, for rarely have nine short words enshrined a reform so massive, the achievement of which would bring a new world and new men [sic] to inhabit it. . . . The simple fact is this: that at rock bottom, veganism is the most recent of the periodic surges which have marked the tide of freedom ever since history began. (1954, p. 9)

By 1979, when The Vegan Society became a formally registered charity, the now most widely recognized definition of veganism was in place, namely as:

> a philosophy and way of living which seeks to exclude—as far as is possible and practicable—all forms of exploitation of, and cruelty to, animals for food, clothing or any other purpose; and by extension,

> promotes the development and use of animal-free alternatives for the benefit of humans, animals and the environment. (The Vegan Society 2014, p. 6)

To those who understand veganism in this way and try to live in accordance with its founding philosophy, there is clearly something fundamentally amiss when an increase in people "identifying as vegan" does not lead to a notable decline in the exploitation of animals (humans included) and the environment. My contention here is that this is *not* a failure of veganism *per se*; rather, it is mostly the consequence of the (successful) appropriation and commodification of veganism in recent years such that they have distorted and deformed veganism entirely. Having outlined the rise of big business to take advantage of "vegan products" and the consequences of this, the chapter will make an argument as to how we can contextualize and frame the plant-based lifestyle trend more appropriately; in addition, it will look to other complementary ways to reanimate the radical praxis and promise of veganism.

The Rise of "Veganism" in Western Society

> Similar to the ballots we cast and the clothes we wear, our diets are statements about the values we hold and the world in which we want to live. (Elder 2019, p. 104)

Business-based analysis of the market for "meat-free" and "dairy-free" foods has identified plant-based diets as a potentially huge growth sector, one ripe for "cashing in on." In this context, veganism and plant-based foods are used interchangeably. For example, under the subheading, "Global brands are riding the vegan wave," Tyler (2019) names billionaire investors such as Jeff Bezos, Sergey Brin, Biz Stone, and Evan Williams among those rushing to invest in vegan start-ups. Many global multinationals are now moving to offering more "vegan" options (including KFC's "The Vegan Burger," McDonald's' "Veggie Dippers," Subway's "Beyond Meatball Marinara"), as are other major companies and supermarket chains. In the U.K., for example:

> Waitrose, Tesco, Asda, Sainsbury's and Marks & Spencer have all recently introduced own-label vegan ranges and products to capitalize on the shift and compete for market share; while on the high street, chains including Wagamama, Pizza Express, Yo Sushi!, Zizzi, Gourmet

> Burger Kitchen, The Real Greek, Las Iguanas and Giraffe are among those advertising a range of vegan options. (Tyler 2019)

At the same time as developing new "vegan" products and creating "vegan" start-ups have become an important strategy of multinationals, their "vegan" portfolios have expanded in other ways. The most significant of these has been the acquisition of smaller, successful "rival" vegan businesses. In recent years, for example, Nestlé USA has acquired Sweet Earth (Nestle 2017), and Unilever, The Vegetarian Butcher (Unilever 2018). What's the problem then? Well, the problem is (at least) threefold, as these parent companies are (1) profiteering from nonhuman animal abuses, (2) profiteering from human abuses, and (3) profiteering from environmental degradation.

Profiteering from Nonhuman Animal Abuses

Far from signifying a golden age for veganism, what we are faced with is an increasingly dominant glut of companies that profit from "vegan" products *and* continue to reap financial reward from their ongoing investment in animal abuse industries. Ethical Consumer (2021) drew critical attention to this strategy, highlighting, among others, Cauldron and Linda McCartney (meat alternatives), Pure and Vitalite (vegan spreads), Swedish Glace (dairy-free ice cream), and Violife (vegan cheese) as "vegan brands" that are now owned by nonvegan companies. The organization argued that of all such parent companies, the best example is the "French multinational Groupe Danone, a company with a 24.4 percent share in the global fresh dairy products market, who in 2016 completed the purchase of WhiteWave Foods, whose brands include Alpro, Provamel and Soya Soleil" (Ethical Consumer 2021). These cases form a particularly egregious demonstration of the moral incoherence of capitalist business and should deeply, deeply trouble every "ethical" vegan who continues to buy from these companies.

Profiteering from Human Abuses

I want to expand a little more on this theme, as it is often conveniently overlooked or ignored by those who position themselves as (strident) social justice activists, but who continue to consume the flesh or drink the milk of other animals. Within critical animal studies and critical animal geographies, for example, the intersectional approach has become an increasingly important lens through which we may understand the interspecies violence and capitalist exploitation present whenever animals are being abused (Cudworth 2015; White & Springer 2018).

While continuing to document the incomprehensible pain, abject terror, and extreme suffering of nonhuman animals, research has also increasingly drawn attention to the financial hardships, mental and physical suffering, and coping strategies of slaughterhouse workers, (see, for example, Johnson et al., 1998). For example, in seeking out the "true cost" of a hamburger, Dillard (2008) found that:

> Common meatpacking injuries [for slaughterhouse employers] range from musculoskeletal injuries, such as tendonitis, carpal tunnel syndrome, and white finger, caused by rapid repetitive motions, to life-threatening injuries, often caused by the deadly combination of long hours, tiring work, and sharp knives designed to easily slice through bone. (p. 3)

The same paper draws attention to the severe nature of the psychological trauma experienced by slaughterhouse workers, particularly in the form of "Perpetuation-Induced Traumatic Stress" (PITS):

> The substance abuse that is symptomatic of PITS is also prevalent among slaughterhouse workers. This adverse psychological impact is also evidenced by the increased usage of alcohol and drugs among slaughterhouse workers. One former hog-sticker (an employee who stabs the hogs to cause them to bleed to death) stated that "[a] lot of [the slaughterhouse hog killers] have problems with alcohol. They have to drink, they have no other way of dealing with killing live, kicking animals all day long. If you stop and think about it, you're killing several thousand beings a day." (Dillard 2008, pp. 7–8)

Dillard's research also reinforces the reality that the violence and suffering in these "hidden" spaces are never contained but rather seep into "everyday" life. Fitzgerald et al. (2009), for example, in drawing attention to the community effects of industrialized animal agriculture, indicate that "slaughterhouse employment increases total arrest rates, arrests for violent crimes, arrests for rape, and arrests for other sex offenses in comparison with other industries" (p. 158). This evidence is deeply inconvenient, of course, for those who profess solidarity with human victims of oppression while still continuing to gorge on the corpses of other animals, willfully ignoring the human exploitation and suffering that make it all possible.

Similarly, an intersectional vegan-anarchist critique of capitalism and the animal–industrial complex also looks at how plant-based foods can be far from cruelty-free. Contemporary research, for example, continues to expose the human trafficking, forced labor, servitude, and slavery that surround the industrial production and harvesting of fruit and vegetables. Focusing on cereal production, Amnesty International (2012) reported on the harrowing working conditions that many migrant workers in Italy's agricultural sector endure. It included evidence of "severe labour exploitation of migrant workers in the agricultural sector in the areas of Latina and Caserta, in particular wages considerably below the minimum agreed by unions and employers, arbitrary reductions of wages, delays or non-payment of wages and very long hours of work . . ." (p. 21).

More recently, Pai (2019) drew attention to the exploitation of African migrants working in Italy, noting how "the country's hard-right authorities keep turning the screw." Similarly, severe labor exploitation has been evidenced across Western Europe, including in Spain, France, the Netherlands, Poland, Portugal, and the United Kingdom (Cyrus 2005; Nye 2018; Braakman et al., 2014; FRA 2018).

Emphasizing the pluralistic forms of domination that exist between groups—albeit based on race, gender, sexuality, *or species*—strengthens (not weakens) our grasp and understanding as a whole. To paraphrase Nocella II et al. (2015), calls for interspecies justice bring new movements together to create more support and room for collaboration, allowing activists to educate themselves on the goals, purpose, history, tactics, and campaigns of movements with which they have had less involvement (p. 11).

Profiteering from Environmental Degradation

It is also important to draw attention to the truth that industrial fruit and vegetable production relies heavily on pesticides (insecticides, herbicides, fungicides). These, of course, are used to poison and kill insects and other creatures deemed to be "pests" (for detailed reflections on the violent implications of categorizing these small creatures this way, see Gunderman & White 2021). Holden (2019) reported that strawberries, spinach, and kale are among the most pesticide-heavy crops and that "conventionally farmed kale could contain up to 18 pesticides." This has implications far beyond the targeted crops: the pollution of soil and rivers is well-documented, and the impact on animals, socio-ecological systems, and the food chain is devastating. As a damning report for *National Geographic* notes: "Insecticides, unsurprisingly, hurt non-target species, and neonicotinoids have been implicated in the worldwide decline of bees. Pesticides may play a role in one-eighth of the species' declines featured in the study" (Maim 2019).

Viewed individually or collectively, these ongoing geographies of violence, oppression, and suffering that go hand-in-glove with contemporary veganism should outrage anybody who believes that by buying "vegan" products on ethical or environmental grounds, they are contributing to the realization of a fairer and more just future society. There is no fair or just society under capitalism, as Watkinson and O'Driscoll (2014) succinctly argued: "as long as we are being played by capitalism we can never affect any lasting change" (p. 12). And twenty-first-century veganism is certainly being played by capitalism. What the "vegan consumer" is unwittingly contributing to, though, is the increasingly successful appropriation of the word *vegan* by big business and its being marketed as a "consumable" lifestyle package—wholly stripped down, uncoupled and divorced from its radical origins (White 2018). All of this presents a significant "vegan dilemma": how can we position ourselves in ways so as to reassert the radical promise that the term "veganism" brought to the world? Recognizing that the vegan *telos* should always "be read as an anti-capitalist venture" (Yates 2017, p. 297), what may we do to ensure that veganism remains (in a meaningful sense) outside of and/or uncoupled from capitalist interests as we enter into the second decade of the twenty-first century? It is the challenge of thinking through this dilemma that this chapter now turns its attention towards.

Reasserting the Radical Promise of Veganism . . .

> Evolution can be retrogressive as well as progressive, indeed there seems always to be a strong gravitation the wrong way unless existing standards are guarded and new visions honored. (Watson 1944, p. 1)

1. . . . by recognizing the power of language: veganism is not "ethical veganism," nor is it reducible to "plant-based" consumerism.

First, and to expand more fully on a key point made earlier in the chapter, it is essential that we pay critical attention to the language and framing of veganism. At the very least, we should be confident in restating the original conception of what veganism is and what it represents. Guided by the understanding that "where veganism is, violence, exploitation, and oppression *are not*," we need to ruthlessly call out anything that claims or is claimed to be "vegan" but falls short of this critical mark. We need to unapologetically defend the grounds upon which veganism stands and use some other terminology or reference to describe plant-based lifestyles. "Plant-based consumerism" is certainly a more appropriate description for capitalist-based forms of "veganism." This arrangement is infinitely preferable when we consider the ways in which contemporary veganism has been broken up and made to adopt banal categorizations, as seen in the ridiculous rise of the "ethical" vegan, for example. Indeed, earlier this year, *The Guardian* reported on the ruling from an employment tribunal that ethical veganism is a philosophical belief protected by law against discrimination (Gayle 2020). The report understood "ethical" veganism and "dietary" veganism in the following way:

> Ethical vegans, like dietary vegans, eat a plant-based diet, but ethical vegans also try to avoid contact with products derived from any form of animal exploitation. It includes not wearing clothing made of wool or leather and not using products tested on animals.

But veganism, properly understood, *is* ethical! The ethical imperative to "avoid cruelty to animals" is not a bolt-on extra; it is an intrinsic quality of being a vegan! Moreover, reinforced by an appeal to an anarchist-vegan praxis, the links between an intersectional human ethic of care and a more-than-human ethic of care embodied by veganism must be reaffirmed: veganism should always be seen as a key intersectional, interspecies form of direct action. It does not "become" or "lead to" activism as an optional extra. Therefore, it makes as much (non)sense to try to talk about an "ethical" feminism or an "ethical" feminist as distant from feminism or feminists. Rejecting the distinction between veganism and "ethical" veganism is important, as is untangling veganism from "plant-based" approaches. Unlike veganism, plant-based consumerism is apolitical, focusing on diet alone and being underpinned predominantly by nonethical reasons. It may well be that some people come to identify as vegan through a plant-food diet, but the terms should never be used interchangeably.

2. . . . through vegan-anarchist geographies.

Secondly, I am utterly convinced that the theory and practice—or rather, praxis—of anarchism and anarchist geographies have a vital contribution to make to reasserting and further extending the radical intent of veganism. But before expanding on this, I find it necessary to offer a few brushstrokes to sketch out a brief context about what anarchism actually is and how it ought to be approached and understood.

The spirit and practice of anarchism, as with veganism, have existed from the earliest times of human society, certainly well before Pierre-Joseph Proudhon declared, "I am an anarchist," in 1876. Though it is neither possible nor desirable to "pin" anarchism to a singular definition, Murray Bookchin (1993) helpfully suggests that anarchism is that which "seeks to remove the domination of human by human" (p. 6). An anarchist praxis can exist in many forms—as "a mode of organizing resistance, as a model for interpersonal relationships, or a way of thinking about . . . our world more generally" (May 2010, p. 1). It is not difficult, therefore, to see how narratives and concerns about domination and freedom involve important *geographies* (Ince 2010; Springer et al., 2016; De Souza et al., 2016; White et al., 2016). As Springer (2013) argues:

> If we are to accept anarchism as the dismantling of unequal power relations and the pursuit of re-organizing the way we live in the world along more egalitarian, voluntary, altruistic, and cooperative lines, then it becomes necessary to appreciate anarchism as a geographical endeavor. (p. 36)

That said, it is mostly true that anarchists have, for most of its history, focused almost exclusively on *human* narratives of freedom and liberation. Regretfully, this has meant that serious and detailed reflections on veganism and the question of (the liberation of) animals have largely been conspicuous only by their absence (Watkinson & O'Driscoll 2014). Some important exceptions have of course been made, and it would be remiss for us not to mention Brian Dominick (1997) and Bob Torres (2007) here. For it was Dominick who coined the term *vegan anarchism* just over twenty years ago in his inspirational pamphlet *Animal Liberation and Social Revolution: A Vegan Perspective on Anarchism or an Anarchist Perspective on Veganism.* It should also be recognized, thankfully, that key animal rights/liberation movements do not bear out the dearth of engagement with veganism/nonhuman animals across "intellectual" anarchist landscapes. Activists in such movements, the most prominent of which were arguably the Earth Liberation Front and the Animal Liberation Front (ALF) in the 1980s and 1990s, have often acted in ways that are highly consistent with—and reflective of—anarchist praxis. The presence of such important activist anarchist interventions makes the absence of "academic" anarchist integration even more lamentable, considering that:

> . . . proper contemplation of anarchist traditions leads to concern for animals. Can a society whose abiding objective is freedom from violence, hierarchy, and oppression confine, slaughter, dominate, eat and wear other sentient creatures? (Socha 2012, p. 15)

It is heartening to note that such "proper contemplation" has been evident in literature spanning the tradition of anarchist geographies, from the nineteenth-century writings of the French anarchist geographer Élisée Reclus through to the works of various contemporary activist-scholars (Springer 2021; Véron 2016; Véron & White 2021; White 2015; White & Springer 2018). Reclus (1901) was certainly far ahead of many of his contemporaries in purposefully insisting that the beautiful ideals and commitments of anarchism be fully extended to include our "animal brethren" (p. 158). Importantly, his critical reflections on the wrongness of abusing other animals did not need to appeal externally to "rights" (and thereby state legislatures), but were articulated in an altogether more internal and aesthetic register:

> It is because of the ugliness of the act [of violence] that we are disgusted. . . . Ugliness in persons, in actions, in life, and in the natural environment are all the enemy par excellence. Let us become beautiful ourselves, and let our life be beautiful. (Reclus 1901, p. 62)

It is important for critical scholars and activists alike to take heed and draw attention to the geographies upon which violence moves, thereby recognizing more fully the deeply matted nature of the "social" and the "spatial" that are ever present whenever veganism is addressed (White & Springer 2018). In the context of this chapter, it is anticipated that vegan-anarchist geographies, by focusing intently on the interrelationships between place, space, and trans-species violence, will lead to an important "re-theorization of place as a relational assemblage, rather than as an isolated container" (Springer 2011, p. 90). Focusing on creative, original, and necessarily complex ways to transgress the *invisibilities* of these assemblages of violence should undoubtedly become of greater importance to social justice activists in the future.

Importantly, veganism and anarchist geographies are highly complementary, and share much common ground. For example:

- Vegan-anarchist geographies accommodate a rich and diverse range of interpretations (i.e., are anti-dogmatic);
- Vegan-anarchist geographies constantly have to address the deepest prejudice, lies, and propaganda deliberately peddled to grossly misrepresent and misinform the public. (*This, of course, is no accident, as both anarchism and veganism serve a radical notice on perverse ways of thinking, such as speciesism, and ways of engaging in the world, such as capitalism, that function only to preserve the unearned and unjustified privileges of a minority, which allow it to dominate humans and more-than-humans*);
- Vegan-anarchist geographies necessitate an ongoing and unfolding commitment to freedom and nonviolence (there is no "end-state");
- Vegan-anarchist geographies are radically intersectional, advocating a radically inclusive vision of the commons as a communal dimension of its politics;
- Vegan-anarchist geographies invite ongoing critical reflection to avoid becoming calcified;

- Vegan-anarchist geographies appeal to a prefigurative DIY praxis; and
- Vegan-anarchist geographies reject a politics of waiting.

Happily, there are certainly strong indications in the broader fields of social justice that anarchism and anarchist geographies in particular are becoming more influential (see, for example, Werkheiser 2013; Springer et al., 2016; De Souza et al., 2016; White et al., 2016). While this is encouraging, the case needs to be aggressively and repeatedly made for extending anarchist questions and concerns about justice to include nonhuman animals. Embracing a vegan-anarchist geographical praxis, then, begins with the recognition that *to act in the here and now,* in ways that are consistent with our understanding of how we can create a more fully nonviolent society, is an important, empowering, and hopeful (in the literal sense) position to take.

3. . . . by taking advantage of the unintended consequences of corporate plant-based consumerism.

The third way to reassert the radical praxis of veganism is to continue to expand vegan imaginaries about what is possible, practical, and achievable. In sketching out the rise of plant-based food geographies, we must recognize that while veganism always is and will be anti-capitalist, moving forward there may be potential advantages in this contemporary plant-based revolution for veganism (White 2018). Ironically, corporate plant-based consumerism has developed plant-based foods in ways that would have been unthinkable a few years ago. Consequently, debates around veganism, for example, have penetrated mainstream consciousness in important and positive ways that have brought new insights into and awareness of vegans and veganism, and we would do well to take advantage of these positive "vegan imaginaries" and, where necessary, continue to further expand them in new directions. These include:

A. Refuting Myths about What Vegans Eat

Another way in which we can reassert the radical promise of veganism is to point to the rise in the quality, extent, and availability of plant-based foods and nondairy milks seen in recent years. The dominant public perception of the vegan diet—that it is highly restrictive, flavorless, unhealthy, and joyless—is something that no longer holds any credibility, as evidenced by the "success" of the vegan market and the demand for new plant-based foods. And this is no bad thing.

B. Refuting Stereotypes around Health and Veganism

The popular propaganda stereotyping vegans as sickly, unhealthy, sullen, pasty, excessively flatulent ("cos beans") individuals has been completely undermined as a consequence of the favorable branding of the significant health benefits that plant-based foods and drinks offer. As Tap Le and Sabaté (2014) note, "compared to lacto-ovo-vegetarian diets, vegan diets seem to offer additional protection for obesity, hypertension, type 2 diabetes, and cardiovascular mortality" (p. 2131).

In stark contrast, meat and dairy consumption has been linked to higher incidences of certain cancers, cardiovascular disease, type 2 diabetes, and Alzheimer's disease. There is no doubt that scientific evidence emphasizing the vitality and energy that vegans *actually* enjoy will continue to emerge. It is also important to raise consciousness of these issues, particularly given the powerful propaganda machine that the hugely influential animal (ab)use industry continues to have at its disposal.

C. Refuting Myths about Who Gets to Be Vegan

It is important that veganism and vegan geographies resist becoming dogmatic. We should always remember that the original definition of veganism includes a significant caveat: *as far as is possible and practicable.* This is particularly important, as it allows for different pathways and opportunities that an individual or group "coming to veganism" will have and/or that will present themselves at different times and places in life. In terms of what is "practicable," again, this allows for an important geography of difference and diversity to be acknowledged. Price, taste, competence, knowledge, and culture are all potentially important geographies that open up or narrow possibilities for individuals and families to be vegan.

"Practicable" should never be interpreted through the shallow prism of *lifestyle* consumer practice, one characterized by convenience. For example (to focus on a spatial geography of food), a middle-class family's decision to buy dairy ice creams because getting the nondairy option entails walking an extra ten minutes to a supermarket a few blocks away from home should not be justified on grounds of "practicability"! The prevalence of meat/dairy "alternatives" promoted through expensive advertisement campaigns has opened up the potential for new levels of awareness of and interest in these foods that could scarcely have been imagined a few years earlier. Certainly, in the U.K., it is no longer true that most people have to go "miles out of their way" to access an incredible array of plant-based foods and drinks. The most inconvenient step may be just raising their hands to reach another shelf at the supermarket for the soy, almond, coconut, or pea milk. That notwithstanding, given the greater awareness of and confidence in plant-based foods, a significant step away from plant-based foodism and towards veganism would be to try—wherever possible—to support dedicated smaller, independent, and local "vegan" businesses. Even without the extreme economic adversity that many retailers are facing as a consequence of measures to address the spread of Coronavirus, an increasing number of established local vegan businesses are already struggling greatly or closing due to high-street, larger chain restaurants and/or supermarkets selling more plant-based foods (Turner 2020).

As with all matters of ethics, being vegan depends on the individual having options (i.e., access to vegan food). Where there is quite literally no choice—*if one would starve as a consequence of going vegan*, for example—then veganism is not possible. At this juncture, it would be tempting to argue that most people living in the world today have the option and, therefore, the choice to live according to vegan-anarchist principles of nonviolence and non-harm. However, it is crucial that we not fall into the trap of making simplistic assertions and erasing the complex geographies that are at play in the world and that indeed surround veganism—one need only think about the concerns raised over the way plant-based foods are grown and harvested, as highlighted earlier in the chapter. What access do most people have to knowledge of the *real* working conditions on vegetable and fruit farms? The possibility of going vegan is always complicated by questions of the information and resources available.

Putting in the time and effort to engage seriously with the question of who contemporary vegans are is important on many levels. There are some persuasive arguments to be made that plant-based foodism, as a consumer-led movement, is oriented towards primarily (affluent) white people. This recognition is another important reason why separating plant-based foodism and foodists from veganism and vegans is crucial. Vegans are far from being an elitist, homogenous, white group, and it is essential that this myth is called out whenever it rears its head. As Amie Breeze Harper asks in *Sistah Vegan*:

> If a majority of Blacks have had negative experiences with "whiteness as the norm" (because of collective experiences of racism/classism), and they have and they have come to believe that veganism or ethical eating philosophy is a "white thing" and in no way connected to deconstructing systemic institutionalized racism/classism, how can sistah vegans and allies present a model that presents veganism and vegetarianism as a tool that simultaneously resists (a) institutionalized racism/classism (b) environmental degradation and 3) high rates of health dis-eases plaguing the Black community? (2010a, p. xv)

When questioned by Vilda Team (2019) as to whether "the vegan movement has a diversity problem," Aph Ko (founder of the *Black Vegans Rock* blog) responded in the following insightful and nuanced way:

> First off, we have to collectively come to the realization that just because people of color aren't in a given space doesn't mean they're not doing the work. This means that people of color have been doing animal rights work for a really, really long time in different ways; however, our efforts typically haven't been seen or celebrated as mainstream "animal rights work." So, focusing on diversity in the mainstream movement bypasses all of the incredible work people of color are doing outside of the vegan/animal rights movement. We have to realize that the vegan/animal rights movement isn't the only movement that advocates for animals. So many anti-racist activists and thinkers have been interrogating animality and animal oppression for years—even before the animal rights movement started. There is a lot of history and literature that proves this. (Vilda Magazine 2019)

Indeed, as Ko has argued elsewhere, the "black vegan movement is one of the most diverse, decolonial, complex and creative movements" (Severson 2017), which speaks well of the radical potential of veganism as both a transformative and intersectional praxis.

4. . . . by telling the truth and always striving to raise "consumer" awareness of the violence of meat and dairy products and the ethical geographies that underpin veganism.

> The realization that the animals we enslave, the animals we turn into *things*, the animals who slave for us that we might eat some luxury from their bodies, are *alive*, are as possessive of their lives as you or I, this realization would throw a wrench into the system [of oppression and slavery]. (Spiegel 1998, p. 92)

Fourthly, it is impossible to underestimate just how powerful are the stories we get to tell about ourselves and other animals, not least because of how these inform our everyday attitudes and actions in ways that either legitimize animal-abusive norms or, alternatively, promote an ethic of care and trans-species solidarity. The battle to colonize our imaginaries is, of course, the main field of attention of animal abuse industries. Literally billions upon billions of dollars are invested each year with the sole intention of deliberately deceiving and misinforming an uncritical public through anti-vegan/pro-meat and pro-dairy propaganda. As Zaraska (2016) argues:

> The meat industry is capable of swinging our food preferences because it is ultra powerful and ultra consolidated. Consider these numbers: in 2011, in the US alone, the annual sales of meat were worth $186 billion. That's more than the GDP of Hungary or Ukraine. Moreover, just four pork producers control two-thirds of the market, and the top four in beef have about 75 percent of the market. Tyson, the largest meat corporation in the US, recently had a revenue of $34 billion—that's over twenty times as much as the GDP of Belize.

The power of truth-telling depends in many ways on the ability to successfully expose and undermine this propaganda. For example, one of the many powerful barriers to veganism has been its being unjustly framed both as economically elitist and, in terms of its racial politics, as a preserve for predominantly white, privileged individuals and communities.

To directly call out these gross misrepresentations and unleash a new vegan imaginary is a key central challenge. For example, as a direct rebuttal to accusations that Western veganism is for the financially privileged, a vegan-anarchist geographer may draw attention to the collusion between government policymakers and animal abuse industries, as demonstrated by the millions of pounds of public funding allocated to directly subsidizing the flesh-food sector. *The Guardian*, for example, reported that in the U.K., "industrial-scale livestock [*sic*] farms have received millions of pounds of public funds"—almost £70 million—in 2016 and 2017. Individuals and companies linked to intensive poultry farms across the U.K. received the most money in subsidies, at £32 million. The operators of pig and dairy factory farms were given £18 million and £16 million, respectively, while the figure for operators of intensive beef farms was £2 million (Wasley & Heal 2018).

A similar story plays out in the U.S., with public subsidies heavily skewed towards industrial, corporate-owned farmed-animal production facilities. For example, Starmer et al. (2006) found that the U.S. "broiler industry gained monetary benefits averaging $1.25 billion per year between 1997 and 2005" (p. 1). This political economy goes some way to highlighting the enormous lobbying power that the agricultural industry has over our politicians and why we readily regurgitate the myth that fresh, organic fruits and vegetables are inevitably costly (or costlier) to produce and, therefore, more expensive to buy.

In addition to ending this hideously unfair flow of subsidies, there are other creative and experimental approaches to making vegan food more affordable and accessible. Increasing opportunities to grow fruit and vegetables in community-owned spaces and to distribute this food fairly within the local community—at low to zero cost—would be something powerful to consider. As Winter (2015) argues:

> Food is something we all have in common, that makes us all feel better, and that can build a community that is also a coalition to fight the forces arrayed against the oppressed groups in the world. . . . When you give someone food, you are in that moment engaging in the very egalitarian mutualism that every system of ethics—including libertarian socialism—see[s] as its basis. (p. 69)

Over the last forty years, Food Not Bombs, "one of the fastest-growing (anarchist) social movement groups in the world" (Heynen 2010, p. 1225), has stood as an excellent illustration of how sharing vegan food is both a meaningful act of solidarity and care and an important intersectional politicized space for individuals and groups to come together. In this way:

> Food Not Bombs works in coalition with groups like Earth First!, The Leonard Peltier Defense Committee, Anarchist Black Cross, the IWW, Homes Not Jails, Anti-Racist Action, Farm Animal Rights Movement, In Defense of Animals, the Free Radio Movement and other organizations on the cutting edge of positive social change and resistance to the new global austerity program. (Food Not Bombs, n.d.)

5. . . . by insisting that animal exploitation is connected to all other forms of exploitation.

Finally, holding fast to the original definition of veganism, all the while rejecting appeals to "ethical" veganism, means being fully conscious of—and committed to ending—"*all forms of exploitation of, and cruelty to, animals for food, clothing or any other purpose.*" In doing so, we must resist the common (and up to a point, understandable) tendency to aggregate cruelty and suffering based on the numbers of animal victims and to prioritize areas of animal exploitation accordingly. Farming, for example, is statistically the most dominant space of animal abuse:

> By the 1980s, farmed animals comprised fully 99 percent of all animals killed by humans each year; the other 1 percent includes all animals used for fur or leather, in experiments or entertainment, and in

> hunting or trapping, as well as those raised as companion animals or euthanized in animal shelters. (Cherry 2016, p. 3)

While a vegan geography never neglects to find ways of liberating farmed animals from the hells they find themselves in, it also recognizes that other spaces of animal suffering are equally deserving of our serious thought, attention, and commitment. In short, you cannot aggregate pain. Anarchist-vegan geographers should act with the full knowledge that the blood and misery of tortured and caged animals, far from being confined within the walls of factory farms and abattoirs, pour from vivisection laboratories, zoos, circuses, canned hunts, and so on (Lyons 2013). The "war" against animals has many fronts (Wadiwell 2015).

It is the four final words, though—". . . *or any other purpose*"—that imply a potentially unlimited extension of veganism, which is, paradoxically, its greatest strength and greatest weakness; one is in danger of seeing veganism as an impossible ideal and getting mired in inertia. When all is said and done, where does veganism begin and end? How does one square radical veganism with the use of products that have been or continue to be tested on animals? In addition to observing that all vegetables and even salt and water have at some time been tested on animals, Linzey and Linzey (2019) argue that "animal products can be found everywhere, not only in food, but also in dyes, glues, paints, film making equipment, clothing, footwear, furniture, household items, most drinks, ceramics, toiletries and even UK five pound notes" (p. 3).

Such dilemmas about what it is to "be vegan" inform much of the spirit of Brian Dominick's *Anarcho-Veganism Revisited* (2015). For example, Dominick problematizes the figure of the transport-using vegan. The car user is framed as one who is "complicit in a method of transportation that kills millions of vertebrates alone every year . . . not to mention the billions more displaced or mangled during construction of our 4 million miles of roadway [in the U.S.]" (p. 23).

Other forms of transport are also implicated: "Even if you rely on public transportation, most of the above is true for you. Just stop to think about the rat poison used in your subway system, paid for by your transit fees" (Dominick 2015).

Acknowledging this is important, not least because it recognizes that the struggle for interspecies peace and nonviolence, like the fight for human justice, will always be ongoing and incomplete. There is no pure space to be found. However, the knowledge that we can never situate ourselves and our actions outside or beyond the webs of violence we are caught in should not be used as basis for the pathetic argument that one may as well do nothing. You should always do something, as Adams (2010) argues: "Veganism is always a question of now. Knowing what I know, *now* what will I do? It comes with an insistence! 'Pay attention!' Pay attention, *now*" (p. 315).

The reassertion of a radical spatial praxis at the heart of veganism through anarchist geographies folds in nicely with calls to envisage and enact a politics of total liberation (Pellow 2014) or "Total Liberation Ecology" (Springer 2021). Vegan-anarchist geographies "embrace the ideas, vision, and practice of total liberation which views inequality as a threat to life itself—for oppressed peoples, species, and ecosystems and is organized around the struggle for justice in all its form" (Pellow 2015, p. 2). That vegan-anarchist geographies help display *how* a radical intersectional politics is being put into *place* needs to be understood and unpacked more fully than is currently evident. The renewed call for a vegan-anarchist geographical praxis to burn brightly in the world is a statement of radical intent and vision that promises to enhance our chances of fighting back—hard—against the exploitation and destruction of all animals and the earth.

Conclusion: Truth-Telling (about Veganism)

> Animal Liberation is not just about liberating apes, cows, chickens, pigs, mice, and bees; it is also about liberating human animals from mindlessness. (Socha 2012, p. 27)

We are living at a time that seems to be continually ceding ground to violent, malevolent anthropogenic geographies that destroy our fellow Earthlings in the billions, make human life increasingly one of misery and survival, and threaten to destroy the very support systems upon which all known life on Earth depends. And yet, mindful of the opening reflections, I still continue to write, and you continue to read. Why bother? I do so because I believe that truth-telling through writing always has the potential to offer something positive to help transgress the crises we face. Here, I am mindful of the words written by Alice Walker, the American novelist, writer, poet, and activist, in her foreword to Marjorie Spiegel's *The Dreaded Comparison*:

> There is hope following close behind the initial despair that one feels on reading [*The Dreaded Comparison*]. Despair because one realizes one has eaten eggs produced by mutilated (de-beaked) beings being crammed four to a cage the size of a record album cover; one has tasted veal from a baby calf ripped from its [*sic*] mother's womb without so much as a goodbye lick or look from her; one has used cosmetics

> derived from products forced out of animals' bodies in great pain. The civet cat, for one, is whipped in the face until it sweats the essence that is the foundation for many a sweet perfume. We are guilty. But that is only a first response. And normal. What do we do with our heightened consciousness, is the question. (Walker 1988, p. 10)

Reflecting on this passage, I hope that as long as there is a *strong* sense of a future on this planet, there exists a real possibility of change: hope reigns eternal. For all of the propaganda of the animal (ab)use industries that profit from violating our *humane*ness by perpetuating myths that promote human supremacy over others, for all of our own epistemic failure, the desire for society to evolve towards co-lived spaces without violence beats strongly (White 2015).

Without doubt, a resurgent vegan praxis has a crucial role to play in opening up new ways of imagining, enacting, and being in the world that can help liberate society from the speciesist straitjacket that binds it to a repertoire of senseless violence, depravity, and ugliness. To make this liberation possible, we must not shy away from telling some home truths about veganism—and what challenges it faces at the current time, the most pressing of which, arguably, is the need to uncouple it from those contemporary trends that center on plant-based foodism and are carried on the shoulders of capitalism. There must, though, be a "heightened consciousness" at play if we are to address this successfully and "make good" on the radical promise of veganism and, more generally, critical vegan geographies. These nine thousand or so words have been committed to this end—as an attempt to try to identify the strengths and weaknesses that characterize contemporary expressions of veganism, in order to reassert the radical and revolutionary spirit of veganism and open up new, emancipatory futures and possibilities. If this chapter has stirred greater critical thought and reflections on the reader's part about how veganism generally and vegan-anarchist geographies specifically can be woven more fully into the broader tapestries of interspecies struggle and solidarity, then it will have more than served its purpose.

2

A "USEFUL USELESSNESS"

Vegan Geographies of Bearing Witness at the Slaughterhouse Gates

Alex Lockwood

Introduction

Your feet are so big. Bigger than I imagined. And yellow. The middle toe on your left foot is missing—ripped off in the cage on the way to the warehouse, we guess, or lost in a fight for space in the warehouse where you were grown. Your skin is dull, your feathers absent. The passenger in the truck's cab hands you over to one of the activists and we're all surrounding you, even though I think this must be adding to your fright. Alina is videoing the event to put online later. Jessica is thanking the truck drivers. They shrug. Everyone else wants a photo with you—nearly everyone. There's one activist not crowding you but standing at the back of the departing truck. His hands rest against the crates carrying six or seven hundred others—your brothers and sisters, crammed ten to a box, being taken away after their purchase to the smaller private slaughterhouse or restaurant that was going to be your fate. You could have been any one of them. Any one of them could have been you.

I arrived four hours earlier for this Save Movement Cancun vigil outside Rastro Municipal, the government-run slaughterhouse. The Rastro is not busy. I'm told that this network of Mexican municipal abattoirs is kept open as a program to keep unemployment numbers down. On the wall outside is the price list for slaughter. A male pig: one hundred pesos. A cow: three hundred. A lamb: two hundred pesos. A female pig: one hundred and fifty. But you didn't come here. The chicken clearing house is over the road. You came in on a truck around 6 p.m., with perhaps five or six thousand others. The activists were watching for you with binoculars, staring west into the setting sun and the traffic, as all the trucks came into Cancun this way and then did a U-turn at the lights down the road. When you passed us, we quickly crossed and stood outside the clearing house waiting for you. On the chicken abattoir gates is a picture of a well-fed, well-bred, fully feathered chicken with firm red comb proudly raised, a red superhero cape thrown around his shoulders, wings planted like arrogant elbows, showing readiness for action—or death, because death is why you are here. You do not look like this; you are defeathered, stressed, pale, struggling to bear weight on your infant legs, comb collapsing to the side.

Jessica knew that not all of you would be slaughtered here. Some of you would be sold on to smaller abattoirs, and sure enough, when the small truck with two men in the front arrived, Jessica was there immediately, speaking to them on your behalf, striking up a conversation, asking them if they knew about you, really knew you, knew that you each have a unique individual personality, that you're intelligent—if they knew what a short life you'd lived, what kind of life you could live if they were willing to give you to us, just one of you, on their way out. They know who you are. They know you do everything together with your close flock members. They know you suffer. So, they promised, they would give one of you, *you*, to us when they left. Then they drove in, and the gates shut, and we went back over the road to keep an eye out for the truckload of pigs that Jessica had told me would arrive around 7 p.m. for the Rastro, after which another truckload of workers would arrive at 8 p.m. to kill them. We stood on either side of our homemade vegan banner, and we ate the rosca, the ringed breaded donut cake that is traditional on this day, Twelfth Night, with the hidden plastic figure somewhere in the dough; whoever finds it will have to offer tamales in four weeks' time. And we waited.

Around 7:30 p.m., I asked Jessica why it was taking so long for the small truck to emerge with its crates filled with chickens. She grimaced. Last time, it had taken four hours. The vigil was slated to end at 8 p.m. Most of the activists had to drive back to Playa Del Carmen. And I was already feeling faint, the first indication of the fever that would floor me for the next week. What if we left before the slaughter men emerged with you, our chicken? I wondered, *Do we leave? But we can't leave, surely? That means you'll die. You'll all die. How can we be called advocates of the Save Movement if we don't stay?* I began to bargain with myself. *Do we all need to stay? Only the Spanish speakers? Or only until 9 p.m.? 10 p.m.? Where do I draw this line today? Ten activists spending half a day, eight hours all-in, to rescue one chicken? Wouldn't we have done more, achieved more, leafleting or protesting in a busy town center? Or rather, Is what we do useless? Does it have any usefulness? Can it be quantified? Does it need to be?*

* * *

For vegan geographers, a starting point for answering these questions is to focus on the space itself—the physical location of vigils outside the slaughterhouse—and its imaginaries. The abattoir, once found in the very center of urban spaces, was moved (at the time, due to Victorian sensibilities) to less visible locations and has thus stayed hidden (Kean 1998; Philol 1995); the same can be said mostly for the changes to North American slaughtering practices—with Chicago as a prime example, especially following the publication of Upton Sinclair's *The Jungle* (Pachirat 2011). As slaughterhouses are found on the periphery of contemporary city spaces, close enough to deliver "meat" products to consumers, but not close enough so that consumers see the animals who are the sources of that "meat" and without graphic signage or windows into buildings where the killing and processing happen, the acts of slaughter are, in the main, invisible and insensible in the everyday lives of most people in Western countries. Civic infrastructures (such as roundabouts, lay-bys, and traffic lights) are investments funded by public money to ensure industrial animal agriculture practices can continue taking place with the same invisibility and on the same scale: trucks are often double-length, carrying up to two hundred pigs at a time on their deliveries to places such as Fearman's Meat Packers in Toronto (10,000 pigs a day) or Tulip Meats in Manchester and Bristol in the U.K. (3,000 pigs a day each).

What I wish to do for the remainder of this chapter is explore a set of attempts to challenge the spatial imaginaries outside and around one particular (and typical) slaughterhouse in the U.K.: Linden Foods abattoir in Cramlington, Northumberland, where I attend vigils. As Rosemary-Claire Collard and Kathryn Gillespie write in their introduction to *Critical Animal Geographies*, this critical approach to "taken-for-granted spatial orders . . . is especially attentive to the power relations that particular spatial orientations and imaginaries reveal" (2015, p. 9). My work is essentially autoethnographic in that I have been engaged as both an activist and a researcher in these spaces; as Kay Peggs (2014) writes, this shift of human researchers from "assumed and invisible creatures [to] exposed reflexive creatures" (p. 48) is part of the work of nudging critical animal studies from the margins to the center of academic practice (if that is a desired thing). I at least agree with Nik Taylor that all scholars and academics are or should be activists too,[1] and I argue that acts of bearing witness outside slaughterhouses are "useful" practices in troubling the power relations that the particular spatial orientation of the slaughterhouse sets in place. The Animal Save Movement's vigils politicize the logic of human domination of nonhuman others on the (often literal) verges between everyday life and industrial locations of nonhuman bodily appropriation. I shall connect (although most probably ineffectively and incompletely) these spatial analyses to Levinasian concepts of ethical responsibility to the Other, a

1. Taylor has made the argument in a number of presentations and places, for example on the Knowing Animals podcast (https://www.youtube.com/watch?v=MjeLG3y2MV0).

responsibility that preempts the Other's call but whose demands can never be fulfilled—and are, therefore, perhaps "useless." I finish by proposing a "useful uselessness" in relation to this form of vegan activism, noting how it opens out the otherwise highly controlled and overlooked spaces of material entanglement between human and nonhuman at the intersection of slaughterhouse and public way. This opening out is a political act that asks, as Collard and Gillespie do, "How can we more justly share space?" (p. 8), as well as demands that bearing witness be understood as a moral duty in the political sphere. Such a duty recognizes as "impossible" the demands without end of animal advocacy, but nevertheless offers a new reading of vegan spatiality that is charged with the ethical obligation to contest the settled terrains of our exploitative relations with nonhuman others.

The Origins of the Save Movement

I've been thinking for a long time about the work of the Save Movement and about bearing witness as an activist practice (Lockwood 2016). I help organize weekly vigils in the U.K., where the Save Movement has grown from one group—Manchester Pig Save, formed in February 2016—to over fifty groups around the country. I stand by animals and watch them go to their deaths once every ten days.

The Save Movement was started in Toronto in July 2010, when founder Anita Krajnc began work to bring visual and sensory attention to the pigs going to slaughter at Quality Meat Packers slaughterhouse in the city's downtown area. The Save Movement is a growing grassroots vegan activist network of more than five hundred autonomous groups in over fifty countries. Central to its activism are the acts of bearing witness to nonhuman animals as they are transported into slaughterhouses; attempting to relieve suffering momentarily (with water, for example, during heatwaves); and bringing awareness to the issue of nonhuman exploitation and commodification through video footage, imagery, and testimony, with the goal of convincing others to practice veganism. The vision of the Save Movement is to bring an end to the consumption of animals by humans, close all slaughterhouses, and institute a vegan world. But on a more pragmatic level, to use Tolstoy's famous quote on suffering animals in "The First Step," the aim is simpler: to have people turn towards, rather than away from, suffering.

The vigil I attended that January day in Cancun was organized by the local Save group. Luckily, the truck bringing you, our single saved chicken, to us appeared before the end of that particular vigil. But that encounter, one of the many I have experienced in the last four years since I first attended a vigil, came laden with the question: Is what we did that day as a collective group of activists a success or failure? One life saved, countless others not.

The Toronto-based scholar Sara Salih explores the concept of a "critical or ethical witness" through three of what she considers "scenes of failed witness" that include both chickens and vigils (2018, p. 57). Her first scene of failed witness was at a celebratory dinner for a Nobel Prize–winning author, when she first realized she could no longer sit down with those eating animal products. She writes:

> The main course (it was chicken) was carried in by the servers, my stomach lurched at the sight of the flesh and bones on the plates, and all of a sudden I was struck with a parallel vision of the live chickens and all these good people (we had gathered to celebrate, after all) chewing on what was left of these animals' bodies. I knew I couldn't watch, and almost against my will, I found myself leaving the room in tears without explaining to anyone why I couldn't stay or where I was going. (p. 58)

Her second "failure" was at a vigil similar to the one I attended in Mexico, but this time in Toronto (where I have also attended vigils). Salih watched as a truckload of pigs was brought into the abattoir, and then again as she was led around the back to peer "over the fence at pigs being prodded off the lorry with electric probes." She writes: "I wondered what we were all doing there gazing at each other, and when I biked away from the slaughterhouse I found I was in tears once again because all we had done was glimpse the pigs, and now they were standing in their pens freezing cold waiting to be killed the next morning" (p. 58). (Her third failure, for the record, was another tearful departure from the house of a friend who had requested Salih's help in serving and clearing up a "meat"-based meal made for paying guests.)

Since these three (and, I expect, more) episodes, Salih has been asking herself what it means to witness, "what it means to turn towards or turn away" (p. 58), and if there is any point to it. I am especially interested in these questions in terms of the spatial and political implications of the vigils held outside slaughterhouses, which have risen in popularity globally over the past decade (Lockwood 2018). Like Salih (although perhaps with a more positive hypothesis), I want to find out "if there is anything in these gestures or whether, as I suspected when I failed to witness, I was merely reacting sentimentally and, thus, not 'ethically' (a word I find increasingly vague and suspect anyway) because my responses had no outcome whatsoever, as far as I could see and as far as the animal is concerned" (p. 58).

The question of where and whom to turn towards, and if such a turn has any impact, is central to Salih's critiques of the vigil she attended and the expansion of vigils worldwide. Her sense of failure in witnessing stems not only from the problematic decision to leave the pigs to die, but also from the impossibility of witnessing—from being unable to witness the chicken on the plate, or rather, turning away from that choice. There are also questions of prioritization: witnessing one scene of suffering inevitably means turning one's back on another that demands equal attention. Salih's specific critique of Save activists' failure to directly interfere with the too-smooth processes of animal agriculture at the slaughterhouse has been echoed worldwide, including by Ronnie Lee, one of the co-founders of the Animal Liberation Front in the U.K., who derides the movement's name: "Do they actually save animals?" asks Lee.[2] Save vigils are also not thought particularly highly of by those in the Effective Altruism movement, who say we'd all be better off performing city-center leafleting and vegan education, or working in high-value capitalist systems and spending our money on in vitro meat development.[3] And yet these vigils, with their love-based manifesto encouraging activists to respond with compassion and love to human and nonhuman actors alike while bringing people closer to the animals within the agricultural system, have caught the imagination of thousands of people around the world. It is for this reason that it is important for us to study and understand vigils in order to further our knowledge of vegan social movements and human–nonhuman relations.

Outside the Slaughterhouse

Linden Foods is a Northern Irish company based in Dungannon, with facilities spread across the United Kingdom that slaughter up to 1,800 cattle and 4,000 lambs per week. One of these abattoirs is found in Burradon, a small village near Cramlington, six miles outside Newcastle in the northeast of England. On most days, cows and sheep are brought to the slaughterhouse, where they are killed and dismembered, often to be sent by truck back to Northern Ireland for processing into packaged "meat."

The spatial logic of this slaughterhouse is similar to that of other slaughterhouses found across the planet. The facilities are surrounded by an eight-foot-high green fence, with one automatized gate for entry and exit controlled by an employee in an office who monitors the cameras and intercom (when he is not distracted playing video games, so explained the manager one time) for approaching vehicles and

2. https://www.facebook.com/photo.php?fbid=10212821502445234&set=a.4413633351834.171331.1618824695& type=3&theater.
3. By way of an example, see, https://forum.effectivealtruism.org/posts/ch5fq73AFn2Q72AMQ/why-animals-matter-for-effective-altruism, and also, http://www.ourhenhouse.org/2015/10/effective-altruism-as-it-relates-to-animal-rights-an-open-ended-approach-to-advocacy/.

arrivals, be it of slaughterhouse workers, administrative team members, farmers with trailers, or large "livestock" trucks. There are no signs letting people know this is a slaughterhouse; the only sign is high on the main warehouse walls and reads, "Linden Foods." There is a verge approximately twenty feet wide outside the gate, on either side of the main entrance, leading to a road that runs perpendicular and leads one way to a busy main A-road, from which direction most "livestock" trucks and tractors and trailers approach.

The activists of North East Animal Save set up their vigil approximately every ten days, generally in the morning. The morning is when most deliveries of animals arrive, in preparation for that day's killing (many slaughterhouses prefer to avoid having animals in lairage overnight in case it incurs costs in terms of water and feed, or damage). On one side of the slaughterhouse is a field used for crop agriculture. On the opposite side is a lane leading to a row of cottages that are found directly behind the slaughterhouse. The road that runs past the slaughterhouse has few pedestrians passing by, but it does carry a number of bus routes and a cycle route between this outlying area and the main civic center of Newcastle. On the other side of the road are more crop agricultural fields, beyond which lies a dairy and beef farm, from which regular deliveries of cows to the slaughterhouse are made (often by a South African farmhand whose girlfriend, he tells us, has been vegan for ten years).

Inside the gates of the slaughterhouse, a concrete space, perhaps half an acre in size, is divided into: a road for trucks to drive down to deliver the animals into lairage; a car park for workers; some smoking areas for workers on break from the kill and processing lines, including a smoking shelter; and space for trucks to back up to roller doors on the side of the main warehouse, where they can be loaded with body parts of cows and sheep in refrigerated containers for transport. These trucks are often seen speeding away from the open roller doors before the drivers slam on the brakes to shift the hanging carcasses of the load closer together inside the freezer containers, thus saving on manpower (it is predominantly men who do this work) to pack the body parts of cows weighing considerably more than humans. All of this action is seen through the fencing at the front of the slaughterhouse, around 200 meters away from where the cows and sheep are offloaded. Around the back, the lairage area initially had gaps in between some of the corrugated building structure, so that animals and workers prodding animals could be seen and images taken. In the eighteen months since North East Animal Save started holding vigils at Linden Foods, the slaughterhouse workers have barred gaps in the lairage with makeshift barriers made of wood and more corrugated metal, so that no images can be taken. Barbed wire has also appeared around the top of an eight-feet-high brick building outside the slaughterhouse fence (and so presumably not part of its private property) that had provided activists with a vantage point to see further into the unloading and lairage areas. Beyond the slaughterhouse and at the bottom of the front garden spaces of the row of cottages is another field, often occupied by a small herd of cows.

The activists employ a number of tactics to disrupt the spatial arrangements of the slaughterhouse's workings; here, I will focus on three of them that bring attention to, as Collard and Gillespie write, "how violence depends in part on specific spatial arrangements: proximities and distances, spatial demarcations such as borders or pens, and controlled movements through space" (p. 10).

1. Stopping and Bearing Witness to the Flow of Bodies

The aim of the activists of North East Animal Save is to bear witness to the suffering of the animals who are brought to Linden Foods. For some, this witnessing takes place only when activists can come into direct bodily or visual contact with the animals—that is, when activists can see the animals, rather than when, as is often the case, the animals cannot be seen because of the construction of the transports and the high sides of the "livestock" vehicles. For others, to simply be present as the trucks pass by is bearing witness enough. However, this bearing witness can normally be done only if activists bring about some disruption to the otherwise

Fig. 1: Activists (including the author) in hi-vis vests obstruct trucks from entering the slaughterhouse. Image © Alex Lockwood

smooth operation of delivering animals to slaughter by stopping the trucks outside the gates for a brief moment. When a truck approaches, some activists stand in front of the gate and raise placards asking for "three minutes to say goodbye to the animals" or proclaiming "no hate for truck drivers, only love for the animals" to encourage the drivers to slow and stop (Fig. 1). Such acts can be dangerous when the gate has been opened in advance and the truck or tractor drivers do not intend to stop. So far, no one has been hit by a vehicle (in the U.K.), although over the course of multiple vigils at this site, the activists have learned not to attempt to stop one particular green tractor driven by a farmer or farmhand. If and when the trucks stop, some activists attempt to make conversation with the drivers and thank them for stopping, while others approach the trucks and, according to the vigil group's guidelines, especially taking the welfare of the animals into account, either bear witness or capture footage of the scenes to be shared later online and via social media (Fig. 2).

Fig. 2: Activists use mobile phones and cameras to record footage of cows inside the stopped transport truck. Image © Alex Lockwood

2. Contesting the Physical Structures of Political Economy

Continuing with this idea, activists at North East Animal Save include artists and makers interested in exploring the ways in which their art and craft can alter and remake the space around the slaughterhouse. Their performances and creations work with structures such as fences and gates that operate as limits that separate

Fig. 3: Hearts made by activist artists adorn the fence alongside the group's banner. Image © Alex Lockwood

Fig. 4: Letters made from scrap material and covered in red paint spell out the word SLAUGHTERHOUSE. Image © Alex Lockwood

Fig. 5: The police arrive to issue warnings. Image © Alex Lockwood

public from private space—challenging those operations, thereby asking others to pay attention to the structures of power that enforce said limits. Each vigil, activists hang a twenty-foot banner on the fence that reads, "Slaughterhouse," with images of animals along with logos and social media contacts. They have also held special "art" vigils, creating temporary installations using the fence as a physical canvas on which to make images. The first of these was a shower of love hearts made with red cloth, wrapped around and in between the gaps in the fence (Fig. 3). The second installation was made of pieces of white fabric wrapped around individual wireframes to spell out the word SLAUGHTERHOUSE (Fig. 4), which were then spattered with red acrylic paint to represent the blood of the animals. Both of these were created on-site, turning the verge outside the slaughterhouse into a temporary art workshop. The activists also have an ongoing practice of leaving flowers tied to the gates, to the fence around the intercom that visitors use to access the slaughterhouse, and to the lamp posts and other municipal street furniture.

During the construction and installation of the red love hearts, the police arrived after a call from the slaughterhouse manager. The police insisted that the fabric be unwrapped from the fencing, otherwise it would be seen as an act of criminal damage and the activists responsible arrested (Fig. 5).

3. Sharing of Food and Drink

Each vigil has an emphasis on the sharing of vegan food and drink among the activists who attend. There is a practical element to this, as vigils are held throughout the year in varying weather conditions; both hot drinks in the winter and cold drinks in the summer are necessary to encourage activists to attend and stay for the duration of the vigils, which often last three hours, sometimes longer. Many activists bring food they have baked themselves to share (Fig. 6), and activists will sometimes offer the food (which often comprises "alternatives" to the standard fare made with animal products such as cake, doughnuts, and "sausage" rolls) to slaughterhouse workers as they arrive for work or the truck drivers who agree to stop. (Very few have taken the food offered.)

Fig. 6: An activist shares homemade food. Image © Alex Lockwood

The Spatial Disruptions of Bearing Witness

Work is beginning to be done on the ethics of bearing witness to animal suffering, building on a surprisingly small body of literature addressing bearing witness in general, mainly in relation to the Shoah (Holocaust) of World War II, to torture, and to American slavery and race relations (Felman & Laub 1991; Hatley 2000; Moore &

Swanson 2018; Oliver 2001). In particular, Kathie Jenni (2018) is beginning to think through the implications of acknowledging that veganism is not quite enough of a moral obligation. She writes:

> Not only must the conscientious abstain from the benefits of animal abuse, but we must carry the spiritual burden of attending to the atrocities that underlie our choices. But we are not absolved from the painful duties of memory and witness by freeing our lives of the products of animal cruelty. Rather, because we are the only ones who will pay proper attention—because we care—we are precisely the ones who must keep animal atrocities before our minds. This is undeniably painful. (p. 175)

Jenni's work here is dealing with the animal dead, rather than those still—albeit barely—alive, at the slaughterhouse gates. But this attention to bearing witness is part of critical animal studies' "call for concrete action by deriving conceptual insights from activism" (Giraud 2015, p. 49). Eva Giraud suggests that attending to activist practice—"and particularly participating in projects where complex political issues are articulated in practice—[provide] valuable insights about how to politicize theories that have proven popular in 'third-wave' animal geography" (p. 36).

When we look more closely at the examples of spatial disruption above, the fact that activists only stop a truck for a few moments means that this act of witnessing "fails" to do anything for the animals in the truck and is therefore, at least for these animals, perhaps useless. (Indeed, as some critics of the movement have suggested, it prolongs the animals' distress and perhaps, when they are being approached by activists in hi-vis jackets, with smartphones projecting bright flashes, makes it worse.) And what of my role there, as both activist and researcher? As Collard and Gillespie (2015b) write in their exploration of the "problematic dimensions of witnessing as a research methodology, . . . this work is often done in service of longer-term future change, but frequently does nothing for the individual animals passing through" (p. 204). Is it useless, then? Researching as an activist does at least shine a light on the ways in which both this form of activism and the research conducted around it are "marked by a central struggle of seeking out encounters with animals . . . and knowing that the conditions of violence, suffering, and asymmetrical power make these encounters possible" (p. 206). Although these tensions remain mostly unexplored, that they are coming to light suggests researchers—and activists—will begin to tackle such questions through both practice and theory; and then perhaps, as Giraud argues, we can find ways of "politicizing approaches that stress relationality and putting them to practical work" (p. 39).

The best way to engage with these problematic issues, suggest Collard and Gillespie, is to learn from the methods of multispecies ethnography, which "invites inquiry into the intimately intertwined enactments of violence, power, cruelty, love, care, and kinship that define the varied and ambivalent relationships between humans and other animals" and, importantly, is "attentive to the places and spaces (or rather, the multispecies contact zones) in which these cross-species encounters occur" (p. 207). For Lestel et al. (2006), this is best conceptualized as an "ethno-ethology" that blends the best practices of ethnology and ethology together into a research method that "grants all living beings the status of relational beings, that is, agents interacting on the phenomenon of 'culture' that was hitherto reserved for human beings" (p. 168).

What the Save activists do by disrupting the flow of animals into the slaughterhouse—even if only momentarily, at risk to themselves—to be able to briefly bear witness is force the foregrounding of these existing entanglements between humans and animals (Gruen 2015). The halting of the trucks is a moment wherein "violence, power, cruelty, love, care, and kinship" are all present, but activists bring attention to the ways in which even such asymmetrical displays of power at the gates of a slaughterhouse can be complicated by the acknowledgment of more loving forms of cross-species encounter—of human encounter between vegan activist and slaughterhouse worker, between vegan activist as bearer of testimony and the general public. Here, the disruption to the political economy of power wielded by slaughter companies and the wider animal agriculture industry is clearly a spatial interruption to the flows of capital and profit. However, perhaps the impacts of such a disruption are seen not immediately in these spatial imaginaries, but on the social media channels where the media footage is shared. But they are also evidenced by the knowledge that the U.K. Association of Independent Meat Suppliers has met with the official National Counter Terrorism Police Operations Centre team to discuss how to respond to vigils and the "threats" of the Save Movement to the industry's physical practices and workflows.[4]

The enactment of art practices outside and on the slaughterhouse's fence is a concrete example of how activists foreground Lestel et al.'s point that it is not only humans who are "agents interacting on the phenomenon of 'culture.'" In this instance, the animals are the agents who stimulate an artistic response from the human activists. This art is made in response to the activists' feelings towards the animals to whom they bear witness and who are transported to this location to be

4. Chas Newkey-Burden. Our Counter-terrorism Experts Shouldn't Be Wasting Their Time on the "Save" Animal Welfare Protest Movement, Independent (U.K.), February 14, 2017, https://www.independent.co.uk/voices/save-veganism-abattoirs-animal-cruelty-terrorism-vigils-animal-welfare-a7579251.html.

slaughtered—feelings that are born out of genuine bodily encounter, often face-to-face and eye-to-eye, and that include physical touch and sensory experiences such as smell, which are shared both ways. And the suffering, although asymmetrical, is shared across species boundaries and articulated through cultural practices of channeling difficult emotions into image-making. As Adams notes, "an emphasis on [the animals'] role as active subjects is rare" (2018, p. 3) in psychological research on nonhuman subjects. Nonetheless, this oversight is being challenged by activists who clearly mark their love for "animals as such" (Shapiro 2017) and by the sharing of suffering among species, whereby the line demarcating levels of suffering is marked spatially by the fence that runs around the slaughterhouse.

And the political potential of the subtle food practices of these activists who prepare and share vegan food is in their recuperation of an autonomous and alternative means of consumption in a space that has been otherwise reserved as an empty public border around a commercial enterprise in which animals are slaughtered and processed—rendered invisible as "meat." As Eva Giraud writes in her analysis of activist food practices, foregrounding of the sharing of vegan food in such spaces "can be used to unsettle categorizations of humans-as-consumers and animals-as-commodities that are ordinarily reinforced" (p. 48) by the standard methods of slaughtering, processing, selling, and cooking animals. Giraud's analysis of the Nottingham-based Veggies group is focused on its work directly outside outlets of the fast-food chain McDonald's. But her analysis of the ways in which the "performative serving of vegan food" can be seen as a way of "altering people's bodily engagements" (p. 49) with spaces that facilitate the normative, pre-existing relations between humans and animals can also be applied to the spaces outside slaughterhouses. While the preparation of vegan food makes for perhaps more direct protest when performed outside fast-food outlets, vigil activists see their cooking and sharing of vegan food as part of the activist practice in developing "affective relations [that] reconnect animal bodies with the spaces in which they are consumed" (p. 50), or in this case, killed and processed.

An Insomniac Ethics in the Spaces of Vegan Activism

Such activist practices do indeed problematize the power relations that the particular spatial orientations of the slaughterhouse establish and protect. Each element of the activism outlined above disrupts or playfully and creatively unpicks the assumed geographies of the public space around the slaughterhouse—up to and including its own fence. The attention given to such a specific space is important, not least because of the now-central locus of and the focus on the slaughterhouse in the contemporary animal rights movement and its distinct forms of activism:

with over five hundred Save groups worldwide already, the Save Movement aspires to have a vigil outside every slaughterhouse on the globe.[5] This space, along with the acts that take place there, is part of the "chains of interaction that constitute industrial agriculture" (Adams 2018, p. 5) and is the point at which activists—and members of the public viewing the acts either live or later via social media—can get the closest to the killing of billions of animals each year.

Here, questions arise as to how best to think through these acts in relation to my starting point in this chapter, as well as just how effective, useful, and impactful such protest against the animal agriculture industry can really be.

Across his work, but especially in *Totality and Infinity*, philosopher Emmanuel Levinas (1969 [1961]) theorizes ethical responsibility as an insomniac call in two ways. First—and as both activists and researchers, we may know this feeling—living ethically will always demand more from us than we could ever deliver, and so it keeps many of us up, awake, insomniac, with attendant threats of burnout and the revolving door. (I could ask our Cancun chicken: "How long would I have waited that night for you to come out of the warehouse gates? All night?")

The second meaning of Levinas's characterization of ethical responsibility as insomniac derives from the obligation to respond to the suffering of the Other even before knowing who the Other is. That is: for Levinas, we hear the call of the Other before we know who the Other is, and this is the way it must be if we were to institute ethics; it is not possible for an ethics to be truly ethical (and as Salih points out, that term has become suspect) if we humans were to create this thing called ethics, and then look around for a subject to respond to ethically. To respond to the call before we know who is calling is to take what Levinas calls a radically passive position towards the Other. As Matthew Calarco puts it, "Levinas's ethical philosophy is, or at least should be, committed to a notion of universal ethical consideration, that is, an agnostic form of ethical consideration that has no a priori constraints or boundaries" (Calarco 2008, p. 55).

Calarco's "should be" is important for the understanding that for Levinas's logical framework to operate rigorously, the "a priori constraints" cannot limit ethical consideration to the human. In Levinas's famously humanist philosophy, the only animal to play any great part was Bobby the dog, who recognized the humanity of concentration camp prisoners. But as others have begun to think about passivity towards animals in activism (Atterton 2012; Halls 2012; Rose 2012), the position here is radical because we have no choice in being obliged to respond to the pain and suffering of the Other; to repeat after Levinas, it is the call of the Other and not the who of the Other that institutes ethics. This "universal ethical

5. List of Save Groups, The Save Movement, https://thesavemovement.org/list-of-save-groups/.

consideration" we need to give to the Other suggests that the nonhuman animal is far from voiceless and, as many have argued (for example, Derrida 2008; Shapiro 2017), has agency. We are called to their aid regardless of "who" they are or what form of language the call comes in.

This ethical responsibility can be easily characterized as useless; that is, if ethics is committed to a universal ethical consideration of who or what demands our response, our response will be, from the very start, always too much and never enough (to quote the title of Jasmin Singer's 2016 vegan autobiography). If our duty to the Other is always grounded in this universality to begin with, then we will never be constrained; our ethics knows no limits. Echoing Carol Adams's call for veganism to be anti-teleological in challenging the idea of continual growth and progress, our ethics cannot have an end-point (Adams 1990). That would be the end of ethics itself and an end to the calls. Rather, says Levinas, our duty is insomniac: to always be listening and ready for when the call comes.

So, this is why Levinas characterizes ethics as an insomniac duty: it is only in being mindful and ready to act and advocate in each moment that we may fulfill our ethical duty towards the Other. And the best way for us to do that for nonhuman animals, as Jenni says, is to keep their suffering in front of us. This is what regular, continual vigils outside slaughterhouses do, perhaps mostly for the activists involved, but also for those witnessing their testimony via video, photo, and sometimes audio (as when activists record and share online the screams of cows and pigs going into slaughter or into the CO_2 gas chambers). As Joy (2010) reminds us: "The goal of all justice movements is to activate collective witnessing so that social practices reflect social values. A movement succeeds when it reaches a critical mass of witnesses—that is enough witnesses to tip the scales of power in favor of the movement" (p. 139).

The logical conclusion from this argument, then, is that bearing witness cannot be "useless," at least not in its totality; rather, bearing witness in this way, even though it may not save many (or hardly any) of the unique and particular animals in the trucks, is the practice of ethics as being mindful and ready to act and advocate. Whoever arrives on the train or truck, be it a pig or a child, a human or an animal, will demand a response from us—a differentiated response, perhaps, but our "rigorous and generous agnosticism concerning the 'who' of the Other" (Calarco 2007, p. 71) is what keeps ethics open, as ethics.

But, as Calarco suggests, "if we are to learn anything from Levinas, it is that ethical experience occurs precisely where phenomenology is interrupted and that ethical experience is traumatic and not easily captured by thought" (p. 73). That is, keeping suffering in front of us, we risk trauma, PTSD, and burnout. This is where the two forms of insomnia—the theoretical ethical concept and the practical embodied experience—meet. So, the only proper practice that can motivate and sustain us is, perhaps, care and love. Not effective but compassionate altruism, then, is the basis for an ethical witnessing that bears the burden of those whom we love who are in pain. Such a practice is what Kim Stallwood (2014) advocates, drawing on Buddhist writer Ken Jones's formulation of compassion as "the daily face of wisdom." Compassion resonates with the call to not turn away—to not physically turn away—but to face what is difficult: the suffering of our chicken and all the animals in industrial agriculture (as well as in the exotic pet trade, in entertainment, forced labor, and other exploitative industries). As such, activist practices outside the slaughterhouse depend very much on the direction in which activists face the trucks, the animals, and the killing spaces. This maps onto Levinas's most famous concept: that it is the face of the Other that demands our response. When asked if animals could have a face, Levinas said: "No, well, maybe a snake does. But no." But if, as Stallwood emphasizes, "compassion is, like veganism itself, not so much a goal as an orientation or journey" (p. 61), then it is the orientation towards the face, not its substantive species, that demands our commitment. As scholars such as Deborah Bird Rose (2011) have argued, Levinas's theory of the face only makes sense if the nonhuman also has a face; otherwise, why would we respond to their call, too? "The daily face of wisdom" could also be a description of witnessing.

Stallwood, in what is a both astute and loving move, notes that our insomniac advocacy is "one we learn to recommit to as much in the breach or inadequacy of our efforts to extend it, as we do through living it" (p. 61). As he reaffirms, compassion or loving altruism is a practice; we must repeat that practice, not only for the animals but also for ourselves, and—here's the thing—we repeat it knowing that it is always already inadequate, often fruitless, mainly useless. Yet to do away with compassion because it is uselessly inadequate, writes Stallwood, is "to deny oneself the very possibility of the sort of change—whether personal transformation or social progress—that could fill the heart and open the mind to still further change" (p. 58).

One of the problems with categorizing the act of bearing witness as useless is that it too simply demeans this advocacy by aligning it, perhaps unintentionally, with the broader social construction of domesticated animals as "useless" animals. Matthew Cole and Kate Stewart (2016) pick up on this in their study on the socialization of children when they say that "the commercialized slaughter of animals . . . demonstrates a murderous alchemy, by which the 'useless' animal is transmuted into profit" (p. 17).

But most of all, this criticism of uselessness sets up a false dichotomy and an overreliance on measurability in refusing to recognize the unquantifiable value of a chicken's life. The same criticism also separates bearing witness from testimony, which transforms moral witnessing into political witnessing. The difference is that the political witness sets out to bring about change. It is bearing political witness through and with testimony, particularly using footage and photography of the suffering of animals in agriculture, that has transformed the nature of animal advocacy and that is no doubt—although I haven't measured it—in part responsible for the rising tide of veganism across the globe.

Bringing attention to the physical acts in space of the activists who bear witness, together with the theoretical constitution of ethics via an a-priori call from the Other, means—to me at least—that such practices cannot ever be only useless, even if, as clearly happens, the specific animals who pass through the space on a given day will have been dead by the time the activists get to work or return home. (Apart from the very, very few, such as you, our chicken.) By attending to the spatial imaginary of the cross-species encounters enacted in those spaces—normalizing both the hegemonic acts of speciesism carried out by the truck drivers, farmers, slaughterhouse workers, and police, and the counteracts of protest that are activists' strategic interventions in the flow of power, capital, and political economy—Levinas's insomniac ethical responsibility shows us that a trust in the altruistic uselessness of standing outside a slaughterhouse is exemplary of the ethical call to action. Yes, it is always already useless. But as I have explained above, that is because for Levinas, the call to be ethical comes before any particular suffering; as Calarco puts it, we must remain agnostic in our understanding of who the Other may be, and that includes in consideration of species. Our duty to another comes before the specific relationship with that other, instituted by a moment or an act such as coming face-to-face with a unique individual animal. Because we are already awake and prepared for the call, we already have entangled agential encounters with the animals.

So, bearing witness cannot be only useless because it is already the practice of ethics. Recognizing uselessness rather than usefulness—or perhaps recognizing a conceptual uselessness as practical usefulness—is the only fully responsible ethical stance in relation to immanent, multitudinous, unbearable worlds of pain. You, dear chicken, don't care much for claims of uselessness. We were useful to you; we were bound, by our already-existing ethical duty, to you, and who knows to how many others in animal agriculture whose lives the Save Movement has brought to light and radically transformed public sensibility of. You get to enjoy perching, dust bathing, living in peace. How many of those acts are useless?

I've addressed this chapter to you, my friend, our Cancun chicken, now resting at Tierra de Animales sanctuary, because I want to take seriously Salih's argument that critical animal studies and vegan geographies risk "rendering the animal body into academic rhetoric which may cause us to forget or overlook the fact that we are talking about the actual physical suffering and death occurring on a scale most of us would be hard-put to imagine" (p. 70). For myself, this address to you is a foregrounding of what Oliver (2001) notes as the "address-ability" that, alongside "response-ability," is at the very core of ethical subjectivity and that, she argues, is established by the performative act of witnessing. You are addressable; you are the other to whom this chapter is addressed; and of course, there is the hope that the "you" is also the collective of your brothers and sisters and—conscious of Derrida's (2008) affirmation that there is no "Animal," there are only "animals"—that the singular "you" can help us turn towards the collective "you" whom we didn't "save."

By the end of her speculation on the act of witnessing and whether or not "meat" has a face, Salih concludes that we have not thought about death enough. And in helping us to do just that, she seems to give the sense that the vigils outside slaughterhouses may not be so useless or pointless after all:

> It is said that humans are a lonely species. Refusing to look or listen to the life that surrounds us, we equip ourselves with elaborate apparatuses of killing which we then spectacularly ignore. This is what vigils outside slaughterhouses are for: to remind us that we are living in the midst of death, indeed, that we have made our lives depend on killing and death. (pp. 71–72)

Back in Mexico, in the car, as we're driving along Avenue de la Luna on our way back into Cancun central, a Coldplay song comes on the radio. Chris Martin sings, "I was just guessing at numbers and figures," which, I think, sounds like a suitable and timely rebuke to those who would not have recommended we be outside the slaughterhouse at all. Never before have I finished a book chapter by quoting Coldplay, and I imagine I'll never do so again. But I'll be honest: as I think of you, our freed chicken, now, these many months later, wondering how you are coping with your new life at the sanctuary (if your torn-off toe is healing) and grappling with the sheer numbing number of your brothers and sisters who go into slaughterhouses all round the world every day, the next line nearly brings me to tears. Sings Chris Martin, "Science and progress never spoke as loud as my heart."

3

ENVISIONING VEGAN AGRICULTURE

Mona Seymour

Introduction

Veganism necessarily engages our food systems. Over 70 billion land animals are confined, farmed, and killed for their flesh, eggs, and milk globally each year (Taylor & Twine 2014). Global demand for farmed animal products is projected to increase by 70 percent by 2050 (Food and Agriculture Organization of the United Nations 2018). These statistics do not account for the vast numbers of farmed insects, farmed and wild-caught fish, and wild-caught animals bound for human consumption. A disturbing corollary to all of this is the elimination of free-living predators in the interest of protecting the lives of (read: investments in) farmed animals. For instance, in 2017, the United States Department of Agriculture's (USDA) Wildlife Services program systematically killed over 2.3 million animals, including coyotes, mountain lions, and wolves, largely to benefit ranchers who graze their cattle, sheep, and other "livestock" on public lands (USDA 2017; Bergstrom et al., 2014).

Vegan responses to the violence against animals that is characteristic of food systems around the world are located in both the production and consumption realms. On the consumption side, veganism is typically promoted and enacted as a set of dietary guidelines for what food items may be consumed and what must be avoided, centering on whether the food is of animal origin or contains animal byproducts. For instance, one of the most familiar definitions of veganism asserts that this "way of living . . . seeks to exclude . . . all forms of exploitation of, and cruelty to, animals for food, clothing or any other purpose"; "one thing all vegans have in common is a plant-based diet avoiding all animal foods such as meat . . . dairy, eggs and honey," in addition to a lifestyle that excludes animal-based and

-tested products (The Vegan Society, n.d.-a).[1] Veganism also informs the work of advocates and activists who target the production side of food systems, seeking to reform or abolish the farming of animals and other violent practices, such as hunting. Activism takes many forms, ranging from indirect intervention (e.g., policy change) to direct action (e.g., open rescue). But how else does veganism inform the production side of the food system beside dictating that it must not involve the farming and take of animals? This is an underexplored question. This chapter engages with veganism and agricultural production spaces in order to consider what more veganism has to say about acceptable human–animal relations on the farm, moving beyond the abolition of animal farming. In short, *how can we envision and enact vegan agriculture?* What might vegan agricultural spaces look like, and what sorts of relations and practices might characterize and shape them?

It is a moral imperative to examine these inquiries in light of the present and prospective scopes of animal farming and suffering. Exploring what constitutes a vegan agricultural space is part of the process to "create necessary counter hegemonic spaces so desperately needed" (White & Springer 2018, p. 170) to challenge and replace the entrenched spaces of violence and oppression of the agricultural industry. A coherent and feasible vision of vegan agriculture can be embraced and promoted as normative by the vegan and animal rights movements and by allies in the food movement.

The central intent of this chapter is to explore what agricultural spaces informed by veganism may entail by developing a conceptualization of vegan agriculture and a set of vegan agriculture guidelines. The next section considers key ideas that may inform these pursuits. It first reviews existing understandings of vegan agriculture, and then considers a particular vegan farming method and vegan discourse on interlocked oppressions to expand upon these ideas. A definition of vegan agriculture and a set of vegan agriculture guidelines based on principles and practices extrapolated from said resources are presented in the following section. Next, a case study of a Stockfree-certified veganic farm in California, U.S., is presented to provide an example of vegan agriculture in practice and to discuss and problematize some of the guidelines. The chapter concludes by suggesting a few further questions and perspectives that should be considered in envisioning vegan agriculture (see footnote on next page).[2]

1. However, note that this heavily circulated definition belies the scope of The Vegan Society's historical construction of veganism. "An ethical practice that always transcended dietary regimen" (Taylor & Twine 2014, p. 12), veganism's ethical substance "centered on compassionate nonexploitation: For other animals, for the self, and for other humans" (Cole 2014, p. 211).

Informing Vegan Agriculture

Vegan agriculture has not been extensively defined, let alone discussed, particularly in the academic realm. Visak (2007) offers that vegan agriculture "is agriculture without animal production, such as meat, dairy or eggs and without the use of manure that results from animal production" that "produces plant food, such as grains, vegetables, legumes, herbs, fruit, nuts and beans" (p. 195). This definition points to non-farmed-animal agricultural products and fertility sources as key elements of vegan agriculture. The attention on manure follows from the routine use of farmed-animal wastes and remains for soil fertility on organic farms and in some chemical-based operations. Visak further suggests that vegan agriculture is being successfully practiced in the form of vegan organic agriculture in Western Europe. Cole (2016), with reference to a study by Fairlie (2010), also identifies vegan organic agriculture as a model of vegan agriculture, along with the vegan chemical and vegan permaculture models.

Visak's definition helpfully provides a basic conceptualization of vegan agriculture, emphasizing that it absolutely must not involve the farming of animals or the use of animal products. However, I suggest that vegan agriculture entails a broader set of vegan-informed practices and relations than mere avoidance of animal outputs and inputs. The remainder of this section describes some perspectives that are helpful for formulating vegan agricultural spaces, beginning with vegan organic growing—the approach to vegan farming identified by Visak (2007) and Cole (2016)—and the associated Stockfree Standards.

"Vegan organic" is defined as "any system of cultivation that excludes artificial chemicals, livestock manures, animal remains from slaughterhouses, genetically modified material and indeed anything of animal origin such as fishmeal" (Vegan Organic Network, n.d.). Vegan organic production departs from organic agriculture in refraining from the use of domesticated animals and their byproducts in plant production. It does not completely exclude animals from the production system though, as it relies on ecosystem services supplied by wild insects and soil microfauna (Schmutz & Foresi 2017). The question of soil fertility in a vegan organic system is posed frequently: "fertility is maintained by vegetable compost, green manures, crop rotation, mulches, and any other method that is sustainable,

2. This chapter makes references to "vegan agriculture," "veganic agriculture," and "vegan organic agriculture." These terms are distinct but related. By way of initial differentiation, I offer that "vegan agriculture" is the most general and heretofore undeveloped of these terms, while veganic and vegan organic approaches can fit within the rubric of vegan agriculture that I develop later in this chapter.

ecologically viable and not dependent upon animal exploitation" (Vegan Organic Network, n.d.).

The Vegan Organic Network (VON) is the core supporting organization for vegan organic agriculture. VON was founded in the United Kingdom in 1996 to research and promote vegan organic growing throughout the world (Vegan Organic Network, n.d.). The organization was established out of deep concern about how vegans' food is grown—predominantly with synthetic fertilizers and/or animal byproducts—which VON's founders felt the vegan movement had largely ignored. Among VON's first accomplishments was the creation of the Stockfree Organic Standards, a set of farming standards developed for the guidance and certification of growers who follow vegan organic farming principles. "Stockfree" refers to a method of growing plant-based foods sans animal inputs (Tolhurst Organic, n.d.).[3] VON also formed a Stockfree Organic Services wing to assist with providing advice, support, and documents related to the standards (Vegan Organic Network, n.d.).

The Stockfree Organic Standards are rooted in vegan values including nonviolence, nonexploitation, respect, peace, and security (Vegan Organic Network, n.d.).[4] The standards consist of seventeen categories, each containing multiple standards pertaining to organic and/or stockfree practices. The Stockfree Standards (Table 1, see p. 65), which focus on cruelty-free, plant-based agricultural practices, are a subset of the Stockfree Organic Standards. These standards guide growers away from profiting from the exploitation of animals, the use of animal wastes and byproducts, and the taking of animal lives; they also advise on animal

3. The standards were termed "stockfree organic" rather than "vegan organic" for ease of communication with farmers, lest farmers assume that they themselves must be vegan to implement the standards (Graham 2014). The term "stockfree" is a modification of "stockless," which is commonly used to refer to arable farming (Hall & Tolhurst 2007). However, "stockfree" is more positive and progressive and connotes that animals are not necessary to agriculture and human diet, while "stockless" indicates that something is missing (Schmutz & Foresi 2017; Vegan Organic Network, n.d.). U.K. growers may apply to the Soil Association, a leading organic certification body, for Stockfree Organic status. In the U.S., Stockfree Organic certification has been offered by a diversified certifier, Quality Certification Services (QCS).
4. VON also identifies unsustainable land use for animal agriculture, in addition to the horrendous, senseless violence against animals that it entails, as a key rationale for stockfree organic growing and standards (Vegan Organic Network, n.d.)
5. See next page. There are some discrepancies in the categorization and level of detail of the Stockfree Standards between the Stockfree Organic Standards and Stockfree Standards documents. In these cases, the table follows the categorization scheme indicated by the Stockfree Standards document and synthesizes the details from both documents.
6. See next page. The full set of Stockfree Organic Standards contains numerous additional standards that are in line with vegan values or that represent good alternatives to nonvegan practices. In the interest of space, the full set of standards is not presented here but will be drawn on to build the guidelines presented in the following section.

keeping. Stockfree certification is available anywhere in the world through grower-to-grower inspection (Stockfree Organic Services, n.d.).

Table 1. The Stockfree Standards[5,6]

Category	Summary of Standards
Keeping of animals on the holding	• Animals may not be kept for food production or commercial gain (including for meat, dairy, eggs; fur, wool; racing; breeding). • Livestock fodder and bedding litter may not be grown. • Companion animals, rescue animals, service animals, and guard animals may be kept. • Bees may be kept as long as they are not harmed or exploited and as long as their honey is not removed.
Main sources of fertility	• Manure, urine, or slurry from animals may not be used as a source of fertility. This includes the wastes of animals legitimately on holding. • Worm compost from deliberate wormeries may not be used.
Supplementary nutrients	• Animal byproducts of livestock or fish origin may not be used (including blood meal, fish meal, bone meal, fish emulsion).
Competing birds and animals	• Animals may not be poisoned or shot. • Animals may not be killed for sport.
Disease, mollusk, and insect pest control	• Biocides based on animal derivatives may not be used. • Hypochlorite-based disinfectants may not be used to sterilize buildings and equipment. • Copper sulfate, copper oxychloride, or copper ammonia carbonate may not be used. • Beeswax pruning agent may not be used.
Labeling for box schemes that buy in non-stockfree produce	• Customers must be notified which items are stockfree organic and which items conform to another organic standard.

The Stockfree Standards clearly evince vegan values, and vegan organic farming is promoted by leading vegan organizations including The Vegan Society in the U.K. (Baker 2009; The Vegan Society, n.d.-b). Thus, these guiding principles on grower–animal relations in and beyond agricultural spaces provide an invaluable baseline for the development of vegan agriculture guidelines.

Yet I suggest that an understanding of vegan agriculture should be informed by additional vegan and vegan-allied perspectives, as the contemporary vegan discourse and praxis suggest that a concern for animals—other-than-human animals—does not define the limits of the vegan sphere of moral concern.[7] For many, veganism and animal liberation also entail a commitment to ending human oppression: this is made clear by arguments about the connections between the oppression and suffering of human and nonhuman groups.[8] The burgeoning field of critical animal studies (CAS) has been particularly adept at illuminating not only the means and modes of nonhuman oppression, but also the intersectional and interlocking nature of oppressions. On the "commonality of oppressions," Best et al. (2007) write that "speciesism, sexism, racism . . . and other hierarchical ideologies and institutions are . . . parts of a larger, interlocking, global system of domination" (p. 5). Speciesism, classism, ableism, sexism, and racism augment and reinforce each other (Nibert 2017). CAS further identifies these forms of domination and oppression as entangled with capitalism in a number of ways, including in how these belief systems function to rationalize the abuses that occur under capitalism (Nibert 2017) and how capitalism amplifies these forms of oppression (Sanbonmatsu 2017). The recognition that nonhuman and human animals are both commodified and are exploited in similar ways by capitalism generates "the ethical duty to oppose these interlocking forms of exploitation and violence"

7. VON, in fact, aligns with this position. While the Stockfree Organic Standards are heavily informed by concerns about animal rights and environmental sustainability, VON itself was established with a broader vision, embracing "an alternative view of market economics, of cooperation, and a movement for land reform and redistribution" and viewing "food production [as] but one aspect of a dynamic vegan culture which embraces justice for people, animals and the environment in a sustainable balance" (Vegan Organic Network, n.d.).
8. Within the vegan movement, there are numerous arguments for actively extending justice and compassion to human groups in vegan advocacy. For instance, the case is made that if veganism is about ending animal oppression, it is also about ending human oppression, as humans are animals; another articulation is that if veganism is about reducing the suffering of all sentient beings, then of course, humans are included in the vegan agenda. Others suggest that if vegans are anti-speciesist, we must believe that humans are as deserving of justice as animals are. However, here, I will point to perspectives about interlocking oppressions of nonhuman and human groups, as agriculture is a sphere in which these are particularly pronounced yet underrecognized. Critical animal studies scholarship is especially enlightening on these matters.

(Matsuoka & Sorenson 2018, p. 5). All of this makes clear the critical importance of contesting speciesism and violence against nonhuman animals, ultimately committing to a holistic social justice struggle and the goal of total liberation for human and nonhuman animals alike (Matsuoka & Sorenson 2018; Nocella II et al., 2014), while looking towards post-capitalist futures (see, for example, Nibert 2013; White 2017a).

The deep intertwining of the oppression of nonhuman animals with that of humans is perhaps nowhere more pronounced than in animal agriculture. As White (2017a) notes: "The dark reality [is] that capitalist modes of exploitation and violence in the farming industry . . . are never just about nonhuman animals. . . . [T]he violence spans 'the species divide'" (p. 275). The violent displacement of Brazilian Indigenous communities by Spanish and Portuguese colonizers to expropriate land for cattle ranching (Nibert 2013); the dual commodification of ducks and Mexican immigrant laborers in the U.S. foie gras industry and the various forms and experiences of violence involved (Joyce, Nevins, & Schneiderman 2017; also see Ducey 2017, and Sebastian 2017, for other recent works on the interconnected oppressions of farmed animals and of laborers); and the "spillover" of slaughterhouse work into abuses against other, less powerful groups in adjacent communities (Fitzgerald, Kalof, & Dietz 2009) comprise only a few examples of the ways in which animal and human oppressions are connected in capitalist agriculture.

Furthermore, speciesism, racism, classism, ableism, ageism, sexism, and other forms of oppression share the same *roots*, the same mentality of domination. Thus, no society that tolerates discrimination based on race, for instance, will ever reject the exploitation of animals (Hawthorne 2016; Joy & Tuider 2016). In the words of Martin Luther King Jr., "injustice anywhere is a threat to justice everywhere" (Best et al., 2007, p. 5; Tuttle 2014, p. 284). Veganism, therefore, must embrace a commitment to ending violence against animal *and* human life through cooperation, alliance, and solidarity with other movements against hierarchy and oppression (Hawthorne 2016; Joy & Tuider 2016; Jenkins & Stănescu 2014; Nibert 2017; Nocella II et al., 2014; Weitzenfeld & Joy 2014; Best et al., 2007).

Recognition of the inseparability of animal liberation and human liberation (Best 2007) carries key implications for the envisioning and enacting of vegan agriculture. For example, vegan agriculture must be cognizant of and avoid the ways in which different groups of humans may be exploited in plant agriculture. And it must function in solidarity with other social justice movements for which these are also focal problems. Critical vegan scholars and activists have pointed out numerous ways in which plant agriculture entails human suffering and exploitation, dispelling the notion that vegan food and its production are necessarily cruelty-free. Instances and types of abuse include slave labor, child labor, and dangerous farm tools on West African cocoa plantations (Food Empowerment Project, "Child Labor"; Harper 2010b; Ornelas 2014); forced labor and dangerous working conditions on the Dominican Republic's sugar cane plantations (Harper 2010b); exploitation through short-term contracts, violent suppression of unionization, and pesticide exposure on Central American banana farms (Food Empowerment Project, "Peeling"); and heat exposure, exposure to toxic agricultural chemicals, sexual harassment, verbal abuse, low wages and contract violations related to wages, and threats of deportation in U.S. fields (Food Empowerment Project, "Produce Workers"; Ornelas 2014).

It is also important to note that the purchase of animal manures, blood meals, and other byproducts originating from farms and slaughterhouses—products that are commonly used to enhance soil fertility in organic plant agriculture—not only underwrites animal exploitation, but also subsidizes an industry that produces dangerous and traumatic working conditions for a low-wage, largely immigrant labor force (see, for example, Champlin & Hake 2006; Dillard 2008). These critiques make clear that agricultural spaces that use or harm no animals in their operations are not necessarily liberated spaces, point to some specific issues that vegan agriculturalists must be aware of, and suggest movements that vegan growers may support and seek guidance from (e.g., the farmworker justice movement). A commitment to critical awareness and solidarity will help vegan growers towards operating in opposition to all forms of oppression that may manifest in plant agricultural systems.

A final key perspective from veganism for vegan agriculture concerns pragmatism and aspiration. One of the best-known definitions of veganism, in describing it as "a way of living which seeks to exclude, as far as is possible and practicable, all forms of exploitation of, and cruelty to, animals for food, clothing or any other purpose" (The Vegan Society, n.d.-a), acknowledges that there are challenges inherent in living as a vegan in a nonvegan world. In the context of agriculture, large farm machinery used in the industrial agricultural production of fruits, vegetables, and grains can harm rodents, birds, small mammals, reptiles, and amphibians. Plant agriculture is not greenhouse gas emissions–free and, thus, negatively impacts animals and the environment (Gruen & Jones 2015). Ingredient lists on bags of soil amendments may fail to indicate the presence of animal byproducts. Guidelines for vegan agriculture must recognize that growers who are deeply committed to minimizing harm and practicing avoidance of animal products will sometimes face challenges in doing so and be limited in their ability to surmount these obstacles completely.

Guidelines for Vegan Agriculture

This section presents a set of guidelines for how veganism may inform growers' practices involving and relationships with different groups of humans and other-than-human animals in agricultural spaces (see Table 2 on pp. 71–73). The guidelines are informed by the perspectives above, as well as by conversations with U.S. veganic farmers and activists about veganism and veganic farming practices.[9] The Veganic Agriculture Network (VAN), a core promoter of veganic agriculture in North America, describes veganic agriculture as "an approach to growing plant foods that encompasses a respect for animals, the environment, and human health"; "this is a form of agriculture that goes further than organic standards, by eliminating the use of products that are derived from confined animals and by encouraging the presence of wild native animals on the farmland" (2008). Some consider "veganic" to be the North American alias for "vegan organic" (see, for example, Veganic Agriculture Network 2008), and in the U.S., "veganic" is more commonly used than is "vegan organic" or "stockfree organic" to refer to plant-based, nonchemical agriculture. However, unlike the vegan organic movement with the Stockfree Organic Standards, the North American veganic movement does not currently have a set of standards to delineate common practices, and, thus, approaches to veganic farming may be more diverse.

The guidelines evince a general understanding of vegan agriculture as *an agricultural system that does not rely on, involve, or support animal ownership, commodification, exploitation, and suffering; that promotes compassion and justice for animals; and that extends these considerations to humans*. While the guidelines themselves engage largely material aspects of agriculture, they should be understood as "representative of an entire social justice worldview of which [products and activities represent] the visible tip of the iceberg" (Pedersen & Stănescu 2014, p. 264). Thus, they are consistent with formulations of veganism that are explicitly political, are cognizant of the interconnectedness of oppressions, and are social justice–oriented rather than merely diet- or lifestyle-focused (see, for example, Jenkins & Stănescu 2014; Jones 2016; White & Springer 2018; White 2017b). Vegan agriculture is also posited as fundamentally incompatible with capitalist agriculture. It refutes the commodification of bodies and the prioritization of profit over all else.

9. These conversations took place in 2016 and 2017 in casual settings, conference settings, and in the context of formal interviews for a separate research project on veganic agriculture in the U.S.

Vegan agriculture may be implemented on farms and in market gardens, in household and community gardens, and in other noncapitalist spaces of plant food production through practices including, but not limited to, those outlined below. The guidelines below cover practices and materials in agricultural spaces,[10] not in homes, offices, or other spaces associated with production sites; thus, the guidelines do not cover, for instance, farmers' diets or the keeping of indoor companion animals. These guidelines are not intended as technical advice—they are guidelines that reflect and promote vegan values and that growers can apply to existing knowledge about farming and gardening.[11] They are intended to be implemented to the greatest degree practicable and possible, with financial, temporal, geographical, and knowledge-based constraints taken into account. Finally, these guidelines acknowledge that vegan agricultural spaces are situated within the broader context of a nonvegan world.

Case Study in Vegan Agriculture: Lazy Millennial Farms

Lazy Millennial Farms is located in Salinas, CA, in one of the most important agricultural regions in the U.S. It is one of approximately fifty veganic farms in the U.S. (Seymour 2018) and is one of two U.S farms to have held the Stockfree certification (Vegan Organic Network, n.d.). The farm is a family-owned, two-acre, diversified operation. In these senses, it is representative of U.S. veganic farms: most appear to be family-owned, small-scale (under ten acres), diversified vegetable and fruit farms (Seymour & Utter, unpublished data).

Brittany and Matthew (Matt) Loisel, both new farmers,[12] founded Lazy Millennial Farms in 2016 and operated it for two seasons. The Loisels made the decision to farm after self-educating about the dominant industrial food system

10. These guidelines were prepared with outdoor agricultural spaces in mind but, with some modifications, are scalable and transferable to smaller sites, such as window-box gardens, and to non-soil-based projects, such as hydroponic grow operations.

11. There are a number of books and websites oriented towards vegan organic and veganic growing methods that may be consulted for technical advice that is in line with the proposed guidelines, though some advice from these resources may contradict points presented here, particularly concerning soil amendments and pest control. Suggested resources include O'Brien (1986), Hall & Tolhurst (2007), Burnett (2014), Bonsall (2015), and the website of the Veganic Agriculture Network. Beyond these, numerous farming and gardening texts give technical advice that is incidentally vegan.

12. The United States Department of Agriculture describes new or beginning farmers as individuals with ten years of farming experience or less.

Table 2. Vegan Agriculture Guidelines

Category	Guidelines
1. Soil health	1.1 Wastes and remains of farmed or otherwise exploited animals are not used to enhance the soil. These include but are not limited to manure, blood meal, bone meal, feather meal, fish meal, and worm castings. 1.2 Nontoxic methods that protect and enhance the soil and soil life are implemented. These include but are not limited to: continuous coverage of the soil with plant matter; use of low- or no-till methods; minimal to no use of heavy machinery during planting and harvesting; and avoidance of chemical fertilizers. 1.3 Plant- and rock-based sources of fertility are used. These include but are not limited to green manures, plant-based composts, mulches, seaweeds, wood ash, and rock dust. 1.4 The following animal-based sources may be used to enhance the soil, to the extent safe (e.g., properly treated) and legal: 1.4.1 Humanure and urine from plant-based humans; 1.4.2 Manure, eggs, and other byproducts from rescued farmed animals, provided that the animals are not being sanctuaried for this purpose; 1.4.3 Manure from free-living animals (e.g., bat guano, bird guano).
2. Weed, disease, and animal "pest" control	2.1 Poisons (e.g., herbicides, fungicides, rodenticides, and other pesticides) and toxic seeds (e.g., Bt crops) are not used. 2.2 Soil sterilizers are not used. 2.3 Substances containing the byproducts of farmed or otherwise exploited animals are not used. 2.4 Animals, including insects, are not purchased (or otherwise obtained) and brought in for biocontrol purposes. 2.5 Animals who interfere in farming operations are not shot, trapped, drowned, or otherwise killed. 2.6 Nonlethal measures are used in the management of weeds, diseases, and animals. These include but are not limited to mulching, hand weeding, crop rotations, companion planting, and barriers (e.g., fences, netting). 2.7 Native predator habitat may be enhanced.

Vegan Agriculture Guidelines (Continued)

3. Wildlife and habitat protection	3.1 Nesting and roosting sites are not disturbed or removed. 3.2 Wildlife are not shot or otherwise killed for food or sport. 3.3 Planting and harvesting methods that have the least potential to injure or kill wildlife and soil life are implemented. 3.4 Native habitat and wildlife populations are preserved and supported through measures including, but not limited to: restoring native habitat; maintaining existing valuable habitat; enhancing wildlife corridors; and installing bird boxes, bat boxes, and feeding stations. 3.5 Maintenance activities (such as mowing, trimming, ditch clearing, and activities involving the use of loud machinery and artificial lighting) are sensitive to daily and seasonal wildlife activities and cycles. 3.6 Any new structures or fields are sited in areas of low value to wildlife populations. 3.7 Injured wildlife, particularly those injured by farming practices, are rescued and rehabilitated (on- or off-site).
4. Animal keeping	4.1 Animals are not bought, raised, used, or sold for products (including but not limited to meat, eggs, milk, honey, skin, and fur), progeny, labor, companionship, or entertainment. 4.2 Crops intended for farmed or otherwise exploited animals at other sites are not grown. 4.3 Sanctuary may be provided for rescued farmed animals, other domesticated animals, and wildlife.
5. Labor practices	5.1 Domesticated animals are not used for farm labor, including for the operation of machinery and the control of animal "pests" (see footnote on next page.)[13] 5.2 Humans who work on-site are ensured safe and fair working conditions. These include, but are not limited to, being paid at least a living wage and overtime (or another mutually agreeable compensation arrangement); working free of coercion, force, and harassment; not being discouraged from bringing working condition issues into question or from organizing; not being exposed to toxic chemicals; and being provided ample clean drinking water and shelter from the elements.

Vegan Agriculture Guidelines (Continued)

6. Community engagement	6.1 A portion of the produce grown is designated for local food-insecure or food justice communities. These community members are consulted on their food and nutritional needs and preferences and on their ability to pay. 6.2 Growers working land that originally belonged to Indigenous groups consult members of the dispossessed community on how they may farm or take other actions in line with land justice and sovereignty struggles. 6.3 The space may be used for education and other forms of outreach about veganism and vegan farming; for community organizing around vegan issues; for other communal activities that reflect and promote vegan values; and for organizing and education related to other anti-oppression movements. In these cases, the space is welcoming, accessible, and safe for all visitors.
7. Resources from off-holding	7.1 Vegan, slavery- and sweatshop-free, and nontoxic food, shoes, clothing, tools, and other materials are the norm for all workers, visitors, and domesticated animals when present in the agricultural space. 7.2 If resources (including but not limited to seeds, water, fertility, energy, and machinery) are imported from off-holding, the grower has done their best to ensure that each product was extracted, harvested, manufactured (or otherwise created) and transported in ways consistent with veganism and with justice for and nonexploitation of all sentient beings.

13. Though see Donaldson & Kymlicka (2015) for an interesting perspective on sanctuaried and other domesticated animals and their inclination or desire to "work."

and becoming disillusioned with corporate life. They viewed starting a farm as a means to forge a more meaningful, ethical, environmentally sustainable, and pro-social life path. Though comfortable with gardening, they had no formal farming education and began to research training options. In 2015, Matt and Brittany entered a ten-month farmer education program at the Agriculture and Land-Based Training Association (ALBA) in Salinas to learn aspects of farming, including organic farm production, marketing, and bookkeeping. Upon graduation, the Loisels were eligible to apply to lease acreage as part of ALBA's on-site farm incubator program. Shortly before signing their lease, Matt and Brittany transitioned from vegetarianism to veganism. At this point, it dawned on them that all of their training had involved the use of animal byproducts for soil fertility, as it is common in organic farming to use farm and slaughterhouse byproducts, including manure, blood meal, bone meal, and feather meal. This forced the Loisels to research alternatives, which led them to veganic agriculture and the Stockfree Organic Standards. They pursued Stockfree certification in addition to their organic certification and began farming and marketing Stockfree-certified organic produce through a community-supported agriculture (CSA) model in 2016. Their diversified vegetable farming operation expanded from one-half acre to over two acres in 2017; each week, they served approximately thirty CSA customers—most of whom were attracted to their veganic growing practices—during the summer and fall of each year. As they got established, Matt retained a full-time corporate job while farming part-time, and Brittany farmed full-time with help from a small number of employees and interns.

In late 2017, after two growing seasons, Matt and Brittany decided to pursue other ventures. They left Lazy Millennial Farms to one of their former employees, Leo Sanchez, who continued to farm the land veganically. However, they generously provided input on the vegan farming guidelines presented above, elaborated on how some of these principles were implemented at Lazy Millennial Farms during their time there, and shared thoughts on the opportunities and difficulties associated with some of the guidelines.[14] Their practices and experiences at Lazy Millennial Farms help to illustrate and problematize how some of these guidelines may inform operations on a commercial, small-scale vegan farm.[15]

As a Stockfree-certified farm, Lazy Millennial Farms adhered to all of the standards presented in Table 1, many of which are reflected in the vegan farming

14. In addition to a phone conversation with Matt and Brittany about the guidelines (2017, November 19), this section is based on participant observation research at the Lazy Millennial Farms site in Salinas, CA, and at farming and animal rights conferences throughout CA in which Matt and/or Brittany were involved (2016–2017). It also draws on media coverage of the farm and on farm-related documents created by the Loisels.

15. Lazy Millennial Farms closed due to theft in the spring of 2019, after this piece had been completed. Its owner-operator hoped to be able to reopen the farm elsewhere in the future.

guidelines in Table 2. For instance, Matt and Brittany avoided farmed-animal sources of fertility (Guideline 1.1) and used exclusively plant- and rock-based fertility sources to build the farm's soil (Guideline 1.3). Their program included compost made from municipal green waste and a grain-based fertilizer (both purchased from local companies) for nitrogen, phosphorous, and potassium; rock phosphate for micronutrients; and cover crops (wheat in 2016 and a wheat-legume mix in 2017) for additional nitrogen.

Since they were certified Stockfree, Lazy Millennial Farms did not incorporate fertility sources from humans, sanctuaried farmed animals, or free-living animals (Guideline 1.4). Matt expressed, though, that he felt that permission to use these sources was appropriate for a set of vegan farming guidelines: he understood these sources to be vegan in a philosophical sense (despite not being vegan materially, as products of animals), as long as the collection process did not entail exploitation of or harm to the "donors." On the topic of using fertility sources from rescued farmed animals, Matt articulated that "we wouldn't have an ethical problem with a farm sanctuary rotating the rescued animals through [our] plot or applying their bedding to a field or composting it" (M. Loisel, Facebook post, March 2017). Indeed, rescuing and sanctuarying farmed animals are very much in line with veganism, and the use of their manures may be considered vegan in the sense that the animals are no longer being treated as property and kept to be used or exploited as resources.[16] Had the Loisels been able to provide sanctuary for farmed animals (they were not, due to lease conditions), they would have considered an integrated system in order to avoid wasting nutrients. However, Matt also acknowledged that the use of sanctuaried animals' manure fails to anticipate the abolition of animal agriculture and, thus, a state in which there are no longer farmed animals needing sanctuary (or at least enough of them that their manure would be a reliable, accessible resource). Therefore, it is critical to have a tried-and-true model of plant agriculture based on non-domesticated-animal fertility sources, ready for a post-animal agriculture future.

Matt and Brittany tended to view the free-living birds and rodents on their acreage positively or neutrally, observing that most of the birds who came onto their farm ate insects rather than damaged their crops, and that the gophers living on their plot primarily fed on a cover crop rather than their cash crops. While they had been instructed in their training program to install bird deterrents and to trap and kill gophers, the former seemed counterproductive, while the latter

16. Lest it appear that I am suggesting that VON's Stockfree Standards do not permit sanctuaried farmed animals' manure on the (technical) grounds of nonvegan materiality, I want to clarify that the prohibition derives more so from the desire to demonstrate that it is possible to grow without manures (J. Hall, personal communication, 2018).

was not acceptable to them as vegans and was to be avoided according to their Stockfree certification. The Loisels instead had planned to install bird boxes someday (Guideline 2.7), and they began to plant cover crop year-round in "gopher areas" of their plot to ensure there was consistently an appealing alternative to their vegetable crops for the gophers (Guideline 2.6). During their first season, Matt noted: "I remembered reading that gophers don't actually like vegetables, they prefer native plants. [Farmers usually] pull out all the native plants and all that is left are our vegetables, and then we kill the gophers [after we have given] them no other option [for food]. I started to do research and found that gophers are a big problem with alfalfa and another cover crop, so I've planted a row of that. So far they have only eaten one lettuce head and have cost me one dollar, and my conscience is clean" (Seed the Commons 2016).

The Loisels' approach to insect control shifted during their tenure at ALBA. In 2016, they moved onto a plot containing flowers, such as sweet alyssum, left behind by the previous farmer. Matt explained that this meant that predatory insects had been supplied with the food and habitat they needed to overwinter on the plot, and so when their growing season began, there were predatory insects in place to control the herbivorous insects that might feed on their crops. The Loisels enhanced their plot with more flowers, especially native species, to attract additional predatory insects (Guideline 2.7) and did not experience extensive problems with insect "pests" during their first growing season. However, in 2017, they moved to a different, larger plot that had only remnant cover crop, which could sustain herbivorous insects but not predators during the winter. The Loisels also knew that farmers on neighboring plots at ALBA would likely use pesticides (organic-approved ones) to eliminate insects; since many herbivorous insects have faster reproductive cycles than do predatory insects, Matt and Brittany expected a spillover of herbivores onto their plot before the predatory populations recovered. They made the decision to purchase and establish predatory species.

While the guidelines prohibit importing insects (Guideline 2.4) on the grounds that this involves treating animals as commodities, Matt focused on a different aspect of this decision that troubled him as a vegan: the predation activities that they were deliberately setting into motion. He remarked: "The area [of farming] I probably agonized the most in is, what level of insect suffering are we comfortable with?" To wit, among the predatory species that the Loisels brought in were parasitic wasp species, which deposit their eggs inside of the eggs or bodies of host insects. Upon hatching, the wasp larvae begin to consume their hosts, which Matt was fully aware of: ". . . it's not lost on me that [this] was the death sentence that we were issuing to the herbivores on the farm." However, the specter of waiting for predator–prey relationships to balance themselves in what Matt described as a highly artificial environment (their farm plot) that was continually influenced by practices occurring in the patchwork of surrounding plots begged the question of the Loisels' livelihood.

While for Matt, these ethical questions about causing suffering arose from the practice of deliberately bringing in animals for biocontrol, they may also be considered in cases in which farmers enhance habitat in the hopes of attracting predators—i.e., when farmers less directly structure predator–prey relationships. While Guideline 2.7 states that farmers may enhance native predator habitat, some vegans may not find this acceptable or may find it acceptable only in cases in which farmer livelihood is under serious threat. The question of whether and how vegans ought to encourage predation may also be considered in light of other Section 2 guidelines that prohibit lethal means of control. Under dire threat to their subsistence, some vegans may find it more acceptable to implement bullets (Guideline 2.5), or rodenticides or insecticides (or Bt tomatoes, should they come onto the market) (Guideline 2.1) if the end result would be quicker deaths, less painful deaths, or fewer net deaths than under a predation strategy. In this case, though, the potential impacts of these substances on farm labor and "non-target" free-living animals must also be taken into consideration. These quandaries point to the contingent, contextual nature of veganism in agricultural spaces.

While Lazy Millennial Farms did not have an articulated commitment to social justice for human groups, Matt and Brittany felt strongly about paying employees a $15-per-hour living wage (the 2016 California minimum wage was $10 per hour) (Guideline 5.2). Each season, the Loisels paid one to two regular employees for supplementary labor to their own and that of an intern (both unpaid).[17] They also extended this wage commitment to ad hoc labor needs. They understood that labor costs constitute a substantial portion of an organic farm's operating costs and that offering higher wages can place new farmers in a precarious financial situation, but they wanted to offer remuneration that was fair and that reflected the value of farm labor and laborers. Matt recalled encountering a different, prevailing perspective on farmworker pay early in their first season, when they fell behind in picking and boxing their lettuce crop. An ALBA contact suggested that they seek assistance from another farmer at the incubator whose day job was farm work. They were advised to ask her how much she and her family members would expect to earn per hour rather than offer her $15 straight out, which their contact remarked was

17. The topic of unpaid intern labor and the extent to which it is exploitative has been controversial in the small-farm community. While I did not delve into this with the Loisels, I thank Alisha Utter for raising this question; certainly, it is another labor-related issue that vegan agriculture must engage.

very high for farm labor. The Loisels were dismayed at this advice, which they felt was underhanded and exploitative.

During their time at Lazy Millennial Farms, the Loisels were quite active in outreach and education about veganic agriculture. Each season, they offered farm tours to the public in an effort to inform CSA members and other interested visitors about their veganic approach to farming (Guideline 6.3). As Matt and Brittany walked tour groups through their plot, they would discuss their business model and crop plans, point out beneficial insects and native plants, describe their approach to building the soil using plant-based inputs, explain their perspectives on various free-living animals on their farm, and converse with numerous visitors who asked questions about their practices and experiences. Matt and Brittany also routinely engaged in veganic education and publicity off-farm, leading quarterly gardening workshops in the Bay Area, presenting at farming and activist conferences throughout California, maintaining a social media presence, and speaking with reporters and bloggers.

Matt shared thoughts on another point about community engagement—regarding a vegan farm's involvement in local food justice work (Guideline 6.1): "I love doing crop plans. . . . If I had the information [on the species of plants that community members wanted to eat], putting together, say, a couple of rows, maybe five rows that are to be donated annually or something like that . . . I don't think it would be impossible." It was the amount of time needed to learn about a population's food needs and preferences that concerned him. "I feel like farmers are just always scraping by, and so some of this stuff might be difficult—the added stuff on top of just growing food is kinda difficult. We had big dreams with . . . stuff similar to this, and it never happened because there was never time to do it. . . . It was very difficult to do anything beyond just functioning, just trying to make a profit."

He then gave an example of a woman, a fellow vegan, who had approached Lazy Millennial Farms, hoping to use her EBT card[18] to purchase CSA boxes. Together, they had decided that the farm ought to acquire an EBT card reader, but even with her assistance, the legwork and paperwork proved to be too much. The growing season ended before Matt was able to complete the paperwork ("I wanted to help her, but we just weren't able to"). How to balance community needs and affordability with farmer subsistence is an important question to consider in

18. An Electronic Benefit Transfer (EBT) card is similar to a debit card, containing the cardholder's monthly CalFresh benefits. CalFresh is California's version of the Supplemental Nutrition Assistance Program (SNAP), a federal public benefits program.

the context of vegan farming that is practiced in solidarity with low-income or food-insecure populations. That "alternative" production methods like organic and veganic may allow growers to charge a premium at market (provided that consumers are familiar with the concept and find it desirable) potentially presents an opportunity. If vegan growers are able to market to wealthier customers willing to pay more, they may be able to charge lower-income community members at a rate that they indicate they can afford. In-kind arrangements, whereby produce is exchanged for farming advice or labor, are another possible approach to sustaining both farm(er) and community. Nonmonetary forms of compensation may help to alleviate the time crunch that beginning farmers like Matt and Brittany experience from scaling the agricultural learning curve, working off-farm jobs, and grappling with questions of land tenure and ownership.[19]

The concerns that Matt expressed about time budgeting in the context of growing produce for low-income communities also characterized his thoughts on a vegan farmer's capacity to research and source fair-trade, sweatshop-free items such as tools and protective clothing for employees (Guideline 7.1). Matt also questioned whether it would be realistic to expect farmworkers to abide by the guideline (7.1). He worried about mandating employees to, for instance, leave leather boots at home and purchase vegan boots, as "most people working in farming are not making a lot of money." Thus, the language of a vegan "norm" rather than a "requirement" appealed to him. To all such issues of capacity, "to the extent possible and practicable" surely applies.

Conclusion

This chapter offered thoughts on what the base of a vegan food system may look like, building on an existing approach to vegan farming. It suggested that vegan agriculture must not only entail growing plants with nonexploitative fertility sources, but also seek to uphold broader ideals, including compassion and liberation for nonhumans and humans alike. Thus, a vegan farm is constituted not only by the materials that flow in and out of the farm space, but also by the relations between the farmers and different human and nonhuman communities.

19. These ideas are not meant to suggest that supporting new or young farmers is an easy fix. In the U.S. and other settings, agricultural policy and the broader political economy are generally inhospitable to the types of small-scale, diversified, non-commodity crop operations in which vegan approaches to farming would otherwise have the most potential to flourish.

A case study of a veganic farm in the Western U.S. illustrated some of the vegan agriculture guidelines in practice.

This extended example helped to identify some practical difficulties, as well as ethical questions that may arise in the implementation of these guidelines and the creation and maintenance of vegan agricultural spaces. Ultimately, Matt and Brittany's experiences suggest that shaping a vegan agricultural space is more than a matter of simply abiding by a set of guidelines for what "to do" and "not to do." It further entails thoughtful, compassionate navigation of conflicts that arise when these guidelines are put into practice in real space and real time. Indeed, to answer the question of "how [we can] more justly share space" (Collard & Gillespie 2017, p. 8) on the farm is a deeply contextual endeavor.

Perhaps most importantly, the case study underscored that *vegan agriculture is possible*. The Loisels, and the sum of farmers and gardeners around the world who are implementing different plant-based methods on their land, show us that there *are* practicable alternatives not only to animal agriculture, but also to animal-based plant agriculture, and that there *is* possibility for these approaches to embrace liberation for nonhuman animals and humans alike. The "radical potential of both intersectionality and prefigurative praxis, which are argued to be absolutely a key to the wider process of achieving spatial emancipation" (White & Springer 2018, p. 164) can be glimpsed in projects and places like Lazy Millennial Farms.

It is my hope that others will expand, refine, and improve the conceptualization of vegan agriculture and the guidelines offered above. While there are many ways in which this could be done, I suggest it may be especially helpful and productive to consider a vegan farm's relation to the neoliberal marketplace; the issues of farmland access, rights, ownership, and sovereignty, particularly in and near food deserts and in regions with settler-colonial histories; questions of plant sentience and plant exploitation in a vegan farming system (Mancuso & Viola 2015); insights from other plant-based approaches to farming such as Shumei Natural Agriculture, the "three sisters" system implemented by Iroquois and other First Nations peoples, and biocyclic vegan agriculture;[20] and case studies of farms with stronger holistic social justice orientations.

Taylor asserts: "Throughout history people have managed to grow food under amazing circumstances and in myriad ways. The fact that it has never been a human priority to develop farming methods that don't rely on animal products . . .

20. The Biocyclic-Vegan Standard (BNS Biocyclic Network Services Ltd. 2017) is an outstanding example of a set of vegan farming standards that incorporate social justice in meaningful, specific ways. The author encourages readers to view this standard for another perspective on what constitutes vegan agriculture.

and that minimize harm to field animals . . . says more about the paradigm of human domination over animals than it does about the viability of developing a sustainable and vegan agriculture." In working to further envision a production base for a vegan food system, we can counter the observed "lack of imagination surrounding the possibility of sustainable vegan agriculture" (Taylor 2011, p. 214) and anticipate agricultural spaces and practices that are just for all.

Acknowledgments

Thanks to Brittany and Matt Loisel for sharing their time and experiences, as well as their perspectives on the vegan agriculture guidelines; to Alisha Utter for helpful comments on an earlier draft; and to Andrew and Richard for their insightful suggestions on how to improve the manuscript.

4

NGURRAJILI—"CONTINUED GIVING"

COMING TOGETHER AROUND YURAAL (FOOD) AS DECOLONIZING PRACTICE

Yandaarra Including Aunty Shaa Smith, Neeyan Smith, Paul Hodge, Lara Daley, and Sarah Wright

INTRODUCTION

In this chapter, we share stories of garlaany (pippies, a small saltwater clam), the Golden Hole, and guuna (shit) that have taught us much about food and our connections. As they have guided us, we ask garlaany, the Golden Hole, and guuna to guide this chapter as we think through what food relationships may mean for decolonizing practice and survivance and how these practices inform debates within vegan geographies. We have written this piece through layers of conversations and experiences together. We have learned from Country, from garlaany and guuna, from our embodied experiences at, with, and as Gumbaynggirr Country; we have talked about and reflected on these experiences, the understanding of yuraal (food) as ceremony, veganism and gluten intolerance, yuraal as colonizing and decolonizing, our relationships and positionalities. We have also written reflections individually, recorded conversations, and then had conversations about those conversations and early drafts of the chapter, which have again been woven through.

Through this, a collective voice has emerged, and in this chapter, we use "we" to acknowledge our more-than-human collaborative process. We also, at times, attribute specific quotes to members of Yandaarra whenever a particular insight or experience has come from a particular person or interaction. We also want to acknowledge the importance of our differences so that this piece reflects our coming together but not our sameness. We aim to neither homogenize nor silence, and we make efforts to speak to this both through the collective voice and in our direct quotes. Country and ngurrajili bring us into relationship, not sameness. In this, we are learning to heed the call of Country (Larsen & Johnson 2017), to attend to some of what Country communicates and teaches (Bawaka Country 2016; Smith et al., 2020), and to acknowledge and learn from the teachings of the Old Fullas.

In sharing our place-based story, we think through and reflect on what it means to honor yuraal (food) as ceremony and connection on Gumbaynggirr Country in a colonized and colonizing, decolonial and decolonizing world. We center Country, rather than veganism, and yuraal as ngurrajili, as relationships of continued giving and receiving, as decolonizing practice. This also means attending to some of the tensions and incompatibilities that exist between decolonizing of food and veganism. We hope that our chapter will support veganism's ethic of care and responsibility, but in ways that invite deeper understandings and engagements with place-based knowledges, protocols, and human and more-than-human co-becomings, particularly within the context of colonization and survivance.

As Yandaarra, we aim to "shift camp together," which is the Gumbaynggirr meaning of the word. Yandaarra is a Gumbaynggirr and non-Gumbaynggirr collective made up of Aunty Shaa Smith, story holder for Gumbaynggirr Country; her daughter, Neeyan Smith; Sarah Wright, Paul Hodge, and Lara Daley, three non-Gumbaynggirr academics from the University of Newcastle; our families; and Gumbaynggirr Country itself.[1] By shifting camp together, we mean working within ourselves, within our relationships with each other, with Country, and with more-than-human others to decolonize ourselves and our relationships. We come together acknowledging our Elders and mentors, and acknowledging Country and its stories. We also come together as Indigenous and non-Indigenous people, knowing that we are differently positioned in relation to Gumbaynggirr Country and Gumbaynggirr Law/Lore.

As we commit to shifting camp in ourselves and in our lives, and as we try to honor Country and live in ways that nourish and support our co-becoming, we have come to see yuraal (food) as an important focus. Yuraal is ceremony and connection. Yuraal has the potential to connect us with each other and with Country. Yuraal is a way in which Country nourishes us, and in our respectful

1. *Country* is an Aboriginal English word meaning "homeland," a place of more-than-human co-becoming, lived with and lived as (Bawaka Country 2016; Hsu et al., 2014; Rose 1996). Rose (1996) describes: "Country in Aboriginal English is not only a common noun but also a proper noun. People talk about country in the same way that they would talk about a person: they speak to country, sing to country, visit country, worry about country, feel sorry for country, and long for country. People say that country knows, hears, smells, takes notice, takes care, is sorry or happy. Country is not a generalized or undifferentiated type of place, such as one might indicate with terms like 'spending a day in the country' or 'going up the country.' Rather, country is a living entity with a yesterday, today and tomorrow, with a consciousness, and a will towards life. Because of this richness, country is home, and peace; nourishment for body, mind, and spirit; heart's ease" (p. 7).

engagements with the beings we hunt and gather and grow, eat and shit, we nourish Country, too. We do so in ways that link us to Country, and we support Yandaarra as part of Country from our different positions as Gumbaynggirr and non-Gumbaynggirr people. This is ngurrajili—continued giving, and giving and receiving, in Gumbaynggirr.

The Gumbaynggirr Nation is on the heavily populated eastern seaboard of Australia, where the colonization of Australia began. The lands reach from the Clarence River in the north to the Nambucca River in the south, with the Pacific Ocean to the east and the Great Dividing Range to the west. While Gumbaynggirr people and Gumbaynggirr Country are often invisibilized by the profound disruptions in human–more-than-human relations that have come with the onslaught of cities, towns, farms, parks, and all that make up the colonizing landscapes of east-coast Australia, Gumbaynggirr people and Country are still here. Gumbaynggirr people and Country survive, continue, rebuild, and create within and as part of these same landscapes. On Gumbaynggirr Country, ngurrajili is one of the many ways this survivance is practiced.

Survivance is a term used to highlight the vitality and active survival of Indigenous peoples (Atalay 2006; Glancy 2008; Vizenor 2008). The character of survivance, says Anishinaabe cultural theorist Gerald Vizenor (2008), "creates a sense of native presence over absence, nihility, and victimry" (p. 1). More than just endurance and survival, survivance is "an active repudiation of dominance, tragedy, and victimry" (p. 15); a "narrative resistance" (p. 1); a continuance of stories, remembrance, and action. We as Yandaarra engage ngurrajili—giving and receiving—as an embodied practice of survivance that is ongoing and that actively continues to nourish humans, more-than-human beings, and Country. As part of engaging ngurrajili, as Gumbaynggirr and non-Gumbaynggirr people, we affirm and come into relation with what is not colonized, through an active presence of ngurrajili on Gumbaynggirr Country. We do this as we care for ourselves, each other, and Country and open ourselves up to be cared for as we live yuraal (food).

While we try to live yuraal as ngurrajili, we are also very aware that much of the food we eat and the practices of agriculture that support it are a significant way in which lands, bodies, and relationships, including our own, are continually colonized. Agriculture proceeds apace on stolen land at the same time that Gumbaynggirr people are excluded from their ongoing sites of food production. Simpson and Bagelman (2018) describe the "imposition of a colonial socionatural order" when examining the case of the Lekwungen territory, commonly known as Victoria, British Columbia (p. 558). They show the way the colonializing present is inscribed in the settler-colonial city—in parks, through the presence of property lines and through settler agriculture—and its effects on a dynamic food system maintained by the Lekwungen over millennia (Simpson & Bagelman 2018). In many instances, Gumbaynggirr people simply cannot access the places where our/their ancestors and Law/Lore tell us/them to go. Or those places do not exist in the same way anymore, being under houses or roads or on cleared and privatized land. Or, for access to them, paperwork must be completed and regulations complied with as laid out by the very systems of possession and authority that also deny Gumbaynggirr sovereignty (Moreton-Robinson 2015). These are the realities of continued colonization of Gumbaynggirr Country.

Underpinning much of the yuraal we buy are disrespectful, colonizing relationships with animals (and with plants, too), resource-intensive agricultural practices, and the inhumane treatment of plants and nonhuman animals. These do not follow or acknowledge the place-based protocols and human–more-than-human relations that have nourished humans and more-than-humans over millennia. Here, the knowledges and agencies and lives of animals and plants and waters and lands are not respected (Burarrwanga et al., 2012). Some of these concerns resonate with vegan and vegetarian critiques (Hall 2009). Many do not and are not necessarily addressed by veganism. Some are in contradiction with vegan ideals.

Given this complexity and the potential for food processes and relations to be both nourishing and damaging, colonizing and decolonizing, we see our relationships around yuraal as part of the cultural interface (Nakata 2002), a complex space of interaction between Indigenous and Western domains. Our research collective of Gumbaynggirr and non-Gumbaynggirr people works at this interface, too. Torres Strait Islander and academic Martin Nakata (2007) has theorized the cultural interface as:

> a multi-layered and multi-dimensional space of dynamic relations constituted by the intersections of time, place, distance, different systems of thought, competing and contesting discourses within and between different knowledge traditions, and different systems of social, economic and political organization. It is a space of many shifting and complex intersections between different people with different histories, experiences, languages, agendas, aspirations and responses.

Within this contested space, knowledges, relations, governance, and power arrangements, including around yuraal, have the potential to be configured in both colonizing and decolonizing ways. Hunting and gathering, growing, buying, eating, and sharing can both enact survivance and embody the ongoing colonization of Indigenous lands and bodies at the cultural interface.

Nakata (2002) explains that there are many points of intersection and sets of relations at the cultural interface. As Yandaarra, we are individually and collectively part of these multiple relations, which make and remake the interface in potentially colonizing and decolonizing ways. The three non-Gumbaynggirr authors must stay attuned to who they are and how they've come to be(ing) here (Snelgrove et al., 2014, p. 5)—in this contested knowledge space and in relationship with yuraal, on stolen land, at the cultural interface. Taking direction from Aunty Shaa, from our different positions, and from Nakata (2002), we need to negotiate the tensions and work the interaction between Indigenous and non-Indigenous knowledge systems in ways that serve Indigenous interests and maintain the distinctiveness of Indigenous knowledges (p. 286).

To do this, Sarah, Paul, and Lara, as we have reflected elsewhere (Smith et al., 2020), must be accountable for both the history and the continuance of disrespectful and damaging relations, including those in research (Bawaka Country et al., 2018; Kwaymullina 2012; Rigney 1999; Smith 1999). It is their responsibility to work hard and self-reflexively to not reproduce these relations—to try to be good friends of Country and respectful guests and to "come into a place of relationship through acknowledging and respecting Gumbaynggirr Law" (Yandaarra 2017; Smith et al., 2020, p. 943). They must also talk back to dominant knowledge institutions, acknowledging how these institutions have disproportionately benefited them, and "create openings with and as Yandaarra for Gumbaynggirr knowledge to shine through" (Smith et al., 2020, p. 943).

As Sarah and Aunty Shaa reflect:

> Sarah: The other thing with us as Yandaarra is about acknowledging that we have different positions. We are coming together and it is about everything; it is our interconnected journey, but we are all different.
>
> Aunty Shaa: I think it is good to give it acknowledgment—we are in this meeting, in this coming from different places and it needs to be honored. So, coming to this place of oneness, how do we live that? How do we practice that together?

As Yandaarra on Gumbaynggirr Country, we see that yuraal, the beings and co-becomings we hunt, gather, grow, harvest, give, sell, buy, and are given, are in relationship with us. They make us; they make—and are made by—the cultural interface in ways that colonize and in ways that decolonize or refuse to be brought into colonizing relationships. This is not abstract. It is in Country; it is in our positionalities and relationships, the ways we make and remake survivance and (de)colonization. As Gumbaynggirr people, Aunty Shaa and Neeyan have different relationships with Country and food-as-Country than do Lara, Paul, and Sarah, who come as non-Indigenous vegetarians and vegans seeking to decolonize their relationships with and as Country and yuraal insofar as they can through careful, invited steps as they live the cultural interface. Country is there, too, holding it all—the colonizing and decolonizing, persisting, continuing, creating. This is what we aim to affirm and support: those parts that can never be colonized, that refuse to be brought into colonizing relationships—Country and practices of survivance.

Yuraal and Ceremony, Yuraal as Ceremony: Garlaany (Pippies) at Mylestom Beach

Our first camp together was at Mylestom, New South Wales, by the beach. Garlaany were center stage that weekend, as they often are, Uncle Bud (Aunty Shaa's uncle) tells us, when custodians come together by the sea in ceremony. This first camp at Mylestom was the initial coming together of the Yandaarra collective, family and friends, Gumbaynggirr and non-Gumbaynggirr, as part of a five-year collaborative project led by Gumbaynggirr custodians. After we waited to be invited, the time came for us to wander to the shoreline with our "pippie bags" in hand. With Aunty Shaa leading the way, we gradually, tentatively got into the rhythm of the movement, wriggling our heels, hips, bodies, anticipating the giving over of the garlaany, the feeling of joy once received, and the same over again (Fig. 1). There was ceremony to this movement—together. Gumbaynggirr and non-Gumbaynggirr moving together, laughing at how some of us lacked coordination, swimming together, talking together, connecting together.

Through these connections, gathering garlaany, we were caring for Country and as Country, caring for each other, for our connections, relationships, and co-becomings; and Country was caring for us too (Bawaka Country 2013, 2016).

Fig. 1: Aunty Shaa in ceremony with garlaany at Mylestom. Source: Yandaarra

Yuraal was a focus as we came together; it is always a focus. Yuraal is ceremony and connection. Through the ways we eat and hunt, we respect Country—we are Country. We are there in Country, in the sand with our feet sliding down, in the water, not separated out or external to place. And when we eat, we take those beings inside of us. We respect those beings and ourselves. We acknowledge them and their Law/Lore. The gathering—the being with Country—is an important part of that. If you look at our relationships and how we are building our relationships, it's around the whole. This sense of wholeness is also strong in other places where Country cares, gives, and "gifts" *in relation*. For the *Koyukon Athabascans* in Alaska, an ethic of hunting involves "becoming animal" (Watson & Huntington 2008, p. 260). Stories, places, and ancestors are "assembled during the hunt" (Watson & Huntington 2008, p. 259) as an intuitive knowing connects moose and Koyukon in co-responsibility and respect. Only when the time is right, the moose gifts itself to the Koyukon—"the hunter warbles his call as he is becoming-rutting bull" (Watson & Huntington 2008, p. 268).

Ceremony and connection are also a fundamental part of co-becoming in Bawaka Country, Northern Territory, Australia. To gather yuraal is to connect to the patterns of the universe: being relationally, co-becoming as a responsibility "between humans and nonhumans, between Country and all of its beings" (Bawaka Country 2013, p. 192). The connections between plants, animals, and people are co-becoming time and place.

> Gaypal, the wattle, is flowering now. The gaypal is a messenger that tells us the time is right to hunt miyapunu. . . . The djinydjalma, mud crabs, have a lot of meat on them, too; the bapi, snakes, are laying their eggs; and the guya, the fish, are fat. That is what the gaypal tells us when we see its masses of yellow flowers. (Bawaka Country 2013, p. 193)

Back at Mylestom, garlaany bring times together as part of the wholeness, part of the ceremony, and also part of the layers of a more-than-human existence. In our conversations within and as Yandaarra, we reflect that the garlaany are ever-present: they live in the sea that the two sisters made. (Aunty Shaa tells a story of the creation of the sea and all that is within and part of it.) So the garlaany continue to connect us to the two sisters. They show us that the creation time is here and now. Aunty Shaa likens this more-than-human existence to ceremonial cycles—of garlaany, tides, seasons. Eating yuraal (food) embodies the wholeness in ceremony. For Aunty Shaa, eating yuraal is about "promoting the continuation of that cycle of giving and receiving," connecting to "the first garlaany hunt" arising from the two sisters' creation. The garlaany, then, bring us together to be together in place and in time. The garlaany are in all times and they gather all times—the times of the ancestors, which are, after all, the time now, and the times of the future. Ngurrajili—continued giving—in the ways described here is visceral, bodily, and sometimes hard to put into words. As Aunty Shaa reflects, this embodied knowing with the ancestors in ceremony:

> is a feeling, a sacredness, a ritual that infuses all of the things we are doing. There is an intention . . . maybe ceremony is about doing things in purpose or with purpose, living Country, living the dreaming now (Country leading the way). Listening and trying to tune in. Living the connections.

The garlaany are omnipresent, always in existence. And they are in cycles, always in their own time. They live and die and grow in ways that are themselves a ceremony. The seasons for the garlaany are connected with the cycles of the tides. So, if you are a coastal person, that's a big part of the knowledge that you carry—knowing the tides, knowing the cycles, that water, the yuraal, the seasons. It's in living this connection, in the now, that you wouldn't be singing in ceremony *about* garlaany. You would be singing the continuity. It's what's happening when you say it. How could you bring that back? For Aunty Shaa and Yandaarra, that's what we're trying to do. The continued giving is the garlaany saying, "It's time to create now!" When Aunty Shaa talks about *living Country* and *tuning in*, it is about connecting, being Country, nourishing Country and being nourished by it.

The continuity, the connection, the ceremony also—always invite playfulness. Country has fun with us in this wholeness. For example, when we were collecting the garlaany, Country played tricks. Lara talks about "pippies playing with us," recalling bending down to pick up a pippie then realizing it was a pippie-shaped rock! We all laughed. Seeing that way of being and being in it. It's our connection to the two sisters; they are playing with us, too. Even the waves come to you and play with you. Having a go. Rising unexpectedly. Getting wet.

At Mylestom, we put the garlaany on the barbeque. We were all there together. There were lots of garlaany. We had a feast, a wonderful feast, and they were so good—they just tasted so good.

But we weren't *always* there together. As a vegan, Paul shares some of his anxiety and positionality as he worked through what it means for him to be vegan in an intercultural context. When garlaany are ceremony and connection, what does it mean for him to not participate in order to stay true to his veganism, whatever that is? Paul ponders whether this might mean continued complicity in the colonial project:

> When we arrived back to cook up the pippies, I started to feel anxious. I even sat back away from where the food was being prepared, and away from Uncle Bud, Aunty Shaa, and Neeyan. One minute, I was part of a collective rhythm and movement. Sharing. Laughing. Talking. Giving. Receiving. Now, I was intentionally disconnecting myself from ceremony—from Uncle Bud's stories, Gumbaynggirr Country's invitation, the two sisters.

But something shifted for Paul. In his coming down to the beach, a shift had actually already taken place. The often-hard edges of veganism, for Paul, had washed away like our footprints in the sand, and a more nuanced, contextual version emerged. If veganism is about *living* an ethics whereby non-hierarchical relations of care for our nonhuman kin are paramount, then *living Country* and *tuning in* as we come into relationship with garlaany on Gumbaynggirr lands offer such an ethics and something else besides. Grounded in place, co-becoming with garlaany embodies a decolonizing practice in creation time now. To feast together at Mylestom on and with garlaany as a vegan is to embody a practice of veganism that is respectful to the cultural context. Participating in this cycle, in this practice, at this time is, as Aunty Shaa says, "sharing the spirit and continuation of life—it's a oneness." The garlaany are ceremony. The garlaany are ngurrajili. The garlaany are life. The story of the garlaany is the way we as Yandaarra come together. We do this on and with Gumbaynggirr Country.

Fig. 2: Garlaany on the BBQ. Source: Yandaarra

Yuraal and Connection to Country/as Country: The Golden Hole

Early in 2017, we had a three-day cultural camp and clan gathering, *Gaarrawaygam* or "The Returning," at the Golden Hole on the southern edge of Gumbaynggirr Country (Fig. 3). This was a chance, as Neeyan wrote in the plan for the weekend, to "initiate a space of sharing with, listening to and guiding each other, while bringing in the strength of who we are as a family and as custodians of Ngambaa to continue the dreaming of our Country with the support from our 'Old Fullas'" (Smith 2017; Fig. 4). This camp was an additional layer of sharing, as we talked with family about Yandaarra and our five-year collaborative project and what it might mean on Country, with family on the Mid-North Coast.

We met at the Golden Hole, where the Macleay River and Clybucca Creek converge, as it is an important place at which to gather. Aunty Shaa says that the Golden Hole is so rich with yuraal, it can have a lot of people go there and feast. This is a gathering place of tens of thousands of years of continuous occupation and custodianship. The Country there can hold many people. The middens of the Golden Hole reflect the thousands of generations of people who have gathered and feasted there, the shells and bones of fish and oysters and yuraal that layer in a more-than-human co-becoming that has literally become the land. It is reportedly the largest midden in a temperate estuarine location in the Southern Hemisphere (Connaughton 2012).

Fig. 3: Camp site, Golden Hole. Source: Yandaarra

This is part of the connections between Country and people: the ways in which practices and yuraal and ceremony are connected. Elsewhere on Gumbaynggirr Country, in a place like Mutton Bird Island, Coffs Harbour, only certain clans are allowed. This limits the number of people going there because Country can hold only so many people. The richness of beings on Country leads us, tells us where to camp, where to gather. Country, if we can attend, calls and teaches (Larsen & Johnson 2017; Bawaka Country 2016). As Larsen & Johnson (2017) point out, place convenes our being together, and place-based ceremonies "acknowledge and renew the spirit of place, and the intrinsically life-supportive value of our being-together-in-place" (p. 78). This, for us, on Gumbaynggirr Country, means ngurrajili.

At the Golden Hole, Country showed us the wholeness, the potential for wholeness, what it felt and tasted and looked like, and ngurrajili, the continued reciprocal giving ceremony and the coming together. There, Aunty Shaa talked about coming together and we could all feel it. Neeyan, Lara, and the younger women went to get oysters: being in the moment, getting into it, finding the big oysters. Paul, Matt (Sarah's partner), and other men were off getting paperbark to

Fig. 4: Uncle Bud at the Golden Hole telling stories of connection to Country where Macleay River and Clybucca Creek converge. Source: Yandaarra

cook the fish in. Aunty Shaa, Sarah, and Fee (Paul's partner) were with the kids, watching them swim and play on mud slides. We were all there, different people doing different things, taking on different roles, yet connected. We were renewed by—and renewing—the spirit of Country. There was the fish on the fire, everyone standing around the fire, everyone gathered around it, someone having caught the fish and sharing that. We had a feast. And the kids played, holding an impromptu "Golden Hole's Got Talent" dance competition, a reworking of a popular television show, with tunes played on phones with poor signal, under the camping gazebo. The kids were expressing the joy of feeling and being connected.

As we gathered together, we acknowledged a multidirectional ngurrajili. It was about being cared for by Country, by the fish and the oysters and the fire that called us to stand around. It was about receiving that care honorably. This was not a one-way giving, though, in which Country just gave and gave and we took and took; to understand it like that imposes a disconnection and mistakes the multidirectional and more-than-human care involved. Nor was it a transactional quid pro quo whereby fish was exchanged for planting a tree, or hours spent caring for children were repaid with yuraal by parents. Rather, the giving is also a receiving, and gifts come from different directions including through more-than-human relationships, from and as time, from and as place. This is the balance of it all, the web of life that continues as we are all connected, as we become together. It is the relationality, the knowledge, the sharing, the caring of the seasons, the tides, the fish, the laughter, the dance, the time spent gathering. Yuraal brings us back to all that—in and as connection.

At the Golden Hole, beings and people and yuraal were integrated together as part of the landscape, as Country. So much of the Western way makes yuraal separate. It is often grown on a distant farm, away from other parts of life. At the Golden Hole, around yuraal, things were drawn together. There was playfulness, being together, relating, family, the sun, ceremony. And so being together at the Golden Hole was a victory in the ongoing nourishment. As we added to that midden there, with people and/as Country still getting nourished, if there ever was a thought that there would be a loss of culture or a dying out, it was like, "No, we *are* here." It was a celebration of connections. We were that midden, adding to the midden, joining and connecting with those more-than-humans who had added to the midden for millennia.

Food—yuraal—and at least the kinds of relationships to/with/as yuraal we lived at the Golden Hole are a way in which Gumbaynggirr people live their refusal and survivance. It is one way of living Country outside a politics of recognition, outside being judged or valued on terms set by colonizers (Coulthard 2014). When Neeyan was gathering oysters, she was living an ongoing relationship with the oysters, living Gumbaynggirr Country as nonlinear time and place, co-becoming through *Maangun*, Gumbaynggirr Law/Lore. Lara, in going with the group of women and gathering herself, was coming into relationship with the oysters as a vegan navigating the cultural interface, learning and practicing relationality as Country. The connections were with Country, with each other, as Country. Here, Lara reflects on what this means/meant for her:

> There was an awkwardness in my being at the Golden Hole. This was a special place and a special camp for the Ngambaa Smith clan coming together, returning, (re)living and continuing their relationships to Country as family and custodians. I wanted to respect those relationships and be open to where I may or may not fit. At one point during the weekend, I was invited to join the women—cousins, sisters, mothers—to gather oysters. The laughter, joy, and excitement of driving in convoy down the sand track, trying to find the right spot, and then running rock to rock searching for "the big ones" was infectious. Being vegan became far less relevant as I was encouraged to get an oyster from the rock and eat it. This was not only eating another being but an invitation to relate to the oyster and Country differently, to become with the oysters in their place on/as Country. It felt my responsibility to relate in this way: to learn to relate, care for, and be nourished by Country in the proper way, guided by the women. And also, an invitation which calls upon me to relate with deep care and respect as someone whose history and presence can be, and also is, dispossessing. That felt more important than being vegan at the Golden Hole. I may not always eat oysters, but being brought into those relationships of continuance on Gumbaynggirr terms shifted my understanding of Country: to understand it as strongly constituted by food relationships and Country itself as food—the midden we camped on and were adding to; the oysters on the rocks; the fish in the waterways.

Yuraal, too, and living as Country are a way to live nonlinear times as part of survivance, the continuation of Maangun as non-ruptured. At the Golden Hole, through "The Returning" or Gaarrawaygam, Aunty Shaa and Neeyan and their families were able to live and practice and nurture the parts of themselves, those relationships, that remain uncolonized, that can never be colonized. This is a returning and a re-returning, a cycling that connects past, present, and future—now. So, that survivance through ngurrajili, through and as yuraal, includes relationships with time, nurturing and being nurtured by times that go beyond linearity, being in/as time with the midden, the midden that manifests thousands of generations, being with and as the oysters, with and as the fish, the paperbark. All the different timescales of human, animal, plant, tidal, geologic, river activity—the times of Country that co-become. We all added to the midden, and we were those relationships. For Aunty Shaa and Neeyan, this is kin made manifest—their ancestors who lived and gathered there. For Paul, Lara, and Sarah and their families, this was an invitation to begin to nurture different kinds of relationships with Country, to shift something of themselves and their relationships at the cultural interface through the being asked, through ngurrajili—the continued giving of Country.

Neeyan and Aunty Shaa reflect:

> Neeyan: Amongst all the colonization, still, there are intelligent systems we have learned and we are still learning. We haven't lost our traditional beings; we still have them among all this colonization. Still, the Western stuff is still valid; it is here.
>
> Aunty Shaa: For me, listening to you, it's about we are able to hold both and to speak from that place, from the place of oneness and from the whole, and which starts with us in ourselves. And we do, the core of our beings is expressed from that place, the place that cannot be colonized and can never be colonized. So, we are holding all of that.
>
> Neeyan: That place of oneness, inside that can't be touched.
>
> Aunty Shaa: Or violated. That's that place that the healing can come from.

While Neeyan and Aunty Shaa share the strength in holding this place of healing and oneness, challenges remain in the creation time now, and we are not meaning to make the camp sound perfect, romanticized. We stopped at a Woolworths supermarket on the way. There were things wrapped in plastic, sliced ham; the kids had juice in Tetra Paks. We weren't always at one with each other or ourselves either. We had disagreements. There were feelings of hurt and anger. But that is part of it. To have to always be perfect is part of the colonizing. Hurt is a part of colonization, but so is the pressure not to be hurt and to be perfect, to just "get over it." We are living, living protocols, living our hurting and our healing, our care for Country (Smith et al., 2020). And yuraal—hunting, sharing, buying, and swapping—is central to that. As Sarah reflects:

> It seems like another colonizing move is to say Gumbaynggirr can't incorporate the Western on their terms or food can only be ceremony if it is done in some rigidly understood "traditional" way, when the very way Gumbaynggirr people might access and nourish those relationships has been disrupted.

And there is no denying the structures and processes that continue to work to disconnect us from each other and from Country, and to keep making instead of unmaking colonialism—those "generative structures" not of decolonization but of capitalism and colonialism (Coulthard 2014). We are always fighting against things that try to colonize time, stop the continuity of place—things that are the opposite of our meeting on/with/at/as the Golden Hole. In terms of caring for Country, there are forms from Fisheries, Department of Agriculture, and regulations to control, direct, limit, and stop people eating, catching, caring for, and being cared for by the land (Fig. 4, see signage stating restrictive regulations for the adjacent national park). There is an intensity to those structures that are there purportedly to care for Country, in the ways they regulate people's access to yuraal and act as barriers—a gatekeeper. The forms and regulations that disconnect are doing so in the name of protection. The very ways of thinking and being that are creating the problem—separating humans from nonhumans, from the land and nature when, really, we are all connected—are being used to try to fix the problem.

As Aunty Shaa reflects:

> To prepare for the weekend, we had to do all a lot of paperwork and get licenses from Fisheries. We had to say how much we were going to get, how many people, how many fish. Hannah and Neeyan had to spend hours doing that, all this information that was so irrelevant. You've got Fisheries and Parks and Wildlife carrying that Western law in this Country and yet Gumbaynggirr Law/Lore is not recognized, it doesn't carry weight. It's just so complex.

That is what it means to live in a colonizing place, on the edge of cities and holiday homes. Neeyan reflects on the devastating irony of these rules aimed to preserve rather than to shift relationships and ways of being: "If the colonizers would follow the law of the land in the first place, we wouldn't have to have all these regulations, the layers of bureaucracy."

Yet in spite of this, there is ngurrajili. Aunty Shaa saw potential even in the forms as a means of coming into relationship with Fisheries. And with being on the Golden Hole, in relationships, there is an active presencing. This is not Gumbaynggirr people or Gumbaynggirr Country being victims, but an ongoing flourishing of Country and people and the worlds that nurture us. Neeyan evokes this flourishing: "The Golden Hole was different. With the Golden Hole, you had to go through those forms, which were kind of like blockages but then, when we got there, we were just being in it."

Another Colonization: Food as Separation

When we as Yandaarra come together around yuraal to nourish and be nourished, we also acknowledge a disruption of ngurrajili, some separation that needs mending. There is a colonizing of land and bodies—human and more-than-human—in food, too, which can at times disrupt continued giving and at other times exist in tension with it (Watts 2013). There has been a colonizing of multiple bodies, human and more-than-human, through Western diet and industrial food production—a colonizing that breaks some of the threads of Gumbaynggirr food knowledges and practices, changing diets and also affecting relations.

As Aunty Shaa reflects:

> Not feeling connected to what we are eating is a big part of it. The joy and participation isn't there. And the food is not tasty—it is so processed! Since colonization, there have been big changes around food so that we are not fishing enough in the proper way, following Maangun.

Colonized relations infuse the whole process of how food is created in the first place and how we are connecting (or not connecting) to Country. For example, when we shop at Woolworths, there is a disconnect from so much of what we buy and ingest. This disconnect is underscored by colonization on many levels. It is not simply that much of industrial food production involves monocultures, damaging chemicals, and cruelty, but the food production process is separating people from Country. Agriculture has produced forms of land tenure that exclude Aboriginal people. For at the most fundamental level, most food production in Australia is premised upon land theft and the ongoing dispossession of Aboriginal and Torres Strait Islander peoples (Moreton-Robinson 2015). The food production process is part of that continued taking, which needs to be healed by a returning back to Country, back to fishing, to continued ngurrajili. It's about mending the threads that have been broken by colonization and it's about the prior Law/Lore of this place.

The taking plays out in everyday ways, too, as we buy and ingest food from which we are disconnected. Neeyan reflects on how this serves to disrupt Gumbaynggirr food knowledges and practices as she thinks about butchery as a profession:

> Butchery is a whole professional industry, where people learn how to become a butcher and so people become licensed to do that. We Gumbaynggirr people are not licensed to get our food. And we have to get permission to get our food our way! So, we've got this butchery profession to get our meat for us and we have to go buy it at that shop, which takes away our ability to learn how to gather our own food. We

> are reliant on professionals and money to get food. This means there is no connection to anything; it's not supporting any cycle, and the important part is that we are not learning with Country.

Feeling connected to our bodies and our yuraal is an integral part of ngurrajili—continued giving—with and as Gumbaynggirr Country. When we have dug the garlaany out of the sand or caught a fish, there is more desire to sit and enjoy it; we are connecting, participating. However, when we are not connecting with our yuraal, that has a big impact on our minds and bodies; we are not connecting with Country, and Country is not being properly nourished. This is a material reality, felt in our bodies. As Aunty Shaa shares, the becoming one with another being through devouring it is a sharing in that spirit—a continuation of life. On Gumbaynggirr Country, humans and more-than-humans depend on each other for that to happen. This is a bodily interdependence in which human and more-than-human beings are giving and sharing. As Neeyan explains:

> When you think about it, it is not just us humans that have been colonized. It is the animals that have been colonized—their way of being and living. They have lost their way, too. They would have relied on that connection with us just as much as we have relied on that connection with them.

From a Gumbaynggirr perspective, hunting on Gumbaynggirr Country is about being in the cycles of continued giving. It is not taking from Country because it is being all present on/as Country and eating on and as Country. It is all in the cycle. When you fish, it is a human and more-than-human process. It is not just you and the fish; there is the tide, the dolphin who may hunt the fish towards you. Everything is connected at the very moment you throw out that fishing line. In these hunting practices, humans and more-than-humans' bodies and relations are being nourished. Neeyan gives an example of this from a time she was fishing:

> We burleyed up the water to make it easier so that the fish came to us. But ten minutes later, something huge in the water came up and scared the fish away. Probably a shark or dolphin. So, we helped that dolphin get a feast!

Yuraal, including eating other beings, is about a process of living the cycles and continuing the purpose of everything. Colonization has brought a breaking of some of the threads of food knowledges and practices, getting in the way of Gumbaynggirr people accessing Country, disrupting the human and more-than-human protocols of continued giving. There are barriers to humans as well as more-than-human beings living their purpose. As Neeyan shares, we are not seeing the purpose of the animal anymore. On Gumbaynggirr Country, simply not eating nonhuman animals doesn't necessarily attend to ngurrajili and a retying of the threads that have been broken through ongoing colonization. Continued giving on Gumbaynggirr Country, in this context of colonization, means pulling some threads back together around relations to and affinity with animals to really get to a stronger place of connection with and care for Country.

As Yandaarra, a collective of Gumbaynggirr and non-Gumbaynggirr people with different histories and relationships with and as Gumbaynggirr Country, we connect to yuraal as Country differently. Paul and Lara, for example, come into the circle as vegans, and this calls upon them to reflect and to shift as we find a way to be together as Gumbaynggirr and non-Gumbaynggirr people on Country. Lara reflects on this from the cultural camp, Gaarrawaygam, at the Golden Hole:

> Standing around the fire, with the fish that one of the men caught, with everyone being together and sharing the fish, I wanted to also eat the fish as, for me, this feels a part of respecting relationships with Country—the relationship of catching the fish, the relationship between family, the deep and long relationship the family has with the Golden Hole. Eating the fish was also to respect the fish itself who was there at the fire, offering nourishment. To me, this is an entirely different thing from walking into a fish shop and buying a fish, which involves a whole process that demonstrates little respect or care. Eating fish from the fire is part of my learning to relate to Country guided by Aunty Shaa, Neeyan, and their family.

Certain relationships with food, then, reflect the way colonization has empowered and been empowered by a fabricated nature/culture dualism that draws a distinction between people and the environment, people and animals, animals and plants, and more, imposing rigid boundaries and locating agency within certain humans, to the exclusion of more-than-human others (Plumwood 2000; Hall 2009). As Sarah reflects:

> I look at a cling-wrapped cabbage or something from a supermarket and I see it as a manifestation of so many layers of colonial relations and layers of separation. It is like the plastic is suffocating us all. On whose land was [the cabbage] grown; with what chemicals that killed what animals; what stories are held there, both told and untold, now; what death brought that cabbage here; what erasures and violences made it possible for me to be here, buying it? So, I think of the ways to reconcile

> with that cabbage, to acknowledge its agency, and to reconfigure my relationships with food that are so central. As a non-Gumbaynggirr person living on Gumbaynggirr land, I am part of that colonizing. I am standing in that shop knowing that that is me, that my life has proceeded from it. Yet even though that is always there and always to be acknowledged, I must still work on changing my relationships to land and people and all the beings of Country, including food. So that is where I am coming from.
>
> I have been a long-term vegetarian—somehow, it's thirty years now—but I think of it in terms of responsibilities of coexistence with place, learning from place, walking with place. Rather than starting with it being about not eating meat, I feel an importance to be responsible through my relationships with other beings, being in good relationship, not avoiding relationship. And I have learned from wonderfully generous Indigenous mentors that sometimes it means eating the hunted meat that comes from a place of connection and respect for Aboriginal Law, rather than buying the packaged soya product flown in from afar. It's not respectful to say no to these gifts—what would I be refusing? What would I be empowering by doing so?

It is not just people and animals, then, who are colonized, but plants, too, and land and Country and relationships. This is the Gumbaynggirr people being stolen from the land and its relationships, and the land and relationships stolen from them. Plants, even more than animals, are often understood within a colonizing framing as a backdrop against which other struggles around yuraal may be played out. But there is knowledge and law and integrity in animals and plants, in trees and tides and stories and dreams. The protocols and relations of ngurrajili, which have been disrupted by colonization, are also, importantly, relations with plants as yuraal and Country. Like the tree fern that Aunty Shaa tells us about in the following section. And like guuna (shit).

But Shit Don't Hold Us Back: The Moon Man

Ngurrajili doesn't end when we eat together in ceremony. To eat is to shit. The yuraal we eat is a physical and bodily connection to and with Country. We ingest to be nourished and to connect and relate to Gumbaynggirr Country as ceremony. Yuraal becomes us. We become Country. And it is in this co-becoming with yuraal that we continue giving. To shit is to uphold ngurrajili as we return nutrients our bodies no longer need to Country. Country absorbs, retains, renews, and gives back. Guuna (shit) is important, too; it has its special shit place—guunamiirlarl—with and as Gumbaynggirr Country.

Aunty Shaa tells a story of Moon Man, a figure of fun in Gumbaynggirr, and the plant people who carry him when he gets the runs (diarrhea):

> There is a battle between Nymboida and Richmond people at Nymboida in Gumbaynggirr Country. They had a good go, the Richmond and Nymboida people. They stand opposite one another in straight lines and throw their spears. But Moon Man is hiding behind a tree a lot of the time. He's not a warrior; he's not a fighter. So, when he does come out, he throws his spear and it misses everyone, and then it comes back and spears him in the butt, giving him the runs. And the Moon Man is of the Garrabuung section, so the relationships that should help him are the elder brothers, younger brothers, and brothers-in-law. They should have helped but they didn't want to carry him because he had the runs. They wanted to move camp and abandon the old fulla.
>
> But then, the plant people, the ferns and grasses, step in and stay to carry the Moon Man. The plant people take turns carrying him; he's got shit all over him and he is putting shit all over them, but their concern for him is more important, so they continue carrying him. And Moon Man doesn't even want to get down on the ground to sleep and says to the tree fern, "I am going to sleep here on your shoulders."
>
> So, the plant people carry him to his special place, Giidanyurrgala, his resting place. Moon Man says to the plant people: "You all carried me on your backs, you will be all around me here and you will never die. When you die, you will rise again. Go off together and scatter far and wide and flourish, all of you. I am remaining on this hill here; I will stay in my Country. On the other hand, those men will all die."
>
> So, the ferns and grasses, they have eternal life—they keep generating and regenerating, and people are a bit different.

Guuna (shit) is a part of relationships and continued giving. The guuna has given the ferns eternal life as they return after fire, generate and regenerate. You can still see the color of guuna on them in the fine brown hairs that cover them.

We describe guuna here as practice, as more-than-human agent, and as metaphor. As a more-than-human agent, shit is as much a part of co-becoming in practice as is any other part of connecting with Country. Hunting, sharing, eating, shitting—these practices are all part of the cycles that nourish us and, in turn, nourish Country. Yet when we talk about shit, we are also talking about it as metaphor. Shit is the baggage we each carry, and the histories and presences of ongoing colonization that we are also faced with from our different positions as Gumbaynggirr and non-Gumbaynggirr people.

The Moon Man story is a story about ngurrajili, about what happens when relationships are strained, what it means to step up when times get hard, and about the capacity of Mother Earth to continue regenerating—"carrying the shit of others." Just as the plant people carried Moon Man, relationships, very strong ones, are sometimes forged through the carrying of others' shit. The continued giving of the tree ferns reminds us that things can be rebuilt in bad times, hard times, that relationships can be renewed and new relationships can emerge.

Colonization and modern life actively separate us from our shit as practice and metaphor. Toilet cubicles, doors, locks, sprays—each works to distance humans from bodily excrement and to disrupt a practice of continued giving, of returning nourishment to Country. Even the thought of being "in relationship" with our guuna could be seen as offensive, or at least humorous; perhaps, like Moon Man, we are letting the humor teach here. Just as animals have been colonized and miss out on bodily co-becoming with humans, Neeyan explains, Country, too, misses out on the bodily receiving that comes with shitting. And Yandaarra is also affected by this disconnect. At Mylestom and the Golden Hole, for example, our modern lives and habits of separation dictated that the use of conventional toilets, which meant hiring a portable toilet for the Golden Hole, was a given. Setting up an eco-toilet option was not something that was considered or discussed: colonization has a way of normalizing the breaking of ngurrajili.

Likewise, there are attempts to keep the shit of colonization at a distance, separated from the present. The collective amnesia towards Australia's violent making, past and present, works to keep uncomfortable histories and realities distant from the lives of non-Indigenous people living on stolen lands. They enable public discourse to treat invasion and Indigenous dispossession as an event rather than an ongoing reality. Yet shit—this shit, colonization—doesn't hold us back (not always). As Yandaarra on Gumbaynggirr Country, we shit garlaany, oysters, fish *now*, as ceremony and as ngurrajili (even if it is in a toilet!). In Yandaarra, we aim to carry each other's shit in bad times, in hard times, and in spite of the shit we face, acknowledging always that our shit is situational and different as we come from different places in relation to colonization. We each have our special shit place that needs acknowledging. This is to recognize that we each carry our own shit, and that this shifts and changes, too, as Yandaarra and our relationships with each other and Country shift and change.

At certain times and places, particular members of the collective are better placed than others to carry the hard shit. Realizing this—honoring this idea of the shit we all carry—helps to keep Yandaarra generating and regenerating. To keep Yandaarra strong. We are living the shit, the shit of colonialism, but we are also surviving as Gumbaynggirr and non-Gumbaynggirr, mending and remaking relations as Gumbaynggirr and non-Gumbaynggirr, in spite of this shit and as it composts. Like the tree ferns that carried the Moon Man, to give and care and mend the threads of that which has been broken is to live under, with, and against colonizing practices. This is an "active repudiation of dominance" (Vizenor 2008, p. 1), a survivance through practice, in much the same way as the Lekwungen people in Victoria, British Columbia, tend to the *camas* fields as part of their ancestral food system, doing so on park lands without permission (Simpson & Bagelman 2018).

Yuraal as Ngurrajili

Yuraal as ngurrajili is ceremony and connection on Gumbaynggirr Country. As we come together as Yandaarra in our more-than-human beings and co-becomings, we try to hold each other and Country as we negotiate the cultural interface, however difficult it may be, as decolonizing practice. The food knowledges we have reflected upon and shared in this chapter embody our attempts to enact an ethic of continual giving—ngurrajili—and relationality. And while yuraal is colonizing, too, it is the relationships with and as yuraal that we are making explicit as a practice of survivance on and with Gumbaynggirr Country. Yet, as Yandaarra, we are positioned differently. Survivance means different things to the human members of Yandaarra.

As Gumbaynggirr people, Aunty Shaa and Neeyan have different relationships with yuraal-as-Country than do Lara, Paul, and Sarah. In this chapter, we have shared conversations about what this means for each of us as Gumbaynggirr nonvegans and non-Gumbaynggirr vegetarians and vegans. By sharing our collective and individual stories of coming into relationship with garlaany (pippies), fish, the Golden Hole, and guuna (shit), we have offered place-based examples of what it means to persist, continue, create around yuraal in colonizing and decolonizing times.

Aunty Shaa talks about "the practical work of Yandaarra" when referring to the strength in being in relationship with place and knowing your place (see also Smith et al., 2020). Coming into relationship with garlaany (pippies) is one example of this "practical work" of maintaining protocols and one way that Yandaarra is trying to decolonize our practices and relationships including, centrally, around yuraal. While this deep recognition aligns with many of the important ethical concerns and generative relationships that vegans and vegan scholars are advocating and practicing in new ways, it differs and sometimes diverges from vegan principles, too. Our approach through Yandaarra is one that centers the building of relationships and the honoring of protocols, beginning with the need to recognize the violences of colonization and separation and to support practices of decolonization where we can, as we work and live the cultural interface with and as yuraal on Gumbaynggirr Country.

For Lara, Paul, and Sarah, coming into relationship with garlaany, fish, or hunted meat to center relationships and honor protocols embodies the "practical work" of knowing one's place while refusing separation and ongoing violence. The kinds of more-than-human co-becoming shared in this chapter provide a contemporary example of the ecological animalism described by Plumwood (2004), Adams (2003), and others who have questioned the way veganism's "dualistic account of human identity" (Plumwood 2004, p. 55) relies on a human/nature dualism by its refusal to acknowledge cultural difference when it comes to human–nonhuman relationships. To quote Plumwood (2004):

> Ecological Animalism insists we must consider context to express care for both animals and ecology, and to acknowledge at the same time different cultures and individuals in different ecological contexts, differing nutritional situations and needs. (p. 53)

For Yandaarra, yuraal as ngurrajili acknowledges and embodies Gumbaynggirr Law/Lore. This is to acknowledge and honor the agency of animals, plants, guuna, tides, the midden, the Old Fullas. This honoring and teaching are ceremony, too, and this is the practical work of ngurrajili with and as yuraal, with and as Yandaarra. To share this more-than-human co-becoming is to invite new relationships with food, including contextual veganism, in ways that deepen our understandings of and engagements with food knowledges within the context of colonization and survivance.

Acknowledgments

We acknowledge and honor the Old Fullas of Gumbaynggirr Country for now and for all time. Yuraal as ngurrajili is to continue Gumbaynggirr Law/Lore and uphold ongoing responsibilities to the Old Fullas and the sacredness of life. Sharing this chapter is also ngurrajili—sharing the knowledge that will make us strong. The research for the project was supported by a Linkage grant from the Australian Research Council [LP160100366]. Wright is also supported by a Future Fellowship from the Australian Research Council [FT160100353].

5

ANIMAL-BEINGS, ANIMAL-THINGS

RECONSTRUCTING (ARCHIVAL) ANIMAL-BODIES

Catherine Oliver

A vegan geography fundamentally requires a reconsideration of how we define the animals and the ways in which they are imagined, constructed, and lived-with. By questioning the binary of animal bodies as Thing or Being (as we have questioned the binaries defining humans), we can elucidate new ways of relating and caring. Feminist and postcolonial geographies have questioned binary constructions of human bodies, but the "apolitical, safe and sanitized discourse" (White 2015) of animal geographies has failed to address the Being/Thing distinction in our relationships with and representations of animals. *Animal-Beings* are constructed as sentient, feeling *subjects of [a] life*, capable of pain and pleasure (Singer 1975; Regan 1983; Ryder 1989), although this too often rests on human beneficence (Whatmore 1997). *Animal-Things* are positioned as supplementary—at best, teaching us how to be human (Oliver 2015). This binary is historically contingent, built out of human–animal relationships, reaffirmed in animal activism, and troubled by an anti-speciesist veganism.

A rejection of binary animal-Beings/animal-Things moves instead to inhabit a spectral "in-between" and a desire to move beyond veganism as an animal rights discourse—to reposition veganism as a political, ethical, and social issue. To do so, this work operates in the speculative mode of "as if," which breaches spatial, temporal, and species difference to imagine far enough out of the self to empathize with other species, but not so far that the human location is lost (Godlovitch 1971). The (in-) between and the beyond are used throughout this chapter as spaces in which it is possible to reframe animals as existing between Being and Thing as we think about and live-with animals. While entangled, these two spaces are not identical.

The (in-)between considers animals as shifting and vital agents, who are simultaneously object and subject. The beyond is used as a way of imagining *past* archives and animals themselves to inhabit a space of openness and possibility, negotiating multiple and complex ways of being and doing. To work both between and beyond, the archival reader must listen through and past the archive to reach those who cannot respond. *Beyond* the archive are the stories and lives of animals; working between and beyond animals and archives offers the possibility for multiple relations to history, and, thus, to reality, to be read and interpreted. Inhabiting the beyond and the between, then, is an imagining that has been extended to maneuver through history and distance, proximally and somatically, in a past that affects the present (and, thus, the future). This politics of the possible is enabled and enacted by working in the speculative mode of "as if" to breach spatial, temporal, and species distances to renegotiate our shared futures.

The research in this chapter draws on archival encounters and relational histories to propose a reconstruction of animals as between beings and things, and beyond the present. Archives are opened to an imagining of the spaces and beings/things existing beyond them, to challenge the anthropocentrism in archival research. Moments of emotion, anger, and political impetus in the archive are entangled with (archival) animal-Bodies, as shown by excerpts from field diaries kept throughout the research. These excerpts are used as examples of the breaching of distance and emotion through histories and animal-Stories from *beyond* the archive. Veganism is situated in relation to animal rights movements, their failures, and their histories, and it is argued that vegan scholarship must necessarily construct animals as between animal-Being and animal-Thing, as a political and ethical impetus for us to imagine and, thus, enact vegan futures.

The chapter uses materials from Richard D. Ryder's archive (The Ryder Archive) to explore the shifting and contingent processes that order and organize animals' existences in more-than-human worlds. The first section of this chapter questions "Animal-Constructions," the ways in which animals are constructed as *either* Being or Thing, reflecting on how we currently position animals within this binary. This is entangled with the power of both proximal and somatic distance. In the next section, "Archival Animal-Bodies" are situated within the multiple histories of humans, animals, and the political entanglements between them. The archive of Richard D. Ryder and Ryder himself are introduced to contextualize their positioning with respect to animal rights and vegan histories. Anthropocentrism and the challenges of working through human worlds of memory are counterbalanced by the idea of reaching for animals and stories *beyond* this archive. Following this, archival materials are then used to illustrate the reproduction of oppositional "Animal-Beings/Animal-Things" in activism, positioning this binary construction as perpetuating systematic and intimate violence against animal bodies. This section centers on an emotive archival encounter with a chimpanzee, imagining and constructing what exists beyond the archive and the capability of archival animals to share their anger and pain in the present.

The next section, "Animal-Machines and Speaking Pain," considers The Case of the Brown Dog, whose vivisection abuses were exposed by Lizzy Lind-af-Hageby and Leisa Schartau in 1902, in relation to vivisection in the U.K. and to the question of whose bodies matter and how. The brown dog's story asks how thinking around how pain can or cannot be *spoken* and how archival animals can, in reshaping worlds, become symbolic.

The final section, "Animal-Food and Food-Animals," reflects on animals as food by exploring how the export of live animals allows the manipulation of animals' being-ness and thing-ness as politically contingent in food production. This is considered in conjunction with the U.K.'s McLibel campaign of the mid-1980s, and the two narratives are juxtaposed to explore the permeation of binary animal-Beings/animal-Things. Animals are then briefly considered as "Animal-Strangers" who threaten the foundations of binary world(s), before concluding with speculation on "A Politics of the Possible" in working with archival animals for vegan scholarship and veganism.

Animal-Constructions

Before we *re*construct animals as between Being and Thing, how animals are currently constructed as one or the other must be considered. To suppose that assigning being-ness to animals will do the work of bringing about equality and liberation would be dangerous, resignifying knowledges that have already exposed the flaws of oppositional worldviews (see, for example, Braidotti 1994; Irigaray 1996; Butler 1990; Haraway 1984). Rather, a more entangled existence of human, animal, and the earth must be attended to (Barad 2007). This is not a call to shift the animal condition from animal-Thing to animal-Being, but rather a spectral inhabitancy of the ability to exist in between the subject and the object. When located at the constructive moment, this binary non-exists in the same way as any other (Derrida 1978; Lykke 2010). A deconstruction of this notion can provide the basis for political representation, moral inclusion, and a vegan, more-than-human future.

If "Being" is that which separates "Man," the human-Being, from "Animal," what are the defining features of the human that couple with being? Not all human bodies are beings. Rather, the coupling of human with being is extended to those near to centers of (white, cisheteropatriarchal) power, proximally, socially, culturally, economically, or politically (Puwar 2004; Cuomo & Gruen 1998). In defending the comparison of human and animal bodies, Spiegel (1996) positions the line "arbitrarily drawn between white people and black people" (p. 20) as echoing in the line dividing human and animal. This separation is a ranking of human *above* animal in a hierarchy of whose bodies matter (Butler 1993) within a speciesist society. The same networks of power perpetuate historical cycles of violence (White & Cudworth 2014), situating animals within the "interlocking and multiplicative systems of domination and submission" (Fiorenza 1992, in Pui-Lan 2009, p. 193). As these lines are drawn, the basis for granting recognition of being-ness to *some* is also decided: being-ness is afforded to bodies no longer deemed "stranger," to bodies coded as safe and (self-)same. The not-yet-known bodies of strangers are incompatible with Being-ness (Bauman 1990).

"Being/Thing" is a deliberately clumsy phrase, defined in relation to the human being/thing. To define a being in opposition to a thing would be to work in a mode of binary thinking against contemporary geographical understandings of the body, relationality, and intersubjectivity. A body is at once subject and object—at once subject and subject—but a dissociation from body-objects and body-subjects creates dissonance with other bodies (Weiss 1999). There is a somatophobia (Grosz 1994) involved in this process of dissociation, a rejection that cannot be controlled or rationalized away positions the body as an obstacle to the "truth" of the mind. Human feelings towards others are influenced by their own worlds (see, for example, Moule 2009; Banks & Ford 2008). The character and intensity of feeling towards the or this animal is an ordered and organized process, not an unhappy accident (Joy 2010). In striving to understand the mind–body–world entanglements, Gruen (2015) considers the vitality of this sense of closeness, whether physical or emotional: "When people *do* care, that care is often limited to those closest to them or most like them, but not beyond" (p. 82).

The archive can hold the potential to one such beyond, to the re-placing of animal beings/things to be proximally close to us, not distanced from us, both physically (White 2015) and emotionally (see, for example, Kunst & Haugestad 2018, on linguistic dissociation from food-animals), as they have been. Reading animal-Stories through the archive requires imagination and circumspection in order that we may consider what an ethically and politically vegan future may look like. Understanding our history situates our research and vision for a more caring world within these complex relationships of bodies, thoughts, emotions, and affects.

To reject the animal-Being/animal-Thing binary, we must somehow center *this* animal's body, whereby *this* animal (as opposed to the collective "*the* animal") is an individual. When we meet others, human or nonhuman, we see not their being but their (re)presentation (Goffman 1956). That representation is interpreted through a human somatic (non)recognition, communication, and networks of space and society. This moment of encounter with this animal is also the moment of "construction," constituted in relation to their body's socio-historical position. This moment is the moment when the/this animal becomes *who* or *what*, when the/this animal, by being questioned, becomes a question (Ahmed 2016). We must ask, then, how reconsidering the/this animal might inform the theorization and practice of animal "rights."

Archival Animal-Bodies

The Western animal rights movement has failed and for veganism to succeed as an ethical-political commitment, it is necessary to understand veganism's rooting in the failures of historical and contemporary animal activism. Veganism's histories are situated in relation to animal rights movements and their failures. This section reads along the archival grain (Stoler 2009), to consider how the perpetuation of the animal-Being/animal-Thing binary has underpinned these failures.

Richard D. Ryder and the Ryder Papers

The material in this chapter is from the archive of Richard Ryder (held at the British Library). Ryder's archive reflects his involvement and history in animal activism, notably his work on speciesism (and later painism: Ryder 2001). The Ryder Papers provide a lens into the U.K.'s contemporary animal rights movement, beginning with a story on the roots of speciesism:

> Ryder's coining of the term "speciesism" in 1970 marked the beginning of a new era and renewed interest in an evolving relationship between humans and animals. Ryder, in a 1998 interview, told of how he had grown up assuming animals were "like him," reflected in his earliest memory of seeing a dead blackbird on the street that ignited a moment of recognition. Ryder talks of his mixed and inconsistent feelings towards animals, which inevitably turned him towards the animal rights cause. Ryder's story of the word *speciesism* (1998) begins in a bath in his Dorset estate. He first published this idea in the leaflet *Speciesism* and circulated this around Oxford in 1970. Oxford was an important place for Ryder and for the academic history of the animal rights movement, with Oxford University serving as an intellectual hub for animal rights philosophy. In 1971, along with Ros and Stan Godlovitch, and John Harris, whom Ryder was introduced to by novelist Brigid Brophy, he

> began what was later referred to as the Oxford Group (Godlovitch, Godlovitch, & Harris 1971). The group was a collective of postgraduate students, largely philosophers, who acted and spoke against the use of animals. This informal group later included Peter Singer, whose book *Animal Liberation* is heralded as a key text of animal rights philosophy. (Field diary, November 2017, The Ryder Papers, uncatalogued)

Archival stories center human relationships, placing animal-Bodies out of immediate reach, beyond the archive, as not immediately evident but rather a ghostly, absent presence. Animal voices are suppressed by human stories. Those animal bodies are lost in representation in the centering of the human. The Ryder Papers can be constructed and read in such a way that they invite the reader to read *along* the archival grain (Stoler 2009), orienting towards the actual and symbolic animal(s) beyond. When archived, animals fall under a regime of power where their stories become one-dimensional, objectified, and reduced to marginality. The "archival body [is] temporally situated and yet also always in motion"; the "collections are . . . constituted by stories of . . . experiences, and encounters that might elicit alternate affective movements" (Lee 2016, p. 34). The archival body—and the bodies therein—awaits engagement, becoming a holder of that which has not *yet* become necessary (Hetherington 2004). Archival stories of animals and humans are thus entwined in political and temporal relationships and in histories of representation, action, and pain.

Through the archive, entanglements between times, places, and bodies are found and refound, and the animal's construction as Being or Thing in these animal histories becomes relevant to our present actions. For Farge "The reality of the archive lies not only in the clues it contains, but also the sequences of different representations of reality. The archive always preserves an infinite number of relations to reality" (p. 30). These relations to reality expand and multiply, constantly shifting, as the researcher works with and in the archive to shape ways of knowing and relating to historical events and historical bodies. The archive is a holder of historical trajectories, of overlaps, of comings-together and fallings-apart. Understanding the interconnections and entanglements of the "there-and-then" and the "here-and-now," archives "always stand in active, dialogic, relation to the questions with the present put to the past, and the present always puts its questions differently" (Hall 2001, p. 92). The archive remains elusive, never complete—but always reaching through and allowing the present to arch back to the pasts that led to this moment, which in turn weaves into the future.

Anthropocentrism in the Archive

Animals struggle to speak in the archive. Our storing of history and our engagements with the objects that allow us to remember history and (re)imagine historical subjects are entangled with the stories that are told. In the archive, animal stories are forever entangled with human worlds. We coexist and our lives reinforce one another. Our histories cannot be told in the singular, but rather are inseparable, coming together and falling apart in disturbances of the myths we tell about humankind. These myths are held in part in our archives, our storage of memories. This language of discontinuity, transformation, and rebuilding in relation to archival storage and reading (Foucault 1972) resonates with an imagining of a vegan future, which is yet to be acted upon:

> Scholars wrestle with finding a term that disassembles the hierarchical nature of speaking about other animals . . . similar to privileging race by terms such as *non-white* or finding language for incorporating what or who has been socially constructed as Other into mainstream discourse. (Merskin 2011, p. 145)

The human speaks from one experience of the world—that of being human, or rather, of being *this* human. This is the position of subjectivity from which to reach out, to recognize or create an affinity between the self and others (Thien 2005; Bondi 2003). In recognizing the necessity of "decentering human agencies, as well as remaining close to the predicaments and inheritances of situated human doings" (Puig de la Bellacasa 2017, p. 12), we simultaneously recognize the impossibility of such a task. The animal-Being/animal-Thing binary reverberates with discourses on the non-White, non-Male, non-Western body. How animals are included in this rhetoric is, however, problematic, and these comparisons must be approached with caution and sensitivity (Twine 2014). Yet it remains the assumption in human–animal relations that for animals to be considered, their experiences can only be ascertained in relation to what we know of the *human experience* (Spiegel 1996; Adams 2010; Singer 1975; Harper 2010a; Wrenn 2014):

> To discover what is best for an animal, we are to a great extent dependent upon our ability to imagine ourselves in the lives of that animal. We cannot really know what makes any given individual happy. We could not even give a definition of human happiness that would satisfy everyone. (Masson 2005, p. 203)

The anthropocentric theorizations and practices of animal rights rely upon human superiority or beneficence, affirming in turn humans' immovable centrality to living with animals. This is evident in theories that argue for the inclusion of animals within a human framework, rather than a call to change the framework itself. Sentience and pain defined animal-Beings: this is the basis for the inclusion of animals in moral communities. Two theories typically underpin animal rights philosophy: Singer's utilitarianism (1975), centered on suffering as the moral impetus to do no harm, and Regan's deontology (1983), which poses it as a moral right, or duty, to include animals within these frameworks. However, these do not remove the human framework or value an animal intrinsically, but rather assume that the animal can be imagined, molded, and anthropomorphized to fit human constructions and organization.

A third approach—Ryder's (2002 [1983])—is painism, which focuses on the pain of the greatest sufferer. Painism draws upon Singer's measures of suffering, based on the aggregate suffering of all bodies, and Regan's conception of animals as subjects-of-a-life, as beings who matter to themselves, regardless of their inclusion in human worlds. Their pain is inviolable to their self. These theories acknowledge that pain, as embedded within sentience, is a necessary experience of any subject and, despite their differing definitions of the least-harm principle, remain nonetheless within human conceptualizations of rights, duties, and ways of being in the world.

Anthropocentrism upholds animal-Beings/animal-Things in theories of animal rights and welfare, and the practices they have informed and continue to inform. What lies beyond these ways of relating to animals, and how can a turn to geographical thinking about the body deconstruct this binary? *Beyond* the archive are historical animal-Bodies read through their political representatives and representations. This beyond is thus a space for imagining the exceptional animal, as a premise for reimagining each animal as exceptional.

Animal-Beings/Animal-Things

Animals struggle to resist discourses that construct them simultaneously as wholly body and as representations without a body—discourses that prevent animals from inhabiting the in-between of abstraction and objectification. But how do these meanings come into existence from the human? In our listening to those humans in the archive who have acted as political representatives for animals lies potential to consider the animal "condition" and our own position within this co-construction of animal and human. The following is taken from a response to a questionnaire in 1997 about people's reasons for supporting the animal rights movement:

> Sheer cruelty out of perversion makes me hate with a passion. That is why I am involved—motivated by hatred and detestation and anger, and they are very strong driving forces. . . . It's not dying that I find objectionable, in many ways that is a blessed relief, it's suffering and deliberately inflicted suffering . . . that I struggle to prevent, and I think that is a far cry from "animal rights," whatever that may mean. (Response to questionnaire sent by Richard Ryder, uncatalogued)

Anger is a political act that can propel us into radical thought, organization, and action (Holmes 2004). Anger is not necessarily violent, but it can conversely be significant to nonviolence (Sharp 1973) and can be an integral political force in enacting vegan worlds. For Ahmed (2014), "the response to pain, as a call for action, also requires anger: an interpretation that this pain is wrong, that it is an outrage, and that something must be done about it" (p. 174). The anger that this writer is expressing appears to be motivated by pain more so than even by death. It is the violation of being-ness while animals are still dying that suggests a typically welfarist perspective.

Nonetheless, "anger is not simply defined in relationship to the past, but as opening up the future" (Ahmed 2014, p. 175)—entangled with reasons for action, but also as a political move towards something else. The writer speaks his anger at this cruelty and pain and, crucially, at the animal-Being/animal-Thing binary in the history of animal rights that is the writer's "'animal rights,' whatever that may mean." This could be read as a nod, perhaps unknowing, to an understanding that through theorizations and practices of rights, the human has determined and defined animals as only able to exist within our terms, within our systems of order and organization, within the ways the *human* has understood and interpreted the world. Of course, this, too, could simply be a welfarist position, but by considering the sentiment, a small historical significance opens out new meanings. It also points towards a wider questioning of what indeed animal "rights" are and how these frameworks are upheld by political representatives for animals. It appears that it is not the violation of rights that propels action, but rather suffering, cruelty, or pain.

Theory is not simply conceptual but slippery, leaky (Ahmed 2014), and it informs the practices of animal and vegan activists. Binary animal-Beings/animal-Things are historically, socially, culturally, and spatially contingent, connected with the ways of knowing the world. A rejection of this binary is critical for breaking veganism out of animal rights discourse and repositioning it as a political, ethical, and social issue. What is risked in the retelling of archival animal-Stories is multiple, but the first hesitation we must come to is the *anthropomorphism* of animals: an identification of the animal as who they are not, an assignment of value not to themself-as-their-self but to their "human-like" qualities, read as evidence of being-ness and subjectivity. If anthropomorphized liberation were plausible, it would undermine the very understanding of subjectivity that we have come to organize around, that of difference as existing on a spectrum between object and subject, where "the body is less of a thing/being than a shifting/changing historical meaning that is subject to cultural configuration/reconfiguration"—"a battlefield, one that is fought over again and again across particular historical movements and particular social spaces" (Yancy 2005, pp. 215–216).

Through (hi)stories, some animals can (re)claim and be ascribed a sense of individuality and identity. But it is only *this* animal, not all animals. This animal becomes exemplary—the replica that reflects our vision of our own ideal image—in the rarity of their exception to "the animal" (Derrida 2005). This body is instilled with meaning by being ascribed human-like qualities. *This* animal has found a method of enacting their struggle that the human can interpret—for we can recognize a desire to be free in ourselves. Through struggle and pain, this animal who exists beyond the archive, suspended in a historical moment yet still breaching and affecting the present, can speak:

> One of the pivotal moments in Ryder's biography was the circulation of the *Speciesism* leaflet around Oxford. There are several copies of this leaflet in Ryder's archive, but each time my hands found it, or I return to look at it, the image contained shocks me. A tiny chimpanzee, curled over, seemingly weak, emaciated, and covered in scabs from injections of syphilis during experiments. I recognize pain, I empathize, and his distress breaks through the archive with a sudden kick of pain. The image, the first time I saw it, dragged me out of my almost trance-like state of searching archival materials (see Derrida 1996) into the current moment, in a recognition of a shared feeling, of a desire to reach out to this body in pain. (Field diary, October 2017, The Ryder Papers)

This moment was not in the here and now; rather, the chimpanzee exists beyond the archive, and it is through the archive itself that they can reach into and affect my present. This beyond is a critical space, then, in which the visceral moment of this body image can call humans to recognition where words alone have not sufficed, by creating a "sameness," a positioning of this animal as *like* the human. In the case of the exceptional animal (*this* animal), the problem is not that they are being situated in relation to the human, but rather that this animal must be (re)presented as having a different *essence*—a somatically closer body and meaning—for them to become a body that matters. The anthropocentrism that permeates constructions of the animal, and of animal rights, is underpinned by the logic that to engage those who do not care with a speciesist discourse in which they conceivably can care, the human must be maintained as the most valuable. What we must move towards, instead, is an understanding of the interdependent relationality between human and animal.

In the archive, this animal cannot be the narrator of their own story, so attention is given to those who "ask questions in service of those one is speaking of and engaging with" (Merskin 2011, p. 147). All we can know of the intimate lives of animals is restricted to our observations, interpreted through our human-being-in-the-world. So that we may represent and voice their interests, what we know as communication requires "intimate interaction and empathetic partaking of the perspective of the other [as] the major sources of this knowledge" (Sanders & Arluke 1993). Through the archive, we can reach those others who have been representatives for animals.

The centering of human knowledge returns in the dual and intertwined problems that this understanding of our relation to the nonhuman reveals. First, the opening to the other as distinct is already a disconnection from and barrier to intersubjectivity and relationality. Meaningful encounters are halted when sameness cannot be recognized in another because they are too far removed to invoke such an understanding—this understanding being the ethic upon which relationality and, thus, communication are based. This relational positionality is complicated further by species differences in unrecognizable animal bodies. This critical, reflexive positionality is necessarily concerned with making, in a process of determined self-recognition, subjects uncomfortable. This un-comfort-ability is essential to critiquing our own beings and doings (Berlant 2011), requiring a move "from an ethics of sameness, through an ethics of difference towards an ethics of relationality, responsivity" (Oliver 2015, p. 21), and reciprocity.

When the powerful speak, they reassert structures of oppression and silencing (Spivak 1988). This stands at odds with the notion that animal activists act as a "voice for the voiceless": rather, as suggested here, we are not attentive nor attuned to animal voices. This assertion of voicelessness upholds animals as things rather than as agentic subjects enacting voice, or communicating, in other-than-human ways, calling us to "consider that human language . . . rather than separate from the animal, instinctively returns to it" (Massumi 2014, p. 91). Declaring voicelessness for this animal, then, is an exertion of power, a symbolic violence, whereby the ability to inhabit the in-between of being and thing is again denied. Decentering the human by way of reimagining voice and listening can itself be perhaps even painful. Complicity is, therefore, an active process manifested in a speciesist relation to and within the world. Articulating this complicity breaches our doing of our relationships with animals, opening an imagining of an enhanced political engagement with an expanded and entangled community of humans, animals, and the world.

Animal-Machines and Speaking Pain

The Case of the Brown Dog

> In 1902, Lizzy Lind-af-Hageby and Leisa Schartau, Swedish-British feminist activists, enrolled in a medical course at the London School of Medicine for Women at UCL. They were not, however, medical students in the sense that we might expect. Rather, they became among the earliest undercover exposers of animal abuses in the name of "science." In *The Shambles of Science* (2012), the story of the Brown Dog is told. The women first met the little brown terrier in December 1902, when Professor William Bayliss undertook the first vivisection on the dog, cutting open his abdomen to demonstrate a medical procedure on his pancreatic duct. Two months later, in the activists' next encounter with the dog, Bayliss's assistant cut open the terrier again to inspect the previous wound, before clamping shut his abdomen and handing the dog over so Bayliss could cut open his throat and attach electrodes to his salivary glands. Bayliss stimulated these nerves over the next hour, and Lind-af-Hageby and Schartau watched as the dog was inadequately anesthetized, struggling, his body cut open, clamped and tied down to a wooden board, his mouth muzzled. The brown dog was then handed over to future Nobel Laureate Henry Dale, a student at the time, who removed his pancreas and finally killed him with a knife through the heart.
>
> This is a story that tested Britain at the time as a "nation of animal lovers." The case went to trial. Three years later, a memorial was erected at a park in Battersea, inscribed, "Men and women of England, how long shall these things be?" infuriating medical students against anti-vivisectionist activists. This statue became the site, representationally but also physically, of the question of *whose bodies matter.* (Field diary, February 2017, The Ryder Papers, uncatalogued)

The Brown Dog was no longer killable, even though he had been killed. His body became symbolic and memorialized—the representative for the political ideologies behind anti-vivisection action. This projected a "geography of suffering" (Garlick 2015, p. 810) of animal-Beings becoming scientific-animal-Things—through the breaching of subjectivity, the disturbing of the invisibility and distance that characterize animal-Machines. The Brown Dog, his memorial, and the spaces of action this story fueled are positioned as a critical moment in the history of animal rights. Just as humans, animals, and the world are entangled, so too are the there-and-then and the here-and-now of violence, brought closer through pain.

Closeness is more than just proximal or somatic; it is also read through threats to the body—through the threat of pain (Anzaldua 1987). The Brown Dog's pain connected "society" to his body as a body that came to matter. It is in feeling pain that we become most ourselves—above pretense and presentation in the absolute unshareability in/of the moment of pain. This "absolute split between one's sense of one's own reality and the reality of other persons" (Scarry 1985, p. 4) cannot be reconciled until after the pain or unless through a representative. The inability of another at the moment(s) of pain to experience the body-in-pain is the power of pain to (un)make worlds—"because the person in pain is ordinarily so bereft of the resources of speech, it is not surprising that the language for pain should sometimes be brought into being by those who are not themselves in pain, but speak on behalf of those who are" (Scarry 1985, p. 6).

It is pain that overwhelms this animal, the Brown Dog, in life as in death, and through pain, this body tells a story beyond embodiment's impossible political and perceptual enunciations. As a physical, material reality, the pain of animals as a basic principle has been established since at least the end of the eighteenth century (Ryder 2000), but pain's violation of subjectivity and the destruction of self can be invisible and unspeakable. Spivak (1988) asks of the difficulties in theorizing and enacting voice, "are those who act and struggle mute, as opposed to those who act and speak?" (p. 33) The distinction between action and the speaking of action is the determinant of how that struggle is represented, how it affects and is affected. This calls into question whether those who struggle in a linguistic vacuum are inconsequential—whether their struggle simply does not exist. It is not that those struggling do not attempt speech, but rather that the reciprocal of speech—the act of listening—is incomplete. The archival reader as listener learns how to listen through the archive for those who cannot respond.

The unspeakable can be heard through the body. Through body-stories—of pain and otherwise—this animal can (re)claim and (re)assert their relational self as the center that their life orbits. As Spivak takes the oppressed as the subjects of life, this animal's need for the human representative "to establish conditions where the prisoners themselves would be able to speak" (Deleuze, in Spivak 1988, p. 27), which, too, are the conditions for the complicit human to be able to listen. The impetus remains on humans to imagine and construct spaces in which animals can be heard. This listening space exists between subject-constitution and object-formation—a between-space where the animal-as-thing and the animal-as-being are reduced or expanded, where thing and being are one and the same: inseparable and simultaneous. Until we understand this animal (body) as simultaneously matter and being, we cannot reimagine the future.

When we listen to body-stories, an attachment is formed to this animal, who becomes the "doer" even as they are the "done-to." This animal becomes exceptional, but the animals who are not this animal remain somatically and proximally distant. The becoming of this animal-Being is contingent upon—and reinforces—continued violence against animal-Things: "Of course this knowledge is an imagined positioning of space, as the feared constellations of violence that swell in one place are never constructed in isolation from other sites of violence. Instead, violent narratives are collected from a wider matrix of the stories-so-far of space" (Springer 2011, p. 94). The Brown Dog is one such "story-so-far," and in the space between the questions of who *I* am and who *they* are, my body is not this dog's, but we exist in relation, through our bodies, through time and space. There is possibility within the tensions and movements between *us*. Our bodies speak in the subjunctive tone, in the tone of "as if"; I empathize *as if* I felt the pain of the Brown Dog. I can speak as if I were a representative for his pain, in the between-space of our bodies' coexistence. It is the as-if itself that allows for the creation of an in-between and an imagination of the beyond. In the disappearance of the Brown Dog, space was changed. This dog's body spoke *and was heard* through and beyond human–animal–world entanglements, reordering and creating new places of memorialization and of protest. The dog's body as Being became symbolic of a wider anger giving rise to an ethical questioning of "how long things shall be this way."[1]

Animal-Food and Food-Animals

The animal-Being/animal-Thing binary finds its starkest example in food-animals, bred only to be consumed. To consider the process of "thingification," we must consider what food *does* and *means* in the defining of (human) identities. What, where, how, and whom we eat constitute a defining and distinctive process and experience of everyday life, informed by and informing economic, social, and political circuits of culture (Cramer et al., 2011). Food communicates the stories of people and communities; it is "a receptacle of cultural memory" and is "symbolically

1. This is the inscription on the original Brown Dog's memorial on Battersea's Latchmere Recreation Ground (1906–1910).

associated with the most deeply felt human experiences" (p. 59). Food-animal-Things are positioned within human circuits of consumption and are integral to the stories of human-Beings.

To comprehend the myth that "loving" animals is possible while one eats them, we must consider animal-Bodies as not only products to be consumed, enforced through economic interests, but also a culturally validated habit of hiding pain (Ryder 1998). Food-animals are viewed in the context of "necessary evil" rather than that of cruelty for cruelty's sake. Food-animals are out of sight (White 2015), physically distant and psychologically divorced from the human consumer (Fitzgerald 2010); this visible invisibility (Yancy 2005) of the less-than-human body is seen and felt in moments of encounter with overflowing bodies. These processes of animal suffering are breached by the somatic and physical closeness of suffering in unexpected and discomforting encounters (Garlick 2015), such as when a slaughter truck passes by, with its permeating sights and smells, or when a food-animal's body is not "clean" and being-ness is exposed as stray hairs, eyes, or feces. Through these breaches, *this* animal who exists *beyond* food reveals what has been buried by the self who has chosen not to know (McDonald 2000).

The construction of animal-Things for food by those working on behalf of animals as activists, as political lobbyists, and in animal welfare organizations is evident in these archival materials. In the following case of welfarist activism, the animal-Thing's consumption is justified by its very opposite—animal-Being-ness. The food-animal-Thing is used to assign the very rights it is denied because of species. The thing-ness and being-ness of food-animals are not reproduced, therefore, solely on an individual level or in the relations between one body and another. Rather, the binary (and the resistance to it) are scalar, reinforced by the collective-Subject:

> The SELFA campaign was, and still is, a Royal Society for the Prevention of Cruelty to Animals (RSPCA) campaign focused on the transport of live animals between the UK and Europe, whose end goal was for food-animals to be slaughtered before transport so as to reduce their suffering (Ryder Papers). The transportation of these animals was subject already to some laws regarding the space afforded per animal, rest breaks, food and water, but the RSPCA was suspicious this was not happening and as such trailed the drivers of the lorries transporting food-animals (see also Saunders 2002, pp. 42–43). In its most recent statement on the SELFA campaign, the RSPCA calls for the European Commission to cap transport of live animals at eight hours (RSPCA 2017), which it claims will end exports from the UK. In the 2017 campaign, it calls upon a "country of animal lovers" to end the suffering of animals on their way to slaughter. (Field diary, March 2017, The Ryder Papers, uncatalogued)

The RSPCA used the suffering of animals not to end their murder but rather to maintain the consumption of animal-Bodies, using pain to justify this—using their Beings as temporally contingent to ensure their ultimate objectification, fragmentation, and consumption (Adams 2010). Food-animals are constructed as lively commodities (Collard & Dempsey 2013), existing as beings until they "necessarily" become things. Their existence as Being or Thing as the only possible conditions is fundamental to their death, exposing the flaws of the logic whereby in-between-ness is denied. The rejection of animals-as-food can become a multilayered political act.

Food-animals, and the "food" that they become, can help to tell human stories of being-together and of who we are, through the rituals and traditions of eating. To reject this can be to reject the norms of a society. Animal-Things within societal manifestations represent and tell stories of the cultures and societies within which we live, but they also reflect and mirror society's stories. The wrongs done to animals will outlast and tell the story of our societies, cultures, and politics—through future traditions and future readings of the past, which is our present.

The actions of the RSPCA, as a welfarist organization, may well seem unsurprising, but this example has been drawn from the archive because of the very stark way animals are positioned as either/or, their being-ness exploited to maintain and placate the desire to continue consuming bodies "ethically." The archive not only traces these organizational animal-food histories but also contains materials from "radical" animal liberation movements, although from a more distanced perspective, and it can be seen here too that the binary is perpetuated. The McLibel case, even as it stood in radical opposition to the RSPCA's welfarist position, exemplifies this persistence of animal-Beings and animal-Things. While there is a definitive role played by large organizations in perpetuating and exploiting the binary construction of animals, it is vital that we also consider how this binary is perpetuated and reinforced at grassroots levels, as these visions of the animal are slippery and leak through scalar entanglements of activism.

McLibel began with an action against McDonald's (and a suit for libel by McDonald's) in the mid-1980s (Wolfson 1999; Morris 1999). The Ryder Papers are used in combination with the web archive of McSpotlight to understand how animal-Beings/animal-Things underpin even movements whose approaches stem from a more holistic orientation to animal-Bodies:

> After a few months of working in the Ryder archives, I became increasingly frustrated with what I had come to see as the "respectable" side of animal histories being shown, tied up in bureaucracy, paperwork, and platitudes. I had a strong desire to turn away from this and

engage with more diverse activisms. I kept coming across allusions to London Greenpeace but could find little more information. Ryder is a respectable face of animal rights, and his archive reflects this. Yet there were allusions to his wider interest in the radical animal liberation movement: subscriptions to their magazines and newsletters; personal correspondence with people working under the umbrella of [the] Animal Liberation Front; and more radical views expressed in private, at times evident in his actions. Tracing these histories solely within the confines of this archive was impossible, but what I could find was clues to where else to search further, leading me to McLibel, which can help us to understand the continued perpetuation of Beings and Things even in cases seen as radical.

I turned to the web archive of McSpotlight, and here I found the *What's Wrong with McDonald's* leaflet, produced and distributed by Helen Steele and Dave Morris. In the leaflet, they astutely tie together the interconnecting issues of colonialism, capitalism, health, and the environment with the torture and murder of animals. It seemed to be one of the few cases where a food justice campaign had interweaved with veganism, where, rather than clashing, the campaigners had carefully considered the connections between food, animals, and food-animals. (Field diary, October 2016, The Ryder Papers, uncatalogued)

> In the slaughterhouse, animals often struggle to escape. Cattle become frantic as they watch the animal before them in the killing line being prodded, beaten, electrocuted, and knifed. . . . [McDonald's] sells millions of burgers every day in thirty-five countries throughout the world. This means the constant slaughter, day by day, of animals born and bred solely to be turned into McDonald's products. . . . Some of them—especially chickens and pigs—spend their lives in the entirely artificial conditions of huge factory farms, with no access to air or sunshine and no freedom of movement. Their deaths are bloody and barbaric. . . . It's no exaggeration to say that when you bite into a Big Mac, you're helping the McDonald's empire to wreck this planet. (*What's Wrong with McDonald's* leaflet, www.mcspotlight.org)

McLibel presents the premise that liberation begins in your stomach, but does this position reject the binary? Undoubtedly, the Being/Thing binary persists here. This campaign is an entangled and scalar vision of animal and food justice, encompassing the individual human, economic imperialism, colonial invasion, and human rights violations involving slaughterhouse workers (Giraud 2019).

Despite the McLibel campaign's roots in the idea that liberation begins in the consumer's stomach, the animals' bodies and stories cannot be found here. Their voices are again suppressed by this binary, their bodies made into Things, cogs in a malevolent machine. The figure of the animal currently defines and is defined by both animal and food justice movements, and it is at the conjunction of these intersecting movements that we *should* find a vegan ethic and politics. Until the visions of animal-Beings/animal-Things can be reconciled, this ethical-political positioning of veganism as an anti-speciesist movement will remain divorced from a wider liberation agenda.

It is the juxtaposition of the permeation of animal-Beings/animal-Things throughout these different locations, throughout different manifestations, in a mode of thinking *with* entanglements, then, that reaffirms the need to return to and reconsider the non-innocent processes of caring-for, and living-with, animals "aware of troubling relations and seeking a significant otherness that transforms those involved in the relation and worlds we live in" (Puig de la Bellacasa 2017, p. 83). The exemplary animal breaches processes of ordering and organization in becoming cared-for and rupturing the distance that opposes this animal to this human. "To be exemplary, infinitely universal" (Derrida 2005, p. 238) is to simultaneously be singular and irreplaceable.

Animal-Strangers?

Where the animal is imagined as the stranger, they can reduce social and, therefore, spatial life entirely. Their supposed inability to exist outside of the opposition between friend and enemy, being neither yet simultaneously embodying the possibility of both, means they "can no longer be included within philosophical (binary) opposition, resisting and disordering it, without ever constituting a third term" (Derrida, in Bauman 1990, p. 145). These animal undecidables are to remain always neither/nor, exposing the fragility and nonexistence of any binary. This is the animal-stranger not as the not-yet-decided but as the decidedly undecidable. Animals-as-strangers do not only question the opposition between Being and Thing, but rather question opposition at all:

> the very principle of opposition, the plausibility of dichotomy it suggests. They unmask the brittle artificiality of division—they destroy the world. . . . They must be tabooed, suppressed, exiled physically or mentally—or the world may perish. (Bauman 1990, pp. 148–149)

The stranger becomes the stranger when they refuse to stay in the faraway, becoming of concern only when their status of friendship or enmity must be deduced. Because the stranger does not remain distanced and cannot be defined by or within opposition, they threaten how we know the world. The animal-stranger can become proximally close, but has remained somatically and representationally distant. It is through the breaching of distance that the animal-stranger becomes threatening, in exposing us to those we have tortured, consumed, and destroyed. This proximity in one sense but not the other prevents recognition and a relation of care. It is only through a turn to the between-ness of animals, outside of binaries, that this second sense of proximity can be imagined.

Even as we reject opposition, it continues to define our social worlds. We are yet to find a way of being-in-the-world that we can live, not just theorize, and that does not revolve around opposing that and who we are not. The threat to opposition, even when welcome, ruptures the social worlds that are defined by and for the collective. Where we find ourselves is always situated in the rupture; the relational subject exists only in relation to this ambiguity. The stranger is embodied in and embodies the unknowable, which threatens the foundations upon which binary worlds have been built. To embrace the between-ness is to embrace the unknown—through the figure of the stranger—as essential to existence:

> We can't make sense of living without others, and that includes other animals. We are entangled in complex relationships and rather than trying to accomplish the impossible by pretending we can disentangle, we would do better to think about how to be more perceptive and more receptive to the deeply entangled relationships we are in. (Gruen 2015, pp. 63–64)

Gruen's alternative ethic considers a transformed way of being- and living-with animals and the world, but is it possible that we have somehow overlooked the fact that transformed relationships must be based actually on a transformed construction of the animal? In rushing to the enactment of an alternative ethic, have we missed the fundamental questioning of how we ought to live (Quinn 1992)? Reconstructing animals as beyond binaries, as socio-spatially fluctuating and historically contingent beings/things, requires an anti-hierarchical, anti-speciesist emancipatory agenda that not only demands the impossible (Perlman 2018), but also rethinks the boundaries that can possibly align with ethical and political beliefs beyond the human, orienting towards the animal as a mutual constitutor in worldly transformations of the future.

A Politics of the Possible?

> Only if the future is open is there any ground for a politics which can make a difference. (Massey 2005, p. 11)

History is an attempt to pause time and take a cross-section, as if by becoming completely still in the here-and-now, we could observe the past—from our orientation, through an assumed linearity of time—as static. The position of the researcher in the present can be dissected, her scales, objects, and interactions carefully curated (Werner & Zimmerman 2006). But to read history, "One must have no idea. It is necessary not to know" (Royle 2003, p. 11). A politics of possibility must be assumed in the archive, the same political imagination that allows us to care differently, to expand how we care and whom we care about, and that has been imagined here as enacted through moving simultaneously between and beyond archives, their characters, and their stories. And so "imagining what *might* be was as important as knowing what was" (Stoler 2009, p. 21). Stoler reads possibility backwards by "'developing historical negatives' to track a microspace of the everyday through what might become and could never be" (p. 21). This is the first way in which we must understand a politics of possibility: as a means of imagining what might be as crucial to enacting vegan worlds. It is through this imagining and striving for what lies beyond that we can live-with animals between and beyond Beings and Things:

> Not only history but space is open. In this open interactional space, there are always connections yet to be made . . . relations which may or may not be accomplished. . . . Space can never be that completed simultaneity in which all interconnections have been established, and in which everywhere is already linked with everywhere else. . . . This is a space of loose ends and missing links. *For* the future to be open, space must be open too. (Massey 1995, pp. 11–12)

Because space and, therefore, time are always an open system, the past can be read alongside a vision of the future. A "relational politics for a relational space" (Massey 1995, p. 61) entails an interweaving of ourselves and the nonhuman, an expanding of our worlds not for but with animals. Reading possibility backwards, through the archive, opens up the beyond as a space for relational connections between the here-and-now and the there-and-then, as well as for relations between subjects and objects across times and spaces. To study history is a political act, one that suggests a desire for a different future. To go backwards is a call for a reimagined future—it is to enact a politics of the possible. To distance oneself is always to become already closer, to become preoccupied with the imagined space between the self and what or whom it is moving away from. The multiple trajectories of animal lives and the lives of those humans who have oriented towards animals spatialize our stories and allow us to understand how these relations have been opened up and how they can continue to open up. The failings of animal rights can be understood because of and also within the construction of animal-Beings/animal-Things. To reconstruct animal-Bodies, we must turn away from the violent pasts of human–animal relationships and attempt, insofar as possible, to approach those animal bodies we live with in the here-and-now that will become the there-and-then.

This chapter has enacted this imagining of and for the future through the beyond and through thinking about the beyond, opening up "a new figuration of subjectivity in a multi-differentiated non-hierarchical way" (Braidotti 1994, p. 1). This way of thinking embraces in-between-ness, positioning the body as at once Being and Thing, never wholly subject or wholly object. Thus, the body is "a point of overlap between the physical, the symbolic, and the sociological" (Braidotti 1994, p. 4) through which we experience and enact living-together, but also shift between these states of Being-ness and Thing-ness, fluctuating within this spectrum, both in the present and beyond, towards the past and towards the future.

If, then, we follow Bordo's (2004) conceptualization of "the body as not 'me' but 'with' me," and "at the same time inescapably 'with me'" (p. 2), then each of us, human or animal, inhabits the world through this dual "withness" of the body. The body that is with me, therefore, becomes a medium and a metaphor for culture and social scripts; the body that is "with me" is the body that is read by another, but it is not wholly "me." This body is constructed through everyday reproductions, which become part of a double bind whereby Being and Thing—human and animal, self and other—are mutually exclusive, tearing the subject in two. Bodies consume bodies as bodies are consumed, visually, socially, and physically. The bodies that we are and the bodies that we meaningfully encounter coexist as a social flesh, reinforcing one another, relying on one another to exist, where to live is to live-with. A philosophy of "as if," then, is a philosophy that allows us to live "as if some experiences were evocative and reminiscent of others" (Braidotti 1994, p. 5). Then, political priority must be given to reconsidering animals' (re)presentation(s) as multiple selves, as between subjects and objects, as embedded in networks of relationality that not only are in but extend beyond more-than-human worlds, through time as well as space.

To maintain this life-sustaining web, to nourish our social flesh, to enhance our ways of living-with, and to create worlds of nonviolence, we may find our answer only in presupposing and enacting the as-if—by living as if we already lived in the world we want to create. This mode of "as if" has to encompass the ability (of ourselves and animals) to shift between subject and object, human and animal; it also has to embrace the possibility of reaching beyond the present moment, arching backward to imagine forward. The beyond, then, is not only history, but also the space of the future. To enact new worlds, we must "begin with the geography closest in—the body" (Rich 1984, p. 212). It is here, in the body and the embodied, that we must place the animal in our veganism. To live-with animals is to orient towards not only their bodies but their whole, individual selves—as between subject and object, as valuable—both in relation to and as separate from our own. Veganism may be the first way in which we enact our as-if, but it cannot be the *only* way. There has to be thoughtful and careful consideration within, between, and beyond our present, human entanglements with animals.

Acknowledgments

I would like to thank Phil Emmerson for his generous comments and engagement with this chapter. I would also like to thank all of the editors of this collection, and particularly Paul Hodge, for their guidance, feedback, and encouragement.

6

CHECK YOUR ANTHROPRIVILEGE!

Situated Knowledge and Geographical Imagination as an Antidote to Environmental Speciesism, Anthroparchy, and Human Fragility

Simon Springer

Introduction

It is difficult to know where to begin in writing about anthroprivilege, precisely because it is so overwhelmingly pervasive in our contemporary world. What I mean by *anthroprivilege* are the social norms that reinforce anthropocentrism and confer automatic, unearned benefits upon human individuals. Perhaps the best place to begin, then, is in the somatic domain, as anthroprivilege is something that we as humans all embody. The expression of anthroprivilege is encapsulated in the following reactions. Upon reading my title, you have rolled your eyes or snickered under your breath. You've immediately dismissed the idea as navel-gazing. You reject the connotations it has for questions of race, gender, sexuality, and other positionalities wherein privilege and normativity are key spheres of struggle, which you feel are ultimately incomparable. You have thought to yourself, *Here come the vegan police again*, in the same contemptuous way as the alt-right regards so-called "social justice warriors." Anthroprivilege is fundamentally made possible by such an aversion to critical reflection on human positionality. As with all forms of privilege, it is undergirded and enabled by a deep cognitive dissonance and an outright denial. Yet the implications of anthroprivilege are no mere thought experiment. Instead, anthroprivilege is a tangible and demonstrable planetary scourge, for it forms the foundations of human supremacy. It is only through anthroprivilege that processes like extractivism, anthropogenic climate change, and factory farming become possible. The consequence of such hubris is simple. If we don't begin to get this profound sense of human entitlement in check, it will ultimately be our undoing.

Since I have suggested that critical reflection on human positionality is potentially the key to confronting the invisibility of anthroprivilege, it is worthwhile to consider this more fully, particularly in relation to situated knowledge. Positionality, of course, refers to the political and social context that creates one's identity, influencing and, indeed, biasing one's perspective of the world. Usually, the concept is reserved for referencing race, class, gender, gender identity, sexuality, ability status, and age. We could, however, extend this further and be more thoughtful about our "human" status as another stratum of difference, and as such, an understanding of human positionality could consequently become central to any movement towards greater social, political, or environmental justice. For Lisa Jean Moore (2012), "beginning with species as a classification that has led to social injustice offers opportunities for dialogue . . . whereby all humans can confront their own social location" (p. 13). At the heart of this call for an appreciation of positionality is Donna Haraway's (1988) concept of "situated knowledges," which she views as epistemic positions that are at once partial, embodied, and localized. For geographers, this concept has been useful in deepening our understanding of how geographical knowledge is produced. Within the geographical literature, as Audrey Kobayashi (2009) outlines, discussions of situated knowledge have followed two major strands: the first focuses on reflexivity as a way of understanding ourselves in relation to others, and the second emphasizes how the "Other" is constructed through geographical imaginations.

While Kobayashi (2009) stresses the importance of reflexivity in moving towards a more critical geographical praxis and as a necessary component of situating a researcher, she is also cognizant of the "ironic result of resituating the researcher in a position of privilege." With regards to the question of the animal "Other," that privileged epistemic position arises precisely because of our own social situation as humans. Kobayashi also asks us to consider an argument advanced by György Lukács, who maintains that privilege (of the capitalist class) inhibits one's ability to understand exploitation, while those who are underprivileged (workers) possess an awareness of their own lives and those of their oppressors.

To extend this to anthroprivilege, most nonhuman animals, through encounters with humans over the course of hundreds of thousands of years of evolution, have developed a strong instinct to avoid us. A fear or weariness of humans even extends to apex predators. So, while humans so often fail to see our exploitative behavior, our nonhuman victims are acutely aware of human cruelties. One of the few instances in which humans become partially aware of our own supremacy is when we visit places like Antarctica, where wild animals, like penguins, have evolved free of human contact and, accordingly, have no natural fear. The dodo bird is the most well-known example: since they had never encountered any other animals who could hurt them, their trust in humans ensured their extinction.

The point I want to make is that all knowledge, even of nonhuman actors, is context-specific, or situated, which provides a conceptual basis for appreciating that all knowledge has a geography. Thus, while we can speak of anthroprivilege and identify its consequences, there is not a singular experience of being human. Accordingly, privilege is going to vary across space and time. It is also going to intersect with other identity categories such as gender, sexuality, and race. Any analysis of our own positionalities "requires not simply discussions of oppression, domination, and resistance, but also understandings of diverse interrelations between power and privilege that congeal to form our . . . geographical knowledges" (Browne 2008, p. 146).

Geographical imaginations, or imaginative geographies, are powerful ways of thinking about the world. The term encompasses multiple meanings ranging from mental maps to social discourses about culture and difference (Gilley 2010). Drawing on Foucault's (1980) recognition that the exercise of power and the sanction of particular knowledges overlap, Edward Said (1978) identifies imaginative geographies as constructions that operate by demarcating conceptual partitions and enclosures between and around "the Same" and "the Other," which configure "our" space of the familiar as separate and distinct from "their" unfamiliar space that lies beyond. For Derek Gregory (2004), the power to represent and imagine geography and its subjects like *this* rather than like *that*, is at once a process of articulation and one of valorization. In this sense, a geographical imagination is paramount in the process of understanding "Self" versus "Other." Since we operate, through social interaction, in constantly unfolding "webs of significance" (Geertz 1973), the so-called "reality" is shaped by the discourses we reproduce and internalize rather than by external, independent, or predetermined characteristics. As far as the definition of the Self is concerned, the idea is central to the subjective world in which humans operate (Sanders 1990). Consequently, notions of Self are not static but rather imagined, with our nations, cities, communities, and individual bodies all forming part of the geographical imagination of what it means to be human. The ongoing construction of the Other is accordingly a process of imagining geographies of inclusion and exclusion. In other words, imaginative geographies are pivotal in developing a critical understanding of the significance and contingencies of social location and, thus, of who resides inside and outside places of privilege. In short, geographical imaginations are spatial strategies according to which situated knowledge is engaged to produce difference (Kobayashi 2009), which, for our purposes, invokes the animal as "other."

Animal geographies, and in particular, critical animal geographies, have sought to interrogate the privilege and power that constitute human geography and the geographical imaginations that are mobilized to produce difference. There has also been a parallel movement towards so-called "more-than-human" geographies (Whatmore 2006), along with similar movements within the social sciences towards posthumanism more generally (Wolfe 2010). With the exception of some studies in critical animal geographies (White & Springer 2017), these movements in the literature, while they question the parameters of the "human," have often been peculiar in their notable lack of reflexivity with respect to the ethics of using animals for food. In reflecting on situated knowledges, Kobayashi (2009) argues that the production of geographical knowledge is "simultaneously a moral and a political project," so one has to consider the privilege that is manifested through the detachment—and dare I say, solipsism—of some of these scholars who ignore the ethical questions invoked by animal others and their consumption. While animal, more-than-human, and post-human geographies are welcome developments, I have yet to encounter work that addresses anthroprivilege in the same systematic way as critical race theory has criticized white privilege and as feminist scholarship has condemned male privilege on explicitly moral and political grounds.

In this chapter, I will begin by examining the issue of privilege in general and in other registers, including race and gender. By familiarizing ourselves with how privilege works in relation to other identity categories, we are better positioned to start recognizing how anthroprivilege functions. I then turn my attention towards the ways in which *others* are constructed as animals and, thus, animals are created as *others*. In the section that follows, I outline an anthroprivilege checklist in an attempt to better illuminate the ways in which humans take our species' positionality for granted. Next, I examine the pervasiveness of what I am calling "environmental speciesism"; here, I take my cue from reflections on environmental racism to assess how human priorities repeatedly supersede those of nonhuman animals. I then outline the similarities and differences between anthroprivilege, anthropocentrism, and anthroparchy, before considering the curious expression of defensiveness when humans are confronted with these phenomena, which I refer to as "human fragility." Finally, I offer some concluding thoughts. If thinking critically about privilege is an attempt to "sensitize us to things we have been taught not to see" (Leavy 2017, p. 1), then as far as anthroprivilege is concerned, this chapter attempts to expose our environments to make us aware of the environmental speciesism that we all have a hand in reproducing.

Privilege in Other Registers and the Question of Being Human

Before we can understand anthroprivilege, we first need to understand the nature of privilege in general and in other registers. What exactly is privilege? In unpacking any concept, I always like to begin with etymology, since it is often quite revealing. *Privilege* is derived from the Latin *privilegium*, which means "bill or law affecting an individual" and which combines *privus* ("private") with *lex* or *leg-* ("law"). There is accordingly a legal basis to privilege, which, on a social level, may not be immediately apparent but makes perfect sense because, as we shall see, the social understanding of privilege comes from an extension of its legal implications.

In law, a privilege is indicative of a particular entitlement to immunity that has been granted by an authority—usually the state—to a restricted group, either on a conditional basis or by virtue of birth (McNichol 1992). This contrasts with the legal notion of a *right*, which is considered an inherent and irrevocable entitlement held by all citizens or all human beings from the moment of birth. The social meaning of privilege remains similar to its legal understanding. The Oxford Dictionary, for example, defines privilege as "a special right, advantage, or immunity granted or available only to a particular person or group" and uses the example of "education is a right, not a privilege" to reinforce the idea that privilege sits apart from the entitlements held by the majority. It is perceived or actual advantages that are at the core of an understanding of privilege, since they are assumed to be available only to particular groups. These advantages can also be emotional or psychological, relating to self-confidence and a sense of belonging or worth. Privilege is consequently a question of social inequality and is frequently invoked with respect to categories like age, ethnicity, race, ability, gender, gender identity, sexual orientation, religion, social class, and geography. Thus, we can speak of adult privilege, white privilege, body privilege, gender privilege, cis privilege, heterosexual privilege, Christian privilege, socioeconomic privilege, and First World privilege. What is missing, of course, is the question of the animal Other.

Sociologist W. E. B. Du Bois (2007 [1903]) was arguably the first to consider privilege in a rigorous academic sense when he wrote *The Souls of Black Folk*, which examines the ways in which African Americans have to have a "double consciousness" of both how they view themselves and how the world views them. Although he didn't define white privilege explicitly as such, Du Bois reflected on the courtesy and deference, unimpeded admittance to public functions, and lenient treatment in court that are afforded to white people, but not extended to African Americans. The benefits of being white were highlighted—a major development in our understanding of how racial inequality is reproduced.

Peggy McIntosh (1989) subsequently brought the idea of privilege into wider academic currency with her essay on white privilege and male privilege. In particular, she describes privilege as an "invisible package of unearned assets" that white people often refuse to acknowledge, that allows them to be oblivious about racial issues while non-white people become alienated (McIntosh 1989, p. 12). Shannon Sullivan (2006) takes a similar approach in referring to white privilege as an "unconscious habit," suggesting that it "operates as unseen, invisible, even seemingly nonexistent." For Kimmel (2017): "[Privilege is] like running with the wind at your back. It feels like just plain running, and we rarely if ever get a chance to see how we are sustained, supported, and even propelled by that wind" (p. 1). In this way, privilege is similar to power, oppression, and domination, all of which function in insidious and complex ways that make it difficult to discern them (Leavy 2017).

Privilege theory considers individuals as being situated within a matrix wherein one's privilege and disadvantage will shift and transform depending upon the context. This character of privilege suggests that it is a distinctively geographical phenomenon. While privilege is often quite visible, operating through categories, such as race and gender, it can also be relatively invisible, such as in the case of citizenship status, birth order, or even alphabetical order. Some privileges, like those based on age and wealth, can shift over time, but most privileges are quite stable. The stability of privilege is in part what makes it so difficult for those that hold privilege to see it. It is always there as something that those who benefit from it simply have, thus making them unwilling to acknowledge it. Consequently, people often seek to justify their privilege using individual attributes, rather than confront it by recognizing it as institutionally embedded across society. Since privilege is distributed along a range of axes, it should not be considered as a zero-sum game in which one either has privilege or not (Coston & Kimmel 2012).

But what happens when that axis is human/nonhuman? Certainly, the question of the animal Other intensifies the cognitive dissonance people feel, and with respect to the recognition of privilege, anthroprivilege is likely to be even more invisible to those who hold it. Many will surely respond in typical speciesist fashion by suggesting that the question itself is somehow inappropriate, pushing back against the acknowledgment of the Other in reactionary ways, as with all forms of bigotry and prejudice. We also know that the disadvantages of certain species are going to be felt differently in different spaces, for example, in the case of dogs seen as pets versus dogs seen as food. But anthroprivilege seems to be of a slightly different character from most privileges, not only because the category of "human" is so ingrained in our cultural understandings of selfhood, but equally owing to the fact that othering can only be properly understood within a speciesist problematic that constitutes an attempt to defend the privileges of an "unmarked" humanness against the imagined threat of an animalized Other. Anthroprivilege provides benefits that are reinforced by anthropocentric social norms based on the speciesist design and historical binary developed by and for humans that create an "us" (human) and a "them" (animal).

When we replace "white" with "human" in McIntosh's (1989, p. 10) assertion that "white privilege is like an invisible weightless knapsack of special provisions, assurances, tools, maps, guides, codebooks, passports, visas, clothes, compass, emergency gear and blank checks," we begin to see how anthroprivilege functions. Yet the category of "human" often functions at an even deeper level than does whiteness or maleness. This is because anthroprivilege has a fundamental intersection with Judeo-Christian thought and its attribution of dominion over the earth and its inhabitants to humanity. Judeo-Christianity continually reinforces a speciesist worldview as a fundamental truth, moving human privilege to the furthest recesses of our thoughts. Just as "whites are carefully taught not to recognize white privilege" and "males are taught not to recognize male privilege" (McIntosh 1989, p. 10), so, too, are humans taught not to recognize anthroprivilege.

In discussing how she came to recognize and ultimately theorize privilege, McIntosh (1989) suggests that by "thinking through unacknowledged male privilege as a phenomenon with a life of its own, I realized that since hierarchies in our society are interlocking, there was most likely a phenomenon of white privilege that was similarly denied and protected, but alive and real in its effects" (p. 10). Taking this understanding of intersectionality a step further, if we are to acknowledge and become accountable for forms of privilege based on whiteness and maleness, we must recognize their coincidence with anthroprivilege. With higher privilege, one has a greater capacity to do harm to others as the invisibility of one's actions is reinforced. Consequently, it should come as no surprise that the owners of factory farms and industrial-scale slaughterhouses are largely white males. But it is not just the butchers who hold anthroprivilege. Anthroprivilege in our societies is systemic.

The hidden mode of operation that characterizes privilege suggests that conscious argumentation against it is often not enough and that other means are needed to combat it. Put differently, we would require more than mere academic writing to begin the process of acknowledgment and change, whereas other genres of communication, such as literature, art, and film, can potentially have a greater impact because of their "subtle emotional work that richly engages the nonreflective aspects of white privilege" (Sullivan 2006, p. 1). Nonetheless, philosophy is needed because of the disruption it creates in the unconscious habit of privilege. Accordingly, change is more likely to arise through indirect, rather than direct, assaults. Owing to the constitutive role that the external world plays in the formation of any habit, the type of indirect assault required is one that "transforms the social, political, institutional, economic, aesthetic, physical, psychological and other conditions" for the composition of anthroprivilege habits (Sullivan 2006, p. 2).

Thus, habit cannot be separated from its environment or the geographical imagination, meaning that the habit of privilege, as obscured as it is, has a geography that resonates as much from the outside as it does from the inside. Habits are not a thin veneer, but rather become constitutive of the Self as the fibers and threads that are woven together into the complex tapestry of privilege. This metaphor also reveals why questions of privilege are always overlapping and intersectional. Such a framework is critically important because it promotes the extension of privilege studies "beyond the domain of race, where much of the scholarly and popular work has been focused, to other important identity markers" (Case, Iuzzini, & Hopkins 2012).

Others as Animals, Animals as Others

In working through a conceptualization of privilege, we begin to see the exclusion of nonhuman animals. If rights, which are intended to extend to all, fundamentally exclude all beings but those who are *human*, then where does this understanding leave *nonhuman* beings when it comes to questions of privilege? For most humans, these questions don't even register. The exclusion of animals from rights is precisely because anthroprivilege is taken for granted as the essential condition of human experience. The assumption of humans' greater importance is like the oxygen we breathe. It's always there. Yet on the basis of our understandings of privilege in general, it should become clearer as to why animal rights are not enough: precisely because they do not address the issue of anthroprivilege in either legal or social terms. To get at anthroprivilege, we need to move our frame of reference away from a rights-based focus and towards the prospect and potential of liberation.

We have seen how, during the French Revolution, the social and legal implications of privilege intersected, with the abolition of privilege through the removal of separate laws for different social classes being one of the revolutionaries' primary goals. It seems unsurprising, then, that the revolutionary social movements of the present would also advocate the elimination of privilege, given that the leveling of the social playing field has tremendous emancipatory capacity. For animal liberation advocates, this revolutionary principle remains, since the objective is to overthrow human supremacy, and anthroprivilege is a key pillar maintaining this system of domination. It is not rights afforded by humans that will change things, as this approach simply maintains a system of human supremacy in the form of the state. Rather, what is needed is total liberation that demands "(1) an ethic of justice and anti-oppression inclusive of humans, nonhuman animals, and ecosystems; (2) anarchism; (3) anti-capitalism; and (4) an embrace of direct action tactics" (Pellow 2014, pp. 5–6; Anonymous 2019).

Anthroprivilege is so ingrained in the social, cultural, political, and economic understandings of our world that it is difficult to find the words to communicate the ideas to combat it. We are so immersed in the unconscious habits of anthroprivilege that we struggle to realize the ways in which value is denied to others simply because of the species they belong to. Our unconsciousness reflects a rigid geographical imagination of animal bodies as other. Anthroprivilege is the height of human hubris, precisely because it is the foundational moment of the construction of the Self and, thus, the bedrock upon which all forms of othering are structured. Racism is premised upon the animalization of the Other (Polish 2016), whereby those who are not like "us" are rendered somehow bestial. Similarly, racial slurs often take the form of comparisons to nonhuman animals. It is considered denigrating to be called an animal. When we speak of the dehumanization of the Other, what is not considered is the way that anthroprivilege structures this framing. Through various forms of oppression, one's humanity is said to be stripped away, and one is deprived of what we may otherwise consider positive human qualities.

But why are positive qualities reserved for humans? Is there not a distinct form of privilege at play in the rendering of *others* as *animals* and, thus, of *animals* as *others*? If we mean to say "degrade," "demean," "subvert," "abase," or "deprave," why do we retain "dehumanize" as a term? The answer rests in the epistemic privilege of our human worldview. We can ask why it should be insulting to be compared to an animal in the first place, particularly if we are able to recognize animals' intellect, beauty, and agency. But the sad fact of anthroprivilege is that these nonhuman capacities are habitually denied.

Misogyny is similarly rooted in a dehumanizing frame, wherein women are made figures of aversion and disgust because their bodies are supposedly "closer to nature" by virtue of processes such as menstruation and childbirth. This imagined proximity to nature, which is decidedly geographical, is actually the ascription of bestial qualities. In the anthroprivileged mind, that someone is "animalized" gives license to violence against them. In a parallel way, Carol Adams (2015 [1990]) demonstrates with conviction how women are sexualized and degraded through comparisons to the dismembered body parts of other animals as part of what she calls the "pornography of meat." In the nexus of white-male-heterosexual-anthroprivilege, the value of the victim is only materialized once they are murdered—either materially or metaphorically—and transformed through objectification into something that is consumable by the privileged positionality. Through McIntosh's interrogation of male and white privilege, we were able to see how those with privileged identities are taught to think of their lives as morally neutral, normative, and also ideal. Any effort by the privileged to benefit others becomes a salvationary gesture that allows "them" to be more like "us."

Anthroprivilege is slightly different in that it is oriented towards the idea of dominion, as opposed to that of salvation. In the Judeo-Christian tradition, animals cannot be saved. They are said to be unable to reason and, thus, are considered beyond redemption. It is only *man*, who exemplifies the intersection of male privilege with anthroprivilege, who was created in God's image. Nonetheless, anthroprivilege is still tethered to a colonial logic that is rooted in the patronizing of the Other. But the connection is actually much more systematic. The entire impetus for colonialism was underpinned by the bestialization of the Other (Said 1978). Colonialism was the process through which human dominion over Earth as in God's idealized view could be expanded; colonialism conferred human qualities upon the Other, saving them from the world of beasts by transforming their bestial selves into something more like "us."

Postcolonial theory has demonstrated that colonialism was and remains a salvationary gesture premised upon a geographical imagination that places Europeans in the hearth of humanity, with its progress, its rationality, and its enlightenment (Sharp 2008). In contrast, colonial thought situates non-Europeans in the wild, unknown domain of animals discursively positioned as wallowing in their own excrement, dying from disease, in need of "our" deliverance (Livingstone Smith 2011). Yet there is a lack of reflexivity that still lurks in the shadows of postcolonial thought, even though postcolonialism rejects the bestial ascriptions that are assigned to the Other. When postcolonial authors critique colonization, it is almost always positioned as a human tragedy. They fail to see the preceding, current, and ongoing colonization of animal spaces for human use that has occurred and continues to occur repeatedly in virtually every nook and cranny of the planet.

To even suggest that the colonization of animal others is of equal importance to that of human others, or that the two processes actually coincide and are mutually reinforcing, is considered offensive and perhaps even obscene. Human supremacy is so ingrained as a situated knowledge of human experience that the anthroprivilege in refusing this connection goes unnoticed. Even within decolonizing praxis, with some notable exceptions (Colling et al., 2014), nonhuman animals are typically an afterthought at best, as we do not often find nonhuman actors explicitly included in ways that promote a view of intersectionality that extends the emancipatory struggle to an interspecies domain. It is oxymoronic, if not callous, to advocate an end to colonial thinking and practice while continuing to trivialize colonization's impacts on those animal others who have experienced it in the most vicious, visceral, and violent manners. The predominant geographical imagination is firmly rooted in a prioritizing of the emancipation of humans in human spaces coopted for human usages. It would seem that the specter of anthropocentrism is ever-apparent, haunting our political commitments in even the most "woke" of spaces.

The Anthroprivilege Checklist

One of the most compelling parts of McIntosh's (1989) essay is her documentation of forty-six privileges that she, as a white person, experienced in the U.S. This checklist format is a useful model in terms of thinking through privilege, and accordingly, it has been adapted to speak to particular forms of privilege in other registers; examples include "the male privilege checklist" (Deutsch 2004) and "the heterosexual privilege checklist" (Killerman 2012). In line with these other attempts to acknowledge and account for privilege, I present forty-six privileges that I experience as a human being:

1. I can be sure that my fear of another animal is not rooted in their species' systematic and purposeful killing of members of my species.
2. Where members of my species build their homes takes precedence over the damaging effects this might have on other species.
3. If I should need to move, I can be pretty sure that it is not because another species has fundamentally transformed the ecosystem that I call home in the interest of solely their own species.
4. I can be reasonably sure that my neighbors will be neutral or pleasant to me and will not try to poison my children and me.
5. Most of the time, I can go about my business fairly well assured that I will not be followed or harassed by hunters who consider killing me to be a source of either entertainment or food.
6. Advertisement inserts in newspapers do not include pictures of members of my species butchered into chunks, with their body parts euphemized in various ways as part of a marketing strategy.
7. I can be reasonably sure that my children can learn from me the skills they need to live happy lives, because they will not be torn from their mother at the moment of birth so that her milk can be harvested.
8. I don't have to worry about making arrangements to protect my children from members of another species who might hurt them just for fun.
9. I don't have to teach my children to be aware of purposeful and systemic violence against my species, perpetrated by another species for its own daily physical protection.
10. When a member of my species hurts that of another species, either inadvertently or in self-defense, my entire species is not demonized as aggressive and threatening.
11. I am never considered a representative or an ambassador of my entire species.
12. I don't have to worry about members of my species being captured and put on display in zoos and aquariums.
13. I am reasonably certain that members of my species are not being forcibly tested on for consumer products such as makeup and medicine.

14. I can be sure that I will never see the decapitated head of a member of my species mounted on a wall, their dead body stuffed and posed on a shelf, or their skinned torso splayed out on a floor. If this were to happen, I am certain that there would be a criminal investigation for murder and bodily desecration.
15. I don't have to worry about my emotions being trivialized to the extent that many don't consider it possible for me to even have emotions based on the species I belong to.
16. If members of my species were forced to race against each other under dangerous conditions, it would be considered not a sport but rather a crime.
17. I can stumble out of the forest and into a suburban backyard without fear of being shot with a tranquilizer gun and potentially euthanized.
18. I am certain that members of my species are not being selectively bred to produce certain characteristics, physical or personality-wise, by another species to serve its own ends.
19. I can be quite certain that when born, male members of my species will not be immediately thrown into a grinder because they are not considered useful.
20. If a member of my species were forcibly impregnated, it is reasonable to expect that there would be consequences for the perpetrator and that the activity would be considered a crime.
21. I can be sure that if I need legal or medical help, the fact that I am human will not work against me.
22. I can expect figurative language and imagery in all of the arts to testify to the experiences of my species in ways that do not minimize them by morphing the characteristics of my species to match those of another one.
23. If I became lost or homeless, I can be reasonably sure that I would not be euthanized.
24. I am certain that members of my species are not being killed so that their skin can be used to make clothing.
25. If members of my species were forced to pull a carriage filled with tourists through the busy streets of a city, I am confident that the general public wouldn't respond with apathy by deeming them "work people."
26. If members of my species were mistreated in a systematic way that resulted in millions of deaths, I believe the general public the world over would respond in horror, not with indifference.
27. When members of my species are bought and sold, it is considered slavery. The general public does not tolerate the enslavement of members of my species.
28. When members of my species are made to suffer, that suffering is not routinely trivialized as somehow inconsequential on the premise that we supposedly can't feel pain.
29. I can invoke "tradition" or "culture" as a reason for killing a member of another species and the consequence will, in most instances, be nonexistent.

30. When my species uses language or tools, it is recognized and appreciated as such.
31. I am treated as an individual with unique characteristics and concerns. I am understood to have a distinctive personality.
32. When members of my species first migrated to different parts of the planet, they were not considered to belong to an "invasive species," even when historical and scientific record indicates that they radically transformed the environment and caused the extinction of many other species.
33. I am certain that the male babies of my species will not be kept for their entire short lives in the dark, confined to metal crates so that they are unable to move so as to discourage muscle growth, only to be executed while still in childhood.
34. If members of my species were routinely being force-fed to promote growth, it would be treated as a criminal offence.
35. If members of my species died in a natural disaster, their deaths would never be written off as a "loss of stock."
36. Photos of the dead, dismembered, and/or decapitated bodies of members of my own species are not being posted to social media as trophies or as part of a celebratory feast.
37. I am not given hormone injections against my will, and if members of my species were being subjected to this practice on a regular basis, I am positive there would be public outrage.
38. If members of my species were forced to live by the tens of thousands in open warehouses, I can be sure that society would not accept the idea that this is "free-range" living.
39. Female members of my species have not been genetically engineered in such a way that they each produce the maximum possible number of eggs in the shortest time frame.
40. Members of my species are not tricked into having hooks shoved in their mouths and being pulled out of their environment either for sport or to be eaten.
41. I am certain there are not businesses whose sole enterprise is to exterminate members of my own species, citing them as "pests."
42. There is not an industry entirely dedicated to killing members of my species as a sport.
43. When derogatory comments are made about others, my entire species is not referenced or mobilized in such a way as to imply an insult.
44. If a member of my species were killed by being anally electrocuted, being shot with a captive bolt pistol, or having their throat slit, I can be quite sure that this would not be considered a "humane" death.
45. I am not considered "food."
46. I can debate the merits of eating other animals or not. I have a choice.

Through questioning the invisibility that characterizes privilege, McIntosh suggests that it is rare for a man to "go beyond acknowledging that women are disadvantaged to acknowledging that men have unearned advantage, or that unearned privilege has not been good for men's development as human beings, or for society's development, or that privilege systems might ever be challenged and changed." With regards to the invisibility of anthroprivilege, are we willing to do more than simply acknowledge the nonhuman animals on this planet as disadvantaged? Can we acknowledge our own unearned human privileges and how they have been bad for the development of our planet? It would seem to me that such a reflexivity about our species' situated positionality is a necessary step on the path of bringing the environmental justice movement to a greater appreciation of environmental speciesism.

Pervasive Geographies of Environmental Speciesism

One of the most overt ways to confront the geographies of speciesism, and in turn of anthroprivilege, is to consider what I call "environmental speciesism." I take my cue from the concept of environmental racism, which was first used in 1982 by Benjamin Chavis, the executive director of the Commission for Racial Justice of the United Church of Christ. Chavis sought to highlight how non-white peoples are disproportionately exposed to pollution due to policymaking, regulatory slack, and deliberate targeting (Mohai, Pellow, & Roberts 2009). The idea has been widely employed and extended since then and is now typically used to refer "to any policy, practice, or directive that differentially affects or disadvantages (whether intended or unintended) individuals, groups, or communities based on race or color" (Bullard 1994, p. 451). *Environmental speciesism*, then, is quite simply those policies, practices, and directives that hamper, impede, and disproportionately affect (whether purposefully or inadvertently) any nonhuman animals based on their status as nonhuman. When we reflect on that for a moment, at least as far as the directives of the state are concerned, we become aware that virtually every decision made is an act of environmental speciesism, since nonhuman actors are either the last to be considered or, more frequently, never considered at all.

If studying environmental racism is important insofar as it helps us understand racism by offering new insights into the subject, and particularly its spatiality (Pulido 2015), then environmental speciesism can have the same implications with regards to speciesism. Unfortunately, as Pulido (2000) critiques, scholars of environmental racism don't often seriously problematize racism, opting instead for a de facto conception based on malicious individual acts. The problem with this approach is that it reduces racism to a hostile, discriminatory act and thereby ignores "the role of structural and hegemonic forms of racism in contributing to such inequalities" (Pulido 2000).

Scholarship on speciesism has worked in the opposite way: reflections on speciesism typically begin with a desire to understand and examine its broad structural underpinnings (Horta 2010), wherein particular acts of cruelty are recognized as localized manifestations of speciesism more generally. While this places understandings of speciesism at an advantage compared to typical considerations of racism, as of yet, the literature on speciesism has not really done the work of examining its spatiality in the same way as critical race geographies and feminist geographies have with respect to racism and sexism. Animal geographies, and more recently, critical animal geographies, have begun unpacking and identifying some of the ways in which speciesism moves along geographical contours (Gillespie & Collard 2015; Urbanik 2012; Wolch & Emel 1998), but as this volume on vegan geographies implies, there is more work to be done to draw our attention to the geographical knowledges that are both produced by and produced from speciesism. While this is a book about vegan geographies, one should not assume that the discussion is primarily about food. It should be clear that the ramifications of anthroprivilege and environmental speciesism extend to multiple other domains in which humans and nonhuman animals come into contact, where a vegan ethic becomes relevant.

Lawrence Blum (2008) suggests that privilege theory should distinguish between "spared injustice" and "unjust enrichment." The injustices meted out to nonhuman animals in the name of science (animal testing), medicine (use of animal body parts), entertainment (zoos, circuses, and aquariums), and nourishment (meat, eggs, and milk) are staggering and incomprehensible in scale. Yet, in the context of anthroprivilege, we need to ask ourselves not only how we have been spared injustices owing to our status as humans—as not being tested on in the name of science, not having our organs harvested to make medicine, not being captured and put on display in zoos, and not being used as a food source are all markers of our anthroprivilege—but also how social justice movements can so often leave the question of the animal Other entirely unattended to or relegated to a secondary concern.

It is hard to imagine that people would not mobilize *en masse* were it to be discovered that a certain group of people was being slaughtered based on their gender or race, and that their dismembered bodies had started showing up on grocery store shelves. With respect to unjust enrichment, the connection to anthroprivilege is arguably even clearer, as examples of environmental speciesism are not hard to come by. The entire world is staked with human proprietary claims, with vast swaths of land marked as the territories of states, which are afforded sovereign rights to processes like deforestation and extraction, not to mention to the lives and bodies of undomesticated animals. These sentient lives are regulated and recorded through a biopolitics of conservation and a necropolitics of governance, with features like hunting and fishing licenses. With respect to domesticated animals, unjust enrichment is also played out in practices like dog breeding, horse racing, and of course, factory farming. The dispossession of nonhuman animals to make way for human settlements is not even considered dispossession, even though it explicitly involves the accumulation of land and resources that were used by others first. These various facets of spared injustice and unjust enrichment all speak to environmental speciesism's problematic framing of our understandings of the world.

The transition back and forth between environmental racism and environmental speciesism is a fluid process. For example, within cities, the politics of NIMBYism (Not In My Back Yard) often represents opportunities to apply not only white privilege but also human privilege. When we remember that othering itself is a process of "dehumanizing," or rendering difference through the ascription of bestial traits, we can start to see that racism and speciesism are fundamentally intertwined and function in parallel ways. Extrapolating from Phil Hubbard's (2005) reflections on white privilege, we can identify anthroprivilege in the series of structures, institutions, and practices that may not be intentionally or maliciously speciesist but serve to maintain the privileged status of human spaces through both spared injustice and unjust enrichment.

Cities in particular are unequivocal reflections of human privilege, even if not in a conscious effort, as they are so tightly regulated in order to maintain their functioning in the service of human interests. We can see this in everything, from shopping malls with NO ANIMALS signs posted at their entrances, hostile architecture such as anti-bird spikes, the numerous businesses involved in "pest control," to the strict regulation of pets through licensing and registration. Dogs not under the command of an "owner" (the term has a shared connotation with the language of slavery that, again, hints at the fluidity between racism and speciesism) are subject to capture, even frequently put to death, should they not be claimed by a human companion. From the perspective of the animal Other, if the city is not entirely off-limits, as wild animals who wander into such a space are tranquilized or even shot on-site, it is highly segregated in its intended and actual use. As urbanization increasingly encroaches on animal habitats, many animals are becoming nocturnal to avoid human contact (Gaynor et al., 2018).

From Anthroprivilege, Anthropocentrism, and Anthroparchy to Human Fragility

Since privilege is often regarded as something that is reserved for those who are considered somehow special, it is not difficult to see the fluidity between anthropocentrism (the belief in human exceptionalism) and anthroprivilege (the advantages enjoyed by humans). With respect to race, we know that a defining feature of white supremacy is the belief that white people are superior. The idea of superiority itself is an affront to anyone who cares about social justice, but when it comes to anthropocentrism—which is, in fact, just another way of saying "human supremacy"—there is a distinct lack of reflection. This realization is, of course, the point at which the question of privilege should be invoked. How can human supremacist values proliferate if not for the foundational privilege that underpins them? McIntosh (2012) is "convinced that studies of oppression will not go anywhere towards ending oppression unless they are accompanied by understanding of the systems of privilege that cause systems of oppression" (p. 204).

Accordingly, if we wish to ever tackle questions of animal cruelty, exploitation, and oppression, we have to begin by viewing anthroprivilege as a system through which the world is made and remade in the service of human interest and advantage. It is only the recognition and acknowledgment of privilege by members of the dominant group—in this case, humans—that will ultimately promote allyship on our part to challenge our own anthroprivilege (Case, Hensley, & Anderson 2014). But understanding anthroprivilege as merely a repertoire of taken-for-granted advantages is not enough. Without an accompanying recognition of the connection between anthropocentrism and anthroprivilege, any acknowledgment of anthroprivilege will result in only a shallow sense of virtue, not a dissection of the institutional arrangements through which human supremacy continues.

Anthroprivilege is a powerful influence on environmental speciesism, yet not sufficient to explain it. For that, we need to ask questions about supremacist ideas. Pulido (2000) argues that awareness is an important distinction between white privilege and white supremacy, but contends that the two ideas occupy a vast terrain that is not always cut and dry. To help us navigate through the maze, she draws a distinction between *intentionality* and *animus*. The former relies on awareness and refers to the degree of deliberateness of one's actions. In contrast to intentionality, she suggests that animus is the outright hostility one may harbor towards a particular group. To relate this to the question of anthroprivilege, it is very common for people, groups, and institutions to act deliberately to enhance the wellbeing of humans at the expense of nonhuman animals without actually wishing them harm.

This is how privilege functions. Where it becomes supremacy is when humans consciously seek to enhance their own positions and to harm other animals out of fear or malice. This practice that is sadly also common is defined by Erika Cudworth (2008) as "anthroparchy," or the social system of attitudes, practices, and institutions through which other species and the natural world have been dominated by humans to benefit humans. If white supremacy is revealed in an attitude of racial superiority, then human supremacy is exposed by what most humans consider to be a foundational belief. Most people simply take the idea of human superiority for granted. It is a predetermined notion in most contemporary human cultures, inculcated in children from a very young age. A pig is just a pig. A dog is merely a dog. Or so we tell our children through the lens of our own animus. But is it acceptable to say the same things with respect to gender or race? While language that downplays and deindividualizes nonhuman animals is commonplace, the same logic, when applied to humans, is flagged as sexist and racist, and rightfully so. How, then, can we explain its acceptability in most circles vis-à-vis nonhuman animals, other than by acknowledging the deeply internalized sentiment of human superiority? When and where this anthropocentric belief is both conscious and expressed with callous disregard are precisely the moment and space wherein anthroprivilege is transformed into the far more sinister system of anthroparchy. But that the cruelty of anthroparchy should be recognized *as cruelty* is not an easy pill for humans to swallow. Critical reflexivity about this issue is often overshadowed by what I want to call "human fragility."

Robin DiAngelo (2018) coined the term "white fragility" to describe the defensiveness and disbelief exhibited by white people when their ideas about race and racism are challenged. She discovered that this fragility is particularly acute when people feel implicated in white supremacy, and she was perplexed by the resistance to the idea, as if the acknowledgment of the presence of white fragility were more offensive than its actual practice and implications. We can ask the same set of critical questions with regards to human fragility and the reactionary responses that vegans receive from those who participate in eating animals. There is a lack of willingness to reflect on the privilege this practice entails and its connection to human supremacist values.

But anthroprivilege is deeper than the self-justifying words of meat eaters; it is embedded in our language, resting below the strata of our conscious thought. Etymologically, the term *meat*, derived from the Old English *mete*, simply means "food." Its contemporary application to the dismembered and decapitated bodies of nonhuman animals represents the ultimate objectification of (formerly) sentient individuals, reducing a life entirely to a unit of human utility. The very idea of meat itself is thus a symptom of human arrogance, supremacy, and privilege. But the objectifying function of meat actually penetrates even deeper into the bedrock of human understanding, as the language of butchery has a specificity and a precision that facilitate a more thorough objectification and commodification of the mutilated animals. So, for example, a slaughtered pig is objectified even further in the transformation of the various chunks of their flesh into usable human units called "ham" or "bacon."

This dissociative reimagination of sentient life is regarded as an ordinary process, but we can see the anthroprivilege when the tables are turned and such disassociation is applied to the lives of humans. We speak of this as "dehumanization" (Haslam 2006), the process of people being "reduced to animals"; in so doing, we normalize the abhorrent treatment of animals all the while trying to bring greater attention to humans who are mistreated. Or, on the other end of the spectrum, we hear of the "bestial" rage of those responsible for particularly heinous crimes. Whether one is reflecting on the victim or the perpetrator, there is a strong desire to place violence outside of the domain of humanity. The need to skirt responsibility for the actions of our species is a key signpost of human fragility. Such fragility can obviously play out in myriad fashions, ranging from an insistence that one is an "environmentalist" even when confronted with evidence of the environmental ruination that meat production entails, self-consolation that one is an "animal lover" while swallowing the flesh of a nonhuman animal, to the animosity towards and defensiveness about veganism that expose one's paper-thin skin.

Much like white fragility, the characteristic behaviors of human fragility are belligerence on the one hand, and silence and withdrawal on the other (DiAngelo 2018). But here, too, we see anthroprivilege expose itself as humans struggle to return to the comfort of anthropocentrism and to maintain their dominance within the species hierarchy after having become conscious of the problem. Expressions like "for every animal you don't eat, I'm going to eat three" emblazoned on T-shirts and bumper stickers make the link between anthroprivilege and human fragility overt.

Conclusion

It is interesting to note that the term *privilege* did not appear in the index of the *Handbook of Prejudice, Stereotyping, and Discrimination* (Nelson 2009). Likewise, until now, *anthroprivilege* has curiously not been a part of the critical animal studies lexicon. This absence is something that I hope my chapter will change. Anthroprivilege is a fundamental lens through which we can recognize and critique the ongoing oppression of animal others at the hands of human beings;

consequently, it is an important point of departure in any critical understanding of human–nonhuman relations.

But drawing attention to anthroprivilege will not be an easy task. Previous calls to put a check on various forms of privilege, while successful at broadening social awareness, have been contested. In recent years, we have witnessed displays of profound white and male fragility in the form of the rise of the alt-right and men's rights movements, which represent not only a refusal of situated knowledge, complete with their appeals to "objectivity" and "truth," but also pathetic attempts to deny the privileged positions of white people and males in our contemporary world. These developments are in many ways to be expected. The principal way in which privilege functions is through the refusal of its very existence. Once attention has been drawn to a particular form of privilege, the best way to preserve that privilege is to simply pretend that it doesn't exist. When that fails, those who really want to see their privilege maintained will often cry foul and adopt a victim complex.

These same reactionary responses play out with regards to anthroprivilege, as when, for example, animal rights activists were labeled "un-Australian green criminals" by the country's prime minister (*Guardian, The* 2019), or American right-wing pundit Rick Wiles made the laughable claim that plant-based proteins are a satanic plot to "create a race of soulless creatures" (Mantyla 2019). In these instances, the imaginative geographies of nationalism and religion are mobilized in an attempt to shift collective attention away from having to address our privileged position as human beings. All of this represents the opposite of "checking one's privilege" and instead serves to reinforce privilege.

Privilege is always an "elusive and fugitive subject" (McIntosh 1989, p. 11), which means it takes both effort and a sense of humility to grapple with it. What, then, does it mean to "check one's anthroprivilege"? Following Tekanji/Andrea Rubenstein (2006), who first wrote about the idea of checked privilege more generally, it first means acceptance and acknowledgment. It is easy to get one's hackles up and to respond in a defensive way. It is much harder to arrive at the realization that every single person reading this chapter benefits from anthroprivilege in myriad ways. This recognition is the first step towards a more liberatory world for all sentient life. Rubenstein reminds us that in order for us to move towards understanding, criticism isn't hatred. To acknowledge anthroprivilege is not to advocate misanthropy. Humans aren't inherently bad for having privilege, but we must find a balance between accepting it and struggling against it in ways that open pathways to greater recognition of the importance of other living beings. We can despise the behaviors, systems, and institutions that humans are responsible for without detesting humans.

Rubenstein then points towards the adoption of a language of respect and equality. The reduction of nonhuman others to their commodity forms—the process through which the dismembered parts of a pig become euphemized as "bacon" or "ham"—is the furthest thing from respect; this language of oppression can never result in a world free from domination. Think about the processes that are involved in the production of commodities like "milk," "eggs," and "veal," and the abhorrent suffering that they necessarily entail. Think about the way certain animals are rendered "pests" while others are deemed "pets," and the privilege that comes from being able to confer those designations. Be willing to call others out on their prejudice and bias towards nonhuman animals.

Finally, Rubenstein suggests that "check your privilege" means "treat us like humans, not 'the other.'" While we have to overcome her own obvious anthroprivilege in the articulation of this concern, it should lead us to think about why we treat animal others in such abhorrent ways, unbefitting of us humans. Nonhuman animals are not here for our pleasure, whether that be as entertainment or as a source of food. They have their own agendas and desires and an inherent right to the freedom of their bodies and minds. The routine use of billions of animals as cogs in the machinery of contemporary capitalism represents a very different set of circumstances as compared to how Indigenous groups living off the land use animals; nonetheless, both practices still imply anthroprivilege, as the animal Other is used as a resource for humans.

Remember, again, that criticism is not hatred, nor is it inherently bad. Anthroprivilege isn't about anyone or any group in particular. It is about how our society accommodates humans and about all the invisible advantages that we possess and regard as normal because of our status as humans. Privilege in any form is not negated by disadvantage in another register—for example, one can't offset their white privilege with the disadvantage they experience as a female—nor does a difficult life exempt one from experiencing privilege (Bhopal 2018). What is bad about privilege is the way in which it obviates the need for the privileged to see their advantage. As with all attempts to check our privilege, it is what we do with anthroprivilege that counts. The hope is that more awareness of anthroprivilege and its impacts may lead to more positive responses benefitting our nonhuman friends.

Acknowledging that we speak from our situated position as humans does not change the fact that our bodies and ideas are still human and, therefore, privileged. The unavoidable conundrum is that no matter how radical we aim to be, our writings and refusals still reinforce the authority of the dominant, human voice. Reflexivity about this inescapable consequence of our situatedness should not lead us to endorse a certain epistemic privilege; rather, it should lead us to act. We all share the same planet, and even as our anthroprivilege attempts to render *our* "domestic" world distinct from *their* "wilderness," if we don't make attempts to wrestle with our privileged position as humans, we risk undoing the delicate balance of all the deeply interconnected planetary systems that sustain life. In other words, our human hubris could well be our own undoing.

For Kobayashi (2009), the production of geographical knowledge is a simultaneously moral and political project, which means that how we understand our situatedness within our world is critical not only to a moral recognition of privilege, but also to our engagement of a politics that works towards greater equity and renewed forms of interspecies mutual aid. By realigning our geographical imaginations with a sense of human situatedness that is connected to and imbricated within the natural world—rather than separated from it—we begin to recognize how our current sense of entitlement is both exploitative of and ruinous to not just our animal others, but also ourselves. Consequently, admissions of anthroprivilege need to be more than mere confessions that reinforce a feeling of virtue, thereby allowing us to avoid addressing environmental speciesism in any systematic manner. We need to do more to realign the relationship that we as humans have with other animals.

Human supremacy remains the principal lens through which most human beings view the world; and so, while a general awareness of anthroprivilege is already well underway, to actually reckon with it is far from the minds of most people. Having come to the end of this chapter, I expect some readers will double down on their anthroprivilege in the same way that some white males have strengthened their commitment to their unacknowledged privilege. It is in these instances that privilege is transformed into supremacy. For those of you who want no part in continuing to sow the seeds of oppression, aligning your morality with a politics of change doesn't have to be difficult. One of the most direct forms of action you can take in addressing your own anthroprivilege—right here and right now—is also exceedingly simple: *stop eating animals!*

7

Anthroprivilege and Bacon Foam

Ethical Veganism as a Counter to the Foodie Movement's Spaces of Exclusion, Exploitation, and Violence

Hannah C. Gunderman

Introduction

As a spatial representation of ethical consumption, vegan landscapes are rapidly populating the urban environment, standing in direct contrast to a long-existing yet exponentially growing foodie culture. The foodie movement is a fine-dining subculture that takes interest in local haute cuisine, transforming the consumption of food from a necessity to a hobby. Characterized by food that is typically high-priced, garnished with supplementary and/or unnecessary nonhuman-animal products (such as bacon foam, a menu item at the foodie restaurant Grace in Portland, Maine, U.S.), and accessible mainly within a heavily whitewashed landscape, the foodie movement is inherently problematic in its support of spatially exclusive divisions within a city.

While it is understandable that humans would derive emotional benefit from consumption that caters to their palate, the foodie landscape is one of significant anthroprivilege in that the culture translates to multiple, intersecting layers of violence and exploitation. Much of the foodie movement highlights the excessive use of bacon, animal fats, and dairy products, particularly in dishes that do not traditionally utilize these ingredients. This creates a food landscape built of the suffering of both humans (slaughterhouse workers, agricultural workers, and consumers who suffer the negative health consequences of many high-cholesterol foodie dishes) and nonhuman animals, as well as a consumptive culture based on racial and economic inequality. Promotional materials for restaurants, food trucks, and festivals that are aimed towards foodies highlight clean, visually attractive arrays of food, in strong contrast to the violence and exploitation that actually produced the dishes.

Foodie establishments tend to follow gentrification patterns in urban environments; buildings that are "revitalized" in gentrifying areas often are home to foodie restaurants, craft breweries, luxury-product retail stores, and other niche businesses. While these businesses may contribute to the strength of certain sections of the local economy, they have a glaringly problematic nature: whether intentional or not, they exclude large portions of the population based on race, income, ability, and class; deepen existing issues of food access across the world; and promote the heavy consumption of nonhuman-animal products (a practice that is, in itself, exploitative on many levels in capitalistic societies). This chapter will focus on the latter characteristic through the lens of ethical veganism, by proxy speaking to the exclusionary and divisive nature of foodie establishments.

Foodie movements show little sign of slowing down or reducing the use of nonhuman-animal products—a projection particularly apparent in the rhetoric of pro-foodie literature, which presents meat and dairy consumption as a spiritually awakening neolocal practice (Ocejo 2014). Considering this, vegan foodscapes (particularly those in urban environments) have an opportunity to create more compassionate and equitable consumption options amid the urban foodie culture. Of course, presenting vegan foodscapes as the more ethical alternative to the purchasing and consumption of foodie products is not a panacea for the increasingly exploitative global foodscape that exists today; as discussed in more detail in this chapter, some vegan restaurants can and do adopt many exclusionary practices. However, it is a step in the right direction—towards ensuring an equitable, sustainable, and accessible urban spatial praxis.

To be clear, virtually no mainstream consumptive practices are free from exploitation, given the deeply complicated global foodways that comprise food production and consumption. However, veganism is a foundational necessity for a more just society if (and only if) conducted in a manner that is anti-racist, anti-classist, and against the exploitation of all beings, human and nonhuman. Scholars have rightfully identified major strands in mainstream veganism that serve to enforce racist and classist structures, despite being built on "compassionate" and "cruelty-free" narratives (Harper 2010b). Accordingly, this chapter will not attempt to erase these very real, and very problematic, issues that plague many strands of veganism. Nor will it present vegan landscapes against foodie landscapes in a "good" versus "bad"/"us" versus "them" binary. This chapter will, however, acknowledge the deeply embedded themes of violence, exploitation, and exclusion present in urban foodie landscapes and outline a framework for presenting veganism as a socially just alternative to these foodscapes, offering practical insight into how *truly* anti-exploitative veganism can and should play a role in urban spatial praxis.

This will be accomplished through analytical case studies of the foodie and vegan landscapes of three cities: Toronto, Ontario, Canada; Edinburgh, Scotland; and Knoxville, Tennessee, U.S. For each city, there exists a vibrant—or in the case of Knoxville, growing—vegan culture that stands in ethical and moral contestation to the landscapes of foodie exclusion present in the foodscape. These spaces of hidden exploitation will be explored via an analysis of foodie promotional materials in each city, which will set the stage for recommendations for practical actions that intersectional vegan activists can take to combat this movement that turns violence into landscapes of luxury experience. Specifically, the juxtaposition of foodie and vegan foodscapes in each city will provide real-world examples of how a vegan landscape provides a more ethical consumptive option, contributing to an equitable and sustainable urban spatial praxis.

More broadly, this chapter contributes to the book's larger goal of creating discourse around the inherent intersections of veganism and a more compassionate and sustainable world. It must be noted that all analyses and recommendations presented here come from the perspective of a middle-class, vegan settler on the Indigenous land of Turtle Island, and that when speaking about vegans of color, low-income individuals, and/or disabled individuals, I aim not to speak over or silence them, but rather to stand in solidarity with them and uplift their voices.

Supporting Literature

Geographic Landscape Analysis

Early work in geographical landscape analysis began, through a humanistic view, to ask an important question: How do actual landscapes become symbolic landscapes? Meinig (1979) posed this question with two subsets of queries: "(a) What are the means of selection of particular kinds of localities for idealization? and (b) How do these chosen scenes become generalized and imprinted in the public mind?" (p. 174). While Meinig's analysis was applied to North American landscapes such as New England and the "Yankee" regions, such a line of inquiry can certainly lend insight towards capturing the rise of foodie culture's largely positive reputation across the world and, conversely, of the often-negative associations with vegan establishments in the landscape (including, particularly from a carnist's perspective, feelings of exclusion, lack of diversity, and privilege).

With inspiration from Meinig, this chapter explores—through the lens of critical ethical veganism—how foodie culture has come to be linked with urban spatial patterns of gentrification and exclusion, and how its image and reputation have been shaped and cultivated over time.

Analyses like the current one fundamentally engage with *place*, a foundational cultural metric employed in landscape studies. Tuan (1977) defines place as "centers of felt value where biological needs, such as those for food, water, rest, and procreation, are satisfied" (p. 4), which can consist of human-built structures, environmental context, objects, and people's daily geographies (Hostetter 2016). However, the *usage* of place in geographical inquiry is subjective and fluid in practice yet retains a consistent theme: the *placefulness* of a landscape is the heart and soul of a geographic space and serves as the emotional driver for the formation of place identities and place attachments. Broadly, place within cultural landscape studies seeks to understand the palimpsest of human activity (Mitchell 1996; Dickens 2017)—the multiple intersecting layers of culture, society, and politics that work to produce and guide our daily geographies.

Another methodology in geographic landscape analysis that is central to this research is discourse analysis of the urban environment, which is heavily influenced by the work of urban theorists and social scientists (see, for example, Beauregard 1993; Mitchell 1996; McCann 2004; Lees 2004). In an urban discourse analysis, researchers should seek the social settings in which discourse surrounding an idea or object is located and the actors, theories, and structures that allow such discourse to occur (Lees 2004). Following suit, this chapter includes geographically specific case studies of foodie and vegan cultures across the world, and a reading of their associated landscapes for practical solutions in creating urban vegan spatial praxis. Such an undertaking pays homage to the importance of landscape analysis in policy and spatial planning.

In this chapter, literary endeavor and case study analysis will be used to engage with ideas of placefulness surrounding foodie and vegan landscapes in order to understand how to create a more equitable and compassionate urban spatial praxis and, ultimately, an urban landscape free from the disturbing geographies currently present in most cities across the world.[1] At the center of this scholarly goal are the fundamentals of reading cultural landscapes, a process that works to see past the visual and engages, rather, with the myriad social and cultural meanings that affect the placefulness of a geographical area.

1. See White's (2015) analysis of the urban environment's disturbing geographies hidden in plain sight within establishments such as veterinary offices, fast-food restaurants, and butcher shops

Urban Spatial Praxis

The scale at which the focus of this chapter lies is urbanized cities. While strands of foodie and vegan cultures are found in rural areas, the exponential rate at which both movements are growing in urban environments is a promising venue for academic attention. The social structures and cultural frameworks guiding the urban environment, as a densely populated center of trade, wealth, innovation, and culture (Clay & Albers 2016), can provide insight into broader cultural discourse; that is, that which takes place in the city likely affects and influences the greater population of its hinterland. The perception of trends (such as foodie culture) in an urban environment is influenced by the way knowledge transfer occurs throughout the dense populations of cities. Asheim et al. (2007) note the circulation of creative tacit knowledge, as associated with face-to-face and buzz communication, among the urban environment. The antithesis of codified knowledge, tacit knowledge typifies the common phrase "you just have to be there" and is highlighted by information disseminated through personal communication and practical experience. Face-to-face communication is essential for the transfer of tacit knowledge.

Buzz, as Bathelt et al. (2004) explain, is the "information and communication ecology created by face-to-face contacts, co-presence and co-location of people and firms within the same industry and place or region" (p. 38). Densely populated cities allow high levels of face-to-face and buzz communication to take place, influencing the spread of innovative ideas and creative collaboration. When applied to foodie and vegan cultures, face-to-face and buzz communication is essential for the spread of tacit knowledge that aids in the growth of strong social movements. Advertisements for both lifestyles rely on testimony and personal encouragement to draw people into their associated restaurants and establishments, as can be seen in the following case studies.

Understanding this interchange between urban dynamics and culture helps to implement feasible strategies (praxis) for equitable urban growth. Urban dynamics encompass not only broader structures guiding a city's culture as a whole, but also (and most importantly for this research) the exceptional and extraordinary—and small and everyday—spaces that comprise urban areas. Saunders (2013) notes the increased tendency for urban geographers to explore a city at a microscale—from the streets and corners to the everyday movements and geographies of the individual resident. Such a focus produces transformative findings on how notions of place are formed and maintained in the broader urban environment, where such transformation is the "making of large, staccato-like leaps in understanding that result from noticeable or momentous changes in our social world" (p. 537). Although foodie culture is not a new phenomenon, vegan activists and scholars should take note of the industry's increased presence in the urban environment when considering strategies for veganizing the spaces and places of cities. This chapter takes inspiration from such scholarly guidance as outlined above, presenting specific case studies and analyses of foodie and vegan restaurants across the world and using the findings from those case studies to make educated and practical suggestions for urban vegan spatial praxis.

Foodie Landscapes

Numerous food scholars agree that, in recent years, foodie culture has blossomed into a thriving, lucrative, and at many times, problematic foodscape. Kamp (2006) documents the journey that the U.S. has taken to develop a foodscape that emboldened the foodie movements now present in culinary landscapes in the country: economic advances, adventurous chefs, and culinary innovation have led to more ingredients, new flavor profiles, and a usually white upper-class population seeking increasingly luxurious dining experiences. These dining experiences tend to utilize unusual—and sometimes divisive—flavor combinations, as in the case of "the trend of making desserts with bacon" (Johnston & Baumann 2015, p. 24). Lang (2007) describes the foodie cultural practice of creating atypical dishes:

> Boursin stuffed kangaroo nachos with roasted avocado corn salad and huckleberry habanero demi-glace. Chocolate-covered caramel topped with Welsh smoked sea salt. Hangar tartare, pickled Asian pear, amaro, Béarnaise ice cream. Roasted red pepper with goat cheese Kettle chips. Has it really all come to this? These actual foods that you can actually order off a menu or buy in a store are emblematic of several of today's food trend innovations. (p. 1)

While the aforementioned examples make liberal use of fruits and vegetables, it is important to note the heavy usage of nonhuman-animal products, particularly in circumstances wherein these products would not be included in the original manifestations of dishes. For example, Kettle chips traditionally consist of potato slices and oil, but a foodie version of the dish adds goat cheese, calling into question the ethical value of the dish, at least from a vegan perspective.

Of course, food scholars acknowledge that ethical eating manifests differently across individual eaters in varying geographic areas, but overall, "many foodies remain devoted sensualists and are committed above all to the pursuit of 'taste' and pleasure" (Johnston & Baumann 2015, p. 112). This taste and this pleasure are derived overwhelmingly from the addition of meat, dairy, and eggs to dishes. However, what distinguishes a foodie from a common carnist[2] is the luxuriation of specialty nonhuman-animal products such as foie gras and veal, two products that require extra—and brutal—manipulation of the body of a living being beyond the typical husbandry of raising that animal to slaughter age. While all meats, dairy, and eggs are rooted in violence, exploitation, and domination, dishes containing foie gras and veal are even more so and are typically reserved for those willing to pay higher prices.

It is important, however, to recognize that foodie culture cannot be defined in a holistic, all-encompassing manner. In the U.S., mainstream foodie culture "continues to position a particular demographic—namely, white and relatively affluent—as the 'normal' eater" (ibid., p. 16). While foodies of color certainly exist, the marketing and advertising of foodie dishes overwhelmingly cater to an affluent white population, effectively erasing people of color involved in the movement and creating a whitewashed foodscape. Further, foodies *can* be vegetarian or vegan. However, scholars pinpoint the purest foodie culture as one that is heavily carnist (Cowen 2012; Holt-Giménez 2017); therefore, foodie landscapes based on animal-product consumption will be the focus of this chapter.

Vegan Geographies as Social Justice

To be positioned as a more inclusive and sustainable alternative to growing foodie movements that heavily promote animal product consumption, veganism should play a direct role in the spatial praxis of urban environments, particularly in the face of increasing urban gentrification and exploitation. A vegan geography fights not only for the liberation of nonhuman animals, but also for all living beings; in its most effective state, a vegan geography is anti-racist, anti-classist, anti-speciesist, and anti-exploitation.

Fundamentally, veganism and anti-speciesist animal rights are inherently linked by efforts to uphold the physical and mental sovereignty deserved by a living being. Almiron & Cole (2016) highlight how terms such as "livestock," "poultry," and "dairy" serve to devalue nonhuman animals and reduce their bodies to commodities. Many agricultural production industries even use the term "units of production" (Yarwood & Evans 2000, p. 100) when referring to nonhuman-animal bodies. Making connections to foodie consumptive culture, materials such as advertisements, commercials, and restaurant menus then add a deeper

2. Here, a common carnist is understood to be someone who eats animal products as a means of daily sustenance or for taste, but not as a pure hobby, as is common with foodies. The author acknowledges that the line between a common carnist and a foodie is subjective.

complexity to the embodied commodification of nonhuman animals by also speaking *for* the same animals with terms such as "humanely raised," "free-range," and "happy animals," thereby robbing them of not only their physical bodies, but also their emotional and mental agency. Just as vegans *should* protest the use of such damaging phrasing when it comes to nonhuman animals, they should also speak against language and terminology that similarly devalue humans.

Speciesism and racism, in many instances, reinforce and support each other to perpetuate spaces of violence. Harper (2011) recalls a story in which speciesism was used in a manner so as to validate and embolden racism:

> A few years ago, French actress and animal rights activist Brigitte Bardot openly expressed distaste for the French Muslim community because of religious practices in which they kill nonhuman animals. I wonder, "Why are white French omnivorous nationals exempt from her disgust? Why is she not concerned about nonhuman animals slaughtered for traditional white French cuisine or Christian religious feasts?" Instead, she used speciesism as a means to racialize an immigrant group as "barbaric," as a threat to the white identity of Christian France.

Jones (2000) highlights that the ethical relationships between humans and nonhuman animals are significantly uneven, lending weight to how quickly speciesism and racism come to reinforce each other. In the same way that humans can readily Other[3] nonhuman animals based on their perceived contributions (or lack thereof) to the human-built environment, humans can also Other humans perceived as deviating from normative social structures. For example, raccoons are often colloquially dismissed as "trash animals" in many Western countries (Nagy & Johnson II 2013) because they are seen as destructive to human-built structures such as trash cans. People experiencing homelessness across the world are often cast out of common view for similar reasons—they are seen as intrusive and unproductive according to capitalist modes of production. A vegan spatial praxis working against the growing popularity of foodie culture is beneficial not only

3. In the context of this research, the Other (also, Othering and Otherness) are defined with inspiration from Said (1978), who demonstrates that representations of the Orient and Orientalism are largely a European invention, entrenched with notions of "romance, exotic beings, haunting memories and landscapes, [and] remarkable experiences" (p. 9). Therefore, the Orient is situated as separate and different from European and American society, creating an "Us and Them" binary comprised of "ideas about what 'we' do and what 'they' cannot do or understand as 'we' do" (p. 20). In this paper, Otherness, Othering, and the Other are used in parallel manners to signify a circumstance or social convention that creates a social, cultural, and/or economic binary between beings, both human and nonhuman.

for nonhuman animals, but also for humans intertwined with globalized layers of exploitation, violence, and capitalism.

City Profiles

Qualitative case-study methodology was chosen for this chapter as the technique to best highlight specific foodie and vegan foodscapes in the cities of Toronto, Edinburgh, and Knoxville. This methodology was deemed suitable after a methods review of published scholarly literature that engages with food landscapes, traditional foods, and food in popular culture. Pearson et al. (2015) describe case study methodology as a detailed description and analysis of an event, program, or person, using multiple sources, including observations, interviews, and documents. Employing multiple research techniques allows for "in-depth examination of a complex singularity, often a person or program, in its natural setting" (p. 1). Foodscapes are deeply complex landscapes, given the multiple intersecting political, cultural, economic, and social factors that affect their development, and, thus, present an excellent opportunity for a case study methodology.

Sébastia (2017) produced an edited volume of research pertaining to traditional foods and cultural foodscapes, all using case study methodology to reveal the complexity of traditional foods in a globalizing world. Gregory et al. (2010) describe a case study methodology applied to research on casual-dining restaurants and their online marketing as a source of guidance on how to navigate their online environment in order to promote the overall goals, messages, and experiential aspects of the establishments. The case studies used in this chapter are inspired by the above frameworks; each example includes a concise, yet appropriate, summary of the city's contesting foodscapes, using foodie/vegan advertisements, observations, and menu analysis, and will serve as a reference for the forthcoming practical strategies for urban vegan praxis.

While foodie culture is rapidly growing across the world, the three cities were chosen as typical, representative examples of foodie landscapes present in increasingly gentrifying areas; these cities tend to receive regional, and sometimes international, attention for the quality and strength of their foodie-aimed restaurant scenes.[4] In each city, a growing or thriving vegan culture is juxtaposed with the landscapes of foodie exclusion present in the city's spatial design. However, these

4. Of course, cities such as San Francisco, CA, and New York, NY—both in the U.S.—are often cited in internationally available sources as examples of urban environments with thriving foodie cultures. However, this chapter seeks to highlight foodie and vegan landscapes in cities whose foodscapes have received more regional than international attention.

foodscapes do not exist in a moral binary of "bad" foodie restaurants versus "good" vegan restaurants; rather, transgressions and shortcomings, as well as the positives, found in both the vegan *and* foodie scenes in each city are used to develop practical solutions for urban vegan spatial praxis to combat the popular and exponentially growing foodie landscapes found across the world.

It must be again acknowledged that each case study is presented from the perspective of a vegan scholar-activist, with the intent of highlighting the manners in which the foodie scene celebrates dishes laden with animal products and often accompanied by high price tags. The cases of Toronto and Edinburgh are presented with reference to local dining guides for foodies and vegans, while the Knoxville example is discussed through the lens of the author's own experiences as a former longtime resident of the city and local vegan activist. For each city, the case study includes sample dishes from a randomly chosen restaurant and the average prices associated with said restaurant's menu for reference. All restaurant information, menu items, and prices are accurate as of the time of this chapter's writing.

Toronto, Ontario

In 2017, David McMillan, a noted Montréal chef, praised Toronto's growing meat-based foodie culture in an interview with CBC News.[5] McMillan, conjuring up Ontario's breadth of farm products, exclaimed, "I've been looking at beef, cheese, chickens, rabbits, lamb, my God . . . I want to cook there!" while lamenting Montréal's lack of growth in the restaurant scene. McMillan's specific reference to nonhuman-animal products when he speaks of the culinary attractiveness of Toronto suggests that the chef associates foodie culture itself with the progressiveness of a city, an opinion that is shared by many chefs and foodies alike.

In 2016, *Narcity*, an online guide to social and food culture in Toronto, published an article titled "14 Bucket List Restaurants Every True Toronto Foodie Needs to Try."[6] A textual analysis of the post reveals featured dishes that use the following nonhuman-animal products: elk, trout, octopus, duck flesh, duck eggs, shrimp, and lamb. It also reveals the featuring of the following phrases: "foie gras–loving Torontonians"; "talk about diversity!" in reference to "everything from

5. Kate McGillivray. "Montreal's Culinary King Crowns Toronto Best Food City in Canada," *CBC News*, April 19 2017.
6. Maria Niderman. "14 Bucket List Restaurants Every True Foodie in Toronto Needs to Try," *Narcity*, April 22, 2021 (updated), https://www.narcity.com/ca/on/toronto/lifestyle/15-bucket-list-restaurants-in-toronto-for-a-true-foodie. Boralia closed in November 2018.

Spanish octopus to Jewish latkes to Chinese Peking Duck"; and "inspired by his grandmother's dishes" and "that 'home-y,' authentic vibe . . . well-pronounced in the restaurant's dishes." As shown, the promotional materials for these restaurants are transparent about the animals being used to create dishes, in addition to using language that alludes to local identity, food exploration and experimentation, and nostalgia for home/family. A restaurant from the list, Boralia, was chosen at random, as were five entrée items from its menu to highlight the typical foodie dishes available: Venison Liver & Foie Gras Parfait, Beef Cheek Cabbage Rolls, Pigeon Pie, and L'éclade (mussels smoked in pine needles and pine ash butter). The average price of the entrées is CA$17.

Conversely, even a simple Google search of "veganism in Toronto" yields several articles and blog posts about the city's growing vegan scene. "It's a very strong position we are taking in food service at the moment," said Chase Hospitality Group president Steven Salm, whose company had just replaced its fast-seafood restaurant Little Fin with the vegan burger joint Planta Burger (O'Neil 2017).

In the same interview, Salm went on to state that much of the city's growth in vegan restaurants is due not necessarily to more demand from vegans but to carnists who want to include more plant-based products in their diet. Jeff Merkel, the owner of The Vegan Extremist, Toronto's first all-vegan food truck, left a career working in a gastropub to sell food as a "self-described vegan extremist, an avowed enemy of meat-eating" (Errett 2016). Merkel's food truck contributes to a growing vegan landscape in the city, particularly with new restaurants along the Bloor Street thoroughfare.

In February 2017, *Culture Trip*, a travel, food, and culture guide for the Toronto region, published an article titled "Toronto's Top 10 Vegan & Vegetarian Restaurants." Similarly, a random restaurant and five entrée items from said restaurant are highlighted: Fresh, a fully vegan restaurant with four locations across the city, with items including Chipotle "Bacon" Burger, Black Bean Burrito, Falafel Tacos, Poutine, and Buddha Bowl. The average price of the entrées is CA$12.

Edinburgh, Scotland

In recent years, Scotland's capital city has been named the supreme foodie destination in the United Kingdom ("*Scotsman Food and Drink, The* 2015). In October 2017, *Time Out*, an online guide[7] to Edinburgh's nightlife, travel, and tourism

7. Jo Laidlaw, Dayna McAlpine, & Arusa Qureshi. "The 30 Best Restaurants in Edinburgh You Need to Try," June 10, 2021 (updated), https://www.timeout.com/edinburgh/restaurants/the-best-restaurants-in-edinburgh.

hotspots, published an editorial titled "The 30 Best Restaurants in Edinburgh You Need to Try," touting the following:

> In spite of Scotland's reputation for questionable foodstuffs (haggis is genuinely delicious once you overlook how it's made), its capital city is a culinary wonderland, with Michelin-starred restaurants living cheek-by-ethically-sourced-jowl with student-friendly curry houses and perfect pizzerias.

Here, in a manner that is less direct compared to the previously highlighted foodie advertisement from Toronto (appealing to "foie gras-loving Torontonians"), nonhuman-animal products are covertly mentioned by proxy of comments on taste and perceived quality of life ("haggis is genuinely delicious once you overlook how it's made," "cheek-by-ethically-sourced-jowl"). The Witchery (https://www.thewitchery.com), a restaurant chosen at random from the original article, creates an allure of mystery and charm in the marketing of its dining room, with mention of the red-leather seating arrangements, historic stone walls, and ancient oak paneling covered in tapestries. The restaurant offers dishes from its "Lunch & Theatre Supper Menu" at confirmed prices of £22 (two courses) and £27 (three courses). The available items include: Baked Smoked Haddock Rarebit, Witchery Fish Pie, Grilled Corn-Fed Chicken Supreme "Basquaise," and a selection of Iberico charcuterie. It is interesting to note that the restaurant has taken care to mention what the chicken consumed while they were alive, which perhaps increases the perceived taste value of the dish.

Now, a few years after Scotland was declared the foodie capital of the region, others are predicting a boom in vegan dining in Edinburgh. McDonald (2017) states that the number of vegans in the U.K. has surpassed 350 percent growth over the last ten years, highlighting Edinburgh as one of the country's most vegan-friendly cities. Craig Tannock, the owner of Harmonium, a vegan bar and kitchen in the city, explains how veganism has ebbed and flowed in Edinburgh:

> Whilst Edinburgh has been well serviced by vegetarian establishments for decades, there have never been very many vegan places at any one time. . . . Since then [the early nineties], Glasgow's vegan scene has steadily developed, and then exploded in the last few years, whilst in terms of fully vegan eateries Edinburgh became a bit of a desert. (McDonald 2017)

This has, of course, changed with the burst of vegan restaurants in the city, as well as of community groups dedicated to supporting the vegan lifestyle. Scottish online politics and lifestyle newspaper *iNews* featured a guide in March 2017 to the best vegan restaurants in Edinburgh.[8] Henderson's Vegan Restaurant (https://www.hendersonsrestaurant.com), randomly chosen from the list, features items including "Haggis," Stuffed Butternut Squash, Tofu Teriyaki, Raw Chili Bowl, and Winter Salad, with an average price of £11.78. The restaurant's haggis dish, made from steamed and pickled turnip, invokes Scotland's place attachment by providing classic Scottish fare without taking the life of a sheep.

Knoxville, Tennessee

Compared to Edinburgh and Toronto, Knoxville is a markedly smaller city, with a population of 187,500 (as of 2018, according to the U.S. Census Bureau). Despite its smaller size, its exponentially growing foodie scene (followed by a smaller yet strong vegan movement) makes for its inclusion as a case study in this chapter. Despite the lack of regional (and international) acclaim for Knoxville's dining scene, a local's perspective on the city's foodie and vegan landscapes demonstrates how its restaurant selection is rapidly changing in both exclusionary and equitable ways.

The foodie scene in Knoxville is similar to those of the aforementioned cities in that several restaurants, such as Oliver Royale and J. C. Holdway, offer meat-heavy cuisine at prices considered high for the area (at least US$15 a plate on average). A random selection of dishes from J. C. Holdway's most recent menu includes Wood-Roasted Pork, North Carolina Catfish, Spring House Angus Beef, Wood Oven-Roasted ½ Chicken, and Slow-Cooked Farm Egg,[9] with an average price of US$21.80. Other restaurants, such as Boyd's Jig and Reel, a Scottish pub and restaurant in Knoxville, have lower food prices but continue to present menus that rely mostly on animal products. Along with its restaurant service, the Jig and Reel regularly hosts specialty-themed nights, such as the beer, bacon, and whisky event held for Father's Day on June 22, 2017.[10] As can currently be said for many towns, cities, and regions across the world, the consumption and glorification of bacon are at an all-time high in Knoxville and ever-present in its growing foodie culture.

8. Gillian McDonald. "A Vegan Guide to Edinburgh: Animal-Free Eating, Drinking and Shopping, March 24, 2017, https://inews.co.uk/inews-lifestyle/vegan-guide-edinburgh-animal-free-eating-drinking-shopping/. This article was updated on July 3, 2020.
9. Hilary Dixler Canavan. "How a Beard Award Winner Is Heating Up Knoxville's Dining Scene," September29,2016,https://www.eater.com/2016/9/29/13109728/joseph-lenn-jc-holdway-knoxville.
10. Boyd's Jig and Reel. "Father's Day Beer, Bacon & Whisky Tasting," June 22, 2017, https://jigandreel.ticketleap.com/fathers-day-beer-bacon--whisky-tasting/dates/Jun-22-2017_at_0630PM.

At the time of this chapter's formation, only one single all-vegan restaurant, Sanctuary Vegan Café, existed in Knoxville (regretfully, this restaurant has now closed as a consequence of COVID-19, but is nonetheless featured as an example of an ethical vegan restaurant). While many restaurants in Knoxville *can* offer vegan options, several of the menus do not feature these dishes, which must be specially requested. Sanctuary Vegan Café marketed itself as providing "100 percent plant-based comfort food" with "as many organic items as possible," and was owned by a local animal rights activist, Leslie Naylor. Items from its most current menu included Falafels, Black Bean Chile Dog, Roasted Beet Reuben, Garden Burger, and Lentil Meatloaf, with an average price of US$11.15. A local food truck, Dinner Bell Fresh (now also defunct), also served a 100-percent vegan menu, alternating locations between bars, restaurants, and office parks across the city.

Online groups devoted to veganism exist, including Knoxville Vegans and Compassionate Vegans of Tennessee (both on Facebook), each boasting hundreds of members. *Knox Vegan*, an online guide to all things vegan in the city, is also a thriving resource for information pertaining to vegan dining, shopping, and activism in the community. 4Them, a farmed animal sanctuary (https://4themsanctuary.org), is located forty minutes outside of Knoxville and draws vegans (and nonvegans) to the area. It is clear, then, that Knoxville holds the potential for a growing vegan scene, given such strong community support; however, what remains unclear is whether the city's location in the American South, a region known for its love of barbeque and meat consumption, will hinder any forward momentum of veganism, particularly as COVID-19 has impacted much of the established range of vegan options in the city.

It is important to reiterate that the previous case studies are not meant to contextualize the vegan and foodie landscapes of Toronto, Edinburgh, and Knoxville in a moral binary of good versus evil. These case studies, however, do highlight certain themes and trends that are common across thriving foodie cultures in urban environments, as well as the vegan landscapes that may provide a more compassionate placefulness in the urban spatial praxis of cities. Toronto boasts a foodie culture that is unapologetic about its heavy consumption of nonhuman-animal products, and a vegan culture that is growing stronger thanks to vegans *and* nonvegans desiring more plant-based options. Edinburgh employs heritage, place attachment, and Scottish identity in advertising its thriving foodie scene, offering traditional dishes without an extended focus on the processes leading up to the dishes' creation ("haggis is genuinely delicious once you overlook how it's made"). While vegetarianism in Edinburgh has had a long-standing presence, the strength of the city's vegan culture has varied over time; nevertheless, its vegan landscape is now considered one of the strongest in the U.K. Knoxville, as a much smaller city, hosts less than a dozen foodie restaurants and only one dedicated vegan restaurant, but its ability to craft a thriving foodie scene looks promising and bodes well for a potential, adjacent vegan culture. Before practical recommendations are given for vegan scholars/activists to combat these thriving foodie cultures, it proves useful to briefly discuss the implications of the findings from the case studies.

Foodies have a tendency to seek out meat from an animal considered to have been humanely raised, and such information is often provided with the presentation of meat and dairy dishes in foodie menus, advertisements, and marketing strategies.[11] As seen in the foodie promotions from Edinburgh, the terminology of phrasings such as "cheek-by-ethically-sourced-jowl" is used to delineate foodies' meat consumption from that of non-foodies, creating an Othering within the carnist community. While arguments have certainly been made for consuming "humane" meat as part of an enactment of animal rights (UPI NewsTrack 2006), from an ethical vegan perspective, the terms "humanely raised," "cage-free," and "organic meat" lend little comfort. To apply these monikers to the stolen life of a killed nonhuman animal is the ultimate act of anthroprivilege: in doing so, humans place themselves in a position to dictate how that animal felt about their life. Such language is also used to paint certain nonhuman-animal products as conducive to a more luxurious taste experience than others. This process robs the nonhuman animal of not only their physical body, but also their mental and emotional agency in determining the quality of their life. However problematic, this terminology shown in foodie promotions from Edinburgh is common in most foodie landscapes in the world and will likely continue to be a deeply embedded discourse in foodie culture.

Knoxville's Boyd's Jig and Reel capitalizes on a growing trend in foodie culture: themed events merging alcohol and meat. These events are generally marketed with promises of camaraderie: the Jig and Reel's Beer, Bacon, and Whisky Father's Day event merges meat consumption with a widely celebrated holiday. Following suit, multiple festivals around the world such as the Beer and Bacon Classic (alternates locations within the U.S.), the Topsham Beer and Bacon Festival (occurs yearly in the U.K.), and the Bacon Brewfest (occurs in Australia) advertise shared enjoyment of alcohol, craft bacon, and usually live music. It is important to note that, as is the case with most manifestations of foodie culture, the violence and exploitation that produced the nonhuman-animal products consumed at these festivals are largely hidden from view. When foodies attend themed nights involving alcohol

11. Aaron Carnes. "Humanely Raised Meet from Fogline Farms," August 16, 2017, is a representative example, https://goodtimes.sc/restaurants-dining-eating-out-reviews-wine/foodie-file/humanely-raised-meat-fogline-farms.

and meat consumption, it is not common among them to consider the individuals working in abattoirs, the tortured nonhuman animals, and the environmental degradation that resulted from the production of the meat provided for these events. Foodie events and festivals use themes of camaraderie, nostalgia, and decadence in their promotions, promising class and luxury in a dining experience. Yet even a superficial analysis of the processes behind these events uncovers their discriminatory and exclusionary nature.

It would not be inappropriate to point out similarities between the foodie and vegan restaurants mentioned in the case studies above. As particularly apparent in promotional materials for vegan restaurants in Toronto and Edinburgh, current vegan "booms" in cities across the world run the risk of becoming as exclusionary and discriminatory as foodie restaurants in many aspects (cost, accessibility, representation or lack thereof), and many have already reached such negative placefulness. For example, in Toronto, it was shown that much of the demand for vegan food doesn't come from vegans, but comes from carnists living in the city who want a good meal—whether it contains nonhuman-animal products or not. Arguably, this signifies a moral lapse in which taste preference continues to hold precedence over justice and the ethics of animal liberation; such a lapse cannot grow or sustain an ethical veganism.

Of course, one may argue that the increase in vegan restaurants and community support, regardless of the causes for demand, is a step towards reducing widespread nonhuman-animal consumption. While true, this assertion does not necessarily address the underlying issues of human exploitation (for example, agricultural workers, usually persons of color and/or of low income, working for low pay in harsh conditions), nonhuman-animal exploitation (for example, free-living animals being displaced as a result of deforestation), and environmental exploitation that can *still* result from vegan foodscapes. Therefore, while veganism certainly presents a more compassionate, sustainable, and equitable alternative to foodie culture, it must not be taken for granted as a completely virtuous lifestyle.

Given this caveat, it is necessary to implement strategies that ensure future foodscapes will be *ethically* vegan—that is, against the exploitation of all beings. Food itself is complicated, and the geographical context of global foodways is situated within multiple layers of capitalism, colonization, corruption, and violence. Therefore, it must be reiterated that vegan foodscapes, while they are a step in the right direction towards a more ethical world, may *still* involve exploitative practices. However, removing the production and consumption of nonhuman-animal products from a given food culture certainly eliminates a source of physical, mental, and emotional violence against humans and nonhumans alike.

Recommendations for Equitable Urban Vegan Landscapes

To shift the current perception of foodie landscapes requires shifting the *placefulness* associated with foodie establishments. As Tuan (1977) asserts in his seminal geographic work in experiential place theory:

> Place is whatever stable object catches our attention. As we look at a panoramic scene our eyes pause at points of interest. Each pause is time enough to create an image of place that looms large momentarily in our view. (p. 161)

Currently, the placefulness of the foodie movement is seen as overwhelmingly positive, at least in a mainstream sense—among (mostly) white, affluent, and gentrified populations. However, as discussed in this chapter, it is clear that the underlying processes that enable foodie culture are built on violence, exploitation, and injustice. By fostering an accessible, equitable, and representative vegan movement in the urban foodscape, vegan scholars and activists can work towards a truly compassionate and sustainable urban spatial praxis. Such a process, however, will undeniably take time and effort on the part of ethical vegans. Foodie culture has long established itself in elite global foodscapes (Kamp 2006), and to dismantle strong cultural hegemonies requires pervasive small-scale and grassroots efforts to change individual perceptions of the hegemonies themselves.

Casey (1997) explains the process by which a culture shifts: culture itself is comprised of a placefulness that entrenches the spaces of a culture. Space, as an abstracted geographical landscape, surrounds each individual within a culture. Place, as space entrenched with social, historical, cultural, and political meanings and context, surrounds each individual and works to comprise a broader culture. Therefore, to change culture, one must change the placefulness of the spaces that comprise said culture. In the context of this chapter, changing the placefulness of foodie landscapes by juxtaposing them with ethical vegan landscapes can happen through grassroots efforts to ensure that *each* vegan restaurant or business is a space of justice and compassion for all beings, human and nonhuman.

While it can be upsetting to witness the increased luxuriation of nonhuman-animal products in foodie environments, intersectional vegan activists/scholars can use the prevalence of these establishments advantageously in organizing for a future of vegan spatial praxis. The following three practical strategies for ensuring vegan foodscapes that are more ethical, inclusive, and socially just alternatives to foodie culture are meant to not only outline a framework for direct action, but also create opportunities for vegan geographers to supplement their scholarly endeavors with community outreach. As discussed in the case studies, some current vegan landscapes, such as those of Toronto, run the risk of becoming exclusionary and discriminatory in their pricing and advertising. It can even be argued that many vegan restaurants, promotions, and social networks already lack representation and exclude large portions of the population by whitewashing the movement (Harper 2010a, 2011; Wrenn 2016) and discriminating based on income (through high restaurant prices and vegan festival ticket costs, for instance). Accordingly, the following strategies should be implemented into vegan spatial praxis immediately to shift the placefulness of foodie landscapes and concurrently facilitate widespread urban ethical veganism.

Strategy 1: Ensure Equity and Representation in Vegan Landscapes

Most foodie advertising targets (mostly) white affluent urbanites using undertones of nostalgia, place attachment, and national identity/pride (as shown previously in the case of Edinburgh). Foodie restaurants often serve dishes that are priced higher than those served at non-foodie establishments and can require reservations well in advance. Such characteristics certainly exclude a large dining clientele based on income; by proxy, the exclusion can also run along racial lines and further distinguish foodie culture as the luxuriation of exploitation, Othering, and violence. Given this, ethical vegans have an opportunity to promote veganism as a more accepting and nondiscriminatory social and dining network that can serve as a moral alternative to foodie culture.

However, it cannot be said that mainstream veganism has succeeded in representing the diversity of individuals practicing the lifestyle. Harper (2011) grapples with many of mainstream veganism's transgressions of racial equity and representation, noting how veganism itself is based on the practice of *ahimsa*—which comprises kindness, compassion, and justice for all living beings—yet is mainly associated with "white people of privilege" (p. 222). Harper's statement gains further context when considering the severe lack of representation (and the overwhelming whiteness) of vegan cooking and lifestyle books and magazines, in activism campaigns, at Vegfests, and at animal rights conferences (Wrenn 2016). Such materials and spaces often present the typical vegan as white, thin-bodied, and of high income, erasing the thousands of vegans of color who are significant advocates and activists for the movement. Dunham (2010) discusses the difficulties of being vegan, Black, and a woman:

> Involvement in animal rights issues as a Black woman for me means injecting myself into a subculture where Black women are rare. It means going to protests and holding signs decrying abuse of animals and wondering why no other Black people are there, also raising their voices. It means going against the grain of my own cultural norms to participate in the bigger social issue of eradicating animal torture. It means using my one Black voice to try and sway an entire Black Nation, in one fell swoop. (p. 42)

As Dunham notes, veganism is situated in a complicated structure of race and gender, and for vegans of color, practicing veganism is more than simply abstaining from the consumption of nonhuman-animal products—it is also navigating a culture in which representation of their own race may be limited. Considering how major vegan news and advocacy outlets such as *VegNews* and People for the Ethical Treatment of Animals (PETA) rarely, if ever, comment on issues of police brutality, racism, gendered violence, income inequality, and homophobia—let alone practice equal representation of vegans of color—it becomes apparent why veganism is often dismissed as a "thing that rich white people do." Further, it is rare for mainstream vegan activism to acknowledge and support the sustainable relationships between Indigenous individuals and animals, systems that were violently disrupted by colonization (Watts 2013).

This being noted, in order for veganism to stand in contrast to the exclusionary marketing of the foodie lifestyle, it must first grapple with its own lack of representation and inclusion. Vegan business owners (particularly owners of restaurants) are advised to use their spaces as areas of social justice and equity. Of course, to sustain themselves, these businesses need to make a profit, but alongside the sales of food and drink, there should be community-based and online engagement with local, regional, and international issues of injustice and violence. Further, in the same way as foodie culture and foodie landscapes encompass not just restaurants but also promotional materials, magazines, festivals, and so on, ethical vegan foodscapes should use the platform of veganism to speak on a wide range of issues, including nonhuman-animal exploitation, police brutality, racism, discrimination against people experiencing homelessness, or against the LGBTQ+ community, to name a few. These messages should be directly incorporated into promotional materials. While this may dissuade more conservative diners from patronizing these spaces, it is essential to solidify veganism in the collective mainstream as a fight for liberation for all beings. Vegan restaurant owners should prioritize hiring employees from underrepresented populations, and local and national vegan advocacy groups should ensure that their promotional materials fully represent the racial diversity of veganism, as well as openly denounce social injustices through an ethical and moral lens. Seemingly small changes within an establishment, such as gender-neutral restrooms, free literature that educates patrons about race and racism, and jars for donations to community organizations are all further steps towards the creation of a more inclusive and representative vegan foodscape.

Strategy 2: Ensure Affordable Prices

To begin, it is fully acknowledged that eating at restaurants, and having the geographical access and financial means to choose to eat at a specific kind of restaurant, whether foodie, vegan, or otherwise, are all the result of privilege. The goal here is to outline a framework for accessible and affordable pricing at vegan restaurants, but even a full implementation of this strategy recognizes that it is a geographical and fiscal privilege to eat meals outside of the home. That said, vegan restaurants have an immediate opportunity to offer a dining experience at a much lower price compared to most foodie restaurants, given the high costs associated with nonhuman-animal products. While restaurants need to make a profit to sustain themselves, efforts can be made to provide equitable pricing to customers who seek a vegan restaurant-dining experience.

Mealey (2019) outlines some advice for succeeding financially in the restaurant business, beginning with how to create a profitable menu:

> In order to keep your menu profitable, you must maintain a balance of traditionally low-cost foods such as pasta or potatoes with higher food cost items like seafood or prime cuts of beef. Remember, your food cost should be around 30–35 percent. This means that if you pay $1.00 for something, you need to charge a minimum of $3.34. It may seem like you are charging a lot more than necessary, but keep in mind that you aren't just paying for the food itself. You are paying someone to prepare the food, serve the food, and clean up after the food. Everything in your restaurant, from payroll to the electric bill, needs to be covered by the food you serve. (p. 1)

Of course, vegan establishments would not be serving seafood or beef, but they may use higher-priced ingredients such as oils and plant-based proteins (tempeh, seitan, and so on). When executed correctly, vegan dishes using sources of protein such as beans and vegetables are much lower in cost than foods that would be found in foodie restaurants, thus creating an accessible dining experience for people with more varied levels of income than what foodie culture allows. Vegan restaurants should strive to use whole foods *before* any processed ingredients, and if foods such as tempeh, seitan, and/or soy "meats" (colloquially known as "meat replacements" in both carnist and plant-based communities) are served, they should be house-made, as commercially available versions of these foods can be high in price. Striving for a menu in which at least 60 percent of the ingredients are in-season, local produce will keep costs manageable while also providing healthy meals for customers.

Aside from using healthy, whole foods, restaurant owners and employees can take other steps to reduce their establishments' overall operating costs, which should translate to lower markups on food prices. If it is possible in their area, restaurants should compost applicable food waste to reduce costs associated with waste management. Sanctuary Vegan Café, mentioned previously as the sole vegan restaurant in Knoxville (at the time of writing), composted all food waste in order to reduce overall trash accumulation. Further, it used compostable materials in the packaging for takeout and leftover food, which lowered the amount of plastic used. Such steps require planning and careful execution, but will benefit ethical veganism in the long term by promoting a foodscape of high accessibility, fair pricing, and nourishing meals.

It is important to note that in all of the case studies above, the vegan restaurants boast lower prices compared to the foodie restaurants, and this is a trend that extends well beyond Toronto, Edinburgh, and Knoxville. Ingredients used in foodie dishes, such as beef, veal, foie gras, and other nonhuman-animal products, are consistently higher in price than most vegan foods. Eating out, whether only once in a while or several times a week, has long been linked with global food culture. If vegan restaurants are able to sustain low prices with high-quality, healthy, whole foods, they can exist in the landscape as accessible and inclusive dining options in contrast to the exclusionary culture of foodie restaurants, creating overall more compassionate foodscapes in urban environments.

Strategy 3: Use Ethical and Local Ingredients

The world maintains a complicated foodscape marred by exploitative practices (Okur-Berberoglu 2014; Rawlinson & Ward 2015), and virtually all meals (whether vegan or not) present exploitation in some form. For example, many commercially available vegan prepared foods use palm oil as a substitute for butter and other oils. However, palm oil has long been problematic, as its harvesting can mean environmental degradation due to deforestation, displacement of animals, and exploitation of humans for labor (Gilbert 2012; Obidzinski et al., 2012). Another oil used heavily in vegan prepared products and even homemade vegan recipes is coconut oil, whose troubling mode of production includes forced nonhuman-animal labor.[12]

It must also be noted that the environmental consequences of exporting these oils across the world are significant.[13] While both of these oils are present in nonvegan prepared foods and recipes, they are becoming increasingly prevalent as viable replacements for dairy. Two more commonly exploitative ingredients, found particularly in desserts, are coffee and cocoa. Agricultural practices associated with coffee have led to deforestation and water pollution (Greenwald et al., 2013), as well as unfair and unsafe working conditions for production workers (Jones 2002). Cocoa production holds similar consequences: a growing global demand for chocolate requires significant human labor (a requirement sometimes met by enslaved humans), and the externalities of exporting cocoa across the world include environmental degradation and uneven distribution of labor compensation among workers and producers (Alberts 2010).

Given all this, it is important to reiterate that true veganism should work towards ending (or at the very least, reducing) exploitation of all beings. Outright avoidance of these ingredients, however, is not the ethical answer when considering the human livelihoods attached to these industries—livelihoods that often present the only few economic opportunities in an area. With this understanding, how can vegan establishments position themselves as more ethical alternatives to the foodie movement? Ethical and local ingredients are the key to maintaining a vegan landscape of anti-exploitation of all living beings, and the following two guidelines describe a framework for using ethically sourced ingredients.

First, ingredients should be limited to the region in which the establishment is located; in cases where necessary ingredients cannot be procured in the immediate geographical area, steps should be taken to ensure the ingredients were produced sustainably and without human/nonhuman-animal/environmental exploitation, although it may be impossible to completely avoid all exploitation. In the same

12. Eliza Barkley. "What's Funny About the Business of Monkeys Picking Coconuts?" NPR, October 19, 2015, https://www.npr.org/sections/thesalt/2015/10/19/448960760/monkeys-pick-coconuts-in-thailand-are-they-abused-or-working-animals.
13. This presents an interesting conundrum in comparing vegan and foodie establishments: when considering the environmental impact of using oils that are imported from great distances, it must be acknowledged that many foodie restaurants are striving to present a menu using farm-to-table ingredients, where transportation costs and externalities are reduced. Given this, it is important that vegan and foodie establishments are not viewed in a binary "good" versus "bad" manner, but rather as actors on a spectrum of exploitative to sustainable foodscapes.

manner as many foodie establishments boast local, farm-to-table ingredients, vegan restaurants should utilize products from local farmers as much as possible and reduce the use of ingredients required to travel a significant distance from their sources. For example, many vegan "ice cream" recipes call for the use of coconut milk. However, for someone living outside of countries such as India, the Philippines, and Indonesia, where coconuts are sourced, it is a more environmentally ethical option to use a different base for the dessert, such as avocado[14] or locally sourced plant-based milks.

Second, when problematic ingredients such as coffee, chocolate, palm oil, and coconut oil are deemed essential to dishes, ethically sourced products must be the only allowable option. For cocoa and coffee, buyers must ascertain that the products are independently certified fair-trade and direct-trade, respectively, ensuring equitable and sustainable relationships between themselves and growers.[15] Palm oil *does* provide a steady source of income and livelihood for producers, and when purchasing this oil or products containing this oil, buyers should confirm that its sourcing is sustainable and fair (Schouten & Glasbergen 2011). With coconut oil, experts say it is difficult to find a product containing the ingredient that truly did *not* involve enslaved monkey labor (Moyer 2015), thereby introducing an ethical dilemma.

The production and harvesting of coconuts for oil sustain human life by providing a source of income, yet the actual harvesting process is marred by widespread exploitation. Boycotting this oil absolves one of the guilt of supporting enslaved nonhuman-animal labor, yet it also robs human beings of their livelihoods. Again, an ethical veganism acknowledges that exploitation will exist among all capitalistic, colonized/colonizer foodscapes and that all decisions inevitably benefit some actors to the detriment of others; when purchasing (or not purchasing) coconut oil, consumers should understand the product's complicated foodway.

The three aforementioned practical strategies highlight current trends in vegan dining and advertising that mirror those in foodie culture, including whitewashing and racial non-representation. Although veganism provides an answer to a society's moral failing in creating luxury around nonhuman-animal product consumption, it must be executed justly and fairly in order to truly represent liberation for and nonviolence towards all beings. Some of the strategies, depending on geographical location, ability, and income, may be better suited for some restaurants than

14. The avocado would of course be a local/regional option for those living in North and Central America. A recipe using this substitution is highlighted in a YouTube video by Dr. A. Breeze Harper (https://www.youtube.com/watch?v=428MI6W6COw).
15. Achilles Coffee Roasters. "What's the Difference Between Direct Trade and Fair Trade Coffee," August 26, 2016, http://achillescoffeeroasters.com.

others; the utilization of even *one* of these strategies by a vegan restaurant lays the foundation for more ethical foodscapes that contrast with those of foodie culture. The goal is to reinvent vegan foodscapes as a moral alternative to foodie culture, and every step, no matter how small, towards such placefulness is significant.

As scholars and activists work towards creating ethical vegan landscapes, it is important to be aware of concurrent social and organizational changes in urban mainstream foodie cultures. For example, Brion (2011) notes the growing trend of "koodies," children as young as three who are "eschewing chicken fingers and demanding Nobu's black cod with miso" (para. 2), which is meant to be a humorous thought for readers of the article but manifests itself as deeply troubling from an ethical vegan perspective. While any reasonable vegan can acknowledge that fresh foods benefit a child's growing body more than do processed foods such as chicken fingers, foodie culture normalizes the heavy consumption of nonhuman-animal products at high prices.

If young children, especially those living in cities, grow up with the idea that the exclusionary, discriminatory, and speciesist values of foodie culture are hegemonic knowledge, vegan activists and scholars will have an increasingly difficult time working towards a foodscape of equity and justice. Therefore, it is imperative that the recommendations made in this chapter are enacted efficiently and fully with regards to this younger demographic that is embracing foodie culture, usually under the guidance of parents/guardians. A further trend in foodie landscapes is explored by Velasco (2017), who, reiterating the culture's exclusion of the working class with its high prices and often confusing jargon, predicts that foodie culture will start to work towards educating people about foodways, ethically sourced foods, and organic versus non-organic food. Given this, vegan restaurants (and more broadly, vegan media outlets) need to work on informing consumers about ethical veganism *and* providing a resource for ethical education in global social and cultural injustices.

It is, of course, important to learn from the ethical and sustainable aspects of foodie culture and incorporate those characteristics into ethical vegan landscapes. Many foodie restaurants strive to include local, farm-to-table ingredients in their menus (see, for example, Goad 2014), thus avoiding the environmental impacts of importing food products from across the world. Further, putting the meat, dairy, and eggs in foodie dishes aside for argument's sake, many foodie restaurants are conscientious about using other ingredients from ethical sources, such as fair-trade coffee, direct-trade chocolate, and organic produce. Understanding these positives of the current foodie culture is important for vegan activists and scholars in shaping landscapes that not only portray these same ethical and moral traits, but push themselves further up the metaphorical moral ladder by eliminating all nonhuman-animal products.

Vegan establishments and landscapes, when repositioned as more inclusive, compassionate, and sustainable alternatives to foodie culture, benefit nonhuman animals, humans, and the environment by providing ethical, low-cost, healthy food to the community and creating a widespread platform for speaking out against injustice of all kinds. It remains to be seen whether large vegan media outlets, such as PETA and *VegNews,* will work towards representation of the true racial diversity of veganism in their advertisements (Wrenn 2016), as well as speak out in protest of issues such as police brutality, racism, and economic injustice. Currently, most representations of veganism in these outlets are heavily whitewashed, and rarely do such outlets cover the breadth of injustices taking place in the world. Therefore, vegan foodscapes must serve as examples of an ethical veganism that *actually* fights global injustices against both human and nonhuman animals if they are to truly be moral alternatives to mainstream foodie culture as it exists today.

Conclusion

As foodie landscapes continue to flourish and thrive in urban environments, particularly those that are gentrified or undergoing gentrification, veganism can and should exist in direct contrast to the fundamental exclusion and violence that underpin these foodscapes. In an overwhelming majority of mainstream discourse, foodie culture is presented in the positive light of farm-to-table, neolocal, community-building consumption. However, even the most cursory analysis of this movement from a human and nonhuman rights perspective reveals the myriad exploitative and discriminatory practices driving its foodscapes: the dangerous, unhygienic, and low-wage working conditions in abattoirs and the harsh environmental consequences of meat production—both of which tend to overwhelmingly affect low-income individuals and people of color—and the violent slaughter of sentient beings that is deemed humane and natural due to speciesist logic. The growth of an ethical and equitable veganism, an increase in accessible vegan restaurants, and a broadening of vegan landscapes can provide respite from the injustices emboldened by foodie culture.

Ensuring equitable and representative vegan landscapes, accessible prices, and ethical ingredients are nonnegotiable, necessary steps towards a sustainable vegan movement. Vegan restaurants in Toronto, Edinburgh, and Knoxville, respectively, certainly contribute a more compassionate alternative to each city's foodscape, but as per the practical recommendations, in order to truly counter foodie landscapes, veganism must strive to be a movement that combats the exploitation of all beings. True veganism should entail more than simply abstaining from the consumption of nonhuman-animal products—vegan restaurants, advertisements, and social movements, if they are to successfully work towards reducing the strength of foodie culture, must be fundamentally anti-racist, anti-classist, and equitable.

The recommendations made in this chapter are ineffectual without robust implementation by vegan scholars/activists. As vegan geographies grow in strength and number, the subdiscipline finds itself at an opportune stage, with the potential to merge community engagement with scholarly productivity. Outreach conducted with local vegan establishments and groups using these recommendations not only spreads the relevance of geographic inquiry, but also allows for a transfer of knowledge that benefits the broader community, nonhuman animals, and the myriad human beings who experience exploitation at the hand of a foodie culture built on meat and dairy consumption. Such a transfer of knowledge should both educate the broader community about ethical veganism *and* reveal the dark truths behind the nonhuman-animal exploitation taking place across the world (White & Springer 2018), as well as the exploitation of humans and the environment in the global foodscape. Although problematic foodscapes are still thriving, there remains time to present ethical veganism as a compassionate alternative, and the vigilant work of vegan scholars/activists will be required in order to craft a movement that promotes equity amid a complicated and exploitative global foodscape.

8

BETWEEN FORCE AND FREEDOM

Place, Space, and Animals-as-Pet-Commodities

Zoei Sutton and Nik Taylor

Introduction

> It is through the prevention of motion that space enters history. . . . Even the symbolic definition of space relies ultimately on the potential presence of force. . . . The history of the prevention of motion is therefore a history of force upon bodies: a history of violence and pain. . . . The history of violence and pain crosses species. (Reviel Netz 2004, pp. xi–xiii)

Animal companions exist within a complex web of necessary conditions that construct them as affectionate but not minded, lively but never fully alive (Collard 2014). Contradictory narratives depict human–companion-animal relationships as both "naturally" justified—by animals' instinctive submission to unquestionable human domination—and mutually chosen by both human and animal who share feelings of love and kinship ties (Fudge 2008; Tuan 1984). These narratives, though conflicting, *do* coexist side by side, necessitating a social construction of animals-as-pet-commodities that convincingly deconstructs animals as minded beings and reconstructs them as "lively commodities" (Collard 2014). Companion animals, unlike the many animals subjected to more explicit (yet often more hidden) forms of violence in the creation of consumables, in entertainment, and in scientific testing, remain alive for the duration of their commodity life and, thus, are actively (re)created as commodities until they are no longer considered useful as such. The processes by which this (re)creation occurs are enabled by, and tied to, particular places. This means they can be examined through socio-spatial analysis that highlights the mechanisms by which a positive, affectionate relationship can be constructed on a foundation of unquestionable oppression. Though human–companion-animal relationships in their everyday form do not typically demonstrate the explicit violence and cruelty that are obvious in other human–animal entanglements, the spatial praxis of these relationships is one of prevention of animal agency and the "potential presence of force." This is something that is all too often invisibilized by the affective framing of human–companion-animal "love." Critical analyses of the spatial practices of companion-animal "ownership" can expose, problematize, and seek to change hierarchical relationships between humans and the companion species they purport to love and care for.

Critical Animal/Critical Vegan Geographies

As the chapters in this volume attest to, interest in critical animal/vegan geographies (CVG) is growing. Firmly located in critical praxis, this body of work can be seen as "an expanded anarchist geographical praxis that embraces more-than-human animals when speaking of ethics and social justice, and foregrounds questions of space and place when challenging power, domination and oppression" (White 2015, p. 215). It is critical because it focuses on, and challenges, asymmetrical power relations—in this case, between species—and it is increasingly vegan. This is because of the recognition that "veganism is not just about the abstinence of animal consumption; it is about the ongoing struggle to produce socio-spatial epistemologies of consumption that lead to cultural and spatial change" (Harper 2010b, pp. 5–6). Scholars working in this newly developing area, through examining the spaces and places in which human–animal entanglements occur, are well positioned to identify taken-for-granted "spatial imaginaries" that contribute to the continued oppression of animals (Gillespie & Collard 2015).

CVG is profoundly intersectional in that it recognizes the multiplicity and the overlapping nature of various oppressions (speciesism, racism, classism, and so on). It is also geographical in that it focuses particularly on the interactions of socio-spatial-political dominations of other species. Thus, CVG scholars have drawn attention, for example, to the cultural and colonial biopolitics of space that create human/animal binaries (Narayanan 2017), to similarities between the caged bodies of nonhuman and human animals (Morin 2015), and to how mainstream vegan praxis is itself implicated in creating socio-spatial epistemologies of whiteness (Harper 2010b).

Importantly, for our purposes, CVG scholars not only work within critical—often anarchist—traditions to detail the socio-spatial logics of violence (Springer & Le Billon 2016), but also focus on the idea of spatial emancipation (Springer 2016) and resistance. This resistance is cause for hope and can often be found in attention given to individual animals and their relationships with humans that turn on mutual affection (White & Cudworth 2014). This is not to deny the dominance that often goes hand in hand with that affection (Tuan 1984), but to note it also offers an avenue of potential resistance. We return to this latter point in the conclusion.

Following in the footsteps of these scholars who paid attention to the violence implicit in "micro-geographies of domination" (White & Cudworth 2014, p. 202), this chapter makes visible the asymmetrical power relations in human–companion-animal relationships through an examination of the spatial orderings of the home in relation to the "inside" and "outside." We argue that the spatial praxis of human–companion-animal relations is one characterized by the prevention of animal agency through the prevention of motion and the "potential presence of force." In so doing, this chapter captures the dynamic between place, space, and power as it emerges in interspecies relationships wherein power dynamics between the species are assumed to be minimal.

Animals-as-Pet-Commodities[1]

Nonhuman animals occupy a disempowered position within our social world in that human relations with, and treatment of, them differ largely depending on the uses humans deem them fit for (Cole & Stewart 2014). Arguably,[2] companion animals have the "best of the lot" in terms of their relationships with humans and, thus, their treatment. However, this positive treatment is very much dependent upon their serving "our" needs (as pets, companions, and so on), on our terms. Such an anthropocentric view of companion animals is cultivated from a young age. "Pets" are discursively constructed as "cute," "soft," "cuddly," and "vulnerable," with synthetic versions of "pet" species (such as dogs and cats) sold as stuffed animals, interactive

---

1. While we recognize the problematic nature of the term *pet*, we have elected to use it interchangeably with *animal companion* and *companion animal* for two reasons. The first is that our respondents tended to use the term. The second is that we are deliberately addressing the imbalance of power between humans and animals kept as pets, which often turns on their socially constructed "petness."
2. We are cognizant of the fact that many companion animals are not living in good situations. They are stuck in homes where they receive little attention; some are permanently chained in the backyard or relegated to living outside, away from the humans they wish to interact with; still more are subject to abuse, caught up in human-to-human domestic violence; and others are killed with depressing regularity due to their being "unwanted." Despite this, we use the term *arguably* here as many animal companions do have "good" lives (as far as we can tell), certainly when compared to those who are bred and reared solely for human consumption (be it for food, entertainment, or otherwise). We do not think it fruitful to debate "who is oppressed the most," but do think it worth acknowledging that, ostensibly, some animal companions can have "good" lives.

toys, and care-centric games—such as Tamagotchis and Nintendogs (Cole & Stewart 2014). In keeping with the intersectional nature of asymmetrical power relations, this marketing becomes increasingly gendered as the target age of a product increases. For example, the more nurture-intensive "pets"—such as Nintendogs, which require constant care (as feeding, bathing, and playing)—are targeted at a feminine market, reinforcing an infantilized construction of pets as vulnerable and simultaneously an image of women as caretakers (Cole & Stewart 2014).

Yi Fu Tuan (1984) argues that the (feminized) affection cultivated around pets "softens" the domination inherent in pet-keeping practices, drawing on the human tendency to dissociate domination from the realms of "pleasure, play, and art":

> How can we be said to abuse a plant when we take such pleasure in it, even if part of the pleasure lies in twisting the stem into the shape of an antelope? Is it cruelty to breed a variety of goldfish with dysfunctional bulging eyes if such fish are well cared for and fetch a high price? Was it right for a lady of eighteenth-century England to keep a black boy as a pet? She thought so, for did she not dress the boy in finery and allow him special privileges? Of course, some of us are now inclined to disagree, arguing that the boy's dignity was compromised by his pet status and even by his mistress's acts of favor and indulgence. (pp. 4–5)

This domination turns on the idea of companion animals as commodities, something that is simultaneously hidden and obvious in our relationships with other animals. Consider, for example, how animals are sold in "pet shops," yet there exists a narrative of "saving," "rescuing," and "adopting" them (Taylor 2007). This discrepancy exists because, as Collard (2014) puts it, "commodity status is not intrinsic to things," and, thus, "things" move in and out of this status over time (p. 155). When one deals with "lively commodities"—those that remain alive during their "commodity life"—the commodity/companion dualism is challenged; the lively commodity essentially leads a "double life" (Collard 2014, p. 155).

This double life does not come about without some maneuvering. In fact, complex processes of entanglement and disentanglement, attachment and detachment must take place before the animal can be transformed into a "tradable being" (Collard 2014, p. 156). Drawing on Locke's (2002) and Callon's (1998) works on organ transplants, Collard surmises that for something to be tradable, it must first be conceptualized as "thing-like . . . detachable from the body" (Locke 2002, p. 83). Animals must be similarly detached from their existing social relations and environments, though these initial attachments still serve a purpose as a kind of biocapital (Collard 2014). This detachment is partially enabled by distance. As Netz (2004) states: "The value of the sweatshop is a function of its distance from its clientele. The geographic distance allows a vast separation between the extremes of poverty and affluence" (p. 4). In the context of animals-as-pet-commodities, the value of the geographic and discursive distancing of breeding facilities serves to further reinforce a "veil of affection" behind which the practical elements of "pet" creation can disappear (Fudge 2008; Tuan 1984).

Once an animal has been effectively separated from their social and environmental links, they can be relinked in a manner that reflects their use value to humans (Collard 2014). Living commodities can be made and unmade time and time again, although the success with which they can be remade into lively commodities is affected by animal agency and the damage inflicted by this cyclic process (Collard 2014). So, for example, animals subject to the "revolving door" of multiple (re)homings through shelters may become depressed and/or aggressive, leading to their being designated as "unhome-able" and, ultimately, to their euthanasia. Though in this instance, Collard is considering exotic, particularly wild-caught, pets, similar arguments apply to domestic pets in that their parents, lineage, and socialization, and living conditions prior to sale are often of importance to prospective owners.

Once successfully cast as tradable and sold or adopted into a human home, the lively commodity status of an animal is consistently achieved and resisted in an often circular process. Such processes are inextricably linked to the use—and restrictions of use—of space within the human-dominated home.

Place and Space

The spatial dynamics of human–companion-animal relations are integral to the daily negotiation of these multispecies entanglements. The role of place—a fixed territory that is staked out geographically (Goffman 1974)—and space—a malleable area described by Tuan (1977) as "that which allows movement" (p. 6)—in shaping these relationships is as important as it is underemphasized (White & Springer 2018). In this chapter, we argue that the spatial orderings relevant to companion animals' lives—that is, the distinction between "inside" (the home) and "outside" (any place that is not the domestic quarters of the owner and animal in question)—demonstrate the interplay of dominance and affection (Tuan 1984) that constitutes companion animals as commodities. Importantly, though, we also note that paying attention to these spatial orderings offers a glimpse of the avenues of resistance in which some companion-animal owners engage, in order to rethink the role and place of other animals vis-à-vis humans. In line with Richard White and Erika Cudworth's (2014) work, we argue that a conceptualization of structure and resistance needs to be tied to specific places and spaces, if we are to highlight and create meaningful sites of resistance and develop spaces for change. We return to this idea of resistance later in the chapter, but begin by outlining how the spatial orderings of the home demonstrate the implicit domination in human–companion-animal relations.

Henri Lefevbre (1991) points out that space is socially produced, reflecting and informing broader social relations:

> Everyone knows what is meant when we speak of a "room" in an apartment, the "corner" of the street, a "marketplace," a shopping or cultural "center," a public "place," and so on. These terms of everyday discourse serve to distinguish, but not to isolate, particular spaces, and in general to describe a social space. They correspond to a specific use of that space, and hence to a spatial practice that they express and constitute. Their interrelationships are ordered in a specific way. (p. 16)

And this is very much the case for companion animals.[3] As Emma Power (2008) argues, spatial dynamics are important in the negotiation of human–dog relations both inside and outside the home. In particular, she points out, the home space is:

> more than a simple container for these encounters; rather family relations [are] performed through the home. House structures and home values (e.g., view of home as a clean, ordered, "human" space) [facilitate, shape, and mediate] the relations that [occur] between people and dogs. In turn these encounters [shape] home and how it [is] experienced by people. (p. 552)

Furthermore, "place" is integral to the construction of "good animals"—that is, of those who conform to their assumed inherent "petness"—with animals who stray from their allowed space serving as sources of objection:

> The designation "pet" generally indicates belonging: a place in the home, either sharing space with people, adorning the carpet or sleeping on the settee, or confinement within domestic space as in the case of goldfish, lizards or budgerigars. In the case of dogs, moving beyond the confines of the home is usually under the control of a human. (Griffiths, Poulter, & Sibley 2000, p. 61)

---

3. It is also the case for other animal species that are not our focus in the present chapter. See, for example, Pachirat (2011).

For nonhuman animals, the social relations (re)produced reflect broader anthroparchal structures that consistently position human interests as paramount over those of the environment and other animals (Cudworth 2011). Nonhuman animals are "'placed' by human societies in their local material spaces (settlements, fields, farms, factories, and so on), as well as in a host of imaginary, literary, psychological and even virtual spaces" (Philol & Wilbert 2005, p. 5). However, animals are not passive in this placement, but rather:

> it is animals themselves who inject what might be termed their own agency into the scene, thereby transgressing, perhaps even resisting, the human placements of them. It might be said that in so doing the animals begin to forge their own "other spaces," countering the proper places stipulated for them by humans, thus creating their own "beastly places" reflective of their own "beastly" ways, ends, doings, joys and sufferings. (Philol & Wilbert 2005, p. 13)

Though Philol and Wilbert's text is concerned largely with "wild" animals, the themes of socio-spatial constraint and agency are of relevance to domesticated companion animals, whose lives are perhaps more subtly, yet extensively, shaped by human-controlled spaces.

Existing research has highlighted the extent to which humans allow their companions to enter the home, with Franklin and Crook's (as cited in Franklin 2006) survey showing that many participants allowed their companion animals to occupy at least one room in the house, ranging from the living room (76 percent of participants) to a child's bedroom (35 percent). A 2016 survey of Australian pet-keeping practices (Animal Medicines Australia 2016) broke this household inclusion down by species:

Pet species	Lives exclusively inside	Allowed inside/outside	Lives exclusively outside
Dog	14%	66%	20%
Cat	34%	59%	7%
Bird	52%	Not stated	36%
Fish	69%	10%	24%

Table 1: Household Inclusion by Species

What these findings do not tell us is how often, or under what conditions, companion animals occupy these spaces, and how power is negotiated during these intersections of human and companion animal. The mere fact that we talk about "allowing" companion animals in the home indicates a significant power imbalance in that access to and use of space are something that must be granted by humans. But this power imbalance, and the restrictions faced by companion animals, often go unchallenged when we think only through an anthropocentric lens. As Fudge (2008) states:

> We like our pets' silence because it allows us to write their words for them, and what they say—what we write—reminds us of our power. Lassie tells us she wants to come home. Beautiful Joe tells us how grateful he is for human omniscience. But this, of course, is fantasy. (p. 52)

The reality for many, if not most, pets (not just those in "abusive" circumstances) is a life that is not as free or enriching as we humans would like to think (Pierce 2016). In fact, the home is often a space of physical, behavioral, and emotional confinement, even when it is a "good" home, as we will demonstrate. Although human-owner identity has a significant role to play in shaping relations and the subsequent space-making, companion-animal experience of the relationship is largely restricted to the interactions with and physical layout of the home. Companion animals' experiences of the home depend almost entirely on the decisions and actions of the humans of the household.

A Note on Methods

In this chapter, we draw on qualitative data collected as part of the lead author's PhD project. This broader project used semi-structured interviews and observations in the home with humans and their companion animals to explore the lived experiences and negotiations of human–animal-companion relationships. The sample consisted of 30 human participants (25 female, 5 male), 22 dogs, 17 cats, and numerous birds and fish (we were unable to determine an exact number as several participants were unsure of how many birds or fish they "owned"). Other animals present in interview discussions (but not physically present) included guinea pigs, rats, birds, cows, horses, cats, and dogs. Some of these animals were excluded from participation due to interview location (2 of the 30 interviews were conducted out-of-home at the participants' request), while others were located elsewhere in the home during the interview.

The interview questions were designed to encourage narrative responses that were largely companion animal–centric, covering three main areas: (1) (human-) participant experiences and descriptions of shared life with their companion(s) and how they had negotiated the relationship(s); (2) (human) considerations of how their companion(s) might experience their shared life, including limits the companion(s) might face and their experience of social relationships; and (3) owner reflections on the broader issues and ethics around petkeeping as a practice. Throughout the interviews (apart from the two out-of-home interviews), companion animals were present but not required to actively participate. Animals who elected to stay out of the interview zone in the house were not forcibly brought into the room; however, most free-roaming companions wandered into the interview zone at some point during interviews. The home setting was intentionally chosen to facilitate this participation, which is otherwise made difficult in publicly situated interviews, particularly for non-canine companions. Likewise, the observation component allowed for the inclusion of companion-animal actions and interactions in the data, highlighting these contributions to the social situation rather than solely privileging human voices.

The inclusion of other animals in research is not unproblematic. As Lynda Birke (2014) highlights, a nonhuman animal is not required to consent to participation as a human would be, and this participation tends to occur in situations wherein a clear power imbalance grants the human researcher and human participant dominion over the nonhuman animal. However, moving towards species-inclusive methods—which give serious consideration to ethical issues and the benefits to and potential intrusions on the animals involved—is an important step in creating research with and for companion animals, rather than merely about them (Birke 2014; Hamilton & Taylor 2017). As such, companion-animal input was integral to the exploration of the navigation of these relationships, highlighting the material conditions in which the animals lived. Interview transcripts and observation notes were entered into NVivo and coded thematically. Thirteen themes were apparent in the data, three of which we concentrate on in this chapter: (1) constraint within the home; (2) the reimagining of human–companion-animal relationships through recognizing, and making space for, animal agency within these spaces; and (3) the influence of anthropocentric outside spaces.

Interview data was supplemented by reflections we (the authors) both had on living with companion animals. This includes our (ongoing) conversations on these issues that date back around six years. Both of us have lived with companion animals, primarily dogs but also other species, for the majority of our lives. As activist-scholars and vegans, we are both well aware of the problems inherent to "petkeeping." We are also aware that despite our best intentions, the animals who share our lives and spaces have their autonomy and power curtailed on a regular basis, both within the home and without.

Constraint Inside the Home

Within the home, companion animals' agency is consistently impeded by the actions and decisions of their human owners, who have the power to dictate where the animals can and can't go, their access to resources and amenities, and their behavior in, and use of, space. Environmental restriction was a prominent occurrence, with most of the observed households having rooms or areas the companion animals could not access. One participant who utilized baby gates to restrict their dog's movements within the house remarked: "He can go anywhere he likes. Oh, except up to the front of the house . . ." (Nora).[4] Another enforced an evening restriction of their cat's access to children's bedrooms:

> We don't let him in the girls' bedrooms at nighttime. But that's what we've done since we got him so he, touch wood, he doesn't sort of try to get in or sit there and meow until they let him in or anything like that. (Sarah)

Similar bedtime restrictions were enforced by other participants, who limited their companions' access to a specific area of the house (such as the laundry) or the outside, in contrast to the freedom of movement the animals were afforded within the house at other times.

Some participants restricted their companion animals' movement sporadically to accommodate temporary preferences or uses of space, with one owner explaining, "we restrict access to a few of the rooms when we don't want (a) it covered in fur or (b) them chewing plastic bags if we've got things packed up or put away" (Dawn). Temporary space restrictions were also utilized as a "timeout" when animals misbehaved or weren't getting along with others in the house.

With respect to the matter of toileting, canine companions whose homes did not include a doggy door were reliant on their owners' being present and attentive to their need to relieve themselves. One participant found living in rental accommodation with a housemate a barrier to leaving the back door open for their companion; this meant that the dog would have to toilet in the house if no one was home:

---

4. Participants have been given pseudonyms to preserve anonymity.

> She needs someone to let her out, like, because we don't have a dog door and I don't think the owner would let us put one in. If we had a dog door, I don't think the toilet thing would be a problem at all. (Olivia)

Another participant restricted access to outside toileting to avoid unwanted barking outside and maintain the fly-free home they desired:

> We can't exactly leave the door open all the time, because then we get flies in the house . . . and, like, similarly, because sometimes she goes around that side of the house and starts barking at random people and we're just like, "Well, we don't want you to do that." (Edward)

This introduces the idea of legitimate and illegitimate uses of the home space, with the barking mentioned above clearly defined as inappropriate behavior in the backyard. Similarly, another participant reported having altered the treats provided to their dog to avoid defilement of the garden:

> Occasionally, if I think he deserves a treat or something, I'll get him a bone. He hasn't had one for a while because he buries them in the garden, that's the problem. . . . Find the loveliest plant you can, dig it up and put a bone under it [laughter]. So, I sort of moved to buying him hearts or livers, something like that that he can eat more quickly and not bury. (James)

In this instance, while the dog had shown a preference for burying bones (which conflicted with the owner's view of legitimate use of space), the owner restricted his ability to "choose" this by changing to a treat less likely to be buried.

These restrictions of movement are not necessarily malevolent in nature (for example, keeping one's plastic bag–munching cat away from their favorite pastime is certainly likely to be in their best interest!). However, these demonstrations of control over the home environment, and the companion-animal movement within it, nevertheless indicate a prevention of agency enabled by an asymmetrical power relation between species. Although the examples above may seem trivial in nature, the portrait they paint is one of human dominance—the companion animal in the home has as little, or as much, freedom as they are allowed at any given time, and this can be subject to alteration at the human owner's whim.

Despite these constraints, the dogs included in this study enjoyed more symmetrical relationships with their human owners than many of the other species.

Indeed, their relative "freedoms" were often at the expense of other animals'. Jessica Pierce (2016) highlights the unequal values in society of certain companion species, pointing out that smaller, "starter" pets often fare the worst.[5] The findings from the present study largely confirmed this; marginalized pets included birds, cats, rats, guinea pigs, fish, and a horse—never dogs. However, attention paid to the politics of space reveals the manner in which some animals were privileged over others, along with the justifications given by owners.

Space was commonly used to enforce an intra-pet species hierarchy, with marginalized pets facing restriction of movement or physical removal from the living quarters. For enclosed pets, this removal was overt, as they were placed in out-of-the-way areas, such as the garage or backyard:

> When we had all three [rats], we had this little cage and we had to have them just in that little room there, and [the dog] would always be in that room there, staring at them the whole time, so we had to eventually block them all off. (Edward)

For other marginalized companions, exclusion was less deliberate, resulting instead from a function of space, of the lack of available surfaces or infrastructure to accommodate all species. Consequently, the marginalized pet had to "fend for themselves" alongside the privileged pet (usually a dog), who had free rein. For example:

> Yeah, with cats, he sort of, um, with our cat, we have a cat, she's like fifteen and she doesn't really like dogs and he [the dog] sort of like doesn't give her personal space and sort of winds her up and chases her round and barks and doesn't really understand not everyone wants to be his friend. . . . He just wants to sniff her and give her a bit of a lick, but she'll, like, go *hissss* and arc up, and he thinks it's a game and he'll run, like, we've got a tree in the backyard, the cat climbs the tree and the dog runs around the tree, like, circling and barking; and so, yeah, he's very energetic, and also, he's smart, too. (Audrey)

The cat in this household, though not actively rejected from the home, was still prevented from freely interacting inside due to the presence of the overzealous dog. While the cat's food bowl was kept on a higher shelf to deter the dog from

5. This feature is also highlighted in an endnote in Tipper's (2011) work, in which children displayed significantly less enthusiasm when discussing companion fish compared to all other companion species. Tipper links this to the lesser level of action and interaction opportunities in the human–fish relationships included in the study.

eating the food, no other higher-level spaces were provided for the cat, making it difficult for her to move around without encountering the dog. This then passively granted the dog privilege in the home space (and over the cat), marginalizing the cat through exclusive space organization. This privileging is also evident in the language associated with each of the animals—the dog is "smart" and "energetic," "just wants to be friends"; the cat "arcs up," "hisses," "doesn't like dogs." This latter negativity almost implies that the cat is at fault for not adjusting to, and welcoming, the dog's presence.

Physical removal was often accompanied by a lesser attachment to marginalized animals, which was reported as being either the cause for or caused by the physical exclusion. Few respondents gave overt reasons related to attachment for the exclusion. Instead, marginalized animals were more likely to be considered less interactive or affectionate than their canine counterparts. In some instances, this resulted in increased disposability, as these companions could be traded and were unlikely to be mourned to the same extent as more privileged pets would be. It must be stated that this exclusion cannot be explained by species discrimination alone—other households that similarly included birds, cats, and dogs did not appear to have an observable hierarchy. This implies that the exclusion was reflective of owners' constructions of their companions rather than of anything inherent in the animals. Conversely, the power of owner constructions of companion animals also means that within the privacy and control of the home space, human owners can reimagine their relationships with their companions, intentionally creating space for and accommodating animal agency. These reimaginings will be explored in the following section.

Reimagining Human-Companion-Animal Relationships

> What would our world look like if we worked with and supported the creativity of fish, rather than simply working against it? (Wadiwel 2016, pp. 222–223)

At the start of this chapter, we noted that CVG scholars adopt both critical and hopeful approaches to the idea of spatial emancipation, with the latter focusing on different forms or resistance. In some cases, this hope can be found in paying attention to individual animals and their relationships with humans that turn on mutual affection (White & Cudworth 2014). This may take the form of highlighting close relationships in which humans are aware of asymmetrical interspecies power relations and attempt to reconfigure their own relations to animals. For example:

> Jada has problems with other dogs and, um, I went, "Wow, the people at this club can't help me." They're just like, "Tell her off, just tell her no," and I'm like, "If you're highly stressed, if your kid is scared coz of a thunderstorm and is crying because of a thunderstorm, do you just push them over and go, 'Stop doing that'? Does that help? No it doesn't help." And I started to learn that on my own, and then when I picked up that the dog club just couldn't, didn't get what I was talking about, that's when I did a Certificate III in Behavior and Training. (Hayley)

For Hayley, an awareness of ineffectual and problematic dominance dynamics motivated her to pursue further education in training and animal behavior and to intentionally create space for animal agency in her relationships with her companions:

> Sometimes, you will have to do what I ask you to, but a lot of the time, I'm actually asking them—I'm not telling them. Sometimes, I will tell them—if you've got a kid in the middle of the road, you have to tell them, you have to grab them and get them off the road, you know. But if, um, you know, "Would you like a glass of water?" you shouldn't have to oblige unless it's really important. . . . I want it to be a relationship.

The awareness may also take the form of investigating how engagement with veganism causes individuals to problematize petkeeping and question their own practices, upon seeing the connections between the pet industry and other forms of animal exploitation. Interestingly, participants did not talk about their connections with companion animals as contributing to their decisions to become vegans (as has been the focus of existing research, for example, Rothgerber & Micah 2014), nor did they reflect on the ethical tensions around feeding "meat" to their companions. Instead, their veganism highlighted ethical issues around human–pet dynamics specifically:

> When I went vegan, I sort of started seeing a lot of criticism for [petkeeping] and I sort of. . . . I'd always been a bit on the fence, I'd always been a bit, like, I don't like that they're not allowed to fly around in the wild and that sort of thing. But then once I sort of started making more of the connection, I was like, hmm, it's not really right to be doing this, and I don't really believe in humans having control over other animals, and they're not ours to own. So, I was like, no, I don't want to support pet breeders at all anymore, no matter who they are. I just want to have rescue pets because I don't want to pay money to somebody who's just going to use it to breed again, but then, at the

> same time, the parrots that do exist in the world, and the dogs as well, do need somewhere to live, so that's why I've only rescued. (Willow)

Alternatively, the awareness may take the form of acknowledging the strategies some humans use to resist the socio-spatial orderings that are indicative of interspecies domination. Julie Ann Smith (2003) delves into this idea in her article on creating a post-human home with her companion rabbits. Reflecting on the differences between a human's and rabbit's conceptualization and use of space, she observes that:

> After many years of living with rabbits, I noticed that they liked free corridors along perimeters. Before this, I would dutifully place litterboxes and toys along the walls of the playroom after I had cleaned each day. By night, the room was a "mess." Eventually, I noticed that it was a particular kind of mess: Everything movable in the room was in the middle of the floor. This observation changed forever the way I live in my house, as did my understanding of other rabbit preferences: spaces along borders and boundaries, enclosed spaces with more than one exit, spaces that allow them to see out but not be seen. Rabbit ideas of space management often conflicted with my own aesthetics, but I came to value them as indicators that rabbits were making themselves at home. (p. 188)

Alger and Alger (2003) note similar preferences of the use of space in their ethnography of a cat shelter, in which they observed the cats using space in a particular way that reflected their social roles, relationships, and status in the group. For instance, two cats who had formed a friendship, Bibbi and Lisa, had claimed an empty litter pan as their "home base." Other cats were able to exist nearby but never enter the litter pan, and one of the two cats generally remained in the pan at all times. The symbolic importance of the empty pan was clear, particularly when it was removed and their "spot" was no longer available:

> Upon arriving at the shelter, we notice that Bibbi and Lisa are missing and that their empty litter pan is not in its usual place. One of the copresidents happens to be there and Janet tells her about their attachment to the empty litter pan. The president asks one of the volunteers to bring over a clean litter pan and as soon as it is in place, Bibbi and Lisa materialize and sit in it. (p. 101)

Thus, although we cannot fully understand what the litter pan and the rabbit-constructed space *feel* like for the animals, we can understand by observing their behavior that these things are of importance. And because we are aware that "other" animals have the capacity to shape their living space and engage in enrichment activities, we can hypothesize that they are also able to feel constraint when these behaviors are stifled.

For participants who were so inclined, efforts were made to decenter the human in their homes, and instead prioritizing companion-animal preferred behaviors over their own wants or conveniences. While the underlying power asymmetries remain, the examples explored below provide an entry point for thinking about how we might start to reimagine our relationships with companion animals.

One participant reported having made several adjustments to their home to accommodate the two cats they had adopted:

> Yeah, um, we had to put, um, we had to get, yeah, the doors changed over with the stronger mesh coz they like to climb to the top of that and, um, what else was there? Oh, my daughter started, um, came out and started—her eyes were watering and she'd be sneezing and she . . . We discovered she was allergic to the cats, and we've gone, "Oh great, what're we gonna do?" . . . I had to go get a brand-new vacuum cleaner with the pet filters and everything to try and vacuum everything up, and thankfully, she's sort of used to them now. But, um, have to give her a hay fever tablet before you put her in the car with them, and she's just not allowed to bury her face in their fur like she used to like to do. (Dawn)

This participant opted to limit the humans in the house—by cleaning more rigorously, restricting their daughter's interactions with the cats, and administering antihistamines—rather than the cats' movements. Likewise, in opting to alter the screen doors so that the cats could climb them without causing damage, this participant embraced their cats' agency (letting them climb the doors as they wished) rather than seeking to suppress companion-animal agency by attempting to curb the behavior. However, the cats were limited in other ways. They did not have unfettered access to the outside as they wished; rather, their owners tried to give them supervised outside time as much as possible. They also received food twice daily to avoid overeating. Again, this offers an example of how agency and constraint are negotiated within human–companion animal relationships.

The presence of animal "stuff" is also indicative of how freely animals are allowed to use a space. In many of the houses, there was ample evidence of the presence of "stuff"—scattered toys, beds where you would expect to find walkways, and random objects that owners explained were there to suit the animals' preferences: "There is an empty box next to the wall. Milo [cat] strolls towards it and climbs in, hunkers down, and closes his eyes. I am told it is Milo's box, left there especially for that purpose."

The houses in which animal "stuff" was present were otherwise tidy, indicating that they were not "out of control" but rather part of the negotiation of a legitimate use of space. Companion animals' "stuff" was not out of place but rather indicated that they, too, could place items in the home. This stands in contrast to other homes, in which no "stuff" was observed; it was explained that toys were confined to specific areas, mostly to the backyard, thus creating a clear environment in which the "inside" was for human enjoyment (inside pets, therefore, had to conform to human preferences) and the "outside" was for "other" animals.

Navigations of space also facilitated and indicated a recognition of positive social relationships between pets, as well as an effort made to ensure these continued in the owners' absence. One participant, who owned several birds (as well as a dog), was careful to facilitate social interaction for all of the pets—including through cage placement that allowed for communication between birds while maintaining their own private spaces:

> Cages are placed in an L shape in the lounge room, in a deliberate order which places the birds next to those who have similar communication techniques. The budgies are the only birds currently sharing a cage. Though the birds are often out of the cages—the doors are left open to encourage free flying and interaction—this cage placement encourages them to communicate when in the cages. The birds appear to have constructed a hybrid language—made up of the human words they know, natural bird vocalization, and learned sounds such as those imitating human coughing and the sound of the fridge door opening. When we are not in the room, you can hear one bird "cough," which is then answered by another bird "coughing" back. This goes on for several minutes.

This arrangement was not necessarily making life easier for the owner, who explained that living in a rental property meant they worried about the noise from the birds but that this worry did not change their commitment to facilitating the birds' social relationships. The above examples demonstrate some of the ways in which participants reimagined their relationships with their companions to accommodate greater levels of animal agency. These reimaginings were enabled to a great extent by the privacy and control (human) individuals enjoyed within the home space (Mallett 2004). As will be seen in the discussion below, the influence of anthroparchal structures is much more pervasive outside of the home, demonstrating that while relationships can be constructed as *less* problematic, the fundamentally unequal foundation of human–companion-animal relationships is inescapable.

Interactions with the Anthropocentric "Outside"

The complexity of freedom and constraint in human–companion-animal relationships is perhaps better clarified when we consider the role of "outside"—that is, the broader imaginaries that surround these relationships and the public locales in which they manifest. The social production of these relationships occurs both outside and inside the home, even if the physical performance of a relationship is strictly tied to the home space. Thus, by considering the broader social framings of animals in public space and participant interactions with these, we can start to unpack the tangled patterns of relating that create and reinforce animals-as-pet-commodities.

With the exception of the vet, public space for domesticated animals is almost exclusively canine-specific. While the vast majority of dogs are taken for walks (84 percent) and/or to visit parks and other public space (52 percent), cats are overwhelmingly more likely to remain at home (85 percent), with only five percent being taken on walks in the community (AMA 2016). Thus, the only companion relations expected to be viewed in public are human–dog pairs, reinforcing the kind of canine privileging evident in the examples above. For cat owners in particular, the vilification of "feral" cats meant that it was necessary to take steps to ensure that their companions' "pet" status was identifiable: "I'd have to put collars on them and I don't like them in collars," said one participant (Eric). Even then, it was clear that "owned" cats were not thought to be welcome in outside spaces, in part due to their tendency to transgress private boundaries and violate human-acceptable behaviors in space: "I don't want them to dig up a neighbor's yard and take a big poop in their veggie garden as cats are great at doing" (Tara). When discussing their companions and outside spaces, most cat owners touched on the negative associations between cats and wildlife deaths as a motivating factor in keeping their cats indoors. This outcome was cat-specific; although participants also reported their dogs having killed local wildlife, the dogs' movements were not restricted because of it. This is perhaps partly explained by the current moral panic in Australia induced by cats' killing of wildlife (see, for example, Probyn-Rapsey 2016), resulting in very different attitudes towards cat roaming from those reported in a U.K. context (Fox 2017).

Dogs, though allowed in public space, are only tolerated insofar as they conform to behavioral expectations that reinforce human dominance in society.

It is a condition in most public spaces that dogs be under "effective control" at all times, which, coupled with signs about picking up animal excrement and code-of-conduct signs, starts to outline a "responsible dog owner" identity that is required in public. Thus, the public dog could never be allowed the same level of freedom that is possible in the home; the owner must ultimately be in control (Power 2008). This control is established both explicitly and implicitly through interactions with (and between) owners, not with the animals themselves (Sanders 1990). One owner reported an incident in which they were chastised for not controlling their dog to the extent deemed acceptable by the other party:

> I get really, really angry coz, like I said, eight o'clock is off-lead time, and the number of families that have had the whole day to themselves on the beach, and it's eight o'clock so it's the dogs' turn now and, um, you know, piss off—if you don't like dogs, get the hell off the beach. It's dark, your children should be in bed anyway, go away. . . . And I actually had an all-out [gestures thumping fist into palm] with a mother a few weeks back when she said, "He should be on a lead," and I said, "He is under effective control," and I said, "Your children should not be so scared of dogs." (Laura)

This anger highlights a familiar frustration among participants with dogs: as much as they might respect and create space for nonhuman agency at home, in public space an anthropocentric worldview reigned supreme. As such, many participants expressed that they would prefer to take their companions with them to most outside places but were restricted to very few locations that would allow, and that were suitable for, their animals. Several participants voiced an aversion even to places that seemed on the surface to be dog-friendly, such as the dog park, but that they considered to be sites shaped in accordance with the way dog *owners* wanted to use space:

> I've seen people on their laptops, I can't believe that! One doing their work and, um, not really paying much attention to the dogs, and what do you hear? "Oh, they can sort it out, let them sort it out," and you're going, "No, no way José, you know, sometimes you do need to intervene and you do need to watch." (Molly)

In particular, owners of non-typical dogs (such as those with anxiety or reactivity issues) were acutely aware that public space, where it does allow for companion-animal participation, is shaped around compliant and predictable animals-as-pet-commodities, rather than accounting for differences in personality, interaction preferences, and needs. Much like the marginalized cat discussed above, non-typical canines are edged out of public spaces by other owners who do not leash their companions in on-leash areas or exercise effective control, instead operating under the assumption that they know their companions to be "friendly" and expecting all other companions to be receptive to any advances.

Companion animals' awareness (or lack thereof) of their subordinate, commodity status in an anthroparchal society was cause for concern among participants. One participant voiced her worry that the environment of safety and respect she had created for her companion within the home would render him ill-equipped to navigate the outside world:

> He'd run out to the front and he had no fear, and coz he's totally safe around me, I guess he thinks he's totally safe around the world. And one day, a lady was driving along here and she saw him and she saw me racing along to get him, and she opened her car door to help, and he just jumped straight into her car and that just freaked me right out. Coz I thought, gee, if that had happened and I hadn't seen it and the person had driven away—he's microchipped and you know, but if they pull his collar off that has his name and address and phone number . . . When they're top dog, they think they're in control, but they're not really because the world out there is not safe: cars, people, yeah. (Penny)

The construction of animals-as-pet-commodities is emphasized in the context of the outside, with many owners echoing Penny's fear that her companion would be stolen and sold. Multiple owners, particular those with feline companions, reported a fear of animal theft as one of the most pressing reasons for their decisions to restrict their companions' movements to the home space. This was particularly prevalent among owners of purebred cats, who recognized the commodity value of their companions and considered that their animals' worth would be reduced to this monetary potential outside of the home (where they were respected as individuals):

> Someone would probably try and steal her, which is the way of a lot of Burmese, a lot of Siamese cats, um; that's another reason I don't want to let them out, I'm just scared someone's going to . . . (Eric)

For these owners, this provided a confronting reminder of the juxtaposition of their own loving, affectionate relationships with the commodification of the animals who had facilitated these relationships to begin with.

To navigate the potentially threatening outside world, participants reported restrictions of freedom within the home: cats were restricted to indoors, and dogs were trained to respond to their owners' control. These examples show how owner experiences of "outside" space can filter into the home space, providing a stark reminder that these relationships can never truly be free of the anthroparchal underpinnings that facilitated their existence in the first place. However, in highlighting the broad difference in levels of (constrained) freedom companion animals can be afforded within the home space compared to this anthropocentric outside, we also demonstrate the potential of the home setting to facilitate situationally specific resistance against these oppressive structures.

Conclusion

In this chapter, we have argued that attending to the spatial uses of the home makes visible the often subtle, everyday ways in which humans' dominance over companion animals is enacted and reinforced. While the spatial limitations on companion animals' agency we have noted here are much less egregious than the countless ways other animals are oppressed, they stem from the same ideological place: an anthroparchal mindset that sees any and all animals as worth less than humans. Despite this, we are not attempting to cast all human–companion-animal relations in a negative light and have been at pains to point out that resistance—from multiple species, not just humans—is evident in the negotiations over spatial orderings that take place in multispecies households.

We recognize that this often turns on the anthropomorphizing of other species and their needs and behaviors. However, as Fudge (2008) notes, although it is impossible to fully understand what it is to be animal, doing away with educated guesses would mean the animals "disappear from view." Thus, "[i]f the best we can do is make educated guesses about animals' inner lives then educated guesses are what we should make, even as we recognize that these guesses (which are educated, are based on evidence) are just guesses" (Fudge 2008, p. 60). This does not mean simply imposing a human perspective on nonhuman animals and theorizing accordingly; but rather, it means taking what we know (insofar as we can "know") about the lifeworlds of those animals and thinking about how that may shape experience (Coren 2005; Fudge 2008; Horowitz 2010; Von Uexküll 1992 [1934]).

Such theorizing is evident in Stanley Coren's development of "doggish"—a language taught to dog owners that enables communication beyond the near-useless "doggerel" (human dialect) many speak to their pets in (Coren 2005). Coren's approach requires an acknowledgment that other animals do have rich inner worlds and are "active, communicating beings engaged in world-making alongside humans" (Fudge 2008, p. 56). Furthermore, a lack of the above understanding negates any possibility of positive human–companion-animal relationships, for to create an inclusive relationship requires incorporating the companion animal's wants and needs and "know(ing) how to translate his answer" (Horowitz 2010, p. 19).

Conceptualizing resistance in human–companion-animal relationships is not without its challenges; though positive relations can be, and indeed are, co-constructed (Fox 2017; Irvine 2004), these occur in a broader anthroparchal context in which animals are forcibly bred so that their offspring can become our beloved pets (Cudworth 2011). Animals-as-pet-commodities can be created and recreated as living goods for the duration of their lives, and though many owners may not consider it an option, companion animals can be uncreated at any time and find themselves surrendered or euthanized. This objectification and this constant "potential presence of force" make it difficult to see how any meaningful resistance might be possible within these relationships. However, through paying attention to the "micro-geographies of domination," we may be able to not only make visible the asymmetrical relations between species, but also find instances of resistance that can "effectively challenge interspecies domination" (White & Cudworth 2014). It is our contention, then, that while the spatial orderings of multispecies households demonstrate dominance, they can, and often do, also demonstrate mutual affection, closeness, and attempts by humans to understand other species' needs. We conclude, therefore, that a critical analysis of the spatial practices of human–companion-animal relationships better captures the complexity of these relationships and uncovers "new possibilities and spaces for radical change" (White & Cudworth 2014).

Acknowledgments

The doctoral research from which this chapter draws was supported by an Australian Government Research Training Program Scholarship and a Flinders University Research Scholarship.

9

Vegan Environmentalism

Practicing Care for Socio-Ecological Futures

Andrew McGregor

Introduction: Changing Geographies of Nature

One of the defining features of geography is the study of human–nature relations. This has taken many guises, from the racialized and colonizing approaches of a now thoroughly debunked environmental determinism to the radical, emancipatory origins of political ecology (Castree 2005). Until relatively recently, however, there had been an assumption that humans and nature are separate and distinguishable things, one influencing the other in various ways. It is this assumption that normalizes the divide between human and physical geography on the one hand, and the social or nature emphasis within subdisciplines like political ecology and environmental geography on the other.

More recent research informed by materialist (Bakker & Bridge 2006) and more-than-human geographies (Whatmore 2002) abandons this distinction, arguing that nonhuman nature, as well as a natureless human, do not exist. Instead, humans and nonhumans are always entangled in inseparable knots. Humans are not envisaged as impacting nature, nor nature as impacting humans; instead, humans are seen to "*inhabit* hectic and often unruly corporeal worlds that exert their own material agencies" (Houston 2012). Humans are repositioned as one agent among many, made up of and always co-becoming with more-than-human others to create worlds (Bawaka Country et al., 2013). As a consequence, the geographic study of human–nature relations is transforming into a study of the more-than-human relationalities through which spaces, places, and worlds are co-produced, and in which agency is democratized and decentered to incorporate the vitality of living and non-living others.

As these conceptual developments sweep human geography and related disciplines, a parallel and somewhat overlapping transformation is taking place within the biophysical sciences, including physical geography, as evidence mounts that the earth is moving into a new geological epoch commonly known as the Anthropocene. Humans are positioned as a planetary force that is fundamentally transforming and degrading the conditions that have provided stability during the last 10,000–12,000 years of the Holocene (Steffen, Crutzen, & McNeill 2007). The planetary scale of issues such as climate change, biodiversity loss, deforestation, and land degradation means human influences are now pervasive across the earth's surface. This troubles the study of nature and natural processes, as everywhere bears the imprint of human activity to greater or lesser degrees. Natural scientists are, in effect, studying socio-ecological processes rather than strictly ecological ones, as pristine ecologies no longer exist.

As a consequence, research silos are being breached as recognition grows that human and natural worlds are entangled within one another (Latour 2004a), creating interdisciplinary tensions, collaborations, and new research fields, such as the environmental humanities and Earth systems governance (Castree 2014). While the conceptualization (along with the nomenclature) of the Anthropocene has attracted critique for what it enables and omits (Moore 2016; Malm & Hornborg 2014), as well as grief for lost futures (Head 2016), it is also being seen as a generative moment that can inspire new ways of doing and being (Castree 2015; Haraway 2015). For Castree (2015), a key element of this involves thinking past the techno-scientific "solutions" proposed by Earth scientists and engaging with alternatives that emerge from geography's holistic approach to socio-ecologies.

Building on these insights, this paper makes the case for vegan environmentalism as a necessary socio-ecological response to the conceptual and biophysical challenges of the new epoch. I approach environmentalism as a broad social movement that employs forms of "activism aimed at protecting the environment or improving its condition" (Bomberg & Schlosberg 2013). It is a diverse and increasingly complicated movement with wide appeal, united around a common concern for human–nature relations.

Veganism, in contrast, is commonly considered a more narrowly focused form of praxis, primarily oriented against the use and exploitation of nonhuman animals. Despite, or perhaps because of, much more radical interpretations of vegan politics, veganism has growing but limited appeal outside of animal rights movements, occupying, at best, a liminal space within most environmental movements. I will argue, however, that an ecofeminist-inspired contextual veganism provides an appropriate means for environmentalists to reorganize their politics in a post-nature Anthropocene world. An ecofeminist ethic that prioritizes care and opposes logics of domination provides a platform for building solidarities between animal, environmental, and social justice groups.

In what follows, I first explore the existential crises facing Western environmentalism as core organizing concepts like nature and wilderness crumble and key narratives about protecting nature from humans become harder to sustain. I then briefly compare how technology-centered ecomodernists and care-based ecofeminists are responding to these crises and the different pathways they open up. In the subsequent section, I apply these ideas to a case study of animal agriculture[1] in Australia. I outline the destructive impacts of animal agriculture on Indigenous socio-ecologies and how outdated concepts of nature deflect environmental concern away from agricultural spaces. I follow this by comparing ecofeminist and ecomodernist responses to animal agriculture, as well as the more-than-human worlds created when farmed animals are approached in caring and compassionate ways through a contextual vegan environmentalism rather than as abstract, food-producing "animal machines" (Harrison 1966). The paper concludes with a discussion of the problems and possibilities that arise when veganism and environmentalism mix.

Post-Nature Environmentalism

The growing ontological critique of the idea of nature poses existential crises for Western environmentalism, which has long sought to minimize human impacts on nature. As an example, the mission of one of Australia's most high-profile environmental organizations, The Wilderness Society, is "protecting, promoting and restoring wilderness and natural processes across Australia for the survival and ongoing evolution of life on Earth" (TWS 2017). While not all organizations are as explicit, the idea of nature as fragile and pre-human is never far away. This is expressed in policies oriented towards preserving or recreating wilderness and "natural" ecosystems. It is also consistent with broader campaigns aimed at lowering humanity's ecological footprint.

Implicit in this work is an assumption that nature is something "out there," separate and distinguishable from humans. Nature is most often associated with spaces and systems that have no or little human influence, with place-based campaigns seeking to mobilize people around the protection of seemingly untouched or pristine wilderness areas. However, "the trouble with wilderness," as William Cronon (1996) famously titled his essay, is multitudinous. First, the historic presence of Indigenous peoples in many wilderness areas raises questions

1. I use the term *animal agriculture industries* rather than *livestock industries* to emphasize these industries are based on the exploitation of real living animals, not live "stock."

as to whether any space is actually pristine or untouched. As Willems-Braun (1997) has shown in British Columbia, Canada, and Ginn (2008) in New Zealand/Aotearoa, wilderness areas are often romantic fantasies that violently erase centuries or millennia of Indigenous presence. In Australia, while environmentalist–Indigenous relations and dialogue have improved and diversified over the years (Vincent & Neale 2017), there is still plenty of tension when interests conflict (Langton 2013) and a tendency to underplay, or selectively stereotype, 70,000 years of Indigenous history in wilderness-style campaigns (Langton 1996).

A second challenge to wilderness comes from the aforementioned human-induced changes to the biosphere associated with the Anthropocene. Anthropogenic changes to Earth systems, such as climate change, leave no place "untouched," prompting prominent American environmentalist Bill McKibben (2003) to lament the "end of nature"—as everything, to some extent, bears human influence. A third challenge derives from the human work that goes into maintaining "natural spaces" through things like pest control, weeding, rewilding, and the accompanying policy and political machinations. Kareiva et al. (2007), for example, argue that we are better off thinking about a world of "domesticated nature" where "wilderness is more commonly a management and regulatory designation than truly a system without human imprint" (p. 1869).

Cronon (1996) argues that this celebration of nature and wilderness leads to a spatialization of environmental concern. Wild spaces command most of the attention and resources directed towards environmental issues, while spaces with increasing human influence become progressively less valued. This results in an ever-shrinking and unwinnable remit for environmental groups as human influences become ever more apparent and extensive, thus devaluing large extents of urban and rural land due to human presence (Marris 2011). It also leads to an increasingly difficult, "surreal kind of performance art" (Mooallem 2013, p. 2) as environmentalists attempt to recreate in these diminishing areas the conditions that pre-existed modern influences.

In Australia, the environment being recreated is dated to 1788, the conservation space–time "boundary . . . put around plants and animals . . . [being the] boundary around the European human" (Head 2012, p. 176). Not only does this dating present troubling, underrecognized racial elements (by associating over 70,000 years of Indigenous history with nonhuman or pristine nature), but it also normalizes widespread violence within the spaces that environmentalists care most about. As Ginn (2008) suggests, "it is the techniques of eco-nationalist-informed conservation that renders certain beings killable and certain savable, rather than any supposed intrinsic value." Pre-European animals and plants are protected and loved, while post-European animals and plants are hunted, trapped, poisoned, infected, weeded, and burned in a nationalist effort to conserve a precolonial Australian landscape and rid it of exotic "aliens" (Subramaniam 2001). Environmental care manifests in practices of violence.

While environmental activists are clearly aware of Indigenous and other human influences within valued landscapes, and while environmental campaigns have spread to urban areas and diversified to cover other issues, the dualisms implicit in the narrative of protecting nature from humans have proved remarkably resilient. There are structural reasons for this. A shift away from this central narrative that has powerful emotive appeal could easily confuse or disillusion urban middle-class supporters and further marginalize environmental groups in political debates. There are also discursive and conceptual barriers, as a popular alternative narrative drawing from post-nature insights has yet to emerge. Concepts circulating in human geography and the environmental humanities like "novel ecologies," "socio-ecological systems," "naturecultures," "more-than-human," and "post-nature" have yet to find much public support within movements that remain anchored to pre-European nature. For Davison (2008), this is a missed opportunity, as his interviews with environmentalists in Australia suggest that many are already grappling with more-than-human ways of thinking. Finally, there is the risk that erasing human/nature dualisms would taint and devalue nonhuman beings and processes, opening them up to further exploitation.

The challenge for environmentalism is to respond to these conceptual and biophysical changes in creative and productive ways. If not, environmental movements will surely lose ground as the logics behind their increasingly convoluted attempts to recapture pre-European environments become difficult to sustain. Some have already realized this, the most significant of which is the high-profile, U.S.-based Breakthrough Institute, which produced the influential *Ecomodernist Manifesto* to guide future human–nature relations.

The manifesto begins by recognizing Earth as a human planet, as "humans are made from the earth and the Earth is remade by human hands" (Asafu-Adjaye et al., 2015, p. 6). However, rather than attempt to do away with the human/nature dualism this recognition would seemingly require, the manifesto seeks to reify or reestablish it by promoting mostly technology-centered solutions that "decouple" humans from nature: "Decoupling raises the possibility that societies might achieve peak human impact without intruding much further on relatively untouched areas. Nature unused is nature spared" (Asafu-Adjaye et al., 2015, p. 19). The converse, of course, is that "unnatural," "touched" species, ecosystems, and landscapes are considered degraded and humanized, and therefore of little value within ecomodernist imaginaries. The world is divided into spaces and species that matter and those that don't. Ecomodernists promote controversial technologies such as geoengineering, genetic modification, and nuclear power as means of decoupling humanity from an imagined nature. However, there is diversity within ecomodernism, with many embracing rewilding and assisted migration, challenging simplistic interpretations of decoupling (Symons 2019; Marris 2011). With traditional green politics floundering in many parts of the world, ecomodernism has become one of the most visible responses to the challenges of the Anthropocene.

In contrast, and in line with the conceptual and biophysical developments that contest the very existence of a humanless nature, I see much more potential in a post-nature environmentalism informed by ecofeminism. At a conceptual level, ecofeminism links the male oppression of women to the human oppression of nonhuman nature, arguing that the liberation of one requires the liberation of the other (Adams & Gruen 2014; Warren 1990; Plumwood 1993). In both cases, exploitation emerges from dualistic thinking—"the process by which contrasting concepts are formed by domination and subordination and constructed as oppositional and exclusive" (Plumwood 1992). Common dualisms include men/women, human/animal, white/non-white, heterosexual/queer, rational/emotional, mind/body, culture/nature. Dualistic thinking is critiqued for positioning one side of each dualism as superior to the other and for normalizing a logic of domination that leads to oppression. By thinking through women and nature together, the shared source of their oppression is clear: the logic of domination that positions them as inferior to their opposites—men and humans. The task of ecofeminism is not so much to remove dualisms as to oppose the logic of domination that oppresses not only women and nonhumans, but also anyone who differs from the stereotypical white Western heterosexual male (Gaard 1997).

This is a substantially different approach from environmental ethics based on the more common rights-based arguments, whose aim is to identify particular traits that make certain nonhumans morally worthy of consideration and, therefore, subjects of rights and responsibilities. Within rights-based approaches, the logic of domination is perpetuated rather than confronted, with the aim being to bring a selection of nonhumans into a position of dominance in relation to others (e.g., sentient creatures–non-sentient creatures, natural ecosystems–novel ecosystems, native species–pest species).

In place of the logic of domination, ecofeminists have explored alternative values and approaches that have been repressed by the privileging of white male masculinities. Feminine values such as empathy (Gruen 2013), compassion (Curtin 2014), joy (Slicer 2014), and care (Donovan & Adams 2007) are promoted as important influences for improved more-than-human relations. As such, ecofeminism is not anchored to a nonhuman nature for relevance, and an ecofeminist world is not divided into human and natural spaces. Instead, it radically transforms how environmental politics is approached, seeing the world with a "loving eye" (Warren 1990) oriented towards thriving socio-ecologies, or naturecultures, across all spaces. Donna Haraway (2008) argues for "an environmentalism committed simultaneously to multispecies coflourishing, heterogeneous collective memory, and complex histories," and to that end, "serious projects are required to build and rebuild livable naturecultures in the future." Such a perspective is necessarily partial and situated, reflective of different socio-ecological contexts wherein what may be appropriate in one place may not be appropriate in another.

Core to an ecofeminist approach, then, is a coming together whereby conversations can take place about the appropriateness of different options guided by overarching principles of compassion and ethics of care for more-than-human communities, rather than by universal rights and rules. The concept of nature or naturalness is not a fulcrum depicting right and wrong, nor are "wilder" places necessarily more valuable than more human ones. By advocating actions that incorporate concerns derived from empathy and compassion, as well as from science and rationality, ecofeminism provides a radically different pathway from those outlined in the *Ecomodernist Manifesto*, one that is arguably much more suited to the ontological and socio-ecological challenges of the Anthropocene.

Environmentalism and Animal Agriculture in Australia

How green politics reinvents itself in the shadow of the Anthropocene has far-reaching consequences for all life on Earth. This is the case particularly for farmed animals, whose swelling populations are of planetary significance. Over 70 billion land-based farmed animals are slaughtered every year (Sanders 2018), with their combined weight comprising 65 percent of the weight of all terrestrial vertebrates on Earth, compared to just three percent for wildlife (Appleby 2008). Chickens are particularly exploited, with more than 65 billion slaughtered every year and the standing population of 23 billion chickens weighing three times as much as do all wild bird species combined (Bennett et al., 2018). The scale of this mass animal slaughter has profound ramifications for environments but has traditionally fallen outside the nature-oriented focus of most Western environmental movements. In this section, I focus on the growth of animal agriculture in Australia to demonstrate how important these spaces are for a reinvigorated environmental activism in the Anthropocene.

While Indigenous peoples in Australia had long-established techniques for herding and hunting native animals (Pascoe 2014), it wasn't until 1788, with the arrival of British settlers who brought cattle, sheep, pigs, goats, turkeys, ducks, and chickens with them, that the roots of contemporary animal agricultural systems were established. Since then, these "creatures of empire" (Andersen 2004) have played a key (but underresearched) role in the invasion/colonization of the country. The relatively high food and water demands of cattle and sheep underpinned the expansion of European settlement across the continent, as the dry soils and vegetation covering much of Australia meant that large amounts of land were required to support relatively small populations of animals.

The result has been the establishment of sprawling sheep and cattle stations across much of the rangelands that often override and/or compete with Indigenous peoples' traditional territories and land claims (Holmes 2002). Many of the atrocities committed under the guise of colonialism stemmed from the land and resource requirements of these pastoral industries. Pastoral exploitation of Aboriginal laborers at Wave Hill and Pilbara sparked the national land rights movement, which transformed settler–Indigenous relations and saw some pastoral leases switching to Indigenous control (Gill 2005). However, huge non-Indigenous pastoral stations remain. Anna Station, for example, is 24,000 km^2, or six million acres, bigger than the state of Israel and about the same size as Rwanda.

Not only were Aboriginal peoples dispossessed, but widespread land clearing also accompanied the creation of agricultural spaces. Some of this was for cropland, including the wheat belt that extends across large parts of eastern and western Australia, but pastoralism is by far the most land-intensive industry. Grazing is now the primary land use for over 57 percent of the continent, a startling amount of land to be devoted to a single industry, and this figure doesn't include the land devoted to feed crops (ACLUMP 2006). The environmental impacts of grazing lands are extensive, being the key driver of land clearing and deforestation, and associated issues such as declines in biodiversity, habitat, species abundance and composition; soil degradation, compaction, and salinity; as well as water degradation and overuse, and the spread of artificial watering points (NLWRA 2001). Land clearing continues today, with recent amendments to biodiversity protection laws in New South Wales sparking a rush to clear bush for agricultural production. A similar spike in clearance occurred in Queensland between 1997 and 1999, when a government-funded initiative saw an estimated annual decline of 446,000 hectares of bushland, the equivalent of a hundred football fields an hour. This resulted in an estimated death toll of over 112 million trees and over 100 million animals, birds, and reptiles each year (Cogger et al., 2003).

Animal agriculture industries, particularly cattle and sheep industries, are also significant contributors to climate change. Direct livestock emissions, primarily from enteric fermentation, or cattle and sheep burps, are officially estimated to comprise 10 percent of Australia's national emissions inventory. This seems low when compared to global estimates of livestock emissions at 14 percent of total emissions (Gerber et al., 2013), particularly as Australia is a major consumer and exporter of red meat. A competing estimate using lifecycle analysis and a twenty-year, rather than hundred-year, timescale estimates livestock industry emissions to make up as much as 50 percent of Australia's emissions (Wedderburn-Bisshop, Longmire, & Rickards 2015).

The Food and Agriculture Organization (2006) argues that the livestock sector is "one of the top two or three most significant contributors to the most serious environmental problems, at every scale from local to global." This is not to say that all forms of animal farming have negative ecological effects; indeed, all sorts of new relations and novel ecosystems have formed, including important bird habitats in the artificial lakes created by pastoralists. As a whole, however, the impacts of the industry on land clearing, methane emissions, biodiversity loss, and soil and water degradation, as well as on the lives of the animals involved, have been devastating for those animals and for pre-existing Indigenous socio-ecologies.

Despite the breadth and depth of these issues, pastoral industries have rarely been the focus of environmental politics or campaigning in Australia. Instead, like North American movements, Australian environmental groups tend to focus on protecting wilderness and wild spaces, perpetuating romantic visions of nature as something distinct from humans and in need of saving. The environmental movement in Australia emerged from bushwalking and mountaineering clubs, often involving urban people who seek an escape from the city, where rural issues were of peripheral interest.

In Hutton and Connors's (1999) expansive history of Australia's environmental movement, rural spaces receive very little attention, less than even urban spaces, where high concentrations of environmentalists are located (see also Mosley 1999; Lines 2006). Hutton and Connors argue that rural issues like soil and water conservation lie at the boundaries of the movement, as rural spaces are considered domesticated spaces and, therefore, of less value or interest than "wild" ones. "Wild" animals who live in rural spaces similarly attract little environmental interest, unless they are threatened species; indeed, they risk being relabeled as "pest" species themselves by being "out of place," with often devastating consequences. For example, native kangaroos and wallabies, who prosper in the rural areas of Australia's degraded rangelands but compete with farmed animals for food, have become the focus of regular state-sanctioned culls/slaughters involving millions of animals (Drew 2017).

The main environmental protection activity in rural spaces is the government's Landcare initiative, a national multibillion-dollar program that has been running since 1990. Landcare seeks to align farmers, communities, and industry in programs broadly aimed at maintaining place-based environmental values. Some environmental groups, particularly the Australian Conservation Foundation, which co-founded Landcare, have been very important in such initiatives; however, rarely has Landcare triggered the passionate activism associated with threats to "wild" spaces. Instead, industry and government support Landcare as it aligns economic interests with improved natural resource management through promises of boosting or sustaining agricultural productivity.

Much like the "wise use" movement in the U.S., the Landcare program treads a post-political line, successfully mobilizing thousands of community groups and bringing together diverse interests oriented towards lessening environmental degradation. Large multinationals, such as Holden, Coca-Cola, Esso and BHP Billiton, Apple, and most of Australia's big banks, are involved in Landcare, partnering with community groups to conserve land while boosting their corporate brands. Environmental action through Landcare is significant and important, but notably noncontroversial—aimed at improving the sustainability of existing operations, something that is presented as being in everyone's interests but may actually be sustaining industries that degrade the values they purport to protect. Animal farmers are positioned as the source of solutions to environmental problems, deflecting attention from more critical questions about the size and desirability of animal farming industries in Australia. While a more radical environmental activism has emerged in rural areas more recently through anti–coal seam gas actions, this again seems oriented more towards perpetuating farm industries than towards challenging them. In the absence of mainstream environmental activism, it has been left to less-resourced animal activist groups like Animals Australia and Animal Liberation to critique animal agriculture industries through protests, bearing witness, direct action, animal rescues, letter-writing campaigns, and lobbying.

Engaging Animal Agriculture: From Matters of Fact to Matters of Care

A key question for this chapter is whether and how environmental movements should engage with animal agriculture industries. There are two arguments that suggest they should. The first, more conventional argument focuses on the calculative impacts these industries are having on "wild" spaces and natural systems. For example, the FAO (2006) has identified livestock industries as key drivers, at a planetary scale, of climate change, air pollution, water depletion and pollution, land degradation and soil exhaustion, deforestation, and biodiversity loss, to which can be added crises of animal abuse, fisheries exhaustion, zoonotic diseases, diseases of affluence, global hunger, and antibiotic resistance (Willett et al., 2019, for comparative impacts of different food types).

As Tony Weis (2013) makes clear in his book *The Ecological Hoofprint,* no other industry is as complicit in so many socio-ecological crises as the livestock industry—or what he more accurately refers to as the industrial-grain-oilseed-livestock complex (IGOLC) in order to capture the energy and feed crops required for the industry (Twine 2013). These impacts are accelerating as the IGOLC expands to new territories, bringing about new technologies, knowledges, and bodies that produce animals more quickly, efficiently, and cheaply through brutal production techniques such as intensive farming. By any conventional measure, then, animal agriculture should be a matter of urgent concern for environmentalists, as an expanding industry with devastating implications for forests, waterways, biodiversity, climate, and other aspects of nature and natural systems (*Livestock's Long Shadow* 2006; Weis 2013).

A second, less conventional argument can be derived from the post-nature perspective introduced at the start of this chapter. If there is no longer a nonhuman nature, the ongoing prioritization of natural spaces within environmental politics makes less sense; instead, environmental concern can be broadened to include a much wider range of environments, including rural ones. In Australia, the rangelands that host large pastoral industries house two thirds of the country's reptiles, almost two thirds of its birds, a half of the frogs, and a third of the mammals (Markus 2009). These animals find homes among a large diversity of domestic and introduced species, including cattle, sheep, cats, foxes, dogs, pigs, rabbits, buffalo, goats, and some of the world's only remaining wild herds of camels. Native grasses compete with introduced ones, kangaroos compete with cattle, dingoes hunt sheep, while farmers care for their dogs, raise cattle and sheep for slaughter, and shoot nonhuman animals who interfere with their farms. Overlaying and interspersed are Indigenous territories, sacred sites, land claims, lives, and dreams. A post-nature perspective brings these dynamic relations into view but distances itself from the environmentalist assumption that the more natural something is, the better it is (Mansfield et al., 2014). For a post-nature environmental politics, it is not the naturalness of relations that matters; rather, it is the types of worlds being produced (see also Haraway 2008, p. 288).

There is overlap between elements of these two arguments; however, there are also clear differences. Which argument is adopted matters for the types of politics embraced and for the multiple actors involved. The first argument favors an environmental politics that addresses the environmental impacts of animal agriculture as "matters of fact" that can be solved by science and technology (Latour 2004b). Facts distance those doing the collecting, transforming environmental issues into objects to be fixed. The aim is to change the facts—to decrease the amount of environmental damage caused by animal agriculture industries. This lends itself to greater engagement with ecomodernist-type reforms aimed at decoupling animal agriculture industries from "wild" nature in order to reduce the industries' ecological hoofprints.

The second argument points to a post-nature politics that approaches the more-than-human assemblages formed through animal agriculture as "matters of care." Following Puig de la Bellacasa (2011), care is considered to be "an affective state, a material vital doing, and an ethico-political obligation" (p. 90), directed towards multiple actors entangled within animal agriculture. This aligns with ecofeminist ethics that are sensitive to the vast array of human and nonhuman interests and agencies involved. Rather than decoupling humans from nature, a post-nature approach opposes the logics of domination that pervade animal agriculture, instead pursuing kinder and more caring socio-ecologies (Engster 2006). These options lead to very different kinds of worlds, the compositions of which will now be briefly compared.

Under the first, more conventional, fact-based approach, animal agriculture industries are condemned for the impacts they are having on Australian nature and broader planetary systems. An ecomodernist solution would be to draw upon science and technology to minimize environmental impacts. While some ecomodernist work promotes alternative proteins such as cultured meat as a solution (Symons 2019), other research has been directed towards more efficient creation of meat through an intensification of production and manipulation of animal bodies to improve growth and minimize environmental impacts (see Swain et al., 2013). Such approaches seek to decouple animal agriculture from its impacts on "wild" nature.

Unfortunately for farmed animals, since they are not considered "wild," they are therefore devoid of intrinsic value within ecomodernist discourse. Calls to intensify cattle production or switch to low-impact industrially produced animals like chickens or pigs make sense from a purely environmental perspective, yet they disregard the lives of the animals involved. This is the dominant response from science, government, and industry when it comes to managing cattle industries in the Anthropocene (McGregor & Houston 2018). It has widespread appeal, as it poses no immediate challenge to existing political ecologies of meat, requires no social or political change, and aligns with established narratives about pastoral stewardship. It also fits the human/nature dualisms underpinning environmental movements, some of which offer tacit support for this approach.

A closer look, however, suggests this approach is unlikely to bring many benefits and will ultimately harm more-than-human rural communities. The FAO (2006) neatly sums up the focus of many such strategies: "[T]he basic principle is to increase the digestibility of feedstuff, either by modifying feed or by manipulating the digestive process" (p. 120). With increased digestibility, farmed animals grow more quickly and can be slaughtered earlier. Their shorter lifespans are expected to result in less severe environmental impacts—they simply have less time to eat, drink, burp, defecate, etc. The majority of farmed animals in Australia—particularly chickens and pigs—are now raised in intensive production facilities, while an increasing percentage of cattle finish their lives in feedlots. Of course, ecomodernist arguments like those of Swain et al. (2013) are not the main driver of factory farms; instead, capitalist logics aimed at producing cheap, standardized meat out of the sight of most consumers have resulted in these spaces of abuse (Nibert 2017). However, ecomodernism can add a further layer of legitimacy to them.

The environmental gains from moving more animals into such systems come at a tremendous cost to more-than-human rural communities. Despret and Meuret (2016) liken intensification to extinction, as the socio-ecologies animals inhabit are transformed into something much more brutal:

> Extinction begins when the world to which an animal was associated is reduced to nothing, or almost nothing. Extinction begins when the ways an animal composes the world and composes with the world are ended, when the ways he or she makes a world exist, according to the ways his or her ancestors had created it, have disappeared. (p. 29)

As animal activists have long argued, these are spaces of suffering, hidden from public view, where animal freedoms are severely curtailed, and where horrific acts of violence are committed in production and slaughtering that would be criminalized if inflicted on other animals (Singer 1975; Harrison 1966). When production and slaughter spaces do become public, they are often sources of outrage, as evident in the widespread opposition to the live export of cattle and sheep (Dalziell & Wadiwel 2016), as well as in exposés of Australian slaughterhouses and factory farms (Mummery & Rodan 2017).

There are also costs to rural communities. First are the impacts of intensification on farm and slaughterhouse workers who must participate in acts of mass cruelty on a daily basis, often for low pay and in relatively poor conditions. Research suggests that such workers are exposed to physical and psychological harm, experiencing a "shared suffering" with the animals, and are subsequently more likely to act violently and commit crimes in their own lives (Porcher 2010; Richards, Signal, & Taylor 2013; Fitzgerald, Kalof, & Dietz 2009).

Secondly, a less discussed side to intensification is the fact that it would have a positive environmental impact only if factory farming replaced extensive grazing systems. If the two continued to operate side by side as they do now, intensification would simply result in more animals being produced, with a net increase in environmental impacts. Intensification fundamentally alters farmer–animal relations such that "animals are seen as 'units,' the unproductive or underproductive ones are gassed or electrocuted to death, virility serves as a substitute for thought, compassion is a matter of professional misconduct, and moral values must be sacrificed in the name of productivity" (Porcher 2010, p. 14). The caring forms of animal husbandry some writers have suggested might have some place in an ecofeminist politics (Plumwood 2012; Engster 2006) have no role in intensive animal production systems, "where sensitivity, affection and intelligence have no place" (Porcher 2010, p. 14).

The expansion of intensive farming is likely to further consolidate power among large industry players, forcing out smaller farmers who cannot compete with the production efficiency of capital-intensive livestock production systems. Hence, while the intensification of livestock production systems may bring some environmental benefits by relieving grazing lands, it also intensifies the suffering of animals, farmers, and residents of rural towns, while also requiring an expansion of land and energy devoted to feed crops to fuel what is a very inefficient food production system (Weis 2013). This seems a high price to pay for marginal environmental improvements.

By contrast, if the socio-ecological impacts of animal agriculture are approached as a matter of care rather than a matter of fact, a different pathway unfolds. Rather than calculating the impacts of different technologies on an imaginary nature as the key criterion for adjudicating between different approaches (Mansfield et al., 2014), an ecofeminist ethic of care asks what sorts of convivial relations can be nurtured in rural spaces to enable multispecies flourishing. By opposing the logic of domination that normalizes human domination of nonhumans, as well as the prioritizing of native animals over domestic animals, an ecofeminist ethic of care brings the lives of farmed animals firmly into focus. They are seen as lively beings embedded in the webs of relations that create worlds, rather than as objects for human consumption whose values are only realized at death (Colombino & Giaccaria 2016). Practicing care for these lively socio-ecologies means exploring strategies that enable the flourishing of more-than-human communities, including cattle, sheep, farmers, dingoes, kangaroos, cats, dogs, grasses, frogs, birds, gullies, rivers, savannas, sacred spaces, Indigenous peoples, and many other entities. From this viewpoint, the desirability of animal agriculture industries that cause so much harm by raising and then killing animals for their flesh is much more questionable.

The need to shift away from the logics of domination pervading animal agriculture has led many ecofeminists to advocate contextual veganism, which sees veganism, rather than carnism (Joy 2010), as the default position, while accepting that there may be contextual variations to this practice (Twine 2014), particularly in relation to Indigenous communities (Yandarra Collective, this volume). A contextual vegan response provides a means of practicing a politics of care for the more-than-human communities entangled in animal agriculture. If environmental groups were to adopt a more compassionate post-nature lens, the pursuit of further intensification of animal agriculture would make little sense when compared with a future in which those spaces and practices were avoided altogether. The spaces of suffering associated with intensive and extensive animal agriculture could be replaced with spaces of regeneration involving a broad range of species. If managed well, this could increase the habitat available while reducing the diverse array of environmental pressures exerted by animal agriculture industries. New relations would need to form between humans and cattle, sheep, goats, pigs, and chickens—relations in which ecofeminist principles of care and compassion can provide a vehicle to guide decision-making. This could lead to an expansion of the creative relations already practiced in animal sanctuaries, while new partnerships could potentially involve cattle in convivial soil carbon or soil fertilization projects.

There are, of course, hardships associated with such approaches, particularly for communities currently reliant upon animal agriculture. While some of these communities may find opportunities in expanded plant-based food industries, many rangeland areas are unsuitable for cropping. Research remains to be done on the full impacts on rural communities and how best to mitigate them in compassionate and caring ways, but this aspect could involve land stewardship and carbon sequestration opportunities and would certainly be part of an ecofeminist response (see also Holmes 2002).

Towards Vegan Environmentalism

As mainstream environmental movements have striven for legitimacy and influence, they have become increasingly fact-driven. This has led to what Maarten Hajer (1989) terms the "discursive crisis of environmentalism," whereby the alternative ideas and values that attract many to the movement get converted into more recognizable, anthropocentric arguments legitimized by scientific facts (see also McGregor 2004). In some ways, this also reflects the changing nature of environmental issues, as local, place-based campaigns oriented towards protecting forests or rivers now compete with much larger issues, like climate change, that are difficult to know or grasp without recourse to scientific knowledge. The shift away from place-based issues and towards planetary ones is also a shift away from an embodied, felt politics in which emotion, intuition, and attachment play a large part, towards a more detached, rational politics driven by the calculation and modeling of various scenarios. It is not surprising, for example, that a global climate change movement rallied around the name 350.org—epitomizing the science, rationality, and modeling that underpin contemporary environmentalism. In this context, ecomodernism looms large in the mainstream future of the movement.

The problem with this is that environmental politics has become mobilized around matters of fact, as opposed to matters of concern (Latour 2004b) or matters of care (Puig de la Bellacasa 2011). Facts illuminate and obscure. Facts are amassed by environmentalists to protect nature and to legitimize particular practices that will help rehabilitate or even improve nature. Facts also distance—separating the fact maker, or the scientist, from the issue being studied, objectifying issues, and reinforcing human/nature dualisms rather than working through multiple relationalities. It is for this reason that some ecomodernists have taken an interest in geoengineering and genetic modification, positioning climate and agriculture as objects that can be manipulated as part of a process of decoupling humans from nature. Nature is seen as inert and controllable through science and technology—perpetuating science's feminization of nature (Merchant 1980). Nature remains fragile and vulnerable, in need of saving by the masculine calculations of environmental science. Intensification of animal agriculture makes (some) factual sense within this narrative, but intensifying relations of domination to further exploit human and nonhuman animals makes little compassionate sense.

By contrast, ecofeminism approaches environmental issues as matters of care. By opposing the logic of domination that flows through human/nature, native/non-native, and rational/emotional dualisms, ecofeminism strives for compassionate and empathetic responses to socio-ecological challenges, pursuing means of helping more-than-human communities thrive rather than capital-intensive, technological solutions that maintain the status quo. Emotional, quasi-spiritual relations with more-than-human communities pervade many of the foundational texts of environmental movements (see, for example, Leopold 1949; Thoreau 1854; Carson 1962), and yet these felt relations are becoming abandoned as environmentalism becomes increasingly fact-driven.

The challenge ecofeminism poses to environmentalists is to extend the visceral love of nature readily exhibited in and for wilderness spaces to more obviously domesticated spaces. Just as managed wilderness is celebrated for its dynamic, diverse multispecies interactions, so, too, can rural and urban spaces. The same compassion exhibited towards frogs and quolls can be exhibited towards cows and pigs. This is not to denigrate or ignore facts but to elevate emotion, intuition, empathy, and compassion to the same level as facts. Increasingly futile attempts to protect nonhuman nature can be replaced by an environmentalist agenda aimed at worlding convivial socio-ecological relations oriented towards multispecies flourishing. Facts and science matter in this pursuit, but so do intuition and empathy. However, intensifying animal agriculture for environmental gains has no place in this vision.

The politics that emerges from an ecofeminist approach includes the practice of contextual veganism. Veganism provides a form of prefigurative politics opposed to the logics of domination that underpin animal exploitation—a politics that can be practiced at a household, community, or broader scale (Véron 2016; White 2017). It is a generative practice that seeks to minimize human and nonhuman suffering. In the case of food and agriculture, this includes innovations in plant-based foods and the production of vegan spaces and places. For environmentalists, veganism is both the most rationally effective way to respond to the environmental ills of animal agriculture and the kindest, most compassionate way. While farming industries may disagree based on the hardships this option possibly implies for some rural communities, the alternative—intensification of animal farming—incurs similar, if not worse, problems for rural communities, as intensification replaces traditional animal husbandry.

There are, of course, considerable risks for environmental groups in promoting vegan politics. The most substantial risk is to the mainstream appeal of many contemporary environmental movements. If poorly managed and communicated, veganism could be seen as too extreme a position to take and could alienate supporters. Certainly, it would add fire to conservative attacks on environmental groups. However, environmental organizations have proud histories of controversy and have rallied public support behind the opposition to iconic and powerful industries such as coal mining and nuclear power. In their favor is the heightened and growing public awareness about the environmental impacts of animal farming industries, something that environmental organizations are only beginning to engage with in their campaigns. This would certainly make environmental organizations more consistent with their missions and empower supporters to take immediate action in their everyday lives to address issues they are concerned about. Most people have the option of minimizing animal products in their lives, while fewer have the option of avoiding fossil fuels.

Vegan environmentalism also enables the building of important alliances with animal rights movements, in line with the broader work on total liberation that seeks to oppose all forms of oppression (Glasser 2015). The total liberation framework seeks to build a broad socio-ecological movement, uniting the currently fractured social movement landscape. Vegan praxis provides common ground for animal and environmental groups to forge those types of alliances, together opposing the logic of domination that exploits animals, workers, *and* environments. While animal and environmental movements have overlapped occasionally in the past—on anti-whaling and anti-sealing campaigns, for example (Kemmerer & Kirjner 2015)—an unnecessary socio-spatial division of labor has emerged whereby environmental groups focus predominantly on protecting "natural" spaces and systems, while animal rights organizations focus on spaces of animal suffering in rural and urban environments. Closer alliances can strengthen both movements in terms of strategy, campaigning, resources, reach, and outcomes for human and nonhuman animals and environments. For example, while animal rights campaigns are strong on immediately visible examples of human–animal cruelty, they say very little about the indirect animal suffering associated with cropping and habitat destruction (Fazzino, this volume). Building on the two movements' shared anti-anthropocentrism can provide fertile grounds for discussion and collaboration, as opposed to reification and amplification of difference (Luke 1995).

For vegan environmentalism to be successful, such alliances and associated strategies need to be built. How this is done is beyond the scope of this chapter, but such an endeavor should take into account Dominick's (2015) recent critique of veganism for its lack of strategy. Personal commitments to animal-product avoidance that do not challenge broader hierarchies of power are unlikely to contribute much to bringing about flourishing multispecies socio-ecologies. The animal rights rationalities underpinning much of vegan praxis can act against a broadening of care into all areas of exploitation. Vegan products are not cruelty-free—they may be created with minimal animal suffering; however, other socio-ecological oppressions may be apparent in the procurement of factory or plantation labor or in the production of artificial meats and other plant-based foods.

For this reason, veganism should be pursued contextually rather than as a universal absolute. It should form a default practice for concerned environmentalists, unless there is a compelling and compassionate reason to act otherwise. Dominick (2015) suggests veganism (and anarchism) should be seen as not "do-or-die, go-for-broke ideologies, but rather constellations of values and principles helping us plot our way to a better future" (p. 27). It is with this more reflexive approach that vegan environmentalism can offer much to environmental politics: by broadening the scope of environmental concern to better incorporate rural spaces; by reinforcing the importance of care and compassion, alongside statistics and facts, in decision-making; and by providing accessible and empowering everyday practices for activists to oppose the logics of domination that are inflicting destructive violence on human and nonhuman animals and their environments.

Acknowledgments

I would like to acknowledge the feedback I received on an earlier draft of this chapter from Dr Jon Symons.

10

INFILTRATE THE CITYSCAPES

Resisting Speciesist Segregation with Farmed Animals

Darren Chang

Introduction

This chapter centers the urbanized environment as a key battleground in an ongoing war against nonhuman animals. The war I conceptualize here is a settler-colonial-capitalist war, one in which humans continually exercise sovereign power to dominate other animals (Wadiwel 2015). The relation between capitalism and animals is broadly understood within this context as the institutionalized and systematic ways in which human societies and economies are organized to objectify and commodify animals in order to justify instrumentalizing and exploiting them in pursuit of maximum profit (White 2017, pp. 273–276). The settler-coloniality of this war is understood from an Indigenous position, wherein "animal domestication, speciesism, and other modern human–animal interactions are only possible because of and through the historic and ongoing erasure of Indigenous bodies and the emptying of Indigenous lands for settler-colonial expansion" (Belcourt 2015, p. 3). Taken together, processes of settler colonialism and capitalism are not one-off events; rather, they form enduring structures that aim to continually acquire territories and accumulate wealth through capitalist development, while simultaneously exercising violence against Indigenous populations (Coulthard 2014, p. 125; Wolfe 2006, p. 388).[1]

Situated within a settler-colonial-capitalist war against animals, cities built for humans by humans are structurally anthropocentric and speciesist.

1. The original version of this chapter was submitted as a Major Research Paper in partial fulfillment of the requirements of the Master of Arts degree in the Department of Political Studies at Queen's University, Kingston, Ontario, in August 2017, under the supervision of Dr. Will Kymlicka.

Anthropocentrism refers to a human-centered worldview that privileges human interests and experiences over the lives of those of all other species; speciesism is "a belief that human beings are superior to all other animals, condoning human use and domination over animals because we humans rank above them—either spiritually or biologically" (Taylor 2017, p. 84). As such, speciesist and anthropocentric cities exist as structures and spaces designed with little to no regard for the interests and lived experiences of other animals, while continually reproducing violence against animals through conquest, occupation, and domination. The living spaces of many animals are conquered and destroyed for the sake of cities through outward-expanding processes like urban sprawl and pollution, as well as through the inward flow of resources extracted to be used and consumed by human populations. This "anthropocentric biopolitical colonialism" exceptionalizes humans as not-animals and dismisses animals as not-persons, in order to justify humans' claims of land and space as oppose to animals' (Narayanan 2017, pp. 478, 490).

Whether it's indirect or direct, intentional or unintentional, humans design specific structures to exert violence against animals, resulting in physical harms or deprivations. Architecture in its essence exercises power over bodies due to the way it dissects space to spatially organize bodies and can, therefore, be "conceived or instrumentalized as a political weapon," whether we are conscious of it or not (Lambert 2012, p. 11; Lambert 2016, p. 6). Many examples of architecture weaponized against animals exist in the city: pigeon spikes, roads and other dangerous transportation systems, reflective windows that millions of birds crash into, swimming pools where animals frequently drown, and pet stores and animal laboratories filled with cages and tanks, just to name a few.

Anthropocentric cities deprive animals of their chances to flourish, and pose all sorts of potentially fatal hazards. I argue that for farmed animals and other animals used and consumed by humans, besides the obvious places of killing and exploitation (such as farms and slaughterhouses), stores, restaurants, and even freezers and refrigerators can be understood as political weapons against animal bodies. These instruments and structures continue to dissect spaces and organize animal bodies even after their bodies have been mutilated, processed, and commodified for consumption, thereby serving to continually reconstitute animals as objects, commodities, and property. These further reinforce the "everyday enactment of violence against animal bodies" that has been made ubiquitously invisible in our lives (Collard & Gillespie 2015, p. 209).

With this context in mind, I aim to imagine possibilities of how cities can be remade and transformed from weapons that endanger animal lives to hospitable places where animals can thrive and flourish. In terms of architectural design to make cities friendlier to animals, much of the work has already been underway.

For example, The Expanded Environment (ExEn, formerly Animal Architecture) is a nonprofit organization "devoted to demonstrating alternate ways of responsibly and synthetically integrating biological and ecological agents into the built world" (ExEn, n.d.). Organizations such as ExEn assist various levels of government, as well as organizations, businesses, and individuals to "understand, appreciate and envision a more productive relationship between architectural and biological systems" (ExEn, n.d.).

Despite these efforts, to merely redesign and rearrange our lived environment with an understanding of how architecture can be weaponized would, on its own, fail to offer an adequate "solution" without the necessary constant resistance against oppression within existing conditions (Lambert 2012, p. 166). As I am not an architect, I offer here some theoretical considerations regarding how human and nonhuman animals can interact with each other in radically different relationships across spaces and places, thus enabling nonhumans to play a greater role in a liberation project that is centered on their lives.

To narrow down the scope of my analysis, I focus primarily on terrestrial farmed animals in the context of Western liberal-democratic societies. Here, humans have made farmed animals mostly invisible in urbanized cityscapes by declaring their presence illegal. Unless the dwelling or visiting animals served to further their own exploitation by humans (e.g., as backyard chickens, petting zoo animals, or a means of proliferating the livestock industry's propaganda), most farmed animals exist in cities only as already killed and processed pieces of commodity. However, the analysis presented within this context should also be applicable to cities where farmed animal presence in urban spaces is the norm, because within the framework of a global war waged by humans against animals, all farmed animals exist to be exploited and killed regardless of location and visibility. For instance, Alice Hovorka (2008) observes and argues that while chickens dwelling in urban cities and towns in Botswana exist as influential actors possessing the agency to shape human–animal relationships, their presence and visibility have not been sufficient to stop humans from intensively slaughtering them (p. 111).

In the next section, I reconceptualize the identities of farmed animals with theories of animal resistance to open up possibilities for human–nonhuman solidarities. The section following summarizes critical perspectives on sanctuaries for human asylum seekers and on farmed animal sanctuaries (FASes), by Jennifer J. Bagelman and by Sue Donaldson and Will Kymlicka, respectively. Together, their critical insights elucidate the limitations and challenges that sanctuaries face. Given the challenges highlighted in this section, the one after that examines real cases of farmed animals (and their humans) living in urban spaces who are forced to confront speciesist segregation. Finally, I explore how we can resist and dismantle the existing legal and geographical conditions that restrict farmed animal agency and autonomy, reinforce their lower sociopolitical status, and justify enduring violence against them. I suggest that practices of prefiguratively organizing and building a solidarity city can be productive frameworks with which to approach animal liberation, and that establishing farmed animal presence can be a crucial step in the struggle to create animal-friendly, anti-speciesist cities.

Reframing the Identities of Farmed Animals

Who are farmed animals in the context of war? If they need sanctuaries, can we consider them nonhuman asylum seekers and refugees? I suggest that farmed animals take on many simultaneous identities from moment to moment, depending on how they may be confronting human hostility: they are victims and survivors, captives and prisoners, asylum seekers and refugees, fugitives and escapees, and in some instances, combatants defending their own lives. Ultimately, these identity categories exist more to allow humans to conceptualize and clarify our relations to them than to matter to the animals themselves. Regardless of which of the above identities may be more salient in a given situation, resistance against hostile surroundings is the crucial thread that ties them together.

The concept of resistance I deploy here is informed primarily by two frameworks. First, Sarat Colling argues for an "animals without borders" framework of animal resistance, which builds on an accumulation of knowledge from past studies on animal resistance across historical, geographical, and cognitive ethological knowledge (pp. 30–47). By emphasizing animals' agency to resist and the need for animal advocates to build solidarity with them, "animals without borders" dismantles not only the conceptual divide between the arbitrarily constructed superior human and inferior animal, but also the physical and material barriers dividing humans and animals, such as geographical borders, private properties, and walls and fences (Colling 2013, pp. 47–48, 52).

"Animals without borders" is rooted in decolonial transnational feminist thought, practicing a "from below" method that writes history from the viewpoints of the oppressed and that refuses to allow oppressed humans to be pitted against other oppressed humans or animals by privileging some over others (Colling 2013, pp. 48, 50). Crucially, this last aspect allows for both humans and other animals to share the embodiment of those identities mentioned above and to understand how both oppressed groups can mutually resist and fight back against the material and metaphorical borders exerting violence against them. To illustrate how farmed animals put the "animals without borders" framework into action, Colling recounts numerous stories of farmed animal escapes from slaughterhouses.

Second, Dinesh Wadiwel (2015) offers a framework of animal resistance by directing our attention to the violent technologies and apparatuses "designed precisely to counter resistance" (p. 11). Wadiwel notes that if the animals "were not sentient, autonomous and [did not evade] capture and utilization in the first place," then there would be no need to design technologies and weapons aimed at putting down resistance (2015, p. 10). Temple Grandin's curved corral design, well known for lubricating the process of leading bovines to slaughter, or the low lighting used to weaken chickens' vision to reduce their likelihood of struggle are examples of how these technological designs attempt to stymie animal resistance (p. 11). Since the creators of technologies of violence must "constantly innovate to find ways to make the slaughter of animals smoother," they often adapt to animals' creative resistances by using "animals and their own bodies against themselves" (pp. 12–13). Within capitalist processes of production, these technologies always try to capture the productive creativity of bodies through discipline and subordination (p. 14). Through this analysis, Wadiwel argues that "extreme forms of domination that appear to lack resistance are in fact the product of active forms of creative resistance by those who are subordinated," as the capitalist mode of production always adaptively innovates itself by coopting resistance (p. 14).

Colling and Wadiwel's analyses are central to shifting both the relational and spatial dimensions of human–nonhuman interactions within animal movements. Analyses of animal resistance form the necessary foundation for thinking about how humans and animals can be co-participants in resisting and organizing against human domination. Acknowledging that animals are in fact autonomous agents who do resist, the animal resistance framework holds arguably the most potential to overcome the perniciously prevalent savior discourse within animal movements that delimits animals as voiceless victims, whose liberation can be realized only if humans save them by speaking for them or acting on their behalf.

Lauren Corman (2016) has extensively tackled this issue of voice and the problem of speaking for others in animal advocacy work. Voice can be understood as "the ability to define and assert one's subjectivity, or the power to have one's subjectivity recognized by those who refuse it" (p. 486). Given that "voice is wedded to political agency and resistance," disrupting discourse that paints animals as voiceless enables us to "articulate a form of coalition politics" that transcends "a construction of animals as passive victims to a foregrounding of animals as subjects, and in relation, as agents who can also resist" (pp. 496–497).

This articulation of voice and resistance allows humans fighting for animals to recognize other animals as fellow activists with whom we must consult and dialogue. The stories of animal escapes are powerful narratives of resistance that allow humans and nonhumans to build solidarity and reject the savior narratives that frame animals as voiceless and powerless (Colling 2013, pp. 39, 110). Recognizing other animals as resistance fighters or war resisters enables the humans fighting alongside them to act as *accomplices*, who are "realized through mutual consent" and trust building, as opposed to *allies*, who may advertently or inadvertently coopt a struggle to prioritize other aims or agendas (Indigenous Action Media 2014). By definition, being an accomplice in the context of a political struggle for justice would involve assisting others in committing crimes to break unjust laws if necessary. The position of an accomplice is vital in the prefigurative organizing strategy to be discussed later.

On the relational front, recognizing animal resistance and voice also contests the ambassador identity of escaped or rescued farmed animals. Within farmed animal sanctuary communities, it is common for formerly farmed animals to be characterized as ambassadors, who now represent other farmed animals by demonstrating their social, behavioral, cognitive, and emotional complexities, thus showcasing what countless animals' lives could have been if humans had not subjected them to violence and exploitation. As a means to challenge the dominant discourse that depicts farmed animals as lacking the aforementioned complexities, animal advocates tend to assert that in fact, farmed animals are, for example, kind, gentle, and intelligent beings (Colling 2013, p. 57). This type of counter-discourse "might actually re-colonize those beings defined," as it "freezes nonhuman animals as objects of knowledge production, excluding those who don't fit the representation" (p. 57).

While becoming an ambassador may not be inherently undesirable to a nonhuman animal, and a politics of representation is difficult to avoid given that to some extent we all represent others with whom we share similar identities and experiences, it is nonetheless important to recognize rescued animals as first and foremost individuals with their own unique experiences and relationships. Moving beyond ambassadorship also further disrupts the savior narratives extended to rescued animals, suggesting that through representation, they can help save others still held captive in exploitation. Being a representative or savior should not be considered a main attribute or purpose of an animal. Rescued animals have become primarily members of communities or participants in political movements. The central tasks of formerly farmed animals involve co-authoring new narratives and co-shaping new futures with those who support them, simply by living their lives in ways that can radically challenge and restructure the institutions, relationships, and environments they share with humans so that, eventually, no more animals require saving.

On the spatial front, Colling and Wadiwel's analyses of animal resistance show that the dominant relationship between animals and human-built surroundings is one of constant transgression by the animals, and persistent adaptation to restrict or confine on the part of the humans. In this troubling context, we must think carefully about the uneasy positions and roles of farmed animal sanctuaries. Rural areas and agricultural zones are the primary places where farmed animals live, invisible to urban consumers as they endure exploitation before slaughter. Yet these same rural areas also happen to be the only places where farmed animals are legally permitted to live after they have escaped or been rescued, because they have been barred from living in urban areas. The zoning bylaws have, in a sense, confined and limited the visibility of farmed animal sanctuaries, which in turn reimpose these limits on their rescued animal residents. The next part offers some critical perspectives on sanctuaries operating within these legal and geographical limitations.

Critical Perspectives on Sanctuary Cities and Farmed Animal Sanctuaries

In *Sanctuary City: A Suspended State* (2016), Bagelman's central critique challenges "the dominant discursive framing of sanctuary as a 'positive' practice," and she argues that asylum seekers are often trapped in a "suspended state of deferral" by "the soft and seemingly innocuous hand of sanctuary" (pp. 5, 7). While sanctuaries are commonly (and correctly) understood as protected spaces, portraying them only as such allows advocates to set up dichotomous oppositions of sanctuaries versus camps (e.g., detention centers), zones of peace versus zones of hostility, and absolute security versus insecurity, all of which may conceal underlying issues within sanctuaries (pp. 23–24). Many asylum seekers and refugees residing in sanctuary cities feel that they have been trapped within a "cycle of waiting," whereby they experience "a sense of dependency, uselessness and invisibility" at the mercy of charity (pp. 30, 31). These asylum seekers have neither access to basic services and housing due to the rejection of their refugee status nor the right to work. As a result, the support of sanctuary is generally regarded by asylum seekers as a necessary good, but accepting charity while being forced to wait for an eventual citizenship that may never materialize has left them in an indefinite state of suspension (pp. 31, 42).

In Glasgow, which currently hosts the largest population of human asylum seekers among sanctuary cities in the U.K., asylum seekers have brought their frustrations with the temporal and spatial dimensions of their suspended lives to the surface through enacted plays and mapping projects. In one example, asylum seekers wrote and performed a play entitled *The Roundabout*, in which they reenacted their recurrent discontent from being forced to endure weeks of deferred appointments for medical and legal assistance in bureaucratic circuits, simply because they had "plenty of time" to wait (Bagelman 2016, p. 33). The play took the form of a forum theater, which resists turning the actors into mere spectacles and instead interacts with the audience to incite uneasiness as a means to demand action (pp. 31–32).

In another example, sanctuary city organizers in Glasgow held a community mapping event for which refugees and asylum seekers were asked to draw their experiences of Glasgow in the form of maps. The unexpected results posed a direct challenge to the idealized conceptions of an open sanctuary city. Several maps showed a limited number of very specific locations (e.g., a drop-in center, bus station, shopping center, school); some used arrows to indicate a full day's journey through these places; and almost all of them either measured the travel distance from one location to another by time or included the typical amount of time spent at a given location (pp. 50–53). With squiggly lines representing separation from areas beyond which asylum seekers did not travel, labyrinth-like structures with arrows pointing to dead ends, or identifiable "off-limits" and "scary" places, these maps revealed asylum seekers' sense of being trapped within and constrained by small circuits (pp. 50–53).

The play and the mapping project exemplify unsettling *interruptions* to a politics of ease, a politics whereby sanctuary cities discipline asylum seekers through "a kind of temporal governance" (Bagelman 2016, p. 61). Governing temporally goes beyond controlling physical borders and involves holding subjects "through a temporal extension," protracting precariousness and unpredictability, all the while imposing illusions of hope to appease them (pp. 46, 61). Sanctuary cities invite asylum seekers within this state of suspension to become good aspirational citizens through supplicatory or ritual-like routines, while simultaneously denying them full citizenship (p. 97). The interruptions problematize the perceived innocence of sanctuary cities as alternatives to hostile state apparatuses and present opportunities to challenge sanctuary cities as disciplinary technologies; they embody a refusal of asylum seekers to submit to the "soft yet restricting sanctuary promise: don't worry, hold on, and just wait" (p. 101).

Problematizing Farmed Animal Sanctuaries

In their critical discussions on the political role of farmed animal sanctuaries (FASes), Sue Donaldson and Will Kymlicka (2015) argue for FASes to transition towards an Intentional Community (IC) model from the standard Refuge + Advocacy (R+A) model. Since the beginning of the farm sanctuary movement, FASes have operated within a model that prioritized efforts to assist and advocate for farmed animals by committing to specific principles and practices:

1. Rehabilitate and care for animals who have suffered from abuse, abandonment, and exploitation by individual humans or the animal agriculture industry;
2. Ensure rescued residents can flourish according to their species-typical behaviors and activities;
3. Recognize and respect each animal as an individual with a unique personality and subjective conception of their own good.
4. Refrain from any activities that can be considered exploitative, such as the use and sale of, or other commercial activities involving, animals.
5. Prevent further reproduction among rescued animals in order to dedicate already limited resources to the overwhelming population of currently existing animals in need of rescue.
6. Raise awareness about farmed animal cruelty in the agriculture industry through public education and engagement, using social media, outreach, and sanctuary visitation programs whereby human visitors can learn about the animal residents, who act as "ambassadors" for fellow members of their species who still suffer from exploitation and violence in the animal–industrial complex (pp. 51–52).

Although these principles associated with the R+A model are often grounded in and carried out with the best intentions of sanctuary directors and caregivers, they risk reproducing patterns of power asymmetries and injustices between human caregivers and animal residents. This concern is grounded in power dynamics similar to those found in a wide range of "total institutions" for humans, such as asylums, orphanages, prisons, shelters (for the homeless or for women and children escaping domestic violence), retirement homes, and refugee camps (Donaldson & Kymlicka 2015, p. 56). The specific concern is that in upholding these principles, animal caregivers could become overly paternalistic, such that they could either intentionally or unintentionally infringe upon the rights of animal residents by overlooking residents' individual interests and preferences. There are four main areas of concern wherein animal residents' interests might be traded off in the R+A model:

1. The freedom to associate with any members of their communities, including those of other species.

2. The freedom and desire to reproduce and raise offspring.
3. The motivation to explore a diverse range of environments to enrich their lives.
4. The drive to participate in various forms of work and become contributing members of their communities (pp. 55–63).

The overall concern here can be summarized as the difficulty in finding a just balance between protecting animal residents and possibly restricting their freedom and autonomy on the one hand, and enabling the animals' agency and allowing them to take risks to explore and form their own preferences in their lives on the other. Similar concerns regarding paternalistic patterns existing in human sanctuary cities further validate this transspecies problem.

In response to this potential curtailment of the rights and freedoms of animal residents in FASes, existing examples of ICs for disabled humans demonstrate possible alternatives. ICs are guided by "principles of shared membership and non-hierarchical social relations" (Donaldson & Kymlicka 2015, pp. 64–66). Some main guiding principles upheld within ICs may include:

1. A mutual sense of belonging between residents and the community, whereby residents and community belong to each other on a permanent basis.
2. Non-hierarchical relations between members, wherein residents are all simultaneously giving care and being cared for in differing contexts, as "friends, family, coworkers, neighbors, employees/employers, co-citizens, etc."
3. Self-determination for residents to develop their own subjective, individualized conceptions of their wellbeing through the least restrictive opportunities to explore their preferences.
4. Citizenship for residents, whereby they are recognized as active citizens with the right to participate in determining matters affecting their lives, as opposed to being treated as wards to be merely protected and provided for.
5. Exercise of dependent agency by residents, whereby those more dependent on others' assistance to enact their agency are supported through communication with other community members who are most responsive to their subjective needs and preferences.
6. "Scaffolded choices and reconfigured space," with the exercise of agency by dependent individuals beginning within safe and secure spaces most

meaningful and intelligible to them, allowing them to gradually explore new opportunities (pp. 64–66).

I largely agree with Donaldson and Kymlicka's critiques of the standard R+A model of animal sanctuaries, and I support their proposed IC alternative. However, my main concern with FASes is the impact they may or may not have on broader society, which is a concern Donaldson and Kymlicka raise but do not sufficiently address. There are numerous worries regarding the impact and effectiveness of FASes in the advocacy work they do. For one, FASes are established almost exclusively in rural areas distant from and invisible to most of the humans who actively participate in the daily violence against farmed animals, namely humans who dwell in dense urban or suburban areas. Due to FASes' limited exposure, lack of meaningful relationships with broader society, and the attributes they share with total institutions, they can also be considered what Timothy Pachirat (2011) describes as zones of confinement, existing in segregation and isolation, largely inaccessible to broader society (p. 4). While there are many practical reasons as to why FASes are located predominantly in rural, agricultural communities, such as proximity to necessary infrastructures for animal housing, access to food and other supplies, and access to veterinary expertise for farmed animals, one of the most problematic of those reasons is that agricultural zones are "where current zoning laws create a legal opening" for farmed animals to exist (p. 51).

Due to structural and legal restrictions forcing farmed animals to live in rural areas, there is a deep worry about how such segregation could "reinforce assumptions about where farmed animals belong, what forms of society and behavior are 'natural' for them," as well as what their relationships with humans should look like (Donaldson & Kymlicka 2015, p. 54). As a result, segregation reproduces limited conceptions of farmed animals' capacities, interests, and sociopolitical status, which all contribute to a failure to "disrupt ideas of human–animal hierarchy" (p. 54). In fact, the entire "history of industrialized agriculture is a history of the gradual separation of domesticated animals from human spaces," through bylaws that increasingly restricted, confined, and regulated animals and their bodies and made animals invisible, "from the center to the periphery of urban areas" (Donaldson & Kymlicka 2011, p. 113).

The microsanctuary movement has sprung up in response to these problems. According to the movement's co-founder, Justin Van Kleeck, one of its primary goals is to "demystify farmed animals" by integrating rescued individuals into life in suburbia in an attempt to establish relationships between humans and formerly farmed animals within the household, similar to the current relationships between humans and their cat, dog, or other nonhuman family members (Donaldson &

Kymlicka 2015, p. 54). Even with the microsanctuary movement, however, there is no explicit challenging of the speciesist segregation laws in place that dictate where farmed animals can live. Presumably, even in "suburbia," most of the areas where microsanctuaries currently exist either already legally permit certain farmed animals (e.g., backyard chickens) for the purpose of exploitation or are perhaps the denser parts of a rural region where human residents are allowed to run hobby farms.

If these segregationist laws remain unchallenged, they will pose similar impediments to FASes that seek to attain citizenship rights and status for their animal residents, whether they follow the R+A or the IC model. Under current zoning laws, all farmed animals at best remain second-class citizens restricted to a set of social relations and ways of life and confined to one particular geographic area or, at worst, remain illegal, killable beings subjected to forced removal or capture when they attempt to escape agricultural zones.

However, by definition, ICs may not have the dismantling of oppressive borders or the overcoming of animal residents' lower social status as their goals. Despite the aim of gradually allowing residents to expand their relations and explore more life options while living as co-citizens with their fellow beings, these experimental practices may not require traversing speciesist legal boundaries. According to Lucy Sargisson, ICs can engage in a politics of "estrangement," whereby a "creative tension between intentional communities and mainstream society" is generated by their members, such that ICs can be "sufficiently separate to create a space within which" residents can experimentally "explore a better world," while remaining in enough proximity in order to transformatively critique and influence mainstream society (Donaldson & Kymlicka 2015, p. 65). Unfortunately, if residents and their conspecifics in multispecies ICs are kept invisible by speciesist zoning laws and prevented from having a presence among the city-dwelling humans whom they most desperately need to influence, the transformative critiques and influences of a politics of estrangement may remain quite limited. To better comprehend just how pernicious speciesist legal obstacles can be, below are some recent cases in which humans who lived with farmed animals in urban spaces were threatened by municipal authorities to have their family members forcibly removed.

Farmed Animal Stories from Sites of Informality

Yamini Narayanan (2017) uses the framework of informality to understand the positions currently occupied by urban animals. The concept of informality was developed within urban studies to look at how "citizenship, inclusiveness and agency of human citizens" relate to spaces in the city (p. 481). Informality refers to a combination of spatial, social, and temporal states situated within grey areas, neither formally legitimized nor explicitly illegitimate (p. 482). Instances in which the wealthy attempt to use land for private construction prior to formal approval and in which the poor live in unauthorized housing both qualify as informal processes.

In response to informal grey spaces, urban planners tend to proceed through four stages of action:

1. Ignore the spaces and informal activities by turning a blind eye, which is usually a prolonged process.
2. Neglect those occupying spaces informally to intentionally deny them assistance and to prolong underdevelopment.
3. Limit informal presence through "institutional and at times violent control and containment."
4. And lastly, "whiten"—begin to gradually and selectively address the informal "as spaces and subjects of legitimacy" (pp. 482–483).

The coercive approach to correcting informalities describes neatly how planning deals with urban animal presence—by assuming this presence to be a source of dangers and contaminations, akin to a grey space (Narayanan 2017, p. 482). Nonhuman animals in urban areas fall into a grey space "between being tolerated and violently removed," which adds a blurred binary of human/nonhuman to those of legal/illegal, citizen/alien, and permanent/temporary (p. 482). As urban animals face violent and coercive removal or containment, the grey spaces that they occupy can be considered a state of exception that "enables the complete suspension of universal rights for nonhumans" (p. 483). Applying the informality framework to the following stories illustrates how urban-dwelling farmed animals qualify as informal subjects inside anthropocentric and speciesist cities.

In September 2015, Mike Downey, a resident of Victoria, British Columbia, was ordered by the City of Victoria to relocate his two potbellied pigs, Vishnu and Athena, after "animal control spotted Downey taking his pigs for a walk" ("Victoria Pig Lover," 2015). The City of Victoria cited a bylaw that categorized pigs as farmed animals as justification for the pigs' removal as, legally, they did not belong in the city. By Downey's account, his relationship with Vishnu and Athena resembled those typical for humans who have dogs or cats as family members, who share living spaces inside the home with them and interact with them affectionately through care. Furthermore, Vishnu and Athena were popular in the neighborhood, as children from nearby daycares and schools frequently visited to interact with them and offer them food.

In Burnaby, British Columbia, Alexandra Lezo faced similar challenges in February 2015, when the City of Burnaby ordered her to relocate her two pygmy goats, Toggy and Andy, according to agricultural zoning bylaws that prohibited farmed animals within city limits (Fisher 2015). Fortunately for Lezo, she managed to get a reprieve from the city to keep Toggy and Andy after pleading her case at a city council meeting, where she was joined by around thirty supporters (Fisher 2015). On the other hand, according to Downey's Facebook page, "Save Mike's Pet Pigs," Downey was separated from Vishnu and Athena (minus occasional visits) when the pigs were forced to take temporary refuge at a friend's property outside the city, while he continued to fight the bylaws and explore options to become reunited with them. After over a year and a half battling the city council, Downey stated in March 2017 that he had unfortunately lost the battle with the municipal government; however, he optimistically looked forward to a new life with the pigs, living in a creative off-grid trailer outside the city.

These examples show that not only are bylaws that label certain animals as illegal and impose specific identities (such as "farm" animal) oppressive, but the resulting coercive removal can also disjoint various relationships in a community, producing traumas and burdens for both the animals and their humans. The reality is that such struggles are not at all unique, but rather ubiquitous. A 2014 *ABC News* article detailed two similar cases, one involving a certified emotional-support pig named Tucker, the other a potbellied pig named Sooie, both threatened with removal following neighbor complaints (Lopez, Simpson, & Valiente 2014).

In January 2017, *The New York Times* featured an article titled "Pet Pigs of New York: Illegal, Embattled, Beloved," revealing that there existed "an underground pig network in New York"; a veterinarian who treated these pigs stated that pet pigs were scattered throughout all five boroughs of the city in untold numbers (Newman 2017). These pigs were living there against a city health code provision that prohibited "'all even-toed ungulates,' including but not limited to 'deer, antelope, sheep, pigs, including potbellied pigs, goats, cattle, giraffe and hippopotamus'" (Newman 2017).

The article also featured a pig named Queelin, who was described as a "lawbreaker," who had not yet been discovered by the authorities, as well as a pig named Wilbur, who was not so lucky and already had a sanctuary in North Carolina waiting for him in case his human lost the fight to keep him (Newman 2017). After Danielle Forgione, a resident of Queens, New York, gained media attention for her fight to keep her pig Petey in 2013, a bill seeking to "legalize pet pigs under two hundred pounds statewide" was introduced by New York State Senator Tony Avella, but the bill has yet to pass (*CBS News* 2013; Newman 2017).

These stories of informal farmed animals reveal the arbitrariness of speciesism expressed within bylaws and health codes, which often lump farmed animals together with wild animals or demonize farmed animals on unfounded claims of threats to human health. For example, the health department in New York has made a statement claiming that pigs can become aggressive to humans when raised as house pets and that there are currently no federally approved rabies vaccines for pigs, even though statistics from the Centers for Disease Control and Prevention have shown zero cases of rabies in pigs reported in the U.S. (Newman 2017). As Narayanan (2017) points out, when animals assert their presence against human attempts to make them invisible, "colonial narratives based on fear and contempt are often employed to operationalize human–nonhuman segregation" (p. 479).

These narratives also surface a troubling pattern that is consistent with Colling's concern regarding how certain descriptions of urban farmed animals used to distinguish them from other animals may serve only to recolonize their identities and reproduce borders and boundaries. In an attempt to justify keeping urban farmed animals in the city, human guardians often describe their animals as friendly, gentle, affectionate, smart, and playful. While this may very much be true in the human guardians' experiences, when asserted within the context of their attempting to differentiate their urban farmed animals from other farmed animals, it not only fails to challenge stereotypes about nonurban farmed animals, but may even reinforce them. For instance, Noah Graves, a human defending his potbellied pigs Einstein and Winstin against removal, stated that the two pigs were not "loud or smelly" as a way to justify their presence (Willick 2017). Similarly, in the New York bill proposed to legalize "pygmy pigs," one of the key arguments made for them was that they make "great pets due to the combination of their unique traits such as cleanliness, diminutive size, friendly disposition and intelligence" (Newman 2017).

When human guardians are forced to engage in the recolonizing of farmed animal identities, whether out of desperation to protect their family members or simply as a reflection of existing speciesist norms, they reproduce divisions that undermine animal liberation. To defend their animals, it is typical for humans to try to convince city authorities that their animals are "pets" and "family," as opposed to "farm" or "food" animals, who are "livestock" and serve "agricultural functions." Legitimizing the "farm" designation dictated by speciesist zoning laws effectively suppresses potential opportunities to build coalitions between informal animals facing removal within city limits and those facing routine violence and death in agricultural zones.

To be fair, we should not place the heavy burden of advocating for all farmed animals on a few individual humans, who are right to prioritize defending their immediate family members, given the unlikelihood of immediate institutional changes achieved through their cases. Below, I discuss how support networks can be built among informal urban farmed animals and those living within legalized zones, such as livestock farms, traditional farmed animal sanctuaries, and microsanctuaries, precisely to help reduce individual burdens and address these divisions.

Infiltrate! Prefigurative Organizing at Sites of Informality

Prefiguration describes an organizing practice in which social movements model, or prefigure, the world they hope to build "through the manner in which they [organize]" (Kauffman 2017, p. 57). Prefiguration can also be defined as "the notion that our organizing reflects the society we wish to live in—that the methods we practice, institutions we create, and relationships we facilitate within our movements and communities align with our ideals" (Walia 2013, p. 13). The history of prefigurations to utopian projects traces back to at least the early nineteenth century, when communes akin to laboratories were formed to experiment with redesigning social structures and relationships (Kauffman 2017, pp. 57–58). However, most of these utopian communities were "invariably small and often isolated," and the creators and residents of these communities believed they could transform the world simply by inspiring and persuading others to imitate them, without the need to get involved in conflicts (p. 58).

Based on critical analysis of sanctuaries, existing FASes fit this description of isolated prefigurative communes, currently operating in a mode of containment, largely removed from broader society. To recap, the segregation of farmed animals produces two issues that traditional FASes seem unable to resolve. The first issue is *relational*, whereby a vast majority of the humans who actually participate in most of the violence against farmed animals through financially supporting the animal agriculture industry also happen to find farmed animals the most alien to them. The lack of farmed animal presence in the lives of urban humans means that for most of these humans, possibilities for meaningful, transformative relationships with farmed animals are foreclosed. The second issue is the legal/social standing of farmed animals, with speciesist segregation laws ascribing lower social status to them and forbidding them from entering spaces wherein they can potentially transform their relations to urban humans. I argue that we must contest laws that segregate and denigrate farmed animals and concurrently create opportunities to allow farmed animals to transform their relationships with humans, and that this must be done prefiguratively, at sites of informality.

The strategic prefigurative process is both straightforward and difficult. In essence, it requires anti-speciesist human accomplices to adopt farmed animals into urban homes, find creative ways to ensure they flourish within relatively confined and "unnatural" spaces, and work towards enabling their agency and autonomy within the urban environment. So long as these urban farmed animals are able to sustain their clandestine presence in the face of authorities, they can subversively form relationships with other humans and animals in their environment, as family, friends, neighbors, and so on. These relations can eventually translate into political support should the "illegal" animal residents be discovered and have to fight legal battles for their right to remain, as demonstrated by the earlier stories from informal sites. Anti-speciesist advocates taking on informal living with rescued animals should, as a strategy oriented towards a liberation movement, intentionally bring their political consciousness into existing networks of informal animals and humans in order to build solidarity, which can result in a form of collective consciousness that acknowledges the importance of mutual aid in response to threats of removal. Ideally, the connection of activists to the informal networks of those keeping informal animals as family members produces political solidarity through common interests. Nonetheless, we can anticipate many concerns regarding this radical approach that must be addressed.

First, one may ask under what conditions it would be impermissible for guardians to subject animals to the nonconsensual risks of informal living. My view is that within the context of a war wherein the entire world is hostile to farmed animals, the question regarding the permissibility of guardians and their animals taking on nonconsensual risks becomes less relevant. Rather than limiting our understanding of our relationships with farmed animals to the one-dimensionality of guardian-to-dependent relations, we should return to considering the relations between accomplices and asylum seekers/combatants/fugitives. While less risky options—such as campaigning to change bylaws to allow farmed animals to legally live in urban areas—may be available, the issue as it currently stands is that many farmed animals are already transgressing these boundaries by living informally in cities. Unfortunately, these informal subjects do not have the numbers or the political networks to effectively reach and leverage the whitening stage of the response to informality. It is therefore important for us to acknowledge that one of the ways to move from an established state of illegality to one of legality within a given status quo is precisely to normalize the illegality through resistance and lawbreaking.

Second, there exists a worry that intentionally bringing farmed animals into urban areas to live informally would be a form of instrumentalization—failing to treat the animals as ends in themselves. Within the context of war, such a process can also be viewed as a form of conscription. I argue that the understanding of intentional informal living as a way to conscript or instrumentalize farmed animals as ambassadors so that a movement may achieve certain political aims is misguided. We should instead acknowledge that farmed animals are already always forced to engage in these struggles, given the legally sanctioned and culturally normalized mass violence against them. To assume that there are farmed animals who now possess certain rights after having been rescued is to buy into a fiction, since safety for individuals within sanctuaries is far from citizenship and liberation. To assist farmed animals in asserting their right to remain in a given space as members of a community is precisely to treat them as ends in themselves. By organizing prefiguratively around individual farmed animals living informally, we recognize the uniqueness of each individual's circumstances and struggles and engage with them as fellow participants in a political movement to collaboratively shape new futures and defend each other's lives. Nonetheless, as mentioned earlier, ambassadorship is unavoidable, since each individual animal's struggle is necessarily connected to the wider struggle of their entire kind.

Third, given that the livestock industry and zoning laws have normalized the general understanding in the Global North that only the rural environment can provide farmed animals with an acceptable level of wellbeing, there may be concerns that farmed animals would live in deprivation in urban spaces. The reality, however, is that farmed animals have been known to be highly adaptable to the limited physical surroundings and ecological niches within urban habitats (Hovorka 2008, p. 101). Pigs easily subsist in confined physical spaces within cities that face land scarcity; cows can thrive and produce milk in intensive urban areas that offer no grazing opportunities, which has made them a success story of development in sub-Saharan Africa; and chickens in Cairo manage to carve out their own niches in a city with hardly any green spaces (Hovorka 2008, p. 101). Nevertheless, cities are in fact dangerous spaces for farmed animals in terms of architectural design and urban planning. However, the existing structural risks imposed on farmed animals within cities should not be a reason to retreat from informal living and resistance; rather, they should further motivate us to transform spaces to make them animal-friendly. As Narayanan (2017) argues, urban planning and development should *engage* with, rather than *manage*, animals (p. 489).

Theoretically, what would this engagement with farmed animals look like in urban settings? In her work on the overlaps between animal and disability liberation, Sunaura Taylor offers promising insights in her critiques of Frans de Waal. Taylor notes that de Waal distinguishes between two processes that humans or animals can exercise to support others who are disabled. The first process is known as *learned adjustment*, whereby able-bodied persons gradually familiarize themselves with the limited abilities of certain members in their community, despite not necessarily understanding those limitations initially (Taylor 2017, p. 28). The second process is *cognitive empathy*, which de Waal considers to be a more complex ability possessed by certain species with higher cognitive capacities and which enables one to imagine oneself in another individual's position (p. 28). Taylor argues that the distinction between the two processes is actually quite troubling when examined through a critical disability analysis, as it would suggest that able-bodied humans possessing the capacity for cognitive empathy would immediately be able to imagine accurately what it is like to, for example, have a body with no arms (p. 29). In reality, our imaginations may not be accurate, unless the disabilities and injuries we engage with are already familiar to us, and our interactions with disabilities and illnesses we have never encountered would arguably always be characterized by learned adjustment (p. 29).

Building on this perspective, I suggest that prefigurative organizing with farmed animals at sites of informality must begin with learned adjustment. Not only would the humans and animals need to learn through mutual adaptation and interdependence, but they must also collectively adapt or adjust to their living environment. It is only by extensively learning about other animals' needs that we can begin to creatively transform spaces according to their preferences while simultaneously transforming our relations. The need for learned adjustment, however, does not mean that humans and animals entering into informal living must always begin with zero knowledge of each other. Formal FASes can take on a supporting role by providing resources to assist their informal counterparts in this struggle.

In addition to serving a practical, standard function as places of refuge for informal urban farmed animals who lose their battles and must escape to safety, FASes can provide trainings so that humans living informally with animals may gain basic skills and knowledge regarding animal handling, socialization, and health. Moreover, FASes where residents practice living as multispecies ICs can share knowledge with informal networks as their ongoing experiments with non-hierarchical living expand what we know about possible relations to farmed animals. In effect, what I am suggesting is that just as those in the microsanctuary movement have made themselves "micro" in comparison to standard FASes, the reverse can be applied to our understanding of ICs in terms of size and scale: FASes would become micro intentional communities, while informal animals and their accomplices would work to turn the entire mainstream society into the ideal IC we envision.

By maintaining lines of communication as networks of resistance that cut across speciesist boundaries of segregation, both micro-ICs and informal urban resistance communities would use the knowledge they produce to advise the other's practices for change. For example, micro-ICs can elicit the interests and preferences of individual farmed animals through prefigurative forms of living within models of ideal future communities, while informal urban farmed animals can help us better comprehend how their presence and visibility in urban humans' daily lives actually reshape human and animal's behaviors and perceptions of each other. This process can be a much more productive form of *creative tension*; we should aim for a politics of stronger connections and mutual aid instead of estrangement.

Regardless, it remains crucial that we not trivialize the real fears humans may have about informal living, such as having the animals they have adopted seized by authorities due to their animals' illegal status, and going through the associated experiences, which are traumatizing for both human and animal, as a result. Humans who choose to experiment with informal living but live under residential contracts that prohibit animals may also risk getting evicted themselves. In order to take on these risks, one may need strong networks of community support as a necessary prerequisite for adopting farmed animals into urban areas against the law, and no one should be expected to infiltrate the cityscape with their animals in isolation.

This is where a solidarity network becomes essential as a means to provide informal dwellers with the support they need. Due to critiques of sanctuary cities, the human sanctuary city movement has begun to shift the discourse informing its campaign practices, and this is very instructive for the prefigurative approach I argue for here. Instead of fighting for sanctuary cities, migrants and their allies in confronting unjust immigration and refugee systems now advocate *solidarity cities*. Some of the key organizing principles of solidarity city campaigns include:

1. Breaking isolation and fear by networking and unifying based on straightforward demands, such as status for all, in addition to an end to deportation and detention.
2. Practicing tangible support work and mutual aid, as opposed to charity approaches.
3. Organizing campaigns informed by on-the-ground realities.
4. Building the capacity of mutual aid and support networks.
5. Holding decision makers directly accountable for their policies and actions.
6. And lastly, using direct action to achieve justice (Solidarity Across Borders 2013).

In some ways, animal liberation activists have already begun establishing important groundwork for such networks. Unfortunately, much of this networking is currently happening only online, on social media platforms. For example, the Facebook group Vegans with Chickens has thousands of members in the microsanctuary movement and chicken rescue communities, and regularly shares knowledge and information for new and seasoned chicken rescuers. The Microsanctuary Movement website dedicates pages to "species guides," offering detailed information about a range of farmed animal species that rescuers should be attentive to, as well as a map for finding veterinarians experienced with treating farmed animals (The Microsanctuary Movement, n.d.).

Information regarding available veterinary services is crucial, considering that denial of services to informal residents is precisely one of the repressive strategies used against them. In fact, this happened in the high-profile case of celebrity animal Esther the Wonder Pig, in which animal hospitals denied her and other animals from her sanctuary life-saving medication and medical procedures because they were considered "non-traditional companion animals" (Howells 2018). Fortunately, Esther's humans were able to raise over $750,000 to purchase a massive CT scanner and successfully convinced the Ontario Veterinary College to remove her breast cancer tumors and save her life (Howells 2018). Esther's example shows exactly how effective communities can be in responding to emergencies when they are able to pull together and exercise mutual aid.

Conclusion

When a farmed animal has been successfully rescued, it is very common to find animal advocates who say that the animals will now get to live out the rest of their days in peace at a sanctuary. While farmed animals' conceptions and experiences of time are perhaps some of the less understood aspects of their lives, common expressions about their post-rescue lives nonetheless engender a sense that they exist in a suspended state of waiting similar to that experienced by many human asylum seekers. Although these animals are living, there is also a sense that they are simply waiting to die, waiting to be replaced, or, more optimistically, waiting for a transformed world wherein sanctuaries become obsolete. Perhaps waiting has met its end, and more radical actions need to be taken now.

I have proposed a tangible but demanding strategy to transform the status quo of farmed animal struggles across spatial, temporal, social, and relational dimensions. Infiltrating urban spaces to practice informal, prefigurative living with farmed animals seeks to disrupt both the cultural and ideological hegemony and people's embodied habits that normalize and render invisible human violence against and indifference to farmed animals (Donaldson & Kymlicka 2016, pp. 74–75). If urban humans could experience the interactions between farmed animals and other urban dwellers through interspecies play (imagine goats and pigs at dog parks) or witness farmed animals as they engage in relations of care with others, these activities would have interruptive powers similar to those of the theatrical plays performed by human asylum seekers. Donaldson and Kymlicka (2016) argue that "the fight for animals starts with the battle to belong, to be viewed as members of community, with the right to secure space" (p. 97). My contribution here suggests that cities are important sites of these battles of belonging for farmed animals, and that animal liberation cannot be realized unless we dismantle speciesism and anthropocentrism in urban spaces.

Possible future directions of such prefigurative projects may examine how the theory and strategies shared here could be extended beyond our relations to farmed animals, into the realm of our relations to other domesticated animals, wild and feral animals, as well as those confined and exploited in different contexts, such as animals in laboratories, zoos, and aquariums. How might the presence of all these different groups interact with each other within and outside of cities? The prefigurative strategies advanced here, which defy unjust boundaries and borders segregating human and nonhuman animals, have been informed largely by anti-colonial struggles and can therefore facilitate solidarity with other anti-colonial and anti-capitalist movements. What has been discussed here is only a tiny step towards imagining truly anti-speciesist, anti-anthropocentric, and liberated cities for human and nonhuman animals alike.

11

DO NONHUMAN ANIMALS RESIST?

Critical Geographies, Decolonial Theories, and the Case for Veganism as Multispecies Solidarity

Marco Reggio

> Are those who act and *struggle* mute, as opposed to those who act and *speak*? (Spivak 1999, p. 257)

> There is no collective movement that speaks for each of us all the way through. (Rich 1984, p. 224)

Introduction

In common perception, as well as in academic research and journalistic reportage, animal rights movements are made up of human actors elaborating and acting out strategies of resistance for animal liberation. But is it not also the case that oppressed nonhuman subjects act and resist?

The recent flourishing of animal resistance studies affirms this, eroding the dominant narrative in the animal rights movement, which contemplates only a minority of goodhearted humans fighting for the "voiceless" (Cappellini & Reggio 2014; Cavalieri 2011; Colling 2013, 2021; Corman 2012, 2016; Hribal 2003, 2007, 2010; Kowalczyk 2014; Piazzesi 2015; Resistenza Animale 2019; Wadiwel 2016).[1] Until recently, this paternalistic vision had been undisputed to the point that it had always seemed obvious and had contributed to spreading the image of a movement more altruistic than any other. According to this vision, this would be the only movement whose activists dedicate themselves to destroying a system of exploitation without benefiting from this struggle, and going against their own interests.

1. Corman (2016) illustrates several examples of the use of the "voicelessness" rhetoric by animal rights associations and academics, including Tom Regan (pp. 482–483).

Even to admit the simple fact that humans are also animals—and therefore that animal liberation also means the liberation of human animality and the dismantling of the dominant apparatuses that govern the life of all species, for example—does not appear to make things simple. Not only scientific studies but also testimonies of daily rebellions by nonhuman animals enslaved in zoos, circuses, laboratories, and farms seem to point to a resistance that is impossible to completely dismiss, despite the powerful means of zootechnics, genetics, and all the forces that maintain order in anthropized territories (Cappellini & Reggio 2014; Cavalieri 2011; Colling 2013; Hribal 2003, 2007, 2010;[2] Philol 1995). In this chapter, I present two related arguments: first, that nonhuman animals resist, and that their resistance opens up new ways of thinking about configurations of space and what constitutes language or politics itself; and second, that forms of veganism that refuse species privilege and, in this refusal, recognize nonhuman animals as active subjects embody a "multispecies solidarity," not by speaking *for* animals but by speaking *with* and *as* them.

In the following section, I discuss stories of rebellious animals and propose the need for non-anthropocentric visions of struggle. As part of this discussion, I outline a conception of veganism as "interspecies solidarity." In the section after that, I explore the ways in which critical geographies have approached the problem of animal agency, power, and space, drawing particularly on the work of Michel Foucault and Judith Butler, before highlighting Jacques Rancière's formative contribution to the question of language. Next, drawing on the work of Sarat Colling, I examine key ideas from decolonial feminism, which are particularly valuable for observing escapes of exploited animals in relation to physical and symbolic spaces built on the centrality of the white human subject, to articulate forms of intersectional solidarity. In the final section, I outline a discussion of the political problem of "speaking for someone else" in relation to animal liberation movements.

A theme that runs through all the sections is that of language. In fact, the Western ideas of "public sphere" and "political action" are usually linked to the ability to speak up, formulate claims, and negotiate using (human) language (Cohen 2016; Corman 2012, 2016). I suggest reconceiving these issues from a non-anthropocentric point of view and challenging the belief that the mastery of human language is a necessary requirement for subject formation and political action.

---

2. The Italian collective Resistenza Animale (https://resistenzanimale.noblogs.org) curates a very rich, constantly updated archive containing thousands of stories of rebellion.

Animals Resisting: Outlining a Multispecies Solidarity

Some of the animal resistance stories I draw on in this chapter are quite famous. Tilikum's case is perhaps the best known. A two-year-old orca, Tilikum, was captured in 1983 near the coast of Iceland. He lived from 1992 until the beginning of 2017 imprisoned in a SeaWorld waterpark in Orlando, Florida. His resistance could not be ignored, since he rebelled several times, killing three people while in captivity. In fact, Tilikum attracted a vast protest movement against the conditions of animals used in waterparks and, in particular, against SeaWorld. Despite its marketing, this commercial giant has suffered substantial brand damage—large enough to make it waver at certain times during its history due to Tilikum's acts of resistance and what they uncovered: violent training, harsh living conditions, and denial of the most basic of animals' needs (Hribal 2010, pp. 136–140, 149–153; Hribal 2017).

Tatiana and Tyke shared similar stories. The former was a Siberian tiger detained at the San Francisco Zoo who, in 2006, attacked a keeper, seriously injuring him, and then escaped. The following year, she jumped the wall of her enclosure and fled. She injured two visitors and killed another one. Police shot her dead. Although the zoo faced a series of legal consequences, the story engendered discordant feelings: while institutions rewarded the police officers who killed her, many supportive people made Tatiana a symbol of the struggle for freedom, honoring her memory. In fact, artist Jon Engdahl dedicated a controversial sculpture to her and placed it in the city without the permission of the authorities (Hribal 2010, pp. 21–22, 28–30; Koopman 2008).

Similarly, Tyke was an elephant who, until her death in 1994, worked for the Honolulu circus, where she was the protagonist of several rebellions and attacks, with a number of victims. Trained for many years, Tyke escaped for the first time in April 1993. Two months later, she rebelled and trampled her trainer. In August 1994, during a show, she assaulted him to death and injured two others while escaping. She was executed by the police with eighty-six shots: she died after two hours of agony. Tyke also became a symbol of animal rights. Following her killing, several lawsuits against the owners of the circus for ill-treatment were instigated, and her case inspired various proposals for the regulation of circus activities in Hawaii and in other states (Hribal 2010, p. 55–61).

In Europe, many cases of animal resistance have generated movements of solidarity as well. In 2012, Alexander, a giraffe cub held at the Circus Orfei in Imola, Italy, escaped from his tent. The story ended with the intervention of the local police: a sniper hit Alexander with two doses of narcotics, which caused his death by cardiac arrest within hours. His escape attempt, however, made it possible for his supporters to mobilize solidarity, public opinion, and institutional support. Demonstrations for Alexander were organized, extending solidarity to all animals detained in circuses and questioning these businesses' legitimacy. In many municipalities, a prohibition of encampment for circuses with animals was demanded, negotiated, and often obtained (Cappellini & Reggio 2014; Turrini 2012).

These forms of animal resistance have not been limited to circuses and zoos. In May 2011, for example, a cow who came to be known as Yvonne escaped from a small farm in Germany. For months, she hid in the Bavarian forests, eluding several attempts to capture her. Residents' sightings did not help: when the capture teams arrived, Yvonne had already disappeared. Some supporters managed to find her before the hunters did. Her final destination was an animal sanctuary (Spiegel Online 2011a, 2011b).

In a similar case in Italy, a long escape led to a happy ending. Camilla, a cow who fled from a small farm in Tuscany in the summer of 2014, took refuge in the woods and avoided capture for several weeks. This allowed the animal resistance collective Resistenza Animale to organize and put pressure on local institutions to halt the cull. When Camilla was captured, thousands of emails were sent to the authorities; the media was interested in the case; and various animal rights associations came forward to guarantee her a safe place. The fugitive, in the end, was not brought back to the breeder—she is still living in a place where she is not exploited (Corriere 2014; La Nazione 2014; Resistenza Animale 2014). Two years later, a similar mobilization formed around a calf who had escaped during transport in Sicily and was found swimming in the port of Messina. Renamed Scilla, he was the subject of months of negotiations between local authorities and Agripunk, a farm sanctuary, to which he was finally led after the mobilization of hundreds of people (Agripunk 2016; Resistenza Animale 2016; Rossellini 2016).

Alongside these striking cases are a surprising number of acts of resistance, ranging from aggression to flight, refusal to work to self-mutilation. The episodes we know of—because they are reported by local or national media—are just the tip of the iceberg. Although most of the attempts are doomed to fail, it is important that we consider the overwhelmingly disproportionate force used to stop them. Between human and nonhuman forms of resistance, there is no ontological hiatus, even if the latter are commonly considered "minor" forms of resistance, probably because they often lack planning, a collective character, a "revolutionary strategy," or, more simply, because nonhumans' intentions are not formulated in our language.

First of all, it is difficult to draw a clear line between human and nonhuman forms of resistance. For example, noncooperation, mutism, self-injury, individual aggression, and slowing of production are practices typically used by nonhumans *and* large groups of humans whose conditions do not allow for "more structured" fighting strategies. Furthermore, the ephemeral and unsuccessful nature of most acts of animal revolt seems to derive more from the subjects' location in particularly disadvantageous power relations than from biological differences. For this reason, a genuinely non-anthropocentric vision of struggle must challenge the current notion of resistance that was born to describe human revolts. In this respect, veganism, the most concrete tool for expressing interspecies solidarity at our disposal, can be seen in a different light—not simply as a form of individual coherence, an ethical consumption, or an effective boycott.

If the phenomenon of animal exploitation is systemic, the answer can only be systemic. Veganism can thus be read as the individual expression of a stance for the abolition or destruction of systems of animal exploitation and as a factor causing "disturbance" to the dominant ethos (Simonsen 2012). Therefore, after discussing the implications of the recognition of nonhuman agency, I propose a concept of veganism capable of disarticulating the paternalism of the animal rights movement.

Critical Geographies, Animal Agency, and Language

Critical animal studies introduced the issue of animal resistance in both public and scholarly debate with ethological, geographic, and philosophical studies and, in particular, with the work of historian Jason Hribal (2003, 2007, 2010). In "Animals Are Part of the Working Class" (2003), Hribal argues that animals' bodies and labor have been the very materials for capitalist and industrial expansion: "horses, cows, or chickens have labored, and continue to labor, under the same capitalist system as humans" (p. 436). This perspective challenges the notion that only humans can be considered workers.

This observation leads Hribal to propose a new historiographical methodology—"history from below" (2007)—in which animals are valued "not because of the perceived benefit of their exploitation for humans, but because each individual's life has inherent worth and meaning to them" (Colling 2013, p. 31). The researcher must demonstrate how animals shape their own lives as social agents who practice everyday acts of resistance, such as when donkeys, mules, and oxen refuse human commands (Hribal 2007, p. 103) or when horses resist being used for human transport, which led to their replacement by various technologies (p. 105).

Other perspectives, including those inspired by Foucault, are emerging too. The French philosopher's conception of power is invaluable in animal rights—as in other fields of research and struggle—in making visible the active role of nonhumans in the network of forces, power relations, actions and reactions that inform daily life (Cappellini & Reggio 2014; Foucault 1972, 1976; Kowalczyk 2014, pp. 193–195; Piazzesi 2015, pp. 17–21; Thierman 2010; Wadiwel 2016). This conception allows us to rewrite a history of zootechnics as an incessant struggle between the subjugated (those literally "put under the *yoke*") and the subjugators—a genealogy of the different techniques produced in the struggle to govern animal bodies. Moreover, it is a heterogeneous and potentially infinite list of practices, whose real common denominator is precisely the resistance these practices were designed to respond to: the use of whips, bites, yokes, and enclosures; surgeries, sterilization operations, genetic selection, pharmacological therapies, repression of "unrecoverable" cases; behavioral techniques; rhetoric aimed at breaking interspecies solidarity; health standards, legal norms related to animal ownership; and many others.

From a Foucauldian perspective, processes of subjugation are inseparable from processes of subjectivation: subjugation is not simply a form of repression of the individual, but also a relationship that *produces* subjects. The grip on the subject cannot be distinguished from the production, and reproduction, of the subject.[3]

Given these Foucauldian inflections, a key question that animal resistance poses is what kind of agency nonhumans possess. Animal geographies have addressed this question in relation to forms of resistance that manifest themselves in different spatial situations: transgressions of urban boundaries by synanthropic animals, violations of the spaces assigned to animals in zoos, and escapes from farms and slaughterhouses (Philol 1995; Jones 2000; Philol & Wilbert 2000; Wilbert 2000; Emel, Wilbert, & Wolch 2002; Urbanik 2012; Colling 2013, 2021). In the case of slaughterhouses, specifically, the notion of agency generates a series of meaningful questions from a political point of view: What kinds of material and symbolic boundaries is the body of a fleeing animal violating? How does this influence our notion of "out of place"?

When animals flee, many apparatuses intervene, the purpose of which is to nullify the rebellion. These are devices that are invested in the construction of society as *human society* and that show the place reserved for nonhumans in the organization of life and production. The nonhuman animal who, thanks to a lucky break, manages to escape from the truck that is taking them to the slaughterhouse finds themselves first and foremost in a territory of human scale, unsuitable for survival, fenced, privatized, cemented—a territory that caters to the human community in every aspect, from the design of paved roads with all their barriers and cars moving at high speed to the inaccessibility of primary resources such as water and food sources. They will then have to deal with a human population density so high that it necessitates vigilance and allows for almost complete capillary control over fugitives (large animals, in particular, are unlikely to go unnoticed). On top of this, disadvantages produced by genetic selection, together with habits formed from living in captivity, also function to restrict animals' ability to find

3. Some authors (Dell'Aversano 2010; Simonsen 2012; Reggio 2018; Zappino 2015) argue that nonhuman animalities are performative in the same sense in which gender is.

freedom after they escape. Farmed animals are usually less suited to life in the wild than were their ancestors, and outside of human-run structures, they are rarely able to survive (Borsellino 2015; Colling 2013; Philol 1995). And if these devices fail, intentionally repressive human institutions intervene—this repression stems from the need to ensure public safety (against risks of road accidents, damage to crops, healthcare emergencies, and so on) but actually works by reducing attempts to escape to nonexistence.

Finally, a series of symbolic instruments makes resistance unintelligible, starting with the narratives surrounding episodes of rebellion, which journalistic texts use to reduce these events to anecdotal, folkloristic, or extraordinary tales. In many cases, stories of animals who escaped are able to break the cognitive dissonance typical of consumers; therefore, these instruments are an obstacle to human empathy and solidarity. Such an instrument is the constant use of quotation marks in stories of animal resistance. This simple stratagem is able to call into question—if not completely conceal—the intentionality of nonhuman fugitives: an animal can "abscond" but not simply abscond, can "rebel" but not simply rebel, can "want" to be "free" but not simply want to be free, and so on.

These dynamics call into question "broader concerns about nonhuman agency, about the agency of animals, and the extent to which we can say that animals destabilize, transgress or even resist our [human] orderings, including spatial ones" (Philol & Wilbert 2000, p. 5). It is no coincidence that the first geographical study that addressed animal rebellion proposed to look at nonhumans in the city as similar to marginalized humans, immersed in power relations "from without" as well as "from within," and to read the actions of nonhumans within the framework of "out-of-place phenomena" (Philol 1995, p. 656). Philol identifies the dichotomy between resistance and transgression in order to problematize aspects of the question of attributing agency to nonhuman beings:

> Resistance seems to imply intention—purposeful action directed against some disliked entity with the intention of changing it or of lessening its effects. Transgression, in distinction to resistance, does not rest on the intentions of actors but on the results—on the "being noticed" of a particular action.

Philol notes that transgression can have a symbolic character as the metaphorical crossing of social boundaries (norms, conventions, and expectations).

The problem of resistance has therefore found different solutions in the field of animal geographies. For example, according to Philol and Wilbert (2000), it is not necessary for us to attribute conscious intentions to nonhumans to be able to talk about resistance; at the same time, it can be productive to adopt a "guarded anthropomorphism" (p. 20). If Philol (1995) agrees, albeit for strategic reasons, not to deconstruct the distinction between transgression and resistance, Wilbert (2000) directly addresses this node, stating that we do not need "to go so far as to impute conscious intentionality to animals in order to speak of purposive action" (p. 249). So how do we describe the actions of nonhumans and their relations to humans in a way that "[does] not force us into attributing conscious intentionality to animals and may allow us to talk not just of transgressions but of animal resistances" (ibid.)? Two ways are suggested by Wilbert (2000). The first can be thought of as an approach that seeks to argue that with regards to their actions, in some ways humans and nonhuman animals are not as different as is often assumed. The second emphasizes how agency is a relational effect, something that emerges out of interactions between heterogeneous materials.[4]

The conceptual barriers that guard the boundary between resistance as such and the actions of nonhumans coincide in part with those that serve to maintain a clear distinction between humans and other animals. The barrier separating transgression from resistance is only one of those. On the ethological level, a classical distinction is that between reaction and response, linked to the basic philosophical distinction between voice and speech that, in Aristotelian philosophy, indicates who is admitted into the sphere of the political and who is not, as pointed out by Jacques Rancière (1999, p. 21). An attempt to undo the political distinction between voice and language in the case of nonhumans based on Rancière's theory was developed by Aylon Cohen (2016).

In summary, nonhuman voice can be included in the political sphere if one argues that the domain of language exceeds linguistic utterances and that the political sphere is performatively created by bodily gestures (see also Butler 2015, and Kowalczyk 2014). We can accept Corman's conclusion, according to which, "in a significant way, animals *are* voiceless in the sense that their suffering is not heard by humans," and "we can also say that they *are not* voiceless in the sense that they are seen by advocates as subjects who have desires, perspectives, and interests" (p. 497). Given Rancière's definition of *subjectification*—"the production through a series of actions of a body and a capacity for enunciation not previously identifiable within a given field of experience, whose identification is thus part of the reconfiguration of the field of experience" (1999, p. 35)—nonhuman rebellions can be seen as acts of contestation, as *performative acts*, since they "simultaneously create the parties that engender the act of rupture" (Cohen 2016, p. 241).

4. For a discussion on the possibility of developing a radically relational concept of agency, see Barad (2003).

Therefore, I suggest that the study of animal resistance cannot avoid a redefinition of the concepts of resistance and language. In fact, these concepts are impregnated with anthropocentrism, as they are modeled on the human subject from many points of view (cognitive, linguistic, political).

In addition to these necessary redefinitions, the geographical approach to rebellious animals centers on the animal body in human spaces, particularly urban spaces (Philol 1995, p. 664; Borsellino 2015; Meijer 2013). This is based on the observation that animals negotiate or reject the places that humans have assigned to them, "forging their own other spaces" (Philol & Wilbert 2000, p. 14). Butler's theory of performativity as articulated in *Notes Toward a Performative Theory of Assembly* (2015) is helpful here, as she calls into question the linguistic origin of assembling. The gathering of bodies "speaks" long before speaking, and even the mode of intervention most typically linked to verbalization—assembly—expresses a form of popular will "*before it utters any word*" (p. 156). Clearly, this problematization of the word is invested in not only the whole discussion on the concept of people, which becomes rather articulated in the text, but also the "classical" concepts of revolutionary act, resistance, and public space: "such actions reconfigure what will be public and what will be the space of politics" (p. 75).

The right to appear—along with the very possibility of appearing—depends on the fact that there are "out-of-place" bodies: "at stake is the question of whether the destitute are outside of politics and power or are in fact living out a specific form of political destitution along with specific forms of political agency and resistance that expose the policing of the boundaries of the sphere of the appearance itself" (p. 78). In our case, we must reiterate the questions previously posed: What kinds of material and symbolic boundaries is the body of a fleeing animal violating? How is it able to influence our notion of "out of place"? Moreover, if we apply Rancière's description of the process of conflictual redefinition of the political sphere to the case of nonhumans, it is clear how important bodies' occupation of space is. Nonhumans' actions constitute a "political activity" that ruptures the policing of the community by "shift[ing] a body from the place assigned to it" (1999, p. 30). Following Rancière, we must take much more seriously this emphasis on the term "space" and on the contestation of the assignment of a "right place" for each body.

The Power of Pardon: Stranger Fetishism and a Decolonial Perspective of Animal Resistance

In May 2018, in Paris, Mamoudou Gassama, a clandestine immigrant from Mali, became the protagonist of a story that made front-page news. While going to the bar, he saw a four-year-old boy hanging from a balcony. The child was alone, and neighbors could not reach the balcony; so Mamoudou climbed up the building and rescued the child. A video recorded by a passerby spread quickly, and Mamoudou became a national hero. The mayor of Paris asked for his regularization, and shortly after, President Emmanuel Macron granted him French citizenship (Breeden & Cowell 2018; *BBC News* 2018).

In Italy, a similar case sparked public debate. In March 2019, near Milan, the driver of a school bus hijacked the vehicle with over fifty thirteen-year-old schoolchildren inside, tying them up and threatening to set them on fire. However, one of the kids, Ramy Shehata, managed to phone the police secretly and save everyone (Gemme 2019). His courage was praised on every occasion, in newspapers and on television. Ramy was of Egyptian origin, even though he was born in Italy. Nevertheless, since there was no law in Italy granting *ius soli* citizenship (citizenship based on place of birth), he did not possess Italian citizenship. Public debate ensued on the prospects of granting citizenship to Ramy by virtue of his heroic act. After some days, Interior Minister Matteo Salvini—probably one of the most racist politicians in recent Italian history—agreed to this request (*The Local* 2019).

During the spring of 2009, a small black calf made a break from a New York City slaughterhouse. Molly, as she was later named, managed to break through a fence enclosing the passage between a truck and the pens where she was being led to. She was eventually trapped behind a house, where she was tranquilized and sent to Brooklyn Animal Care and Control, then to a farm sanctuary (Colling 2013, pp. 78–88). "We always think that once they've escaped, they've earned the right to go free," a police spokeswoman said (p. 79).

The similarity between the first two cases and the last one may appear surprising, but it is not. Sarat Colling uses the concept of *stranger fetishism*, coined by Sara Ahmed in reference to the human sphere, to analyze Molly's story and those of other nonhuman fugitives. She writes:

> The recognition and expelling of strangers is in fact often a racist process that supports and maintains certain economic and social privileges. This recognition can also be viewed as a *speciesist* practice in which some species are recognized as others or strangers. Nonhuman animals are expelled yet fetishized by the human community. (p. 7)

Using this interpretative framework, it is possible to explain the functioning of the apparatus of "pardon," an exceptional and individual provision based on an act of generosity by those in power, whose power is not challenged. On the contrary, the pardon granted to a single cow—Molly—reaffirms the normality of the treatment to which billions of animals are subjected on livestock farms and in slaughterhouses. And the granting of "*ad honorem*" citizenship to the two "heroes" does not at all affect the apparatus that separates humans with civil rights from those without rights; on the contrary, it reinforces this discrimination.

In fact, for Sara Ahmed (2000), fetishism manifests itself in both the exclusion and the *inclusion* of the stranger, in particular under the aegis of multiculturalism: "I examine how multiculturalism can function to assimilate 'the stranger' as a figure of the unassimilable. . . . It is the processes of expelling *or* welcoming the one who is recognized as a stranger that produce the figure of the stranger in the first place" (p. 4). The encounter with the foreign body, whether it is an exclusive or inclusive encounter, is first and foremost what the foreigner produces as a figure, as the object of "an ontology" (p. 3), as "a figure which has linguistic and bodily integrity" (p. 6). In this sense, the pardon granted to Mamoudou Gassama, Ramy Shehata, or Molly is not just reaffirming a general condition (that of illegal immigrants or of farmed animals), but also producing otherized bodies, out-of-place bodies, producing and at the same time defining *the place* itself. If Sara Ahmed explains how the encounter can produce "the stranger," we must ask ourselves which kinds of bodies the encounter with a fleeing animal produces, how space is redefined, and how the relation between those bodies and public space is articulated.

To answer such questions, according to Sarat Colling, critical animal geographies must adopt a decolonial thinking. "A decolonial perspective of animal resistance is an approach that emphasizes space and place: how animals both occupy and are excluded from certain locations" (p. 40).

More generally, the "animals without borders" approach proposed by Colling is inspired by Chandra T. Mohanty's (2003) "feminism without borders," which recognizes the existence of material and symbolic boundaries—and, thus, the differences between geographically and politically situated struggles or movements—but at the same time aims to cross, circumvent, break, and discuss these boundaries. A full consideration of animal agency, even if nonhumans are not always aware of the boundaries they are violating (pattrice jones 2009, p. 236), has given rise to an effective expression—"natural anarchism in action"—which makes visible the barriers that separate the spaces assigned to animals by neoliberalism from those reserved for humans, especially those who are white, able-bodied adults. At the same time, rebellions contest the symbolic boundary between Man [*sic*] and "Animal," that general singular whose epistemic violence was denounced by Jacques Derrida (2006).

Furthermore, fleeing animals make the line between "wild" and "domestic" (or "bred") porous. As Hribal notes, the term *cimarrones*—Spanish for "wild ones"—once referred to "escaped cattle, pigs, and horses" (2003, pp. 448–449). This overlap reveals a contradiction with respect to the image of domestic animals that Western urban society has built and that paints them as docile and totally separated from their wild origins: "escaped domestic animals reverse the progress narrative" (Colling 2013, p. 104).

A decolonial reading of animal resistance also sheds new light on the relationship between colonialism and speciesism. The reactions to the sight of an animal running for their freedom in city traffic show all the contradictions typical of the relationship of the Western white subject with non-white otherness, including the coexistence of xenophobia and fetishism, exclusion and exoticism. For example, Tilikum, Tyke, and Tatiana have aroused both terror and sympathy. Tatiana, as a wild and ferocious animal, has especially elicited solidarity precisely *because of* her ferocity, or because of the idea of the "wild beast" she evoked in humans—a stereotypical and exotic idea encompassing the fact that she constituted a possible threat to civilization and at the same time an embodiment of values such as autonomy, freedom, exuberance. (Moreover, exoticism and wildness are the constituent ingredients of shows offered by zoos and circuses.)

Similarly, the flights of farmed animals, such as cows or pigs, arouse mixed feelings. Yvonne, Camilla, and Scilla were hunted because their roles in human society were as meat and milk producers, and their escapes from the farm or the transport truck rendered them unproductive. But at the same time, the public defended them, and the media celebrated them by delivering narratives of "exceptional cases." In this framework, veganism as a "decolonial diet" can be seen as a way to overcome the exceptional character of empathy and to articulate a real interspecies solidarity.

Speaking for Someone Else?

The problem of *speaking for someone else*—raised by decolonial feminists and those in other movements—must also be addressed by animal liberation movements (Mohanty 2003; Hardt 2016; feminoska 2017; Reggio 2017; Resistenza Animale 2019; Kowalczyk 2014; Corman 2016), as they reject pietistic and paternalistic approaches.

Nevertheless, it may be useful to clarify, in a general sense, the terms of this question, starting with what has been elaborated by subaltern/decolonial studies and by Foucault (1972)[5] and Rancière (1999). For nonhumans, the possibility that the subaltern can speak—to recount Spivak's critical intervention—is conditioned

5. Foucault (1972, pp. 207–208) expresses clearly what the colonization of the intellectual speaking for others consists of.

by an epistemological framework that is much more overwhelming than that outlined for the human sphere. This is precisely because the need for interpretation, as highlighted by Cohen, implies that there is someone who holds the power to interpret/represent: "the figure of the subaltern is necessarily mediated by problems of representation" (Chakrabarty 2000, p. 94). Spivak's "native informant" is programmatically deprived of the possibility of accessing their own history, narration of themselves, or elaboration of an idea of a different world. And in the case of animals, this foreclosure is even more profound.

Even when the question is restricted to relations between humans of the "First World" and those of the "Third World," the complexity of the role of nonverbal action as well as its link to *privilege* are apparent. "Voiceless" nonhuman individuals express an embodied critique of exploitation. When Camilla escaped from the farm where she had been chained, obviously, she did not make any direct, written claim regarding her exploiters or the institutions that had enslaved her, but her bodily presence in the Tuscan countryside clearly expressed that she did not wish to live in chains. The duration of Camilla and Yvonne's time in hiding made it concretely possible for the public to develop an effective solidarity. In fact, usually, when news of an escape reaches the public, the animal has already been killed or returned to their owner, and it is much more difficult to do something for them. Camilla and Yvonne's persistence in hiding and evading capture constituted direct and unequivocal resistance to animal exploitation.

In many cases, this embodied critique gives rise to organized struggles. For example, although the giraffe Alexander's flight from the Imola circus was short-lived and ended with his killing, it sparked a debate that continued for months, along with mobilization of supporters and demands to abolish circuses with animals that revealed an extraordinary determination and solidarity. The rebellions of Tyke, Tilikum, and Tatiana even led to serious economic damage, legal trials, and significant legislative progress. It should be noted that in these cases, in order to transcend the focus on a single rebel and develop effective broader movements, human intervention necessarily encompassed more extensive mobilization, legislative or political demands, and lawsuits.

How can those who would like to demonstrate solidarity—to abdicate their privilege, but often without having previously recognized that privilege in all its breadth—allow for the deployment of collective action without "speaking for" others? Here, we are treading on uncertain ground, as suggested by Hardt (2016), between the risk of true paternalism and that of the opposite—of assuming that "only the marginal can speak for the margin" (Spivak 1999, p. 171). On this issue, Adrienne Rich (1984) expresses very clearly some implications of "speaking for someone else": "*You cannot speak for me. I cannot speak for us.* Two thoughts: there is no liberation that only knows how to say 'I'; there is no collective movement that speaks for each of us all the way through. And so even ordinary pronouns become a political problem" (p. 224). This applies to the animal liberation movement. The "politics of location" (Rich 1984) becomes essential to distinguishing "gentle" colonialism from a solidarity based on criticism of one's own privilege (p. 215). Maybe Rich's realization—"it was in writing but also the actions and speeches and sermons of Black United States citizens that I began to experience the meaning of my whiteness as a point of location for which I needed to take responsibility" (p. 219)—can lead us to ask the following: What do the actions of Tyke, Tilikum, and Molly tell us? What do they tell us about our being human? About the meaning of our *humanness* "as a point of location for which we need to take responsibility"? As much as it is difficult for us to ask the opinions of those directly involved (nonhumans) on this point, it is possible for us to listen to the voices of other oppressed subjects who have spoken precisely about the language of the oppressor. As bell hooks (2015) writes:

> Often this speech about the "Other" is also a mask, an oppressive talk hiding gaps, absences, that space where our words would be if we were speaking, if there were silence, if we were there. . . . Often this speech about the "Other" annihilates, erases: "No need to hear your voice when I can talk about you better than you can speak about yourself. No need to hear your voice. Only tell me about your pain. I want to know your story. And then I will tell it back to you in a new way.

The assonance among those fighting for animal liberation with one of the typical problems of mainstream animal rights discourse is surprising. Discursive strategies in favor of animals, such as sharing videos of factory farms or voicing rational objections to meat consumption—even when they do not use anthropocentric arguments appealing to human health or ecological footprint—are always focused on animal pain. From this point of view, these strategies are faithful to the Benthamite principle that asks "can they suffer?"—never "can they enjoy?" or, as proposed by Derrida (2006), "can they respond?" The only condition? "Do not speak in a voice of resistance" (hooks 2015). Again, the Aristotelian conception of animal voice seems to be at work—implicitly accepted by animal rights supporters themselves—as voice is considered a tool capable of showing only sensations of pain and pleasure. And one of the inevitable consequences of these strategies is the victimization of nonhumans (Corman 2016, pp. 474–475). Moreover, utilitarian and naturalistic theories of animal rights seem to rely on an illuminist conception of subjectivity. How the suffering of the "Other" is perceived, according to Chakrabarty (2000), reveals the imposition of a particular model presented as universal: "The capacity to notice and document suffering (even if it be one's own suffering) from the position of a generalized and necessarily disembodied observer is what marks the beginnings of the modern self. This self has to be generalizable in principle" (p. 119).

The encounter between a decolonial perspective and the critique of "classical" theories of animal rights can be appreciated in all its fruitfulness precisely from the point of view of animal geographies, as shown by Gillespie and Collard (2015):

> In some cases, it may be that multispecies justice is found in spaces where distance is sought after more than proximity, difference more than similarity. This may be a world in which the project is not to enlarge the circle of beings that matter, to bring animals "into the circle of morality and subjectivity," but rather to re-examine the practice of circling itself. For what is at the heart of the circle? What or who does the circle defend? (p. 9)

And yet, in hooks's view, the unmasking of the colonist's epistemic violence does not lead to paralysis but constitutes the prerequisite for an invitation to develop a non-paternalistic solidarity (2015, p. 234).

What tools are available to enable an encounter in "that space in the margin"? Certainly, any essentialistic solution must be avoided. Mohanty (2003) uses the expression "imagined community" to indicate an action that "suggests potential alliances and collaborations across divisive boundaries, . . . suggesting political rather than biological or cultural bases for alliance" (pp. 46–47). More precisely, a "community of resistance [is] not based on any ahistorical notion of the inherent resistance and resilience of Third World peoples."

The role of those who are in the position of the oppressor vis-à-vis the slaughtering of bodies is obviously problematic. Hardt (2016) suggests that the desire to join the animal struggle is expressed above all in the claim of "the right not to be a perpetrator." In this sense, one of the most important challenges for an *animal movement of liberation* is to imagine communities of resistance in which human solidarity concretely expresses itself, starting from a deep questioning of species privilege—maybe the least examined among privileges—that brings out the desire not to participate in oppression. And veganism, provided it is redefined, can be a powerful tool for us to express an embodied critique of our species privilege.

In fact, if we define veganism as "decolonizing diet," following Colling's proposal (2014, p. 112), it is possible to relate our privileged location as humans to nonhuman resistance. The irruption of a nonhuman body into urban space, as we have seen, is able to create solidarity, but often not without great contradictions. Even if there are cases of people who have become vegetarian or vegan following an encounter with an animal on the run, people's empathic reactions are usually not accompanied by a change in eating habits. In general, then, veganism is an embodied political practice, but one that does not derive from a real relationship with oppressed subjects: we imagine the suffering of nonhumans and manifest, using a style of consumption, our "closeness" to a collective subject (farmed animals) who has an ideal, and in some ways indefinite, character.

While maintaining this level of "idealization," the "decolonial diet" welcomes requests for solidarity with animal rebels, together with criticism of the modern production system, a criticism that underlines the articulation of social inequalities, human exploitation, environmental destruction along neocolonial lines. It fully highlights our location, which is that of people who cannot be sacrificed, *who cannot be slaughtered*, whose existential vulnerability is minimized as far as is possible, precisely to the detriment of those who do not belong to Homo sapiens. "Non-sacrificeability" implies, for example, the right to free movement—which, with respect to nonhuman resistance, is denied to cows or pigs in farms and slaughterhouses. By redefining ethical veganism in this way, we can overcome the ephemerality of our closeness to the individual who fled the slaughterhouse by connecting this empathy to a system of intensive exploitation of animal bodies that affects billions of individuals, most of whom have not been so quick or so lucky to escape but share the same desires with the "lucky ones."

Within this framework, veganism is a means of deepening one's location at the intersection of axes of power. For example, queer veganism (Simonsen 2012) offers us the opportunity to constantly remember what society constantly removes, that is, the species-/gender-based violence that is associated with social reproduction, specifically with the production, distribution, and preparation of food—heteronormativity and "anthroponormativity" at the same time. Then, if we consider how mainstream veganism is expressed in terms established by the white subject, Black veganism (Ko 2017) enables us to notice how the very concepts of animality and race were modeled on each other during the colonization process. A veganism that is not modeled on the paradigm of the white, heterosexual, male activist, who has a say in place of the "voiceless," is a practice in which solidarity is not paternalistic, as it recognizes the location of the human subject who refuses their privilege but at the same time constantly reminds us that the category of nonhuman, or subhuman, affects even human subjects to varying degrees. Indeed, coloniality unfolds its effects on Black lives, gender-nonconforming people, and other marginalized groups also through animalization.

In this sense, however, it is important to highlight commonality not only in oppression, but also in the capacity for resistance, in agency. Starting from the ability to resist that nonhumans and animalized humans have in common, it is possible to use the decolonizing diet as an instrument of resistance, whereby the human subject is decentralized with respect to nonhuman agency. Veganism is a necessary first step in order that we may use the word *companion* in a multispecific sense: if the etymology of the term (from *cum panis*) refers to the act of eating together, of sharing the table, we can clearly state that there is no conviviality if one "companion" eats the other. Therefore, refusing to eat animals can constitute an act of solidarity towards the rebel and a way of echoing their voice in favor of all the others whose voices are more difficult to hear. In this sense, veganism as multispecies solidarity is one example of a possible interspecies alliance, a practice in which solidarity is expressed through the renunciation of part of the species privilege.

The escapes of Yvonne, Camilla, Scilla, and Molly and the rebellions of Tatiana, Tyke, and Tilikum are not simply acts of rejection of their own oppression. These are proof of the fact that nonhumans have voices that extend far beyond the simple ability to produce sounds, such that we may have to seriously consider redefining the limits of what is or is not "language" and, above all, reconfiguring the political sphere. By confronting themselves as subjects, these animals actually rediscuss who is a political subject. They concretely require us to consider their agency as a fact and to express interspecies solidarity by considering them as active subjects who can take the floor by themselves. Therefore, their political action is aimed not only at saving themselves, but also at challenging the tools that make their material exploitation and their symbolic reification (passivation) possible. All we have to do is take them seriously and take seriously the questions that a non-paternalistic vision of nonhumans poses.

Acknowledgments

The author would like to thank Niccolò Bertuzzi, Sarat Colling, Julie Coumau, feminoska, Paul Hodge, and Giorgio Losi for having discussed previous versions of the article and for their valuable suggestions. A special thanks to the collective Resistenza Animale (resistenzanimale.noblogs.org) for the constant inspiration.

12

FARMING VEGAN FOOD

THE ETHICS OF COMPASSIONATE CUISINE AND CULTIVATION

David V. Fazzino II

SETTING THE SCENE

It is a perfect summer afternoon as I drive from Watkins Glen, New York, to Farm Sanctuary, a small-scale nonprofit organization that rescues farmed animals. These rescued animals will likely live out the remainder of their lives in relative peace, away from the terrors that await their compatriots in many industrial and artisanal operations. At the minimum, their physiology and biology will not be appropriated by humans on an everyday basis; rather, they will serve as the embodiment of what is possible, a partnership between humans and animals in which compassion is highlighted. These nonhuman animals are still serving the particular ideological needs of their human companions, as Farm Sanctuary is an education and demonstration center. The operations of Farm Sanctuary show that it's possible to provide for the needs of animals with fairly standard farm equipment, red barns, tractors with PTO (power take-off) attachments, and a relatively inexpensive labor force.

As I look upon the bucolic scene, I can't help but think of my own farm in Central Pennsylvania. We are in the midst of growing season, and every day is precious in the maintenance of the domesticated landscapes that will be managed to attain specific goals. In the case of my farm, these goals are a mix of providing habitat to wildlife, growing spray-free food, and providing high-quality and nutritious food to local people who may not be able to afford it. For my two neighbors, one leasing in a corn-soy industrial agriculture model and the other operating a Christmas tree farm, efforts are made to produce one or two products for a market, hopefully yielding a return that will allow them to have the lifestyle they want in a capitalist consumer society (Lipsitz 2006).

In each of these settings, the desires of the farmer, as a creator who manifests domesticated landscapes, are highlighted. Hence, what one sees as natural processes is sculpted not only by a series of implements, but also by the underlying ideologies and cultural frames through which one envisions productivity in the landscape. In fairness, both of my neighbors are likely producing greater economic yields in comparison to the approximately 5,000 dollars' worth of produce that I generate on an annual basis. None of our systems incorporates animals directly in order to make the production work; however, the corn is grown for animal feed. Also, both my neighbor and I lose a significant percentage of our crop due to deer and other field creatures.

I provide this brief overview of landscapes to highlight the extent to which they can be viewed through a variety of lenses. In this chapter, rather than sharply contrasting agricultural operations that incorporate animals, in terms of the suffering wrought, with those that do not, I explore the continuum along which we may assess the multiple costs and forms of suffering inherent in different forms of food production, including industrial, semi-industrial, and non-industrial farming systems that provide for vegan diets. Drawing on my own experiences as a vegan, vegetarian, farmer, farm worker, and educator, I consider vegan farming production systems historically oriented towards producing ethical and compassionate cuisine, involving not only food producers but also food collectors, such as foragers, gatherers, and hunters. As an anthropologist, I employ the key concepts of cultural relativism and ethnocentrism in my analysis of the ways in which various foods are cultivated and consumed and reflect on assumptions that I, as a vegan and a food producer, have.

Considering the (Ethical) Landscape

In today's market-based capitalist consumer society (Lipsitz 2006), a plethora of labeling schemes has emerged in order to assuage consumer concerns over the potential costs of product production. "Organic," "cruelty-free," "fair-trade," and the like promise that certain ethics were not compromised in the composition of a product. Hence, a consumer is supposedly assured by the labeling that they are avoiding contributing to negative ethical outcomes or are, in fact, producing a more just and sustainable world through the consumption of particular products. Often, products that are labeled with one or several of the above designators are purchased at a price premium. A consumer supposedly can, in effect, through conscious decisions, buy their way into living ethically. Indeed: "Food labels are loaded with a range of signs and symbols and material values that go beyond nutrition and health. Today, moral discourse has become an important commodity in its own right a medium of exchange" (Irvine 2013, p. 146).

For moral vegans (henceforth vegans), this ethical calculus, applied to the realm of food production, means that in their quest to nourish their bodies, they eliminate animal suffering both directly and indirectly. For vegans, all things animal must be rooted out. This is not easy in an age of increased mystification of industrial and chemical food production processes, whereby both ingredient names and ingredient lists have expanded to create low-cost production and high profits. As Irvine (2013) notes, "vegan discourse also instantiated a new type of consumer, the highly motivated pure ethical vegan" (p. 147). As a vegan, I would often painstakingly scrutinize ingredients to ensure that animals and their byproducts were not present in the foods I was about to consume. This, coupled with knowledge about industrial farming practices in confined animal feeding operations (CAFOs), led me to assume that I was acting in the most ethical way possible by rooting out the often hidden and unacknowledged suffering of sentient beings. Through this process, I thought I would cull suffering from my shopping cart and my plate. However, as I reflect on these past practices now that I have more experience in agroecology, I am less confident that my younger self was as ethical and effective as I thought. I am less certain about my assumption that my diet did not bring suffering upon animals.

What I seek to do in the remainder of this chapter is to consider the ethical ramifications of the production of what are commonly considered vegan foods—that is, foods that have no animal ingredients listed whatsoever. Hence, it is an exploration of common processes of food production at various scales to unveil where animal, including human, suffering may potentially occur. I ultimately argue that scale matters in terms of the potential of creating conditions of compassionate cultivation and hence reducing suffering for sentient beings. Although it is difficult to quantify precisely the amount of suffering involved in the procuring of food, this chapter opens up the possibility that small-scale, mixed food production and food collection systems that effectively incorporate animals so that they live out their lives as contributing members of (agro)ecosystems may, all things considered, produce fewer ethical dilemmas than some vegan diets that seek near-universal bans on the utilization of animals, while leaving systematic suffering throughout the food system unaddressed.

I do this by highlighting the problems of industrial food production and reflecting on my own pathways to understanding food production in different social and geographic contexts. This enables me to interrogate my own complacency as a compassionate consumer and to unearth the troubling ethnocentric foundation of my previous tendency to hold veganism as a universal ideal for our species as a whole.

Farming for a Vegan Future?

I begin with a consideration of Deckers's (2013) vegan project, "which strives for radical legal reform to pass laws that would reserve the consumption of animal products to a very narrow range of situations, resulting in vegan diets being the default diets for the majority of human beings" (p. 187). Deckers excludes the Inuit from the ethical responsibility of being vegan, primarily due to their remoteness and to environmental conditions that do not make the growing of fruits and vegetables possible. In allowing this possible exception to the vegan project, Deckers appears to consider only material and ecological concerns. There is little acknowledgment of the cultural diversity that comprises our species—including our rich biocultural heritage of intense and meaningful interspecies relationships. The intent of Deckers's near-universal "vegan project" suggests that an absolute moral imperative to root out human consumption of animals and animal byproducts has ethnocentric underpinnings. Deckers suggests and potentially enables systems of hierarchical control wherein diet becomes a new means to judge entire groups of people, who consume that which should not be consumed, as immoral and living outside of the law.

In contrast to this view, I suggest, following Hunn (1999), that Indigenous peoples (and others who practice subsistence, from food producers to food collectors) throughout the globe offer industrial consumer societies alternatives to which we would do well to pay heed. Indeed, many of these alternatives have provided fodder for those in Western societies to reimagine food systems. Potentially the most notable instance of this alternative thinking comes from the work of Indigenous peoples in creating the design principles of permaculture (Mollison 1990), which I highlight in detail below. Hence, on nutritional grounds alone, to excuse the continued consumption of animals by the Inuit based on the culturally rooted moral stances of Western academic vegans such as Deckers, stances that make said consumption morally repugnant, forecloses on the possibility and viability of alternative, non-Western ways of viewing the world.

To do so is to seek to undercut the moral grounds for practices that, in the eyes of the many Indigenous peoples, make the world new and possible again in a very real, material, and ideological sense. That is, the consumption of traditional foods and the associated myths and practices make life possible for them both socially and psychologically. To neglect this possibility by framing their actions as moral affronts to humanness stymies cross-cultural knowledge exchange and adds to previous colonial legacies of control that have been justified by ethnocentric assumptions about the supposed savagery or barbarism of the Other and about the lack of refinement in their practices and beliefs as compared to supposedly civilized peoples.[1]

Ultimately, the production of the majority of vegan foods today in the U.S., with its heavy reliance on industrial agriculture, does very little to stem animal suffering at various levels. Surely, this is better than the horrors of CAFOs, but it nonetheless operates according to the logics of capitalist production, which externalizes the suffering of animals and people in fields and in far-off locales. I can live according to my own ethics, and as such, I plan on maintaining the fencing that keeps the dozens of deer who make their way across my farm daily away from my crops. I will likely not incorporate animals into my twenty-three-acre farm because I simply don't want to dedicate time to them at this point. I am unlikely to sit down to what is likely the most sustainable product of my farm, a venison meal, anytime soon.

I am allowed to live with these contradictions in a capitalist consumer society. I rather enjoy them, and I am extremely uncomfortable with broadly defined "development projects" (Escobar 2011)—among which I include Deckers's vegan project—that promise a greater inter- and intra-species good but often serve to justify dominance and oppression. A range of vegan projects is possible, including legislation that calls for greater accounting of the ecological costs of consumption in the prices we as consumers pay, and will likely make for lighter living in relation to currently meat-heavy diets sourced from CAFOs. Nevertheless, Deckers's blanket project, which relegates the majority of people on this planet to a less-than-ethical life because of their use of plants and animals in diverse production and collection schemes, is ethically dubious due to its colonial and ethnocentric underpinnings.

The Need to Feed: Industrial Global Agriculture

Proponents of industrial agriculture argue that the methods of food production employed are necessary for the survival of people today—that is, human lives matter, and the only way to sustain human life is to continue current food production endeavors. The now-infamous phrases "planting fencerow to fencerow" and "get big or get out" attributed to former Secretary of Agriculture Earl Butz continue to dominate food production policies in the U.S. The ends justify the means, as what can be done to produce greater yields must be done in order to appropriately care for our fellow humans (Fazzino 2012). The extensive planting of monoculture crops in

1. For a series of engaging chapters that consider issues of power and colonialism in nutrition and food systems, see Hayes-Conroy and Hayes-Conroy (2013).

mechanized industrial agriculture often necessitates intensive inputs of fossil fuels, water resources, pesticides, fungicides, herbicides, and inorganic fertilizers, all of which diminish the quality of life for present and future generations in the name of producing commodities for today's market.

In industrial systems of production, large swaths of monoculture stretching as far as the eye can see are common. At the most extreme end, every organism in the field that is not this season's marketable crop is considered to be a pest and is eliminated, including through the use of a number of chemicals, the most notorious of which is perhaps glyphosate, a probable carcinogen according to the World Health Organization (International Agency for Research on Cancer 2017). Of course, the impacts of pesticides are not limited to human health, as in the case of glyphosate, but extend to a variety of organisms and ecological processes. The use of these chemicals allows for the planting of monoculture crops in vast areas, leading to high economic and ecological costs, including: public health impacts (acute poisoning, cancer and other chronic diseases, illness from pesticide residues in food); domestic animal poisonings and contaminated products; destruction of beneficial natural predators and parasites; pesticide resistance in pests; honeybee and wild bee poisonings and reduced pollination; crop and crop product losses; ground and surface water contamination; fishery losses; impacts on wild birds, mammals, microbes, and invertebrates (Pimentel & Burgess 2005, pp. 229–252).

I have witnessed some of these impacts in passing. I derive great joy from riding my bicycle out into the countryside and seeing summer's bounty and fall's harvest across the fields of Pennsylvania. These trips, filled with fresh air and bucolic scenes, are all too often interrupted by the smell of freshly applied chemicals and the sight of the mangled bodies of field creatures who have succumbed to either the chemicals or the tractors. Davis (2003) estimates that on a mechanized farm, 60 percent of field animals would be killed at some point during the year's production activities (p. 389). This means 15 animals would be killed on every hectare; with 120 million hectares in production, according to the USDA in 1997, "1.8 billion animals would be killed annually to produce a vegan diet for the USA" (Davis 2003, p. 390). We may argue about the exact numbers of animals killed to produce feed crops for industrial animal agriculture versus vegan food production; however, it is clear that vegan diets based on industrial agriculture contribute to animal suffering and death.

It is also important to consider, in addition to the aforementioned impacts of the production of vegan foods in industrial agricultural production systems, the supply chains that produce all of the equipment, fossil fuels, and chemicals utilized on farms. So, too, is it necessary to consider the transport of these foods to various factories for preparation and packaging, as well as through a series of hubs to be distributed to grocery shelves. The above indicates that considerations of food miles, which highlight the use of fossil fuels and the subsequent contribution to climate change, need to encompass fossil fuel consumption not only in the movement of produce to plate, but also throughout the entire process.

In addition, from an animal welfare perspective, habitat and movement are cut by roads and animals are maimed or killed in collisions with motor vehicles (Hels & Buchwald 2001; Jaeger & Fahrig 2004; Litvaitis & Tash 2008; Riley et al., 2003). Ground transport notwithstanding, the air transport of tropical produce to be consumed in the U.S. and Europe also produces many miles, contributing to climate change and the suffering of humans and nonhuman animals. Melican and Maxwell (2007), for example, highlight the morally indefensible consumption of mangoes, writing that "since the effects of global warming stand to be most catastrophic for the poorest people on the planet, and since we insist on contributing to it due to our personal desires, the following observation at this stage might be usefully formulated: we value our own *preferences* above the *needs* of other people" (p. 209, emphasis in original).

Industrial agriculture emphasizes efficiency along very narrow parameters, while at the same time making unknown the processes of production, including not only the poor living conditions of nonhuman animals in CAFOs but also practices that demean nonhuman lives within agriculture. This is also the case for humans. In the U.S., an agricultural system producing cheap food relies heavily on labor from Mexico to continue to be viable (Holmes 2013; Striffler 2007; Striffler 2002). While slaughterhouse workers are subjected to dangerous conditions that literally put their limbs and lives at risk (Striffler 2007; Striffler 2002), the dangers extend to other operations as well. Farm workers who work with fruits and vegetables, who are generally but not always migrants, face structural violence both in the fields and within broader society that leads to deleterious health outcomes (Holmes 2013; Malkin 2004; Rothenberg 2000). These aspects, as in the case of CAFOs, remain largely hidden, such that one must deliberately seek out knowledge about the social inequality, racism, and ethnocentrism that currently make industrial food production possible in the U.S. (Guthman 2008; Rothenberg 2000).

In neoliberal discourses, narratives of personal responsibility tend to overshadow critiques of structural violence that highlight social inequality. The result is that consumers cannot or are not willing to see how their consumption of foods produced in industrial systems brings harm upon individuals working in those systems, rather than acknowledging only harm to their own persons—such as poor health—and attributing it to a lack of self-care, having no one to blame but themselves (Holmes 2013). As a matter of fact, consumers who eat health foods often do so at the expense of the health of others. As Holmes (2013) demonstrates, in the case of berry production, health benefits consumers gain from the antioxidants in berries come at the expense of those who suffer for each berry; thus, there is an unequal distribution of health in berry production and consumption.

Vegans who focus solely on the consumer end of the spectrum may operate under the assumption that because the food they eat never had a face that could express joy and sorrow, it is without harm. However, food is not faceless; there are always those who have worked to produce it, who are often hidden from view. Hence, as consumers are at the far end of the industrial production system, a certain non-knowing is inherent to them; many can assume to have an ethical diet while ignoring potential violences throughout industrial production processes. Advocacy for farm workers' rights has a long history in the U.S. (Chavez 2002), but those in a capitalist consumer society who practice veganism as the consumption of non-animal products are not necessarily contributing to this work. Perhaps the most poignant critique of veganism as merely a consumer activity comes from Gelderloos (2008), who questions its long-term sustainability, both material and ideological. The above discussion has highlighted the suffering inherent in industrial production systems, adding to what I believe is a key component of veganism—that is, coming to know the processes that make up the production of recognizable food objects.

Coming to Know Food, Part 1: A Personal Narrative

An important part of being an educator is providing opportunities for others to see their world in a new light and to consider the impacts of their own preferences and beliefs. A number of years ago, I was teaching a class on nutrition at an allied health college, and I decided to fill some class time by showing a film about food systems that highlighted the conditions in CAFOs. My intent in showing this to the class was to get the students to consider the industrial production system as a whole and how it might factor into their decisions on how to nourish their bodies.

My attempt at empowering students with knowledge of the world around them fell flat. We never got to the discussion of the current systems of food production and their implications for human health, as a number of students refused to watch the film, particularly as it covered the treatment of living animals as a component of an industrial production system. They resisted an alternative view of the foods that they typically consumed. They resisted alternative narratives to the ones that they shared with their friends and family through the sharing of sustenance. For them, the flesh that they regularly consumed was dense with meanings attributed to it through collective celebrations and everyday life in their family, community, and culture. Ultimately, this was more than a desire not to know; it was a desire to cling to beliefs and practices that they had acquired from their parents and their parents' parents. The knowledge I shared contradicted their understandings of food and self. It was a good lesson for me, reminding me that not all knowledge is desirable, particularly when it challenges basic assumptions about the ordering of the world.

I had assumed that because my transition to vegetarianism and veganism had occurred during my time at university, as had been the case for many of my friends, by showing this film and discussing it with students in my classroom, I would at least be providing the opportunity for these college students to come to their own conclusions about ethical and correct practices in food consumption. My transition to vegetarianism and veganism had certainly helped me define my own sense of identity as a white middle-class male. My journey to veganism was part of my attempt to live as a (semi)autonomous adult. The seeking of peace in relationships with sentient beings through abstention from eating animals and their byproducts comes at the expense of peace in social and familial relationships. Hence, ethical veganism must be considered as part of a series of ethical decisions. Where familial ties are central to one's sense of identity from a cultural perspective, the suggestion of dietary modifications that go against well-set norms can be fundamentally destabilizing.

What I am getting at here is that although my transition to veganism was not met with approval from family members, who expressed concern for my health and, in some instances, the additional burden on them to provide alternative food options for every meal, it was nonetheless part of my process of defining myself as an individual. This journey of self-discovery, however, did not come to fruition for many of my students, who chose to remain utterly oblivious to the ways foods were produced.

Indeed, for me, the process of becoming a vegan was a process of self-education. As a child growing up in rural areas, I was often brought to farms on school field trips. During these trips, there may have been apple picking, baking, farm demonstrations, and interactions with farmed animals—goats, sheep, horses, and the like. I was shown the safe, permissible, and peaceful side of farming in small-scale operations. These glimpses of farm life were consistent with the children's books I read, which highlighted the bucolic, peaceful coexistence of humans, farmed animals, and the landscape as a whole. We were not brought to the killing floors of slaughterhouses or to CAFOs, where there were cries of pain and agony, where the blood of living animals gushed and other undesirable parts were ripped from their sentient bodies. We were likely viewed as too young to be exposed to the graphic origins of what we were eating.

During the 1970s, the National Science Foundation sponsored the Man: A Course of Study (MACOS) program in an effort to enhance critical thinking in children in the fifth grade. This was driven in large part by fears that the former Soviet Union was winning against the U.S. in the space race. The MACOS curriculum included the Netsilik Film Series, made using the ethnographic present of the 1920s and 1930s. The Netsilik in these films demonstrated customary practices of life, including subsistence. Laird's *Through These Eyes* (2003) highlights the extent to which ethnocentric assumptions of superiority destabilized the MACOS program when one child reportedly became sick for days after watching a young Netsilik child eat an eyeball. The program was pulled from schools after a short time due to its "inappropriateness" and "graphic" imagery (Laird 2003).

I have used this film continually in the past ten years to teach university students the concepts of cultural relativism and ethnocentrism. It has been generally taken well by students in the Subarctic, who have typically maintained that the MACOS project would be more likely to succeed in today's classrooms as we, as a society, have become less ethnocentric and more accepting of cultural differences. These are primarily students who grew up in Alaska or the Canadian Subarctic and Arctic and were familiar with subsistence practices of hunting and fishing, either from firsthand experience or from discussions of the history of the region throughout their K–12 education. I again made the mistake of assuming that these reactions would be universal among university students. Hence, I was surprised by the negative and ethnocentric responses from students at my current university when I first used the film *Losing Ground: Shishmaref, Alaska* by Ryota Kajita to highlight the interconnections between climate change, subsistence, and traditional ecological knowledge.

I have since avoided showing this film in class and instead have made it available as an out-of-class exercise. I preface the film with a warning to students about the "graphic" nature of some scenes featuring the butchering of marine mammals, reminding them of the importance of these subsistence practices as a source of nutrition, livelihood, and meaning to many. Acknowledging and appreciating such diversity in food practices should not be dismissed as immoral but are an important element of compassionate veganism.

Coming to Know Food, Part 2

I am still coming to know about food, about the sustenance that not only makes my life possible but also enhances my understanding of and respect for other species, different processes, and more generally, Earth as we know it. I have worked in various capacities on farms in Pennsylvania, West Virginia, Florida, and Arizona. I have completed a second season on my farm in Central Pennsylvania and am just beginning to understand what I can and should do to minimize harm and maximize the potential for life. I sometimes make mistakes, despite my intentions, and animals suffer. Yet I continue to learn and to work the soil with deliberation and care.

Working on the land and helping others to cultivate landscapes have kept my untested ideas for compassionate cultivation in check and produced a grounded account of the possibilities and limitations in balancing what may be competing goals around subsistence or livelihood, sustainability, and compassion. Among my many teachers are those engaged in food production as their livelihood, as well as those homesteading. Most have not been full-time farmers due to a number of circumstances, including economics and pursuits of passion in other areas. I count myself among part-time producers who adopt small-scale agroecological principles with an emphasis on permaculture, which I learned from dedicated and thoughtful individuals in Western Pennsylvania and West Virginia.

Permaculture practitioners are concerned with building systems that live up to the name—developed cultures that can be permanent. Permaculture is based on three ethical imperatives:

> 1. CARE OF THE EARTH: Provision for all life systems to continue and multiply. 2. CARE OF PEOPLE: Provision for people to access those resources necessary to their existence. 3. SETTING LIMITS TO POPULATION AND CONSUMPTION: By governing our own needs, we can set resources aside to further the above principles. (Mollison 1990, p. 2, all caps in original)

Hence, Mollison calls for limits to the fulfillment of human wants and needs in order to maximize care of Earth and of people. This is an oft-used justification for veganism: by eliminating the consumption of meat and other animal products, we can sustain more people while causing less suffering to both humans and other species.

What is striking about the approaches that stem from a permaculture framework is that care is the core concept that governs every action taken. These are carefully thought-out approaches that are based on long periods of observation, reflection, and planning, followed by the implementation of a design that is always subject to change, depending on what is possible in a given area. By working with natural cycles and patterns, permaculturalists strive to build systems that are resilient, adaptive, and self-sustaining and that provide sustenance and livelihood to families and communities. Rather than dreading the supposedly inevitable neo-Malthusian nightmare of a race to the bottom, permaculturalists address issues at the local level. They not only consider the needs of people, but also work to ensure that every element is integrated with every other element so that plants thrive and nonhuman animals live healthy and meaningful lives, with the space to engage in key species-specific behaviors. A poignant example is wildlife farms, which:

> are sometimes established in forest areas. Deer, for example, can lead a natural and free existence before being shot by a guardian of the forest when he determines that the animal should be removed. This type of farming, when conducted correctly, does not degrade the environment. There is virtually no cost involved, and it provides high-quality meat. Even those who condemn the killing of an animal for food must recognize that the quality of a wild animal's life is infinitely better than our cattle experience in typical livestock operations. (Hervé-Gruyer & Hervé-Gruyer 2016, p. 160)

This concern about quality of life, coupled with considerations of subsistence-based economies and the destructive nature of industrial agriculture as previously discussed, caused me to reflect on my own ethical commitments in compassionate cultivation. These commitments continue to cultivate my skepticism over the ethical nature of food consumption in the context of mass-produced non-animal product foods from industrial agriculture. This chapter calls for an expansion of ethical considerations around food production that extend beyond Deckers's (2013) project. Different forms of veganism (personal, collective, and political) allow for critical thinking and reflection with respect to processes of food production that directly lead to suffering of a proximate, visceral nature, as well as indirectly cause harm.

At least for me, veganism also spurs reflection on the scope of suffering caused by industrial agriculture and opens up the possibility that, in some instances, consumption of some forms of non-industrially produced animal flesh may cause less overall suffering, particularly if the processes behind the production of vegan foods are spread across large distances. I cannot know these processes, but this does not mean that I should not consider their probable impacts, given what we know about the suffering inflicted by the industrial infrastructure of contemporary global agriculture. While this chapter has pointed out that the full scope of animal suffering, including death, is unknowable, the story of compassionate cultivation of plants and animals complicates and potentially broadens the meaning of vegan practice at the individual level.

Further, and potentially more importantly, this new narrative should open up the possibility that there is a multitude of ways for us to meet our sustenance needs based on ethical principles specific to cultural setting. Animals must die, in different social, cultural, economic, and political settings, for some of us to live. Animals must die for food unless we are willing to institute heavy-handed, ethnocentric, and, in some instances, colonial legislation that deems some people immoral and deserving of punishment. This is not to deny the horrors of CAFOs and the tales told in Sinclair's *The Jungle*, which first drew me to veganism and helped me confront the morally reprehensible practices that rob animals of any ascertainable joy in life. To be clear, my arguments above do not merely reflect a welfarist perspective that seeks to reform the use of animals, in contrast to an abolitionist stance that seeks to abolish it (Wrenn 2013, p. 380).

Instead, I argue that there is no dichotomy—that is, in any setting, all we really have to fall back on when it comes to sustenance, or any other need or desire we have as consumers, is the welfarist perspective. Despite our intentions to the contrary, we are predatory in the sense that the maintenance of our bodies always necessitates the taking of other life and its incorporation into our selves. Consider the case of Jainism, referred to by Sen (2007) as "the world's most ethical religion." Sen notes: "While in practice it is impossible to survive without killing or injuring some form of being, Jains strive to avoid doing any intentional harm. Thus, they are in theory not allowed to be farmers, because tilling the soil would kill life" (p. 234). In this instance, intentional harm is measured by direct injury to "some form of being." Nevertheless, there is an acknowledgment that suffering is inevitable and that life, sentient or otherwise, is used and sacrificed, directly or otherwise, to preserve human life.

Concluding Thoughts: What's on My Plate?

In this chapter, I have considered animal—including human—suffering in food production, with particular emphasis on industrial channels of food production, distribution, and consumption. In so doing, I have attempted to complicate considerations of morality in eating and to problematize the idea that any one diet can represent the pinnacle of human relationships with the sentient beings we share the planet with. Veganism is compassionate in that it extends consideration to beings who have moral standing; nonetheless, it is cultural—it is rooted in particular traditions. As I have shown above, veganism as a consumer activity (Gelderloos 2008) is a starting point for us to holistically consider suffering and compassion in the food system. There are costs in terms of life in vegan food production at the artisanal and industrial levels, but scale does matter.

It is not my intent to be proscriptive in my approach; rather, I have attempted to reveal the underlying ethical—and hence cultural—underpinnings of various production systems in different environmental, social, cultural, economic, and political contexts, involving various species, including humans, in the quest to sustain humans. While the increased mechanization of agriculture has freed many of us from the manual labor necessary to procure or produce food, it has come at a cost, which is that we now do not know the true costs of food. It is only currently that a small minority of people are able to procure their food locally or from small-scale, artisanal producers who prioritize compassionate cultivation, including in the form of vegan organic production. These small-scale and labor-intensive production operations are noteworthy and innovative responses to the suffering and high resource consumption caused by petroleum-based industrial agriculture. Powering tractors with the energy of living bodies rather than fossil fuels means more people will need to be engaged in agriculture; it also means working landscapes at a slower pace and with more deliberate care so as to minimize harm.

The framework of compassionate cultivation can be scaled up so that we may feed more people with less unnecessary suffering. It is likely that utilizing these protocols will result in an increase in the price of food that, if borne by the consumer, will likely curb expenditures in other areas of consumption. Institutional change, coupled with legislative reform to ensure that the most economically vulnerable of us are not priced out of consideration, is needed. We are witnessing a proliferation of labeling schemes in industrial systems of food production and distribution that promise consumers a kinder, gentler agriculture, whether they deliver it or not.

While not everyone will be involved in agriculture, more people can be, and expertise can be developed with time, practice, and care. This means we ought to promote not necessarily Deckers's vegan project but rather a series of locally based subsistence initiatives as alternative means of providing necessities at the local level (Hornborg 2007). As such, more feet walking on this earth, more heads pondering natural systems and seeking to make them better for all species can lead to a new era that values time-tested principles from most of the world's cultures, wherein compassionate cultivation of plants, our fellow animals, and ourselves is not only possible but highly probable.

Those who have striven towards veganism have often moved beyond Hobbesian notions of the struggle to wrest sustenance from the earth. It is likely that those reading this text have moved beyond this struggle as well. Food, like almost everything that most people consume, becomes a thing that we enjoy to an extent and then discard once it is deemed no longer of value. The product—what appears in our hands or on our forks—is temporary and fleeting; more is on the way, whether accessed via sterile supermarkets or vibrant farm stands. Veganism, for me, was and is always about coming to know food, making known invisible processes of production, and then learning ways to be a more compassionate consumer and, from there, a compassionate cultivator. This is a humbling journey that I am still on.

Those promoting the consumption of vegan foods tend to engage in persuading behavior, telling people what's wrong with their current approach to eating and telling them that they should be vegan consumers. For example, Hooley and Nobis (2015) note that while most people in developed countries are "morally obligated not to support the wrongdoing of the meat industry" and "are obligated to eat vegan," there is no corresponding obligation to grow food in a way that minimizes harm to animals. They explain:

> What anyone is obligated to do depends on what he or she can do, and most people just cannot grow all their own food or eat such a diet: that's not realistic. We are only obligated to take reasonable steps to minimize harms that we contribute to with our food choices, but this is consistent with an obligation to be vegan. Unlike meat and other animal products, there are no readily available alternatives to vegetables and other plant foods grown in ways that kill some field animals. (p. 106)

I disagree: there are alternatives, and if veganism is about a moral obligation to reduce suffering, then vegans should act accordingly. This does not mean vegans are obligated to pick up a broadfork (or even Google the word "broadfork") to join me and countless others in living our truth of a "new, more inclusive and more ecologically aware version of animal advocacy and veganism . . . to make [ourselves] part of ecological processes and feedbacks as much as possible" (Alloun 2015, p. 165). My disagreement is simply that just because you cannot be the one working the soil to create food that results in less harm does not mean that you cannot, in your own way, cultivate compassion for your fellow sentient beings—including humans, with their unique worldviews and perspectives—to ultimately bring about paradigmatic shifts whose final product is a life we can all enjoy.

13

BEAR LIFE VERSUS BARE LIFE

The Political Lives of More-Than-Human Actors

Jennifer Mateer

Introduction

Veganism, as the term was first coined in 1944 by Donald Watson (Leneman 1999), has existed for millennia, across the world and in different cultural and social contexts. However, vegan ethics and ways of being in the world are currently receiving renewed attention in popular culture. As an example, 2018 was proclaimed the year of "plant-based eating" to reflect the increase in the number of people who self-identified as vegan—a rise of 600 percent in the U.S. in the preceding three years and a 361 percent increase in the U.K. over ten years (Hancox 2018; Rivera 2016). In Canada, vegetarians and vegans make up approximately 10 percent of the total population; however, this number is only going to increase, as the vast majority of vegan and vegetarian individuals are under the age of thirty-five and, as such, are predicted to be soon starting families and raising children with the same eating preferences (Flanagan 2018; Thomson 2018). The popularity of the vegan diet has also increased amid the coronavirus pandemic, with approximately 25 percent of people between twenty-one and thirty years of age saying this eating and lifestyle choice "has become more attractive" (Shaw 2020; Dutta 2020).

This new interest in plant-based eating and products has resulted in the growth of the plant-based food market, with "lucrative growth opportunities," especially in North America (TMR Research 2020; Dutta 2020). The U.K. has also been a site of increased interest in plant-based products since the coronavirus outbreak (Ridler 2020). Considering the reinvigoration of vegan ideals and goals, researchers have also become more invested in what engagement with veganism entails. One point of departure for this engagement is animal geographies, which have been a mainstay of cultural and social geographies since the mid-1990s, when a themed issue of *Social and Space* defined, and provided the borders for, this branch of human geography (Wolch & Emel 1995). Alongside this disciplinary avenue, posthumanist political ecologies offer another opportunity for contributions to the burgeoning literature of vegan geographies. However, vegan geography itself offers a new opportunity to challenge human/animal dichotomies and provides new research questions regarding animal liberation and ethico-politics.

Animal geographies take a variety of approaches, including animal studies, human–animal studies (also known as human–animal interactions), bio-geographies, and anthrozoology (Taylor & Twine 2014; Spencer & Whatmore 2001; White 2015). Each of these approaches foregrounds nonhuman life, "bringing nonhuman animals out of the shadows of marginality" (White 2015, p. 20). However, many scholars within these approaches still present apolitical and "objective" discourses and, thus, do not explicitly attend to the ways in which violence towards the more-than-human world is widespread globally (Cole & Morgan 2011).

Although there are critical animal geographers who include ethical questions in their works (see Buller 2016 for a full discussion), vegan geography allows for the explicit demarcation of ethics through an integral opposition with violence against and exploitation of nonhuman beings (Cole & Morgan 2011; White 2015). This approach is a departure from a vegan diet or way of eating, as many individuals may practice a vegan diet for reasons beyond ethics. However, the approach of vegan geographies ought to include a deconstruction, examination, and overall dismantling of speciesism embedded in language, thought, action, and practice, along with a recentering of more-than-human beings.

This chapter argues that in addition to the goals of vegan geography listed above, we ought to consider and include the political lives and subjectivities of animals, as this is a method of recentering the more-than-human as part of a specific scholarship. One of the ways in which we can discuss the political lives of animals is through Giorgio Agamben's (1998) reinvigoration of Ancient Roman legal terms *Bios*, *Zoe*, and *Homo Sacer.* Although these terms refer exclusively to human animals, the lives of humans with *Zoe* are defined as "animal life" or "bare life," meaning that the human individual is alive, performing essential functions,[1] but does not have the ability to remake society or perform politically, as opposed to one with *Bios*, which refers to political life and the ability to participate in and restructure society. However, what would a reading of these concepts mean for vegan geographers?

1. These basic, essential functions include eating, sleeping, mating, etc.

For this chapter, I consider myself a generous accomplice[2] (Oleksiak 2018) to Agamben's work, putting the concepts outlined in *Homo Sacer: Sovereign Power and Bare Life* (1998) in conversation with the politics practiced by nonhuman animals (Flint 2003; Mateer 2018). I begin this discussion with an outline of Agamben's argument before troubling his ideas with a vegan geography praxis, which highlights the political agency of nonhuman animals and, as a result, challenges the idea of the inherent "bare life" of animals, instead recognizing many animals as "*Animal Sacer.*" To highlight the political agency of more-than-human beings, this chapter will use examples of elephants in India, the ocelot and jaguarundi of the U.S.–Mexico border region, as well as mosquitos in Egypt. I have chosen contextually disparate examples in order to demonstrate a cross-section of the political subjectivities of more-than-human beings; however, these should not be considered the only times and spaces when and where animals have engaged in political activities.

Brief Overview of the *Homo Sacer*

Agamben's (1998) *Homo Sacer* discussion provides a framework for understanding politics regarding the rights of citizens and the responsibilities of the State. As described by Agamben, all beings, whether human or nonhuman, are born with *Zoe*—life without political agency or mobility. Humans—Agamben's focus—can be granted political life, *Bios*, in addition to *Zoe* through recognition of the Sovereign. Today, *Bios* is generally recognized by the Sovereign for citizens of a specific age (i.e., the age at which citizens are allowed to vote in an individual country). However, "every man [*sic*] who receives rights as a citizen of a nation-state attains those rights *only insofar* as his birth (the bare life) becomes the excluded-included immediate bearer of sovereignty" (Agamben 1998, p.128, emphasis added). What this means is that citizens with *Bios* are under constant threat of having that *Bios* forcibly removed by the State, upon which they are referred to as *Homo Sacer.*[3]

Under Roman Republic law, the *Homo Sacer* is an individual removed from society and deprived of any civil rights. This person can be killed by anyone but cannot be killed religiously in a sacrificial manner, nor can they be killed by the State (for example, in a public, state-sanctioned execution). Instead, these individuals have the status of an outlaw and are referred to as being outside of

---

2. Timothy Oleksiak (2018) discusses being a generous accomplice to scholarship that he respects and admires, but also seeks to expand on that work—not because it is lacking, but because there is an opportunity to consider the scholarship beyond its original scope.
3. The status of *Homo Sacer* can be bestowed only upon someone who has held *Bios*. This means that the individual does not return to a state of *Zoe*, but rather acquires a new status—*Homo Sacer*—after having *Bios* forcibly removed.

the law—neither protected by the law nor subjected to punishment by law. However, conversely, this status of being outside the law is a legal status that marks individuals as under or not under sovereign authority. What this status means is that the Sovereign, or the State, has codified rules and regulations on how an individual is to be excluded from rules and regulations, so this individual has a legal status by virtue of being designated as without status. Agamben suggests that the ability of the State to force citizens into this legal limbo still exists today and is a tactic that turns (seemingly) democratic states into totalitarian states, taking advantage of emergencies and crises that allow for the erasure of individual legal status—a state of exception—and consequently producing legally unnamable and unclassifiable beings. Agamben points to George Bush Jr., Mussolini, Napoleon, and Hitler as sovereigns who evoked the state of exception.

In analyzing these instances in which sovereigns removed the rights of citizens via a state of exception, Agamben sheds light on previously held notions about democracy and the organization of political power, law, rights, and violence. Essentially, he concludes that there are few differences between democracy and dictatorship, between *Bios* and *Zoe*, between political life and animal life. The concepts are highly anthropocentric, but in the project of vegan geographies, the centering of nonhuman animals must take priority. As such, the question remains: What might a rereading of these concepts include and exclude, or illuminate about the political lives of animals and the global mass violence against them? This question is especially important to consider given Agamben's conclusion regarding the blurred lines between animal life and political life, which provides the main point of departure for this discussion.

Two authors who have put up the argument for animal citizenship are Donaldson and Kymlicka (2011). Although their book *Zoopolis: A Political Theory of Animal Rights* does not directly engage with the work of Agamben and is more inspired by disability studies, they do propose that countries and societies ought to consider nonhuman animals as citizens—which would potentially grant *Bios* to nonhumans. Donaldson and Kymlicka suggest that the suffering animals often endure at the hands (and economic desires) of humans can be adequately addressed only if we move beyond approaches that focus on animal welfare and/or ecological concerns.[4] Instead, domestic animals should be treated as "co-citizens of

4. Donaldson and Kymlicka argue that a welfare approach does not provide rights for animals and will maintain animals' position as subordinate to humans. Further, an ecological approach, which is concerned with the health of ecosystems, focuses too much on animals as part of a system—cogs in a machine, if you will—rather than as individuals themselves. As such, animals within ecosystems will benefit from protections, but those deemed "invasive" may be killed in the interest of the system as a whole.

our territory" (Donaldson & Kymlicka 2011, p. 214) and wild animals as sovereign interspecies communities that interact with human communities. More-than-human co-citizens, although they may not be able to vote or participate in jury duty, are able to engage with what the authors call the thinner dimensions of citizenship, which I discuss below as lowercase-p politics.[5] For example, if domesticated animals were to be considered citizens, then they would be entitled to equal protection under the law, to forms of protection such as emergency services, with personnel trained to assist nonhumans during floods or fires. There would also be public spending dedicated to protecting animals and including them in healthcare, the maintenance and design of public spaces such as parks, and so on.

Although there have been instances in which citizenship was successfully used as a tool for including historically subordinated groups in politics and *Bios*, who would be included in the mixed community of co-citizens? We know that stateless individuals are not included among those with citizenship rights, and thus, Arendt (1951) asks us to consider who has "the right to have rights." So, is citizenship the key to the inclusion of individuals in rights discourses and *Bios*? Today, not even everyone with citizenship enjoys all of the rights afforded the political community or all of the safety and security benefits (Van Waas & Jaghai 2018). This inequality often becomes apparent when one looks at how citizenship is obtained: Is it through birth, or has it been otherwise acquired? Is the individual in question a mono or dual citizen?[6] We also see in cases of "emergencies," when states of exception are normalized, that there is greater inequality with regards to citizenship status if certain individuals are perceived as threats (Van Waas & Jaghai 2018). Consider, for example, people who practice the Muslim faith and their treatment in and outside of the U.S. after 9/11. Thus, it is not uncommon for there to be different classes of human citizens and of citizenship rights, which may significantly impact the potential for nonhuman citizenship rights.

Beastly Politics

Critical scholarship on nonhuman (also referred to as more-than-human) actors examines and discusses the political spatialities and representations of animals. This subdiscipline of (more than) human geography argues that relegating animals to the category of "other" or "less than human" allows humans "to simply

5. The distinction between uppercase and lowercase P/politics is defined by Hobson (2007), who writes that lowercase-p politics includes the politics of the everyday, which can challenge institutions and normalized practices.
6. A dual citizen is more likely to experience a withdrawal of nationality and citizenship than an individual with mono, or one, nationality (Van Waas & Jaghai 2018).

look away and to ignore their fates" (Wolch & Emel 1998, p. xi), as well as to ignore their political subjectivities (Hobson 2007). The inclusion of animals in academic scholarship has interested researchers across all disciplines within the social sciences and humanities; as such, the inclusion of animals is not new, nor are animals new to political analyses. What a vegan geographic analysis offers, though, is overt attention to the ways in which animal beings have always been part of politics, most explicitly through speciesism and through descriptions of the "political subject: the human," wherein the nonhuman animal makes up "the other" (Collard 2013, p. 227). By being othered, animals are made "'faceless' things, [which contributes] to the cruelty many face today" (Jones 2000, p. 281).

What makes humans and animals diametric opposites under the above rationale is that, unlike humans, animals are considered killable or disposable (Haraway 2008). Vegan geographies, therefore, have the potential to undo the dichotomous human/animal divide to enable discussion on animals, not as passive or one-dimensional objects within political and economic relations, but instead as political subjects, and accordingly, to recognize the violence against them as political (Collard 2013; Hobson 2007; Mateer 2018; White 2015). Thus, animals—with their biographies, histories, conscious experiences, and political agencies (Ryder 1998; Masson 2005; Mateer 2018; White 2015)—are centered in the discussion, making them part of lowercase-p politics.

Flint (2003) refers to uppercase-P politics as codified national and international arrangements and negotiations. This form of international relations and political agency is contrasted with lowercase-p politics, which "refers to the spaces, peoples, and practices that . . . challenge institutions through non-traditional political avenues . . . [including] the politics of the 'everyday'" (Hobson 2007, p. 252; Flint 2003). The subjects who make up lowercase-p politics are diverse, moving beyond standard conceptions of the citizenry, and can, as a result, include more-than-human populations. I consider this an anti-speciesist approach indicative of a vegan ethic and geography that subsequently undoes what Braun and Whatmore (2010) describe as a "stubborn attachment of many scholars—liberal and radical alike—to a humanism that finds ever new ways of positing the nonhuman as '*out there*'" (p. xx, emphasis added).

One of the reasons animals and other more-than-human entities have often been excluded from political analysis and scholarship is that they are rarely considered political subjects. Historically, this has been true of other subaltern beings as well. By outlining and exposing the political lives and subjectivities of animals, vegan scholarship can provide new discursive strategies to resist the institutionalized abuse of nonhuman animals and can describe new avenues of liberation (Pedersen & Stănescu 2014; White 2015). This focus on liberation and resistance is the necessary ethical piece delineating critical animal geographies from vegan geographies[7] and, as such, acknowledges the unique natures of all "sentient being which are subjects of a life" (Regan 2001, p. 17, as cited in White 2015, p. 22). With this ethos, vegan geographies provide a necessary agenda for critically challenging speciesism[8] and humans' oppressive domination of nonhuman beings, in order to confront this ruthless era of "abject misery and suffering" (White 2015, p. 24).

A second reason why more-than-human beings are considered to lack political agency is their lack of speech. However: "Nature is highly articulate. Discourse is only one process of articulation" (Haraway 1992, p. 324). More-than-human beings are able to communicate—they have languages and thoughts, even if they cannot present these thoughts in ways that register with humans (Blue & Rock 2014). The distinction we've drawn between human and nonhuman languages is more about "convincing ourselves that we are masters of all things" (Bingham 2006, p. 491). However, this is an anthropocentric understanding of political subjectivities that limits our ability to see that all animals, human and nonhuman, are always speaking "through something or someone else" (Latour 2004a, p. 68). Consequently, "the assumption that only people have politics because people have the capacity to argue, persuade, negotiate and research consensus" (Blue & Rock 2014, p. 507) does not represent reality.

Consider, for instance, work by feminist scholars on the inclusion of individuals with developmental delay and how these people are not wards of the State but full citizens (see, for example, Conejo 2013; Kittay 2001; Kittay & Carlson 2010; Reindal 1999). Such authors critique the emphasis on independence and speech as criteria for political inclusion. Instead, they advocate relational rights and citizenship. As Kittay (2001) writes, "our dependency relations are constitutive of who we are and that, as a society, we are inextricably dependent on one another" (p. 570). Thus, citizens are not isolated—they are interrelated and interdependent actors whose actions are shaped by a relational web and social context. This relational

---

7. Currently, debates in critical geography are routinely "dismissed on the grounds of what is held to be a scholar's unacceptable ethical stance with respect to the human treatment of animals" (Buller 2016, p. 422).
8. Speciesism is the "belief in the inherent superiority of one species over others" (Moore 2013, p. 12). The best example of speciesism in Western cultural traditions is the differences in values and emotions associated with different animals. For example, dogs and cats are generally considered to be capable of love, pain, and interspecies companionship, whereas "pigs, cows and sheep are by and large characterized as objects . . . [whose] sole worth is based on what they contribute to human needs," on whether their bodies can be used "as/for food, clothing, labor, etc." As such, there is a disconnect between these two groupings of animals, which "ultimately enables an acceptance (whether overt or subconscious) of [the] violent treatment and death" of the latter (Gunderman & White 2021, p. 490).

web of interaction and interdependence can also be identified within human and nonhuman political relationships, particularly between some elephants and mahouts in India in the case of the Sepoy Mutiny. This chapter seeks to challenge the assumption that political subjectivity and active participation in politics depend on a particular form of speech or linguistic exchange (Blue & Rock 2014), as these relationships are not predicated on the ability to speak. Such cases allow scholars to see nonhuman animals as political subjects rebelling against state authority rather than as static political tools or objects, which makes animals active resisters fighting certain political practices (Robbins 2005).

Political inclusion and capacity have also been discussed with regards to children and other individuals who may participate in alternative politics. Rollo (2017), for example, discusses a deliberative systems (DS) approach as an alternative means of understanding agency and citizenship. Traditionally, deliberative democracy focuses on the speech and voice aspects of citizen participation, thus excluding many people (and all nonhumans), who do not directly participate in deliberation. DS seeks to correct this oversight by extending our understanding of individual agency beyond "formal sites of political speech designed to inform legislative decisions" (Rollo 2017, p.588). By changing the necessity of agency and political acts, the DS approach provides a more nuanced and inclusive account of democratic legitimacy that overcomes the ways in which limiting political acts and formal political agency to speech "has the effect of erasing the contributions of citizens who are either unable or unwilling to exercise voice" (p. 588).

However, as Rollo notes, there are nonverbal methods of communication, and political action involves more than speech. Rollo does not relate this observation directly to nonhuman beings; however, he does outline those bodily acts and practices that constitute political action beyond speech. More-than-human beings frequently express themselves and their subjective needs in many nonverbal ways. A cat may meow at the refrigerator when dinner is late; a dog may lash out aggressively to demonstrate their aversion to being touched in certain ways; and many animals frequently nuzzle others for affection (Donaldson & Kymlicka 2011). Each of these is an example of communication based on a subjective need or good. Although they acknowledge that some interpretation is needed on the part of an animal's companion to understand their subjective needs, Donaldson and Kymlicka believe that relational agency allows for political expressions as well. Even if a partnership with humans is necessary, these acts and exercises of will by animals become political acts based on the ways in which they contest societal norms, which fits in with the examples involving elephants, ocelots, jaguarundis, and mosquitos discussed below.

More-Than-Human Insurgents

In India, as well as other countries in South and Southeast Asia, human–elephant partnerships have allowed for activities beyond those sanctioned by the state. Sometimes, these have included illegal activities, such as smuggling and logging; however, the coming together of people and elephants in specific lifeworlds has also meant that political rebels have been able to hide from the governing colonial powers (Haraway 2008; Scott 2010). There are examples in which Indian rebels eluded British authorities by partnering with elephants. Evading the British was difficult as they had more advanced weapons and a more heavily armed and well-trained force in comparison to the Indian rebels. Yet in forming relations with elephants, the rebels were able to move subversively to avoid the British troops and governing authority (Malleson 1896; Shell 2015).

For example, during the Sepoy Mutiny,[9] Indian rebels partnered with elephants to cross the Chambal River, a tributary of the Ganges. By crossing the river, the rebels avoided capture, since the horses of the British were unable to intercept either the human rebels or the elephants (Duberly 2009 [1859]; Shell 2015). Another group of rebels also avoided capture by partnering with elephants to cross the Rapti River. It was at a particularly dangerous and fast-moving section of the river, but with the help of elephants, the rebels crossed to Nepal, out of the reach of colonial forces (Howitt 1864 [1873]; Ball 1858). When the British attempted to follow, their troops were trapped by "a sea of black mud" (Malleson 1896, p. 329; Charney 2004). When we consider these examples in conjunction with Rollo's (2017) discussion of the DS approach, we would indeed consider these acts by the elephants political deeds, even though they were unable to voice (in ways recognizable by humans) their anti-colonial sentiments. Rollo's argument reinforces this because the elephants were acting intentionally rather than habitually (p. 589). The elephants with whom the rebels partnered were capable of and yet not accustomed to crossing the Chambal or Rapti rivers, thereby contesting rather than conforming to norms.

Because elephants, due to their size and other physical attributes, do not need to travel by road, guerrilla activities out of the range of state surveillance become possible when they take part in political activities. During the Sepoy rebellion, elephants contributed to an active diminishment of the spaces of sovereignty held by the British colonial state due to their physical sizes and partnership with the Indian rebels. This relationship subsequently expanded the rebels' territory;

9. The Sepoy Mutiny, also known as the Indian Mutiny, was an anti-colonial rebellion staged against British forces between 1857 and 1858 (Malleson 1896; David 2003; Hibbert 1978). This was one of the first amalgamated anti-colonial rebellions in India and an important demonstration of Indian solidarity (David 2003; Hibbert 1978).

without the partnership between humans and elephants, the reclaiming of spaces of sovereignty and refuge for fugitives would never have been possible. As such, elephants were actors actively evading colonial powers and resisting British rule in India (Mateer 2018).

By including elephants in the Sepoy rebellion as insurgents, similar to the Indian rebels, I do not intend to map elephants "onto the pre-existing human world," where they "are dumb actors in diverse polities" (Hobson 2007, p. 257). Rather, my intention is to demonstrate that although the elephants in the above example may not have possessed the *same* political agency as did human rebels, since they could not take part in democratic decision-making processes or *verbally* express their preferences for specific policies or political practices, this does not preclude them from being political actors or from espousing political subjectivities (Hobson 2007; Mateer 2018). Animals, including these elephants, are part of political life and can change how politics is enacted and challenged (Hathaway 2016; Hobson 2007; Mateer 2018).

Another example of nonhumans as actors within political processes involves the ocelot and jaguarundi populations at the U.S.–Mexico border. These two feline populations partnered with humans in a way that compelled the American border patrol to change border security operations (Sundberg 2011); in this case, the partnership between human and feline communities can be considered a "necessary and prior condition for any [political] action to occur including the actions of humans" (Braun 2008, p. 671).

The ocelot and jaguarundi populations live on the land of Lower Rio Grande, which is also the site of the Santa Ana National Wildlife Refuge, as well as the border between the U.S. and Mexico. The dense brush of the area is the preferred habitat of regional feline populations for breeding, hunting, and traveling (Sundberg 2011). However, this area is considered vulnerable in terms of illegal border-crossing, as border patrol has its vision physically limited by the terrain and flora. For this reason, the American border patrol decided to install stadium-style lights to better secure the area.

However, these lights negatively impacted the felines, who are nocturnal and need a dark environment to travel and hunt. In order to avoid detrimental impacts to the ocelot and jaguarundi populations, a collective of humans and nonhuman animals was formed to change the operations of the U.S. border control. This collective represents lowercase-p politics in challenging political, institutional practices with a form of agency that suggests that agency is relational, as per Kittay's (2001) discussion, rather than "an individual attribute or intention" (Sundberg 2011, p. 331). Although, in this instance, the assistance of humans as enablers was required, the physical presence and actions of the felines were necessary components of the political process. The result of their presence during the process was a more formal integration of the animals into public life and space, and political border-making. Even if the felines were not aware of their role in the grassroots activist collective, it does not change the fact that they were agents and participants in the process—because of the way their lives helped shape a shared community of felines and humans.

Border-making processes include human and nonhuman actors, including plants, animals, and topography (Sundberg 2011); as such, borders are made and remade via the "co-habitation, co-evolution, and embodied cross-species sociality" (Haraway 2008, p. 17). In this way, nonhuman subjects at the border play an important political role because they potentially obstruct the work of border enforcement agencies, "[challenging] their presumed authority to dictate life" (Sundberg 2011, p. 332; Robbins 2005). Recognizing the ways in which the felines at the U.S.–Mexico border were part of the politics of boundary-making reconfigures nonhuman agency, since ultimately, the "needs" of the state (using flood lighting for security) were overcome by the needs of the nonhuman animals and their partners who supported their needs.

The agency of the ocelots and jaguarundis must therefore be framed differently from how agency has previously been conceptualized. This agency is not a "product of conscious intention, which restricts it to the imaginary figure of an all-knowing human" (Braun 2004, p. 1354). Instead, the agency of these felines at the U.S.–Mexico border imbues them "with the capacity for affect—the capacity to be acted upon, *and the capacity to act*" (Braun 2004, p. 1354, emphasis added; Sundberg 2011). The management of borders would traditionally be conceptualized as part of uppercase-P Politics (Flint 2003). However, considering the way in which politics was forced to change by the partnership between certain humans and the feline populations, lowercase-p politics is also an important force, with codified regulations being changed based on the needs of informal (to international relations) agents. In recognizing this, we recognize the felines as "participants in constituting the world" (Sundberg 2011, p. 322), rather than as mere objects in politics and political interventions.

Similar to the above example is the case study of the mosquito population in 1940s Egypt, as outlined by Mitchell (2002). In his book, Mitchell demonstrates the ways in which mosquitos, like the felines at the U.S.–Mexico border, shaped and reshaped Egyptian political processes just by virtue of living their lives. It should come as no surprise that mosquitos, and all insects, have this political capacity, given that these beings, "like it or not, have you surrounded, because Earth is the planet of the insects" (Sverdrup-Thygeson 2019, p. xvii). However, insects defined as "pests," universally including mosquitos, are rarely given political consideration.

Instead, the relationship between humans and mosquitos has generally been "forged by a toxic speciesist and human-centric prejudice, one which has manifested itself in a geography of violence and subjugation" (Gunderman & White 2021, p. 490). The main reason for the violence against mosquitos is their reputation as vectors of disease. However, in Mitchell's (2002) description, humans acted as vectors, or partners, in the transportation of the insects from sub-Saharan Africa to Egypt, which then made the mosquitos part of a deadly equation interconnecting war, disease, and agriculture (Mitchell 2002, p. 27).

The mosquitos brought to Egypt were particularly problematic for the local human population because the insects had never been found in the region prior to 1942; therefore, people were both unprepared for and intolerant to the diseases they spread. However, beyond health, there were also significant impacts on politics. This should come as no surprise given the important role that insects play within ecological and social webs of activity—including any number of beneficial activities within given ecosystems (Weisser & Siemann 2008). Why would this be different for our political systems? In Egypt, the mosquitos likely were not aware of their role in the political equation, and yet they did become a part of "a variety of political alliances" that necessitated a new social and hydraulic engineering program by the state (Mitchell 2002, p. 38).

Further, the increased risks to human populations associated with the new mosquito populations provided rationale and impetus for a radical change in land management and distribution, brought about by changemakers outside of federal and local governments. As Mitchell writes, "thanks to the malaria epidemic" and the rest of the previously mentioned deadly equation, poverty was made more "visible, so the question of land reform was now in circulation." Prior to the arrival of the sub-Saharan African mosquitos in Egypt, wealthy individuals had been consolidating political and economic power through the unequal distribution of land, but it was later proposed in parliament to "bar owners of more than fifty acres from acquiring additional land" (p. 40). Grassroots organizations used the mosquitos and the threat of malaria as a necessary impetus for change in land ownership. In this way, the mosquitos were part of the grassroots movement towards the redistribution of land and, by extension, economic and political power. As previously mentioned, the insects likely were not aware of their role in bringing about these radical changes in land management; however, they were still agents in this process.

The case in Egypt described by Mitchell (2002) provides an example wherein political activists sought to establish a symbiotic cohabitation between insects and people, rather than a relationship built upon speciesism in which mosquitos would be deemed as trespassers, those "politically, historically and conceptually circumscribed as being 'out of place'" (Puwar 2004, p. 8; Gunderman & White 2021). The example also provides an avenue for vegan geographies to encourage a politics of true interspecies liberation and justice; to that end, all animals, including insects, must be included in the emancipatory work of this field of inquiry.

The *Animal Sacer*

Political geographies and discussions of political subjects have often omitted consideration of animals and other nonhuman entities. However, vegan geographies offer an opportunity for us to consider the political capacities of animals. In recognizing lowercase-p politics and nonhuman agency as illustrated by the examples above, scholarship in this new subdiscipline can recognize the "individual character, knowledge, subjectivity [and] experience" (Tovey 2003, p. 196) of these sentient beings. Vegan geographies, then, provide the avenue for nonhuman animals to be seen as more than objects of politics, as subjects of politics. By engaging with animal political subjectivities in this way and amending standard ontological approaches to understanding political subjectivities, I aim to trouble the distinction between *Bios* and *Zoe*, particularly as it relates to the rights of animals as part of the project of vegan geographies. Nonhuman animals are clearly part of lowercase-p "politics" (Flint 2003), since nonhuman animals are able to move beyond the codification of "objects"—things to be used for political ends—and become subjects who can be objects *as well as* emancipatory agents in political processes (Hobson 2007).

Zoe, or "bare life," stands in opposition to what Agamben calls the "way of life proper to me" (p. 66). The distinction between *Zoe* and *Bios* is decided outside of the self, through judicial order instituted by the Sovereign. As such, law is what defines what bare life entails and what qualifies a meaningful life. Although Agamben's work does not engage with the "animal question," that life is defined through law can be seen in many modern animal rights laws today; however, these laws still frequently regulate the ways in which animals die,[10] and therefore do not represent how laws are able to grant individuals or imbue them with *Bios*. Agamben cites Aristotle's idea of the importance of interaction with politics, through which one is transformed from an animal state into having a "meaningful" and/or "qualified life," and the importance of the law as the power that separates political beings (*Bios*, citizens) from bare life (*Zoe*, mere bodies). However, the examples in the

10. An example of this would be "humane" methods of slaughter and legal methods of transporting animals to slaughter, which are regulated and enforced in many nations globally. In these instances, rather than protecting life, the law gives license to the killing of animals.

above section demonstrate that the nonhuman animal is political even as they exist both inside and outside of formal political realms. If *Bios* can be gained only through recognition by the Sovereign, then there is no room for fluidity.

The definition that Agamben puts forth is fairly rigid in its understanding of who and what constitutes *Zoe, Bios*, and the *Homo Sacer*; however, nonhuman animal beings trouble this definition.[11] Although under a rigid understanding of these concepts, nonhuman animals would be considered to hold only *Zoe*, the above examples of political agency do constitute a form of *Bios* (perhaps a lowercase-b *bios*). However, if we grant that nonhuman animals have some form of *Bios*, then there is a further argument to be made regarding the connection between animals and the *Homo Sacer* position in society—particularly considering the fates of many animals in industrial meat production and beyond.

This consideration is necessary because while the Sovereign does not perform the killing of the *Homo Sacer*, the Sovereign does not protect them from death, meaning they can be killed by anybody without state intervention (including investigation or justice). In the case of nonhuman animal beings, who are routinely killed and tortured without state intervention, there are laws that regulate the forms of torture inflicted on them. For example, in Canada, animals can be transported for up to three days without food, water, or rest (Shulman 2016). This policy makes the torture of animals legal—and regulated—during transport and therefore situates animals both inside and outside of the law.

Another example of this state of being inside and outside of the legal system is the case of Molly, a pet pig adopted from the SPCA in British Columbia (Canada). After the necessary paperwork had been gone through for Molly to be adopted into a multispecies family (including humans, dogs, and others), she was taken to her "forever home" only to be shot, killed, and eaten by the people who had adopted her. The general manager of community relations for the BC SPCA reported being "devastated" by the incident; however, she also said that although the adopters had signed a contract specifically stating that Molly would never be used for food, they "didn't do anything illegal" because in British Columbia, there is no law against killing one's own animal, who is considered property (Judd 2018). The caveat—that the animal must "die instantly" to avoid suffering—brings together the inside/outside positionality indicative of the *Homo Sacer* status.

Similarly, in Edmonton (Canada), even with animal cruelty laws in place, two men killed their dogs with aluminum baseball bats. Although the men were charged with animal cruelty, when they were taken to court, the judge acquitted

---

11. Women would also not have been included in the original definition of those holding *Bios*; as such, their inclusion as *Homo Sacer* also troubles the rigid Roman understanding of the term.

them, stating, "It certainly is not acceptable to me and many other people in this country to kill a dog like [that], but there is no law" (Labchuk 2016). These are only two of a troubling number of examples that place animals, beings with known political subjectivities, in the position of a *Homo Sacer* (or *Animal Sacer*), because of the ways in which they occupy a simultaneously inside- and outside-legal space.

In the U.S., we find similar examples involving both domestic and domesticated exotic animals. One of the most interesting is that of Grosse Tete's Tiger Truck Stop. This gas station and truck stop in Iberville Parish, Louisiana, was home to a tiger named Tony, who had lived on the property of the business beginning in 2001, when he was just six months old (Jones 2017; Hanson 2017). In 2006, when Tony would have been five years old, state legislature and the Louisiana Department of Wildlife and Fisheries banned individuals[12] from owning exotic cats (Barlow 2015) for the reason that keeping wild animals in captivity causes immense animal suffering and threatens public safety (Jones 2018). However, Tony was considered outside of this legal ban because he had been living at the truck stop prior to the ban, which simply prevented the owner, Michael Sandlin, from acquiring another tiger to live in a metal and cement enclosure on the side of the highway.

Many animal rights groups focused on the size of the enclosure and the fumes from traffic around the truck station in order to engage legal mechanisms against animal suffering and have Tony moved to an animal sanctuary. None of these attempts was successful. Sandlin spent approximately $1.5 million to fight legal suits from animal rights groups, as well as the state's ban on private ownership of exotic cats (Jones 2018; Robertson 2013). Sandlin has even sued the state, arguing that laws preventing the ownership of exotic animals are discriminatory and that it is his right to buy a successor to Tony when he passes. Sandlin justifies this position by saying: "They tried to take my legally obtained property away from me and not even compensate me. This is a violation of personal freedoms" (Jones 2018).

Some of Sandlin's suits have been successful; for example, in 2014, he convinced his state senator to introduce a bill to exempt Tony from the ban legislated in 2006. The 2014 bill created a retroactive exemption, placing Sandlin above a law that applies to all other citizens of the state (Jones 2018; Hanson 2017). As these and other legal battles continued, Tony died, euthanized at the age of seventeen (Hanson 2017; Jones 2017), but animal exploitation continues at the truck stop. Before Tony's death, Sandlin had acquired both a camel and a baby coati and expressed interest in expanding his enclosure facilities at the truck stop to include a petting zoo and alligator exhibit (Jones 2018). However, even in death, Tony

12. Exempt from this legal ban were colleges, sanctuaries, zoos, wildlife research centers, and scientific organizations (Jones 2018).

remains a main attraction, as he has been stuffed and mounted for display and as a promotional prop (Jones 2017).

The legal struggles surrounding Tony's life represent a microcosm of the legal inside/outside distinction faced by so many more-than-human populations as *Animal Sacer*—a system that continues to treat nonhuman beings as property and gives disproportionate focus and political influence to their captors and abusers. Like the laws of many nations, U.S. law designates animals as property; thus, legal battles that pit the rights of "property" against the rights of owners are rigged in favor of the "owners." In Tony's case, Michael Sandlin consistently uses the legality of private property rights to assert that he, as an American citizen, has the right to own Tony.

Throughout these examples of animal captivity and cruelty, although animals do have political agency, thereby disrupting the *Bios/Zoe* distinction, existing legal protection for nonhumans and, simultaneously, the denial of their agency demonstrate that animals may inhabit a position akin to *Homo Sacer* in society. It is critical that vegan geography considers and troubles these political distinctions as it actively shifts ontological approaches to remap the borders of animal rights, human–nonhuman relationships, and animals' political agency, thus allowing for new methods of exploring "the complex nexus of spatial relations between people and animals" and "[teasing] out the myriad economic, political, social and cultural pressures shaping these relations" (Philol & Wolch 1998, p. 110).

Concluding Thoughts

Although this chapter may be taken to be primarily a thought exercise, the questions and considerations presented offer new avenues for challenging standard understandings of animals' political subjectivities and positions. Although the new interpretation of nonhuman political positions will be geographically and temporally specific, it does provide an opportunity for animal liberation—be it more literal, such as via rights-based discourses, or less so, perhaps starting with the recognition that nonhuman animals behave according to logics of their own (Fiege 2005; Keul 2013). Thus, limiting animals' fate to *Zoe* as their "proper place" is inappropriate, considering the nuanced political agency of animals and their inside/outside position in many legal contexts (Braverman 2013).

I also hope that through this chapter, readers are able to better recognize the ways in which animals should be understood as political actors and subjects in their own right (Hobson 2007; Collard 2013). In so doing, I believe we can change how the processes and outcomes of the current political order can be reimagined. In the cases of the elephants in India, the ocelots and jaguarundis of the U.S.–Mexico border region, and the mosquitos in Egypt, we can disrupt the prescribed "proper place" of these beings, based on their roles as political actors taking part in rebellions and border-making, rather than as static political tools or objects (Mateer 2018; Robbins 2005). In recognizing the roles and positions of these and other nonhuman animals in this way, we are not mapping animals "onto the pre-existing human world" or painting them as "dumb actors in diverse polities" (Hobson 2007, p. 257). Instead, we are beginning to identify the ways in which animals have always been makers of history and politics—constructing lifeworlds humans do not or may not recognize and highlighting how political change ought to include a "reconfiguring of [humans'] relationships with nonhumans" (Dempsey 2010, p. 1154). Nonhumans can be seen as serious actors in dynamic environments, including spaces, politics, environmental struggles, and economic developments previously labeled as "human" (Dempsey 2010; Collard 2013). In understanding that nonhuman political subjects are actively engaged in the co-construction of our world, scholars and activists are potentially better able to bring attention to "the violent power relations at work in human–animal encounters" (Collard & Gillespie 2017, p. 2).

Although many humans are bringing the "bloody spaces of slaughter" (Wilcox & Rutherford 2018, p. 4) into their homes and surrounding themselves with a geography of nonhuman animal death, the understanding that the bacon on the stove or the hamburgers in the freezer are the final products of immense violence is strikingly absent. Even if this violence is recognized, because the "process that puts [animals] on our plates . . . is not very appetizing upon closer inspection" (Urbanik 2012, p. 125), individuals may deny animals agency in order to justify the horrific conditions of animal agriculture. However, like mainstream veganism, vegan geographies demand that humans understand that animal bodies are not economic or to be commodified as edible, viewable, or wearable products. It is past time that humans witnessed and understood nonhuman animals as active political subjects who are able to change history, resist authority, create borders, and provide avenues of emancipation.

14

VEGAN GEOGRAPHY

For a Heuristic Radicality in the Environmental Crisis?

Jérôme Lafitte and Nicolas Maestripieri

> For the day will come when the idea that, in order to feed themselves, men of the past raised and slaughtered living beings and complacently exposed their flesh in shreds in display cases, will undoubtedly inspire the same repulsion as the travelers of the sixteenth or seventeenth century, the cannibalistic meals of American, Oceanic or African savages. (Lévi-Strauss 2001)

Introduction

A recent study (Springmann et al., 2018) shows that the food system not only has a major effect on environmental changes, including climate change, but also strongly impacts changes in land use, the depletion of freshwater resources, and the pollution of aquatic and terrestrial ecosystems by excessive nitrogen and phosphorus inputs.[1] According to this study, due to expected changes in population and income levels, the environmental effects of the food system could increase by 50 to 90 percent between 2010 and 2050. Tony Weis (2013) similarly takes stock of the ecological footprint of meat-based diets and livestock farming. The relationship between livestock exploitation and the *carnist* system, as Melanie Joy (2011) puts it (see footnote on next page),[2] is also interesting as a subject of study from the point of view of spatial practices, considering that human–animal relations dominate

1. The authors would like to point out that they do not have the same view on the vegan issue—one is vegan, the other is moving towards flexitarianism—just as their commitments are not the same from an anarchist perspective. With respect to the environment, if their stories of academic and "geographical" life intersect here, they then diverge to meet again on the occasion of friendly and fruitful dialogue. This dialogue may appear to the reader from time to time, without being explicitly indicated.

the social-historical imaginary, structuring the great human/nature divide that underlies many discriminatory sociocultural representations.

Historically, nonhuman animals have been considered mainly as objects of study, and relationships between human and nonhuman societies approached in a unidirectional and apolitical manner. Animal geography, on the other hand, seeks to make nonhumans visible by re-situating and re-politicizing them to ensure that their material (and in some cases, emotional) needs are not ignored. These same nonhumans are considered active partners in the social, ideological, and historical networks of human societies (Johnston 2008; Urbanik 2012). Thus, much more than objects, nonhuman animals are considered as subjects whose distended connections with human societies can be reconfigured or strengthened by the creation of a *zoopolis* that promotes coexistence (Emel et al., 2002).

From a geographical point of view, our position is relational; more specifically, it is "humanimal" (Estebanez et al., 2013). Such a position focuses not only on what fundamentally unites humans and animals, but also on the issue of intersecting temporalities and humanimal spatialities within a shared dwelling.[3] The goal is to define the relationship and interactions between human and nonhuman animal "actants" (Picard 2013). The problems of animal exploitation, representation, and localization contribute to the renewal of geography as a political place (and stake), enjoining the geographer to rethink their view of space. The political and radical dimension with regard to socio-ecological and ethical issues is the keystone of humanimality.

Indeed, we position our work as part of critical animal studies (Castricano & Corman 2016a) or, more precisely, critical animal geographies (Gillespie & Collard 2015), structured by an interdisciplinary approach that allows us to contribute to building a pluralistic field. We raise a question with respect to thinking through a certain unity based on the idea of a continuous transition from the elaboration of knowledge of humanimal relations towards intersectional methods of apprehending humanimal encounters and lived experiences, particularly in the

2. Melanie Joy (2001, 2011) proposes the term *carnism* in order to highlight the normative invisibilization of meat eating on the one hand, and on the other hand, to emphasize the ideology underlying a practice that is hegemonic but increasingly questionable in terms of its effects on health, the environment, and especially morality.
3. Humanimal spatiality is the space captured from (or the configuration and extent of) practices that connect human and animal individuals, human and animal groups (here, of production), and that take place during spatial actions within a system, characterized more often by carnist exploitation than by collaboration. Humanimal temporality is the action and concern, the experience of duration since a humanimal relationship. In this sense, the implementation of a humanimal position can be considered as a strategy.

field (Castricano & Corman 2016b). From then on, the focus will be on justice, social justice, human relations, and therefore ecosocial relations, opening onto a spatial ethic of a shared dwelling that will leave us to never again be alone. Spatial practices and their imaginary, intervening discourses that support the purpose of livestock farming and their criticism by veganism show the power relations and the cruel and violent ordering of the world, structured largely by capitalism.

Livestock farming, particularly industrial livestock farming, seems to us to be at the heart of such a system and its imaginary. A critical humanimal geographical approach that favors a vegan and anarchist perspective is an intersectional approach and is likely to shed light on the current environmental situation, in which the evolution of meat consumption is a key factor in considering issues of ecospatial justice. As such, a vegan geography illuminated by an anarchist perspective (Dominik 2015) pushes radicality on heuristic paths.

The first part of what follows proposes to take stock of animal exploitation and its potential socio-ecological impacts on a global scale, while the second part seeks to anchor this phenomenon in the spatialities at work "on the ground" by opening up the challenge of action to the diversity of prefigurative practices.

Global Animal Exploitation

The main objective of this exploratory section is to paint a picture of the current state of animal exploitation and to highlight its spatial, temporal, and relational complexity. The data used comes from multiple studies in social ecology, agronomy, environmental geography, sociology, and food economics, many of which are based on statistics from the Food and Agriculture Organization (FAOSTAT).

1. The Consumption of Products of Animal Origin, at the Root of a Complex Phenomenon

1.1. The Objectivation of Killing

Although precise quantification is difficult, the most commonly given range for the number of land animals slaughtered each year in slaughterhouses worldwide is from 60 to 140 billion, with both the low and high estimates not taking into account the number of animals who die before reaching slaughter age. The Food and Agriculture Organization of the United Nations estimates the number to be about 75 billion (all meat combined). In addition, 1,000 billion fish are caught each year, not including discarded fish left to die at sea and those killed in fish farms (Faunalytics 2020; Mood 2010).

Such quantitative statistical data objectifies the animals bred and raised for mass meat consumption and suggests the extent of industrial animal slaughter. It also gives insight into our thinking and the way we conceive of our relationship with animals:[4] classification is by species (that is, meat production is expressed in tons and divided into categories such as pigs, sheep, cattle, and poultry); production is also expressed in terms of the "nutritional composition of various meats and other foods per 100 g," or whether the meat is "lean" for that species. It is therefore an expression of the ontological and phenomenological relationship existing between humans, animals, and space. Of course, such a relationship is structured by distance (cultural, ecological, biological, and phylogenetic in particular) and is largely dependent on arguments associated with spatiality and territoriality. The conception of the animal is distanced by a fragmentation of the animal being into body parts and a sequential division of the humanimal relationship that demonstrates a process of objectification through a scientific discourse for industrial and sanitary use. This reification is the result of "divisive practices," since the acts of naming and conceptualizing the living animal show that they are being considered merely in a fragmented way (as pieces of meat, nutrients, fragments finalized according to the human food production system) and are denied their unity with the spatiality they inhabit.

This atomization of animal individuals into nutritional plots, therefore, contributes to the cultural distancing necessary to legitimize the multifaceted global carnist system of exploitation. It connects the farm to supermarket shelves, to protein, to the energy "necessary" for the performance of each human being.

1.2. The Symbolic Horizon of Industrialized Violence

The cruel and violent conditions of the annual slaughter of animals and the trauma of the executioners themselves have led some animal advocates to compare slaughterhouses to the extermination camps that saw the deaths of six million Jews, not counting the victims who died in transport during the deportation. Yiddish writer and Nobel Prize winner Isaac Bashevis Singer (1968) wrote that for animals, "all people are Nazis," comparing their situation to "an eternal Treblinka."

4. See Food and Agriculture Organization (FAO), n.d. Animal Production and Health: Meat Consumption, http://www.fao.org/ag/againfo/themes/fr/meat/background.html.

Historian Charles Patterson (2008) used the expression as the title for his book *Eternal Treblinka: Our Treatment of Animals and the Holocaust*, which examines in detail this historical similarity. Although there are major differences between these two phenomena that must be outlined (for example, that these are two different forms of injustice with different purposes, different victims, and different legacies—the cementing of memory and history as a civilizational issue on the one hand and the invisibilization of animals on the other), there is still room for reflection on this issue.

One point would be to consider the practices of spatial cantonment that make the being, whether human or animal, disappear behind the "population." The spatial concentration of animals, to which an instrumentalizing categorization responds, proceeded by an identity assignment, often reduces lives to pejorative "functions." The reification process reduces the being to a thing, an object. From a phenomenological point of view, the name of the space—for example, "feedlot"—sheds light on this functionalist and industrial reduction. The historical parallels between Nazi extermination camps and slaughterhouses (also mentioned by Porcher 2005) have a twofold significance: in terms of not only the connections between industrial practices, but also their moral and ethical consequences through the processes at work, from the "objectification" of beings to "dehumanization." The limit of our anthropocentric language in describing such processes supports a disturbing questioning of our fundamental and acting categories of thought at the personal level (consciousness and affects) and the collective level (sociocultural representations, collective memory, collective emotions, anthropocentric and humanist values).

This historicized relationship of violence risks objectification as a significant relationship with the world, with others, and with oneself—a relationship that necessarily borrows a symbolic understanding based in particular on language, with its limits. Such "significant practices" of industrialized violence are informed by a social-historical logic constructed by a praxis that returns to the thinking of a way of being characteristic of industrial and consumerist societies.

1.3. The Extent of Moral Questioning: What Measure?

Vegan *praxis* is fundamentally rooted in a positioning of moral philosophy. As Bruers (2015) argues, "all sentient beings (especially vertebrates with functional nervous systems) have the fundamental right not to be used as mere physical means (i.e., against their will) for non-vital purposes, in particular for food and clothing" (p. 287). The right to moral consideration of a being is no longer based on a criterion of rationality (consciousness) but on a criterion of sentience (feeling) (Marshall 2015, p. 432). In this context, do human animals have rights and duties with respect to nonhuman animals? Is their exploitation of nonhuman animals morally acceptable? The literature on these moral questions is abundant (among others, Regan 1986; Francione 2010; Singer 2012; Bruers 2015).

Three major moral frameworks, built by animal ethics, require our attention, as each has a different tolerance towards animal exploitation. For Will Kymlicka and Sue Donaldson (2015), the *welfarist* approach considers animal welfare to be subordinate to the interests of human beings, who presumably have a higher position in the moral hierarchy. The *ecological* approach is articulated by the ecocentric ethics defended by J. Baird Callicott. This ethic is called consequentialist—that is, what must be done is assessed in terms of its consequences for the common good (holistic approach). Callicott believes that "in all cases, the effect on ecological systems is the decisive factor in determining the ethical quality of actions" (Larrère 2006). From a moral point of view, animal welfare is secondary to the interests of ecosystems. Finally, and *in contrast to* the welfarist and ecological approaches, the *basic rights* approach is, according to Will Kymlicka and Sue Donaldson (2011), more radical, since it proposes that "animals, like humans, should be seen as possessing certain inviolable rights: there are some things that should not be done to animals even in pursuit of human interests or ecosystem vitality," that "animals do not exist to serve human ends" (p. 14).

Although they hold radically differing positions on the fate of animals, these three moral frameworks, far from being exclusive, converge in their profound critique of humanity's assumed right to dominate all that crosses its path (anthroparchal system), according to the dominant Western worldview.

1.4. A Multifaceted Exploitation

Products of animal origin (POAO) are the result of a multifaceted and hierarchical spatial operating system that is behind every entity from the farm to the globalized firm. They testify to the systematic integration that industrial and financial capitalism operates, bringing together local micro-territories of intensive exploitation and larger territories through networks of actors, techniques, and globalized spatialities—in other words, actions, representations, and practices. These networks form a productivist chain that follows the metamorphosis of animals as they are slaughtered en masse and cut into portions of meat that are quickly distributed to the plates of consumers around the world.

First of all, a *distinction* must be made between the industrialization of livestock farming and traditional, local family practices. Logic would suggest that locally produced and consumed agricultural products should have a lower environmental impact compared to the same product when imported. Such an analysis should take into account a number of significant "variables," such as: (1) the origin of the products intended as animal feed (import, short supply chain, or self-sufficiency); (2) the mode of transport (container ships, road, or piggyback transport); (3) the distance traveled between the point of production and the point of supply (international or in situ); (4) the size of the holding and the livestock (extensive or intensive livestock farming); and (5) the nature of the holding (agrifood firm, entrepreneurial agriculture, or traditional family holding). Despite the contribution of such an analysis to measuring the "ecological hoofprint" (Weis 2013) of local versus industrial practices, the challenge here is to understand that the socio-ecological impacts of agriculture would not have been what they are today if agriculture had not been industrialized. ("Ecological hoofprint" can be defined as the measured use of space for various uses of natural resources under the condition of sustainability. Tony Weiss's book focuses on industrial animal production systems. Industrial livestock production and the "meatification" of diets constitute a large and growing vector of environmental degradation and worsening human inequality, as well as an invisible, routinized aspect of the deep systemic violence of everyday life.)

Meat consumption is global, massive, and growing at a very rapid rate. Between 1975 and 2009, the amount of meat consumed increased from 175,665,000 tons to 278,863,000 tons, with an increase of more than 125 percent for poultry meat. According to Maeve Henchion et al. (2014), this explosion cannot be explained exclusively by population growth. Per capita consumption, which has also increased by almost 25 percent over the same period, is expected to rise with rising incomes in developing countries, falling prices (in real terms), trade liberalization, globalization of food systems, and urbanization. Henchion's analysis has been complemented by 2018 data, which confirms the trend already observed between 1990 and 2009. This trend is increasing in intensity especially for pig meat (+ 66.5 percent) and poultry meat (+ 60.9 percent) between 2009 and 2018.

While POAO production and consumption are globalized, this remains a phenomenon with strong regional variability, marked by both evolving cultural contexts and extremely variable economic situations, as evidenced by Eugenio Y. Arima et al.'s (2014) analysis of deforestation in the Brazilian Amazon.

Table 1. Global Meat Consumption, 1990–2018, 1,000 tons
(Sources FAO 2021—Food Balances [2014–], inspired by Henchion et al., 2014)

	1990	2009	Change 1990–2009 (%)	2018	Change 2009–2018 (%)
Bovine meat	54,065	63,835	18.1	77,804	21.9
Mutton and goat meat	9,100	12,763	40.2	19,923	56.1
Pig meat	68,692	105,503	53.6	175,665	66.5
Poultry meat	40,173	90,664	125.7	145,910	60.9
Other meats	3,634	6,098	67.8	7,191	17.9
Aggregate	175,665	278,863	58.7	426,493	52.9

Francesca Allievi et al. (2015) show how, despite an increased efficiency in land use for animal products, meat consumption is becoming more significant in most regions. This trend towards optimizing utilization/production processes is also observed in France (and across Europe), although there was an observed 11 percent decrease in annual meat consumption per capita between 1998 and 2013 (Déplaude 2018). The stabilization of the amount of meat consumed per capita (in Africa, for example) would be explained by widespread poverty and the fact that meat is a luxury product compared to other foodstuffs.

In East Asia, the sharp increase in meat supply was coupled with a tenfold increase in meat consumption between 1962 and 2009 (economy-of-scale effect) (Fig. 1). Allievi et al. explain that "while Northern America and Oceania, Southern Europe, and Western and Northern Europe are the regions that present the highest peaks in meat consumption (including 120 kg per capita in 2007 in the case of Northern America and Oceania), they are also the only cases in which the consumption of meat has decreased within the last decade" (p. 145). This downward trend can be explained by, in addition to factors such as price or per-capita income, a higher demand for quality products (Henchion et al., 2014), which will itself vary according to the cultures and societies concerned.

Despite a stronger demand for quality products, the death toll is accelerating at unprecedented rates worldwide. This violence is amplified by a fundamentally anthropocentric relationship with the environment that exacerbates spatial inequalities, injustices, and negative environmental consequences (such as detrimental impacts on land, CO_2 emissions, and terrestrial, marine, and lake ecosystems).

Figure 1. Global Trends of Sufficiency: Total Meat Supply Per Capita (Measured in Kilograms Per Capita Per Year) for Selected Years in the Period 1962–2009 (FAOSTAT) (Allievi et al., 2015)

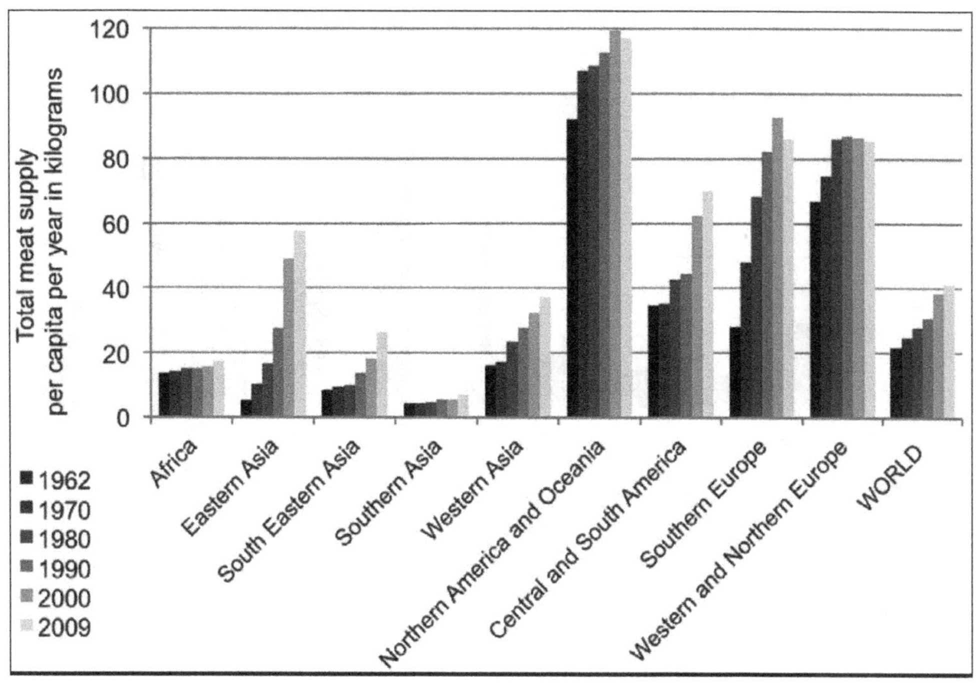

2. Exploiting to Appropriate: The Tip of the Iceberg

This part focuses mainly on land-based animal exploitation, voluntarily excluding aquaculture farms and territories, and marine sampling. Although it is difficult to provide an accurate count of the individuals killed, total global production of fish and fishery products from capture fisheries and aquaculture currently stands at around 140 million tons per annum (World Ocean Review 2010). It should be noted that agricultural practices (mainly intensive), through pollution by nitrogen and phosphorus, also by potassium, drug residues, pathogenic organisms, and heavy metals, are at the crux of the depletion of marine biodiversity due to oxygen loss in coastal areas and the high seas (forming "dead zones") (Heinrich Böll Foundation and Friends of the Earth Europe 2014).

2.1. Agricultural Capitalism: Concentration and Capitalization of Land

A recent report indicates: "According to Eurostat data, today in Europe, 3 percent of farms concentrate 50 percent of agricultural land. At the same time, 80 percent of

Figure 2. Land Requirement for Animal Products Per Capita (Measured in Square Meters Per Capita) for Selected Years in the Period 1962–2007 (Kastner et al., 2012 in Allievi et al., 2015)

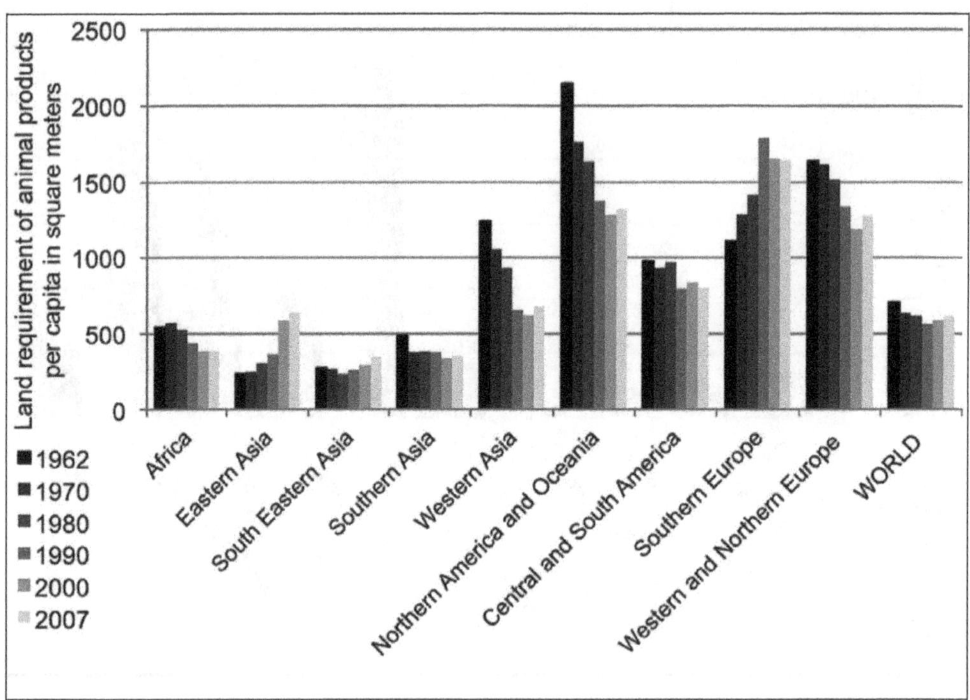

production units control only 14.5 percent of the European agricultural area."[5] The financial aid provided as part of the European Union's Common Agricultural Policy (CAP), not to mention the weight of agricultural lobbyists and agro-pharmaceutical and phytosanitary firms, has a major impact on this strong trend towards land concentration and capitalization. In 1992, a reform (MacSharry reform) aimed at making the CAP market-oriented sought to reduce its budgetary weight by lowering and bringing guaranteed prices into line with world prices (lower than those of the E.U.). Production aid (per hectare or animal) was granted in order to compensate for this price differential. The reform would lead to a concentration and capitalization of land to the detriment of small farmers and livestock, as the granting of this aid was to be proportional to the surface area of farm or the size of livestock herds.

5. Observatoire Des Multinationales. "Concentration foncière en Europe: vers une agriculture sans paysans?" April 25, 2014, http://multinationales.org/Concentration-fonciere-en-Europe; Forum Mondial Sur L'Accès à la Terre (FMAT), 2016. Plan du Document, http://www.agter.org/bdf/_docs/synthese_reunion_16_nov_2015_fmat_cese.pdf.

While these agricultural policies influence territorial dynamics (through production practices), it is the consumption of animal products that was responsible for the highest per capita land needs in the richest regions of the world (i.e., North America and Oceania, Southern, Western, and Northern Europe) between 1960 and 2007 (Allievi et al., 2015). It should be noted that the trend in land use was downward in these same regions for the same period (Fig. 2), caused in particular by intensive modern agriculture and industrial livestock farming, which allow for a reduction in production factors (useful agricultural area) while increasing productivity. A more recent example is above-ground mega farms, including the "thousand-cow" farm in France, the floating dairy farm in Rotterdam, and the farm owned by Zhongding Dairy Farming and Severny Bur with a herd of 100,000 cows.

In France, the number of farms fell from 2.3 million in 1955 to 590,000 in 2003. This notable trend towards concentration has been accompanied by a modernization and professionalization of the sector to the detriment of individual farms (Desriers 2007). This dynamic can also be observed in Canada between 1971 and 2011, with a significant decrease in the number of farms and an increase in the size of farms.[6]

2.2. Land Opening and Degradation

Occupying more than 3.9 billion hectares (30 percent of the world's land area), livestock is one of the biggest land users (Steinfeld 2006), and perhaps the most important, since cultivated land used for animal feed production represents about 70 percent of all agricultural land (Gerber et al., 2010). In the article *Mapping the Global Distribution of Livestock*, Robinson et al. (2014)[7] provide a new perspective on the issue of livestock and its global distribution. The amount of land taken up by livestock raises many questions, including that of land opening and the associated disturbances/damage. The expansion of land linked to agriculture is considered to be one of the main drivers—if not the main driver—of deforestation. Numerous studies highlight this finding (Walker et al., 2000; Barona et al., 2010; Godar et al., 2012; Arima et al., 2014; Nepstad et al., 2014).

However, some authors are of the opinion that "livestock enables the use of land that cannot be used for cropping due to harsh environmental conditions and, thus, helps broaden society's resource base" (Erb et al., 2016). In this view, livestock is

6. Marie-Andrée Hamel and Erik Dorff. Corn: Canada's Third Most Valuable Crop, n.d. Statistics Canada, https://www150.statcan.gc.ca/n1/pub/96-325-x/2014001/article/11913-eng.htm.

7. Robinson, T., et al. (2014). Mapping the Global Distribution of Livestock, *PLOS One* 9(5), e96084, doi:10.1371/journal.pone.0096084.

not fundamentally a systematic vector of environmental degradation, particularly through grazing, as livestock is deemed "necessary" for the maintenance of tropical rangelands (Lambin et al., 2001, p. 264) or seen as "a suitable strategy to preserve this threatened segment of biodiversity under the framework of current agricultural policy and with limited financial resources" (Putfarken et al., 2008, p. 55). Grazing is often considered as a vehicle for opening up landscapes (such as mountains) and is recognized for its carbon storage capacity (see Section 2.1.4.). Some researchers even mention the need to maintain grasslands in order to justify livestock farming (Gaigne & Ben Arfa 2011; *Jeunes Agriculteurs* 2018).[8]

This instrumentalization of the ecological argument in favor of capitalism rejects any moral argument. Grasslands could exist without requiring the commercial exploitation of animals, who could be allowed to maintain these areas freely (Karasiak 2015). In exploring the biophysical space available for feeding the world without deforestation, Erb et al. (2016) explain that the move to human food, more specifically vegan (or vegetarian) food, is a determining factor in halting land appropriation, insofar as vegan/vegetarian food requires half as much space in terms of cultivated land, half as much grazing intensity and overall biomass harvesting, as does meat-based food.

The socio-ecosystemic dimension of animal exploitation is not limited to the surface area taken up by livestock but extends to all the agricultural components necessary to feed livestock (representing an interweaving of the local and the global). A study of the soybean sector in France (2008–2010) carried out by Natural Consultants[9] shows that national consumption in 2009 amounted to 4.7 million tons of soybeans, of which 3.1 million tons were used as oil cake for animal feed by the meat production industry. Of the 3.7 million tons imported, 72.5 percent came from Brazil, 9.9 percent from Argentina, 8.2 percent from Belgium, and 4.2 percent from Spain. Thus, the expansion and industrialization of grain and oilseed production (particularly soybean) and the expansion and industrialization of livestock production are mutually reinforcing (Weis 2013).

A spatial interdependence is then created, mixing animal exploitation and violence at the local level with complex socio-ecological dynamics in South America. Examples of this interdependence include changes in the regional distribution of production, the displacement of other crops, the expansion of agricultural borders, migratory processes and urban changes, and land-grabbing (Craviotti 2016). Rachael D. Garrett and Lisa L. Rausch (2016) also specify that

8. *Jeunes Agriculteurs*. Lettre Ouverte au Président de la République, October 11, 2018, http://www.jeunes-agriculteurs.fr/lettre-ouverte-president-de-republique.
9. Consultants Naturels, n.d. Étude de filière—Le soja en France, http://consultants-naturels.fr/service/etude-de-filiere-le-soja-en-france/.

"soy production is only one of many land uses pursued in the Amazon biome and by no means the largest proximate source of land-cover change; cattle production and small-holder agricultural production are the primary land uses in the region" (p. 477).

2.3. Associated Pollution

Animal exploitation, from captivity to killing, generates environmental degradation that varies greatly not only according to production methods—whether the methods are intensive or extensive, organic or otherwise—but also according to the animal species being exploited (De Vries & De Boer 2010). Within the food system, "the farming stage is the most important source of impacts [of greenhouse gases]" (Xu et al., 2015, p. 1272).

Pierre J. Gerber et al. (2010), in analyzing the environmental consequences of the growth of the livestock sector, explain that "GHG emissions arise from feed production (e.g., chemical fertilizer production, deforestation, cultivation, transport), animal production (e.g., enteric fermentation and methane and nitrous oxide emissions from manure) and as a result of the transportation of animal products" (p. 245). M. de Vries and I. J. M. de Boer (2010) propose a review of life-cycle assessments to compare the environmental impacts of livestock products, such as: (1) acidification from manure in buildings and storage facilities, from grazing and fertilizer application in the field; and (2) eutrophication (caused by ammonia [NH_3] emissions and leaching or runoff from nitrogen oxide and phosphate). Pierre Gerber et al. (2005) also explain that, "the geographical concentration of livestock in areas with little or no agricultural land leads to high impacts on the environment (water, soil, air and biodiversity), mainly related to manure and waste water mismanagement" (p. 264). Further, desertification in arid, semi-arid, and dry, sub-humid areas is exacerbated and facilitated by the animal agriculture sector (Koneswaran & Nierenberg 2008).

Analyzing the carbon costs of different diets based on the Carbon Benefits Index, Searchinger et al. (2018) conclude: "Shifting from beef and dairy would reduce those emissions by 70 percent. Although animal products offer health benefits for the food-insecure, we estimate much larger climate benefits than others if the wealthy consume less beef and dairy" (p. 252). Smith et al. (2013) also write that a reduction in the consumption of animal products could significantly decrease the need for food, since the efficiency of the conversion of plant material to animal material is around 10 percent and about one-third of the world's cereal production is for animal feed.

In the end, the ecological footprint of livestock farming is significant in terms of environmental impact and climate change. As such, chickens, one of the first domesticated species, have been extensively modified for food consumption. The impact of industrialized farming is so massive that chickens make up the most numerous vertebrate species on Earth (at 23 billion). Since the 1950s, their population has grown at the same rate as has the human population, as has our consumption of fossil fuels, plastics, and other resources, making chickens one of the main markers of the Anthropocene.[10] Their bones are found in all parts of the world. Today, this animal, who is modified for human food needs, can only survive for a few months, being unsuitable for a free life in the wild. The world's largest chicken producers are now investing in vegetable proteins, which seems to attest to the fact that a ceiling has been reached in terms of the production and consumption of chicken meat (Bennett et al., 2018).

While vegan practices, which are developing rapidly in the Western world, represent a radical challenge to livestock farming and, consequently, to its environmental and climatic impact in the age of the Anthropocene, the demand for meat from demographic giants and emerging countries does not make us optimistic. However, the conception of the Anthropocene as a great, uniform narrative, both scientific and normative, does not take into account the diversity of relationships within the carnist system. It masks the diversity of moral sensibilities to animal suffering and remains uncritical of the close relationship between the anthroparchal carnist system and capitalism (Moore 2017). A vegan perspective brings out the human supremacy, backed by a technoscientific ethic, that structures the narrative of the cleavage between humans and animals.

Empirical Analyses: Spaces and Life Stories (Socio-Ecological Complexity)

In this section, we explore the spaces and spatialities involved in relations of production, consumption, and carnist exchange. We consider these spaces by anchoring them as much as possible in a lived reality on the one hand; on the other hand, we try to consider the spatiality of the actants at play, actants being understood as individual and collective human and humanimal actors within a

10. The Anthropocene is considered to be the third geological epoch after the Pleistocene and Holocene. Much more than a new era, the Anthropocene is a new great narrative that identifies humanity as the primary cause of the ecological crisis and that is designed to highlight significant environmental changes on a global scale (Castree 2014).

more-than-human world.[11] Finally, some critical points of view from anarchist thought are drawn on to question the system at work.

1. Spaces and Spatialities

From field to plate (from subject to object), farmed animals are actors and vectors of social connection. They become actors the moment they interact with their breeders and become link vectors once they are reduced to pieces of meat. Slaughterhouses are found between these two spaces, where nonhuman animals are ethically and politically invisible, thus allowing human societies to manipulate, to exploit, to displace, to consume, to waste, and to torture nonhuman individuals with impunity (Jones 2000). The travel between the farm and the slaughterhouse also needs to be considered, as the transport of animals often involves extreme violence. In Canada alone, 700 million animals are transported each year; nearly 2 million die in transit, while an estimated 12 million animals are injured or fall sick en route (Gaillard 2019).[12] Moreover, in order to limit the scope of this chapter, we have not approached the topic of retail spaces and direct sales from the farm.

For the analysis of the aforementioned spaces, we use the concept of anthroparchy, advanced by Erika Cudworth (2008). Cudworth emphasizes the systematic relationships of economic policies of meat production with capitalism and its patriarchal forms. Such carnist policies are exemplary of humankind's domination of nature. Anthroparchy—as a social system—builds relatively stable relationships *by* and *in* which the environment is dominated through a social organization that privileges the human (Cudworth 2005, 2007). This notion overlaps with speciesism as a form of discrimination that is related to others such as racism, sexism, or classism. Indeed, according to Jonathan Fernandez (2015), anthroparchal logic, built on criteria that are just as arbitrary as compared to other forms of discrimination, entails "masking behind a veil of objectivity, a natural screen, a reality that is only the result of power relations" (p. 67).

However, anthroparchy particularly emphasizes that human societies are organized around a "hierarchy in which the needs, desires, interests and even

11. The dichotomous expression of "human/nonhuman animal"—and the term "more-than-human," which can be brought closer to a transhumanist perspective—both raise epistemological or even ontological problems. Despite efforts made to break the order of an exclusively humanist discourse, here we can only recognize that the boundaries of our language are the boundaries of our world.
12. Canada's animal transport regulations are among the laxest in the Western world: livestock can be transported for thirty-six hours without rest, without stopping, without drink or feed, in trucks without heating or air conditioning (Gaillard 2019).

whims of human beings shape the kinds of relationships we are likely to have with nonhuman species" (Cudworth 2008, p. 34). Anthroparchy develops different forms and practices of power that feed into oppression, exploitation, and marginalization. Cudworth identifies five arenas of action that constitute the anthroparchal social system from her study of different systems of animal exploitation, from breeding up to slaughter.

Figure 3. The Anthroparchal System and Its Five Arenas of Action, According to E. Cudworth (2008)

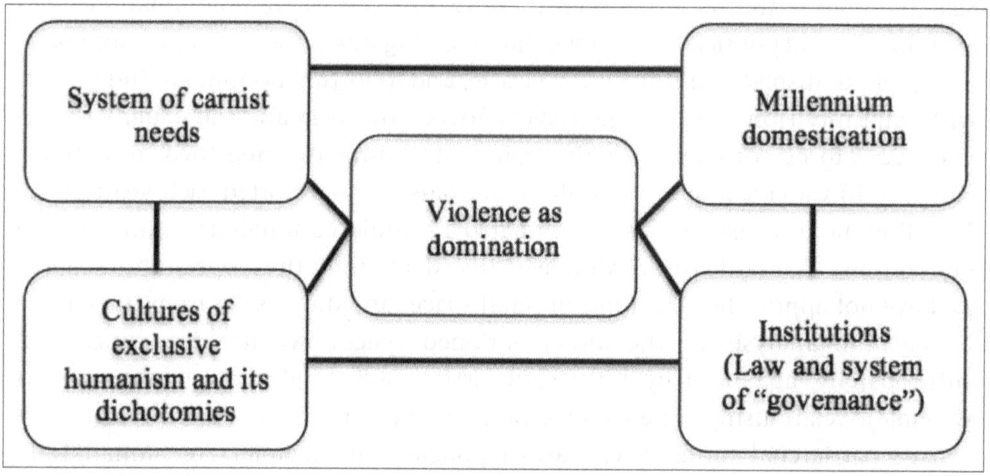

The first arena (or theater) of action is constituted by the *system of carnist needs* and corresponds to the set of relationships that emerge from our production needs (for example, food and fuel oil), which are largely subject to industrialization, thereby generating an increase in the ecological footprint of most societies globally. The second arena, *domestication*, takes place over millennia. It is a major innovation on a human scale but has been undergoing a problematic intensification for two centuries. The *political* theater refers to the *institutions and practices of "governance"* that influence relationships of systematic domination. The arena of *systematic violence* is the nodal point of the system. Lastly, there is the arena of *cultures of exclusive humanism* structured around dichotomies such as humanity/animality, which produce yet other dichotomies that shape practices like meat consumption.

1.1. The House and the Plate (Ritual, Conviviality, Consumption)

The relationship between humans and farmed animals, at least in terms of frequency of interactions, is a carnist relationship—in other words, it is manifested in food consumption. As previously mentioned, the animal's being and domestic animal spatiality are rendered invisible by being fragmented into pieces of meat and identified as such, or by being reduced to portions of protein. The distance between the consumer and the animal killed by this parcelization, which renders the animal invisible to the point of being considered as no more than quantities of proteins, also promotes a generalized biotechnological equivalence that is mobilized within the framework of a health regime compatible with a transhumanist horizon. From a vegan perspective, health remains an important argument.

Amie Breeze Harper (2010b) shows how a vegan path leads to the liberation of many Black women from health disparities. This can occur as a process of decolonization of bodies that have been poisoned by junk food, as the African American community has a higher incidence of common diet-related diseases such as type 2 diabetes, high blood pressure, and cardiovascular disease. For marginalized populations, the combination of poor diet, lack of exercise, and inadequate medical guidance and care is becoming increasingly lethal.

Veganism allows Black women to enter a global process of decolonization through a reclaiming of power over the self in the face of a neo-colonial identity assignment that stigmatizes an accumulation of "defects," giving rise to plural discriminations against one who's a woman, Black, and obese. However, to suggest a break with colonial food practices based on excessive sugar and meat is also to entreat the Black community to move beyond the idea that a healthy or vegan lifestyle is a "white" thing; and to fight political and cultural ghettoization through health-oriented activism, along with a commitment against environmental degradation and a resistance to institutionalized humanimal racism.

Amie Breeze Harper's book (2010a) builds an intertextuality of vegan life experiences that testify to this recovery of power over oneself, which begins with one's plate, practices, and family space. Indeed, in such a space, meat consumption remains a ritual to affirm or accomplish masculinity (Simonsen 2012). It is a fundamental component of the patriarchal system and contributes to the "narrowing of the field of compassion" (Adams 1990) by reducing animals to mere fragmented objects of consumption. Otherness effectively translates to non-subject status, not only to nonhuman animals but also to other oppressed groups, and contributes to social and emotional—as well as physical—degradation. But a vegan position also addresses neighborhood-level political issues, combating food deserts by demanding that grocery stores be supplied with quality non-meat food products, thus revealing the links between political choices and environmental racism and its corollaries (speciesism, ecological devastation, health disparities, institutional racism, overconsumption, and other social injustices) (Harper 2010a, p. xix). The life experiences related in Harper's book thus attest to an intersectional emancipatory struggle that addresses anthroparchy as a node of a multi-discriminatory system.

However, we have seen that the change in meat consumption is differentiated around the world. The demographic giants of East Asia and the African continent are tending to increase their meat consumption substantially. China, among other young and populous countries, is increasingly adopting a meat-heavy diet. Compared to 14 kg of meat per person in 1980, China consumed 60 kg per person in 2010, a figure that is close to France's 85 kg and the U.S.'s 107 kg (Parmentier 2014, p. 35). In Western countries, the trend towards lower meat consumption is progressing rapidly. The relationship with meat consumption therefore paints a social relationship on a global scale.

On the other hand, a recent study by Dalhousie University shows that, in Canada, about 10 percent of the population is vegetarian (compared to 5 percent in France), with regional variation. However, of the approximately 6.4 million Canadians who deliberately limit the amount of animal protein they consume, 63 percent are 38 years old or younger (Charlebois 2019). Though still less than common, food practices that are at odds with carnism are therefore likely to develop.

The limitations of this chapter do not allow us to address other spaces around the plate that give rise to convivial food practices that reflect the global importance of carnist culture (e.g., barbecues, sports events). The carnist tradition of Western societies therefore remains strong despite the growing popularity of flexitarian, vegetarian, and vegan alternatives for the most well-known foods. The projected increase in global meat consumption is not without moral dilemmas and environmental issues related to greenhouse gases (GHGs).

1.2. Slaughterhouses

Before arriving on the plate, animals are cut up into various pieces in slaughterhouses. Such spaces are one of the key features of the industrial dynamics of carnist production and consumption. They have gradually been distanced from fairs and marketplaces, and cut off from public squares and, thus, from the sensory and physical perceptions of humans. This division of space is further affected by a relationship with the law, since slaughterhouses are non-legal spaces for farmed animals. Such spaces, as studied by Erika Cudworth (2008), are arenas of systematic violence par excellence.

In Canada, specifically in Québec, the law remains problematic with respect to violence against animals, particularly farmed animals. While the Canadian criminal code identifies two main offences—cruelty (s. 445(1) (a)) and negligence

(s. 446(1) (b))—there are significant difficulties in its enforcement because of the need to prove beyond reasonable doubt the willful nature of the act of cruelty or negligence. Section 128 of Canada's food safety regulations, which governs the killing of animals in slaughterhouses, addresses the issue of preventing avoidable animal deaths from human actions, but Section 127 specifies that "avoidable death" does not apply to animal slaughter for human consumption. As long as a practice is common in the industry, it is exempt from provincial animal welfare legislation—regardless of the suffering caused, according to Sophie Gaillard (2019). This provision allows the industry to regulate itself—in other words, to decide for itself what is acceptable or not in terms of animal welfare. Florence Burgat (2001) makes the same observation for France, among other countries, noting the primacy of economic activities over ethical considerations related to animal suffering.

Such cases of "disharmony" in the law related to animals' situation are found in many countries (Burgat 2001, p. 68). While upon the first reading such disharmony reflects an evolution of animals right, a second reading reveals that it greatly limits concrete progress in the relationship between humans and farmed animals. The farmed animal *ultimately* remains a good, custom-made animal (through genetic selection, for example). Indeed, in both French and European laws, farmed animals "are in *fact* a set of raw materials destined for various transformations involving almost all the killing"; "what is protected is more or less destroyed, everything that is not protected is still destructible" (p. 67).

European directives and European law give priority to human, particularly economic, interests as well as to the sovereignty of states in terms of animal protection legislation (Büschel & Azcárraga 2013). In Canada, in general, while it is sometimes possible to convict individuals for certain practices of breeding and killing farmed animals, agribusinesses are never held accountable. In addition, it remains impossible to represent the interests of animals unless the state is involved. The primary mission of the Ministère de l'Agriculture, des Pêcheries et de l'Alimentation du Québec (MAPAQ), for example, is to promote agriculture while also being in charge of animal protection. It therefore serves as both judge and jury. Consequently, due to these lawful agro-industrial uses, animal protection measures in the context of livestock farming seem ineffectual in limiting the violence and physical and/or mental suffering induced. This illustrates the anthroparchal system at work.

However, with regard to slaughterhouses, Erika Cudworth (2008) speaks of endemic and not accidental violence. In these arenas of systematic violence, animals, regardless of their gender, are metaphorically feminized and abused by slaughterhouse staff through the use of gender-specific, animal-based terms ("cunt," "slag," "bitch," "dozy cow"), often used to hurry them along. These discursive practices serve as a complex way of distancing oneself not only from the daily horror of killing, but also from that Other whom one kills and cuts. Distance is preserved by the use of masculinized, hypersexualized humor promoted by the macho workplace culture. The male supremacist attempts to gain comfort by suffocating his natural sensitivity under a fantasy of physical pleasure driven by the systemic violence of anthroparchy.

As early as 1990, Carol J. Adams already linked male sexualized culture—rape culture—to the butchering and fragmenting of animals. In her chapter on "the rape of animals and the cutting up of women," she shows that "cutting" up the animal is transforming them into an "absent referent," literally and figuratively cut off from their unified, sentient state in order to pass from living animal (ontologically unified) to meat (parcelized for consumption). Colette Guillaumin (1972) refers to an "altero-referential" racism that is based on a system of domination wherein the dominant group creates the concept of an Other who is different (equivalent to women or animals consumed as "meat" in our case). These racialized groups thus become "natural groups" that seem to have pre-existed the social and power relations that produced them (Roux et al., 2006). Racialized otherness naturalizes social identities that become active through such discursive practices, reinforcing the presumed superiority of the dominant group in the social imagination.

It is necessary to connect animals' suffering to that of slaughterhouse personnel subjected to infernal production rates under the tight control of current managerial techniques. The work of Jocelyne Porcher (2001) sheds light on the absurd speeds of the kill-line, denounced as such by slaughterhouse staff—for instance, an increase in number of pigs to be slaughtered from 500 to 700 per hour without any increase in staff, thus exacerbating violence perpetrated against the animals and, in turn, their suffering.

An anarchist perspective radically opposes such violence as an act of domination that reflects an unjust power balance. Indeed, the anthroparchy that manifests itself in the slaughterhouse, through or with the support of the state, is outside the laws of humanity (Springer 2018). The creation of slaughterhouses as non-legal spaces for animals reinforces the animals' status as objects from birth to death, as exploitable resources divisible into different pieces. According to Florence Burgat (2001), "it is the human use of the animal that determines the value and status of the animal, and each time defines the scope of treatments that are or are not authorized" (p. 67). Indeed, human ownership of an animal defines the animal. It is the human who is protected above all, in law and in deed. "It is not objective criteria of sensitivity to suffering that constitute the guiding principle of regulations, but anthropocentric and cultural reasons"; rather, Burgat argues, "protection confirms the state of alienation" (p. 67). Moreover, it is the sensitivity of the human being, who is shocked by the spectacle of cruelty, that is spared. The space of the slaughterhouse and the violence that takes place there reinforce the anthroparchal system and the resonances between forms of domination, whether physical or moral.

1.3. The Farm, a Sedentary Matrix

The spatialities associated with the operations of a livestock farming space vary in that they refer to a set of spatial actions that construct an encompassing spatial arrangement, which manifests the inhabitation of the human and nonhuman actors involved. A vegan position could immediately refuse to consider livestock farming areas on the grounds that they embody practices of animal exploitation par excellence. Nevertheless, it seems appropriate for us to consider these spaces—first of all, in view of the humanimal reality we currently experience; secondly, because an analysis of such spaces opens the door to the construction of a critical position from a vegan point of view; and thirdly, because of the socio-ecological impacts of industrial livestock areas.

However, a distinction must be made between industrial and artisanal livestock farming. Of course, between industrial farms, such as "above-ground workshops" or *feedlots* with several thousand farmed animals, and artisanal farms, which sometimes hold organic certification, a whole range of farming models exists, even if the meat consumed worldwide comes largely from industrial farms. In addition, certain aspects of industrial farms can be found in so-called "artisanal" farms by virtue of various standards, such as those related to health and accounting. Then, from a vegan perspective, any livestock farming leads to the deaths of animals raised for human food needs. However, reflection on the distinction between different forms of livestock farms leads us to narrow, as far as environmental issues are concerned, certain foundations for their root causes.

Industrial "Farms"

Industrial livestock farming is based on a division of labor and a specialization of tasks and spaces, the purpose of which is to exploit domestic animals with a view to transforming them into consumer goods, according to timeframes of mechanical and violent acceleration, as well as to spatiality that is compartmentalized but reticulated from the local to the global. It is therefore intensification by increasing the frequency of all aspects of livestock farming (fattening of the animal, reproduction, diseases, as well as human labor, etc.). These humanimal productivist temporalities generate a massification of "goods" produced on a just-in-time basis for markets that are in constant search of outlets.

On an ecological level, the co-spatiality of ecosystems and the anthropogenic, productionist system of the industrial farm are where the dynamics of not only violence and suffering but also pollution are concentrated. Catherine and Raphaël Larrère (2001) insist on the productivist model of "above-ground workshops," a model that dissociates animals from the natural environment. Poultry are absent from farmyards; pigs are no longer in pens; and cows and calves disappear from the meadows: "the animal-machine is locked in an industrial building" (p. 11). Such a concentration produces massive amounts of effluents, such as nitrates and pesticides, that pollute ecosystems and destroy the complex relationships between surface waters and river and groundwater systems.

In Québec, a controversy over industrial pig farms revealed the fact that the agricultural sector was responsible for at least 60 percent of nitrogen released into waterways, equivalent to the amount of nitrogen released by a population of 7.3 million people, not to mention the problem of cyanobacteria and odors related to manure spreading, generating toxins and allergens (Proulx 2007). Studies conducted during this controversy (Proulx & Sauvé 2007) have shown that the agri-food industry generates significant GHGs. However, the carbon dioxide balance did not take into account the impact of the pork industry.

Catherine and Raphaël Larrère (2001) show that according to the science, the development of zootechnics after the Second World War contributed to the naturalization of livestock as a "living machine with multiple abilities" (p. 9), while research and applications related to reproduction and selection, particularly genetic selection, have promoted entrepreneurial management based on technoscientific data. In such an industrial system, the animal and their carcass[13] become a measured number (Cudworth 2008, p. 39).

Farmers learn to apply this technoscientific knowledge, all the while documenting the process and benefiting the agricultural management sector through industrial development and the use of computer equipment monitoring their activity. Such advanced equipment as well as the development of the industrial farming space also benefit the farmer, but at the cost of alienation and multiple "distancings" within the farming space, right down to the farmer-entrepreneur's own *interior psyche*. Indeed, objectification through the division of tasks, spaces, and affects builds an infinite distance between the farmer and the animal being, making him see animal beings as sources of income, future pieces of meat, and simple functions in an industrial system.

13. Ton of carcass equivalent (TCE) is a unit of measurement that includes inedible parts, such as bones and tendons.

Here, the metric for apprehending distance, which is of an anthropological nature and internal to the industrial space—including the farmer-entrepreneur, who is himself a stakeholder in the mechanical system—is topographical, or thought of in terms of surfaces. The industrial farm is marked by multiple discontinuities: real spatial boundaries, for example between animal confinement areas, where violence, suffering, and pollution converge, and the epizootics that result from intensive production and confinement systems, not to mention the suffering animals endure during transport to slaughterhouses. The industrial farm is part of a hierarchical network and part of the national and global meat sector. Industrial farms implement "a unique production model based on the standardization of animals and human skills around a single objective: increasing human and animal productivity through quantitative performance . . . and combating 'unproductive time' in the production cycle" (Porcher 2001, p. 30).[14] An economic-environmental temporality structures the humanimal metrics of this highly hierarchical productivist system. The "divisive practices" that organize human relations are at the heart of the anthroparchy at work. Here, space reveals the system of human exploitation of animals in all its institutional and systemic violence.

Artisanal Farms

Artisanal farms distance themselves from the model of the "animal-machine," which draws on modern scientific technology, coupled with a developmental and resourcist vision of the environment. Moreover, such farms are part of a "heritage" or tradition in terms of making use of know-how that draws on the imagination and "craft" practices. Unlike industrial farms, where humanimal contact is mediated by technological equipment that contributes to the objectification and naturalization of the "animal-machine" (as an assembly of potentially valuable pieces), "artisanal" farms practice a humanimal co-presence that is not only physical, but also emotional and spiritual. Humans and farmed animals share a longer life together and moments of shared attention.[15]

14. The authors would like to specify that the duration of breastfeeding for pig farms in Brittany has decreased from 48 days in 1971 to 26 days in 1999. The interval between weaning of piglets and mating decreased from 20 days in 1971 to 10 days in 1999. "The pig farming sector is one of the most intensive in the world" (Cudworth 2008, p. 39).
15. The pressure of materialist and idealist (e.g., health-related) technoscientific standards regulates agricultural practices in a systematic way. This results in increased control and technical investment, which often lead to insurmountable constraints for many "artisanal" farms.

In her work, Erika Cudworth (2008) notes that "in non-intensive systems, where farmers may see the animals over some months, there may be some element of human compassion" (p. 36). From a vegan perspective, anthroparchal power relations remain a constraint—in this case, translating to exploitation or even anthropocentric and patriarchal inferiorization-marginalization, following Cudworth's model. Moreover, death for the purpose of producing meat food causes a brutal rupture in the human experience. However, the temporality and interspatiality of artisanal farms as compared to industrial ones are not the same: the co-spatiality of artisanal farmlands and ecosystems does not lead to the same levels of pollution or disease among herders and farmed animals; these farms are more integrated into the inhabited environment, topographically speaking; and as places of production, they sometimes operate in a network, but only on a bioregional or local scale.

In addition, artisanal farms contribute to the preservation and opening of mountain landscapes. Only this type of relationship between humans and livestock is capable of combating wasteland on steep slopes such as mountains, or of contributing to biodiversity and soil regeneration. However, living soils, which are strongly affected by short-sighted agricultural (excess pesticides) and urban (excess concretization) practices, are the best guarantee of CO_2 sequestration, as stated by Gilles Bœuf.

On the other hand, artisanal farms should not be idealized. A multitude of activities associated with them (ecotourism, for example) generate a large need for transportation, mostly by car. Indeed, the neo-peasant goal of re-habiting isolated lands may require costly developments in municipalities, when reforestation—even if anarchic—can be considered as universally favorable in terms of CO_2 sequestration and as no longer a mere matter related to local socio-ecological issues.

In the end, from a vegan perspective, both industrial and artisanal livestock farms are places of life and death, with the same purpose of transforming farmed animals into meat. The main difference is therefore not only in the amount of human suffering caused, but also in the duration of the life shared by breeders and livestock, as well as in the humanimal spatialities at work, which have socio-ecological implications. The abolition of livestock farming will therefore have a certain cost from an environmental point of view. In addition, the relationship of ownership that structures the humanimal breeding system requires the appropriation of the territory of many species.

Farmed animal species are themselves confined, controlled, and appropriated down to the smallest cell through breeding practices; so, too, are most moments of their life and most of their movements controlled. However, it seems that the violence perpetrated by industrial livestock farming in particular, through multiple ruptures in the socio-ecological interspatialities at stake, exacerbates environmental problems by creating a tremendous ecological footprint and a "division of reality" that is harmful at a time of socio-ecological challenges.

2. Which Spatial and Discursive Practices Remain as Avenues for Change?

2.1. The Spatialities of Resistance

In the previous sections, we have shown the influence of animal exploitation on environmental changes, in particular the climate crisis. To do this, we have aligned ourselves with a radical vegan perspective grounded in social criticism renewed by aspects of not only feminist theories, but also anarchist thought in geography. This crossover of theoretical perspectives therefore leads us to consider solutions. At the root of the thinking that characterizes these three perspectives is the *praxis* that makes reflection and action inseparable as deliberative thinking. However, this point creates tension. Indeed, militant movements remain suspicious or even distrustful of academic reflections, whose social position is often aligned with the ruling powers.

A "critical" discourse emanating from an elevated position can instrumentalize the reading of social struggles in service of their academic interests, or even scrutinize counterproductive discourses that weaken these struggles "in the field" (Castricano & Corman 2016b). From an academic point of view, vegan positions favor an understanding of the humanimal relationship based on morality. These positions overlap with transhumanism, some branches of which defend "the well-being of all sentient beings." A priori, transhumanist positions are in radical opposition to an ecological point of view because they reaffirm the omnipotence of the human being by extolling the power of technoscientific domination to benefit most of all the biotechnological lobby. However, transhumanist positions are diverse, and crossovers between ecology and transhumanism may be found (for example, in the case of techno-gaianism, as developed by Anderson, 1987, among others) (Carle 2017; Dorthe & Roduit 2014).

In the field, militant struggles for the abolition of all human domination over animals imagine radical spatial realities through the systematic questioning of the practices and values underlying the most violent aspects of anthroparchy, as well as its most obvious environmental impacts. Indeed, militant organizations such as L214 in France play a major role in expanding this radical vision, whether it be by organizing interventions denouncing the transport of farmed animals, mass animal slaughter, and other violent practices on industrial farms or by delivering images of the cruelty of these practices to a carnist society that prefers to turn a blind eye.

These actions of public resistance and denunciation are often at risk of breaking the law, as Stevan Harnad (2019) points out in the case of activist Anita Krajnc in Toronto, Canada, who was convicted for giving water to pigs arriving at the slaughterhouse (Craggs 2017), or in the case of anti-whistleblower (ag-gag) laws in the industrial agriculture sector in the U.S. (Bittman 2011). This gag order paints activists as terrorists under the pretense that agriculture is a "vital" sector. What is more, this arbitrary application of the law by the state directly opposes other rights (animal welfare, the right to health) and principles (avoidance of cruelty, violence, and suffering). Ultimately, it is the right to property that prevails in such debates, which reduce animals to a state in which they are perceived as mere goods, designed for nothing more than servicing human development.

As spatialities, these practices of resistance transgress the boundaries of the law and the boundaries of farmed animal confinement territories. By making use of traditional public and media spaces and global social media networks, they contribute to building a public space that connects anthropogenic humanimal places, where violence is perpetrated against animals. To use the interpretation advanced by Doreen Massey (2004), the videos produced by activists and relayed by the media develop scenarios that give rise to humanimal awareness. Such awareness is crystalized on a national scale through a questioning of the law and its practice, such as is the case with the SPCA in Québec (Gaillard 2019). But above all, the same videos affect the sensitivity and affectivity of people beyond state borders by tracing unexpected humanimal continuities of emotion and intelligence that are increasingly well-documented (Bekoff 2013; De Waal 2018). In this way, they demonstrate a reticulated *praxis* that is part of an anarchist geography of struggle against anthroparchal domination.

In addition, according to Simon Springer (2018), following the work of Chantal Mouffe (2005a, 2005b), an anarchist perspective tends to conceptualize the public sphere as an agonistic space, wherein the conflict between discourses and visions, coupled with the challenge of making room for a diversity of voices, is considered to be a major contributing factor of democracy. However, the question of decision-making, and its exclusions, necessarily remains. Furthermore, these struggles question in even broader terms our anthropological conceptions of human relations, including to the environment and climate change, linking what is on our plates to the cosmos. Thus, two extreme scales, one being involved in the daily bodily spatiality of the individual and the other being a planetary scale, are linked by the closure of the world. This world, thought of from a socio-ecological point of view, makes sense and system.

2.2. From Prefigurative Practices to Collaborative and Benevolent Human Spatialities

Other spatialities are emerging in terms of prefigurative practices, a concept that is found in the anarchist movement. Veganism, as a *praxis*, can be conceived as a prefigurative practice insofar as it "anticipate[s] or enact[s] some feature of an 'alternative world' in the present, as though it has already been achieved" (Yates 2015). In relation to the individual, it reflects a life choice, an experience. This person imagines an alternative world on a daily basis and within a system that they wish to radically transform. Like-minded individuals come together to share their views and contribute to an ideal, which becomes gradually more attainable as a critical mass forms.

Grégoire Autin (2016), however, urges that we keep a critical eye on prefigurative practices. Indeed, these practices can be implemented along a broad continuum, from anarchism to totalitarianism, and are subject to tensions and ambivalences, in particular that of opening/closing or protesting/action. However, it seems to us that through veganism, such practices could spread, although they still mainly take the form of discursive practices. Indeed, the ideas of veganism and transhumanism converge on certain points, such as the issue of livestock farming and the challenge of creating alternatives to farmed meat (the first molecular meat product dates from 2013). In the vegan academic world, there is fiercely discussed literature on these questions of the possible links between vegan stances and the avenues proposed in transhumanism (Reus 2018b, 2018a). An ecological view of the question of relations between humans and animals, coupled with a critical and particularly anarchist stance towards a capitalist system that pushes for ever-greater efficiency (time to efficiency ratio) through technoscience and ever-greater division for the sake of profit, can enable us to consider other avenues for improving humanimal relations (White 2015).

Aside from the model of sanctuaries that save and care for farmed animals,[16] Jody Emel, Connie Johnston, and Elisabeth Lisa Stoddard (2015) discuss farming experiences rooted in a shared and more vibrant socio-ecological way of life based on permaculture. On these farms, animals are considered to be cooperators or collaborators in farm work. But as the authors point out, the various

16. R. J. White (2015, p. 29) mentions the example of Hillside Sanctuary in the U.K. (hillside.org.uk). In France, L214, which campaigns to reform the conditions of animals raised and slaughtered for consumption, lists several farm sanctuaries (https://www.l214.com/faq/quels-sont-les-refuges-pour-les-animaux-de-ferme-en-france), as does the Toronto Vegetarian Association (https://veg.ca/sanctuaries). In Québec, the mainstream media covered the opening of the first sanctuary for farmed animals in November 2015 (https://www.journaldemontreal.com/2015/11/21/un-premier-refuge-pour-animaux--de-ferme-voit-le-jour-au-quebec).

contractual conceptions that connect humans and farmed animals only serve to euphemistically evoke the inequality of the terms of the contract, especially if death awaits the animals in the end. Agriculture that is in collaboration with farmed animals and that is based on landscape maintenance and the use of animal products remains, according to the vegan position, an exploitation to be abolished, even if particularly benevolent attention is given to the animals. Nevertheless, these reflections raise the question of the mass populations of domesticated species, created for human food needs, that would therefore no longer be needed, thus raising important geographical problems of an ethical and ecological nature.

Another perspective, brought forth by Kymlicka and Donaldson (2011), starts from the observation that animal rights theory (ART) has simply established a list of *negative* rights—such as the right not to be possessed, killed, confined, tortured, or separated from one's family—for any living being (animal) with a subjective existence. The challenge is to take into account *positive* rights, such as the human "obligation to respect animals' habitats, or obligations to design our buildings, roads, and neighborhoods in a way that takes into account animals' needs, or obligations to rescue animals who are unintentionally harmed by human activities, or obligations to care for those animals who have become dependent upon us" (p. 16). The authors then propose an expanded, citizenship-based ART that potentially "helps to integrate universal negative rights with positive, relational duties" (p. 29). Citizenship is the key concept put forward by the authors, who consider domestic animals as fellow members and citizens of our (human) community, whose existence must be taken into account in our political and social decision-making.

Drawing on work on disability theory and comparing the handicap or lack of rational reflection in some disabled humans and in domestic animals (pets and farmed animals), Kymlicka and Donaldson aim to show that "absence" of reflexivity is not an obstacle to the exercising of citizenship abilities. On the contrary, the ability to express a subjective good, to participate in political life by virtue of their sheer presence and positioning in a relational context should allow domestic animals to be considered as citizens. Nevertheless, despite the protections and democratic "liberties" that it affords, citizenship also comes with obligations to the state. Membership in a human community does not guarantee "a place where individuals are free to cooperate with each other, equal in all respects, not before some legal or sovereign guarantee (which imposes new forms of authority, membership criteria and rigid territorial boundaries)" (Springer 2018). Therefore, radical democracy—as a vector of mutual aid and free association—is an effective means of dismantling and recreating places conducive to the inclusion of nonhuman animals.

Kymlicka and Donaldson's proposal may provide only medium-term solutions, as the inertia of animal-based food systems suggests a potentially differentiated and generally slower transition than envisaged in vegan theorizations, given the durability of cultural norms and carnist tropism. Indeed, we have seen that the demand for meat in densely populated areas such as China and India is growing, fueled by pro-meat lobbies. In addition, social issues and farmed animals are linked by the essential role played by many poor farmers raising small numbers of animals. Those who adopt the prefigurative practices mentioned, first and foremost a vegan position and diet, remain in the minority. The vegan and intersectional practices mentioned by Harper (2010a) explicitly engage with environmental justice actions and seek to draw "vital connections" (Jones 2010, p. 187) not only to the living spaces of animals and the spatiality of their bodies, but also to their minds. Ecowomanism is yet another practical perspective from the Black community that attempts to build spirituality and ecosocial engagement (Phillips 2010). Such prefigurative practices call into question certain analyses that point to the difficult association or even opposition of vegan, ecological, and critical positions.

In the end, veganism reflects radical spatialities in terms of the relationship between humans and animals, in this case farmed animals. Practical—or simply, theoretical—perspectives (the moral perspective and the associated dilemmas, or radical stances that question the spatialities at work) shed new light on environmental and climatic questions. As for the intersection of veganism with an anarchist perspective—termed "veganarchism"—we could go back to the work of nineteenth-century anarchist Élisée Reclus (Springer 2018, pp. 52–53). The crossover between veganism and ecologism seems to constitute an additional guarantee, given our collective self-referential and subjectivist consciousness that consecrates human supremacy, to avoid certain transhumanist drifts of disconnection from the nonhuman. Moreover, a synthetic meat industry would require huge investments and advanced technology that could only reinforce socioeconomic inequalities and benefit multinationals in rich countries. A more likely solution would be soy steak, with natural meat being still consumed but as a rare and luxury good, similar to quality wines.

Conclusion

In this chapter, we have discussed the relationship between veganism and environmental issues, particularly with respect to climate change. To this end, we have focused on livestock farming, specifically industrial livestock farming (excluding fish farming), due to its socio-ecological impacts. Most of these negative impacts on the environment, such as greenhouse gas emissions, are a result of industrial livestock farming.

Vegan *praxis* provides radical solutions to such environmental problems, since it rejects all carnist consumption and, beyond that, demands the abolition of all human exploitation of animals. This radicality is not so radical when we consider the long history of the anthropological perspective, as illustrated by Claude Lévi-Strauss in the epigraph that begins this chapter. Looking at the relationship between veganism and environmental issues from a geographical point of view has a twofold advantage: on the one hand, we can better apprehend veganism by anchoring it in territories of life and concrete spatialities; on the other hand, we can show the complexity of socio-ecological interspatialities in considering both the materiality of environmental impacts and the organizational framework of capitalism, which fundamentally structures an activity sector considered as "vital" from a both geopolitical and experiential point of view. However, veganism questions this quasi-anthropological basis by raising the issue of animal suffering; the most radical positions even consider doing away with "domestic animals" for either food or companionship altogether. A fundamentally protean movement, veganism is driven by a radical imaginary aimed at preventing animals from being exploited and killed. However, the multiplicity of identities (veganarchist, healthy vegan, capitalist vegan, and ecological vegan) and approaches (abolitionist/extinctionist, "threshold" views, and views based on the theory of co-citizenship) leads to the emergence of blind spots (religious, capitalist, transhumanist, intersectional links) that should be highlighted.

The intersection of a critical anarchist approach with the vegan point of view reinforces a heuristic radicality that addresses, above all, the anthroparchy of the carnist system and particularly of industrial livestock farming as a system of domination and multiple violences affecting human and nonhuman bodies and minds. These diverse theoretical and practical struggles give rise to spatialities whose resistance to prefigurative practices reveals the complex territorial and reticulated socio-ecological interspatialities that cross both humans and farmed animals. They enable a radical questioning of the violence of the anthroparchal system that controls hegemonic food practices and raise ethical questions and moral dilemmas about animal suffering and socio-ecological issues. In a very practical way, the choices we make have an impact on society, and therefore on democracy, by virtue of the entry of humanimal equality issues that cross a new socio-ecological normativity.

Acknowledgments

Thanks to Sophie Gaillard, Lawyer & Director of Animal Advocacy in Montreal at The Canadian Society for the Prevention of Cruelty to Animals (SPCA) in Montreal,and Francesca Allievi for the permission to use the figures from her article.

Afterword

BACK TO THE FUTURE OF VEGAN GEOGRAPHIES

Towards a Post-Speciesist World

Ophélie Véron

Introduction

Berlin, November 17th, 2071. It is a grey, cold November day—weather that brings me much joy. I remember too well the warm autumn months of past decades, the trees that stopped losing their leaves, the never-ending summers. I am grateful for the crisp morning air and the bare trees, for they make me appreciate all the more the long way we have come. After almost a century of devastating cyclones, wildfires, and drought, we may be on the verge of reversing climate change. This bleak weather could not have been more welcome on this precious day. Today, hundreds of thousands of activists converged in front of the Reichstag to celebrate the first anniversary of the abolition of animal exploitation in Europe.

To mark this major event in the story of humanimalkind, I have the honor to write the afterword of the new edition of this now-classic work in geography and to commemorate over a century of struggle—for not only animal but also human liberation. Today, the issue of animal rights seems obvious. And yet, not so long ago, nobody would have imagined that our society would progress in that direction. In order to understand this trajectory, I will look back at the history of veganism and animal rights, before developing in more detail what led us to such an evolution and examining the challenges we still face.

From the Exception to the Norm: Veganism, Fifty Years Later

Looking back on my youth, I keep trying to remember what it felt like when I stopped eating animals in the late 2000s. I was a young carnist who had fed on meat and cheese for all my childhood, and I will never forget the feeling of surprise

I had when I tried a "veggie" burger for the first time. I remember thinking back then, *Why would I take a veggie burger when I can have a* real *burger?* I would like to tell my younger self that now, almost seventy years later, we have dropped the "veggie" in "veggie burgers," as "real" burgers are *naturally* vegan, and it is impossible to find a restaurant in Europe whose menu is not entirely plant-based. Veganism has become the new norm, and it is difficult sometimes to remember that things have not always been like this. People can now go shopping freely without the risk of running into a dead hen at the supermarket or a live lobster at an ominous market stall, waiting to be murdered in boiling water. My grandchildren hardly believe me when I tell them that when I was young, vegans were regarded the way we regard meat eaters now—as the exception rather than the norm.

The word *vegan* is actually slowly disappearing. There is no need for it anymore since almost everyone is vegan. It is likely that the word *carnist*, engraved on the few restaurant windows in the few regions where animal flesh is still being served, will soon disappear, too. The increasingly strict regulations in these places make it more and more difficult to keep selling or cooking animal flesh, and global meat consumption has never been so low. It was estimated that 70 billion land animals were killed by the animal agriculture industry in 2020; this number rose to 143 billion—its highest—in 2052, before falling to 5 billion in 2070. While one nonhuman animal being killed each year would already be one too many, if the current trends continue, global meat consumption could completely collapse by 2079, according to the FAO.

Public opinion has also shifted massively in the past decades, even in places such as the U.S., where animal exploitation is still allowed. According to a recent U.S.-based survey, nearly two-thirds of Americans say that abolishing animal farming should be a top priority for the president and Congress. Compared to just a decade ago, this share has grown considerably. Many of the respondents complain of having to pass by shop windows in which pieces of animal bodies, eggs, or cow's-milk cheeses are being displayed. Even though most of the animal products sold in the U.S. come from local organic farms, animals are still being slaughtered, calves still separated from mother cows at birth, and male chicks who can't lay eggs killed soon after they are born. As the conservative government holds on to power, it likely won't last very much longer because popular dissent is now so strong. The same goes for East Canada, Western Australia, and the North Island of New Zealand,[1] where political change seems inevitable in the near future.

1. The Democratic Confederation of West Canada, the Federation of Neighbourhood Councils of East Australia, and the Autonomous Council of Te Waipounamu (formerly known as South Island) all formally abolished animal exploitation between 2067 and 2070.

What research also shows is a generational discrepancy in public attitudes towards animal exploitation. Older generations of Americans are more inclined to think that eating nonhuman animals is normal and natural, whereas younger generations are more engaged with abolitionism than are their parents and grandparents. Those who now oppose the abolition of animal exploitation across the Atlantic are the children and grandchildren of those who opposed the abolition of the human death penalty back at the beginning of the century. It is important to note geographical differences here, as older generations of Europeans and Africans are more likely than those of North Americans to fully support the abolition of animal exploitation. This can be explained by the different stages of legislative progress in these different continents.

Whereas the U.S. is one of the few places in the world that still haven't completely banned animal exploitation, many African regions were among the first to pass laws against animal farming. Of the now seventy-eight states, federations, and autonomous regions of Africa, sixty-seven consider killing an animal being—whether it be a cat, a cow, or a pig—a crime punishable by lifetime imprisonment. There are now more and more young scholars from the North who receive training in animal rights law, humanimal ethics, or multispecies politics from renowned Nigerian, Kenyan, or Nilotic universities, which were among the first to offer such curricula. It is an ironic twist of fate that once so-called "underdeveloped" regions look with abhorrence upon the few—mostly Western—countries in which meat eating is still allowed.

It is also important to note an ongoing phenomenon experienced by older generations worldwide and yet not reflected in statistical figures—that is, the struggle to overcome the guilt associated with animal exploitation. According to a recent report published by the International Center for Humanimal Psychology, older generations are ten times more likely than younger generations to suffer from guilt and remorse. Former meat eaters find it difficult to come to terms with their complicity in the animal rights abuses of the past centuries. As stated by the president of the European Multispecies Reconciliation Commission, "a whole generation has to deal with the shame of having taken part in a genocide, while thinking all it was doing was having lunch." Research also suggests that even people who had been vegetarian or vegan before animal exploitation was abolished feel guilty for what animals have endured.

While I do not want to suggest that individuals should shuck off their responsibility, I believe public debates about guilt should rather target former state institutions and multinational corporations that had a concrete role to play in what happened to nonhuman animals. It is likely that in a few decades, legal commissions all over the world will investigate the crimes against nonhuman animals committed by former prominent members of the political and economic establishment, leading to the greatest trials in humanimal history.

From Climate Change to Autonomous Politics: How the World Went Meat-Free

The picture I have painted of the current public perception of and the international legislation against animal exploitation may give the impression that change happened overnight. Although much has happened in only fifty years, nothing could be further from the truth. Change has taken time and effort. Sadly, it could have happened sooner and taken a less devastating toll on humanimality. For decades, animal rights advocates tried to speak out against animal exploitation and fought speciesism, but their plea was not heard until human lives were directly impacted.

While scientists had warned us as early as at the beginning of the century that the human population would have to reduce its meat consumption massively to help curb climate change (Springmann et al., 2016), avoid catastrophic global food and water shortages (Jagerskog & Jonch-Clausen 2012), and prevent pandemic zoonoses (Espinosa et al., 2020), it was almost too late when measures started to be taken. Scientists also told us that half-measures and cosmetic changes would not suffice, and they were right. Zero waste, Meatless Mondays, and bamboo toothbrushes did not save us. What saved us was political, economic, and social change—structural change. If efforts towards ending animal exploitation and towards environmental and social justice had been limited within the parameters of the neoliberal, statist politics of the first half of the century, we would probably have faced even more sinister disasters. Regrettably, humans would probably never have taken such steps if they hadn't been *forced* to out of necessity.

I identify three main factors that account for the evolution of our relationship with nonhuman animals: zoonotic pandemics, the climate emergency, and the animal abolitionist movement. As it turns out, the first two could have been easily avoided if more attention had been paid to the third, and if the decentering of the state and delegitimization of capitalist relations had been initiated earlier.

When the 2020 COVID-19 pandemic struck and, in many respects, changed the world, its origins were clouded by uncertainty, but it was generally recognized that the virus had resulted from human consumption of animals. What is sure, however, is that it was sadly not the last zoonotic pandemic on Earth. Eight years later, in 2028, an outbreak of SARS-CoV-3 began in a U.S. slaughterhouse and soon infected 1.5 billion people all over the world, killing 150 million in three successive waves. Again, in 2040, an unusually aggressive strain of avian influenza killed 270 million people, making it the deadliest pandemic in human history. In 2053, a new variant of spongiform encephalopathy affected not only bovines but also poultry, pigs, and sheep and quickly spread to humans, causing thousands of deaths and millions of cases of neurodegenerative disorders worldwide. The resulting international public health crisis led a majority of governments and autonomous administrations to temporarily ban the consumption of beef, poultry meat, pork, and mutton. This move was facilitated by the absence of political lobbying from the meat and dairy industry, since the 2049 European Law prohibited climate-damaging lobbies and nongovernmental organizations.

When the ban was lifted five years later, consumption patterns had already been transformed massively, and widespread fear about meat led many consumers to not purchase it ever again, making it easier for animal advocacy groups to promote long-term meat-eating bans in many countries. In 2058, the Autonomous Administration of North and East Syria, more commonly known as Rojava, was the first region in the world to strictly ban meat; it was quickly followed by other more traditional political regimes. The countries that opposed such a ban were unfortunately among the most severely affected by the resurgence of the disease in 2059 and 2060.

In France, where conservative groups close to the government had warned about the "new puritanism" of plant-based diets and organized public demonstrations to put foie gras back on restaurant menus, the new outbreak sparked such a major healthcare crisis that the right-wing president, Edouard de la Haute, was forced to resign. His successor, Aminata Gueye, a French-Senegalese climate activist who was inspired by vegan environmentalism (McGregor, this volume) and had been calling for the end of animal exploitation since the early 2030s, immediately established a roadmap for transitioning the country away from meat. She also initiated major economic reforms, as well as a series of constitutional amendments towards a decentralized, direct system of government. Incidentally, this led France to be the first country in Europe to cut greenhouse gas emissions by 50 percent in only two years.

Environmental concerns also played a major role in helping to build the post-meat world of today. After years of foot-dragging, the European Parliament declared an official climate emergency in 2019, with the goal of reducing emissions by 55 percent by 2030. However, meat and dairy lobbies still exerted much influence on public policies, and emissions from international air travel—not the livestock industry—were the focus of the greenhouse gas ruling. Yet, with the dramatic drop in airline traffic and the near collapse of the aviation industry due to repeated world pandemics, politicians were forced to face the truth: slowing climate change would take much more than just reducing emissions from air transportation. It was time to address the elephant in the room.

In 2052, after Great Britain had suffered its third hurricane in only a year, which forced millions of people to evacuate London, a massive grassroots campaign of civil resistance succeeded in overthrowing the British government and declared an autonomous administration of South England. Headed by a popular council guided by direct democracy, decentralization, and libertarian-socialist aspirations, the new region immediately appointed a popular Environmental and Climate Commission, whose first move was to announce a moratorium on environmentally harmful animal farming. This measure was supported by a three-year adjustment assistance program to aid those in animal agriculture in transitioning to plant-based proteins.

In 2055, the Autonomous Region of South England was the first region in the world to pass a bill banning factory farming, which by then constituted 85 percent of animal farming in the U.K. The bill also concerned fish farming, which climate activists had pointed at for years for its negative impacts on nearby ecosystems and for the pressure it put on populations of wild fish species used as feed for carnivorous farmed fishes. As the international fishing industry had already been greatly restricted in the mid-2040s due to the imminent risk of saltwater fish extinction, this meant that people almost completely stopped eating fish and meat de facto. By 2060, the region had managed to cut food-related emissions by 55 percent and was considered an example worldwide. It should also be noted that it was one of the world regions least affected by the spongiform encephalopathy crisis. The Northern regions, still under the control of the British government, gained their autonomy in 2061, forming with the autonomous administrations of South England, Scotland, Ireland, and Wales the new Democratic Union of the British Isles Communities.

Inspired by such a role model, many countries quickly followed suit. The 2060s were probably the decade that brought the biggest political changes on the planet. In many cities in Europe and the world, citizens took to the streets, rejecting unethical and environmentally disastrous neoliberal statist politics and pushing for new regimes. While mass protests were violently repressed by conservative governments in some places, as was the case in the U.S., the transition of power was mostly nonviolent, and decentralized, direct systems of government mushroomed all over the world. The new administrations passed strict environmental laws and adopted measures to transition away from animal farming and global industrial agriculture.

Deprived of traditional manure, an increasing number of farmers turned to plant-based composts to fertilize the soil, and vegan agriculture, which had until then been regarded by many as a niche of the food system, started gaining momentum. Large-scale, intensive farms gave way to smallholder farming cooperatives. Since vegan farming not only entails growing plants with non-exploitative fertility sources, but also upholds broader ideals of compassion and liberation for animals and humans alike (Seymour, this volume), it played a major role in changing practices and mentalities, eventually helping a fairer, more compassionate food system to come to the fore. As a matter of fact, 2065 was also the first year when the world achieved carbon neutrality. Things evolved so quickly that only five years later, the European Union of Egalitarian Communities was the first supracommunal political entity to abolish animal exploitation in its territory.

Such measures would probably never have been possible without the relentless efforts made by vegan activists. Moved by the belief that the individual interests of nonhuman animals needed to be recognized and protected, they had been fighting to abolish animal exploitation for more than a century. In academia, the "Oxford Group" had developed a range of powerful arguments in favor of animal liberation and against speciesism as early as at the beginning of the 1970s. However, it was not until the 1980s and 1990s that animal ethics became a subject of study in philosophy departments, and then law schools, in Europe and North America. Although an increasing number of academics had become vegan, the shift started reaching other scholarly disciplines only in the 2010s and 2020s, with vegan geography, a subdiscipline of critical human geography, leading the way. Despite initial resistance from more conservative circles, this new scholarly effort soon expanded research horizons in social science.

The move was facilitated by the growing popularity of veganism with the general public. From being seen as hovering on the fringe, the movement became increasingly mainstream from the late 2010s onward. When *The Economist* declared 2019 "the year of the vegan" and forecast a plant-based future, it could not have been closer to the truth. Whereas only 0.4 percent of the population in the U.S. were vegan in 2015, this figure rose to 15 percent only fifteen years later and to an astonishing 35 percent in 2050. Until the 2010s, meatless products could be found only at organic shops and were viewed by the general public as something for macrobiotic hippies, but by the end of the 2020s, they had come to be sold everywhere, from your local Aldi to the nearest gas station. Vegan restaurants popped up like mushrooms in most cities in the world, and in many public institutions and private enterprises, vegan options became the "default" cafeteria food.

However, this vegan boom would never have been entirely successful if veganism had not been reclaimed as not the exclusionary, apolitical niche business it was increasingly becoming, but a radical movement for social justice. Vegans of color in particular played a major role in decolonizing veganism and making it more accessible and inclusive. They also sought to overcome the misperception—then widespread in mainstream vegan circles—that a universal vegan lifestyle was the sole answer to most of the world's problems. Similarly, an intersectional vegan-anarchist critique of capitalism helped reassert the radical promise of veganism (White, this volume).

By recognizing the deep intertwining of the oppression of nonhuman animals and that of human animals, and their entanglement with capitalism, this perspective reaffirmed veganism's commitment to ending animal *and* human exploitation. Guided by this wider struggle for total liberation, more and more self-managed communities arose all over the world—the most famous of which being, of course, the Esperanza Commune. Founded in 2042 by a small collective of vegan womxn of color in Mexico, it was the first farmed animal sanctuary and eco-communalist community in the world that was turned into a fully independent commune, inspiring thousands of similar projects in other regions of the globe. With two million inhabitants today, it is still the biggest commune of the Democratic Confederation of South Mexico.

Without this attempt to reclaim veganism as an intersectional, accessible praxis, it is likely that political measures to curb animal exploitation would not have been so well accepted by the general population. Veganism would have been increasingly associated with an upper-class, elitist, white demographic or, at best, reduced to plant-based consumerism, akin to an exclusionary foodie culture (Gunderman, this volume). Animal rights advocates had a crucial role to play in raising awareness, challenging speciesism, and changing consumption behaviors.

In the next decades, historians will also likely dedicate hundreds of research projects to understanding the women who, in the long patriarchal history of animal rights activism, made up and helped build most of the movement. Often silenced, forgotten, or relegated to the kitchen, they nonetheless played a major role in founding the first animal rights organizations, weaving together the oppression experienced by women and by animals, popularizing access to plant-based food, as well as opening sanctuaries and caring for rescued animals. Without them, nonhuman animals would probably still be in cages as I write this.

Fostering Rights, Dismantling Speciesism: Challenges for the Future

What has been and probably still is the hardest challenge in the fight for animal liberation is to attend to the power asymmetries and the politics of space at work in our relationships with animals—spatial orderings that Sutton and Taylor shrewdly analyzed in the case of pets (this volume). Animal exploitation may be over in many places in the world, but this does not mean that discrimination and injustice are. More than ever, we need to reverse the geographies of domination embedded in our shared spaces and to develop, to paraphrase Donna Haraway, a sense of multispecies *companionship*. Although most people are now supportive of animal rights and would not think of going back to animal farming, they are not so keen on relinquishing their anthroprivileges (Springer, this volume). This is an ongoing private as well as public process. In the same way as people of color, women, and disabled people have long been infantilized, and children patronized simply for being children, animals are still looked down upon and marginalized in our society. We do not kill them anymore, but that does not mean we take their interests fully into account and give them the moral consideration that they, like all sentient beings, deserve. The legacy of animal exploitation is still widely felt across the world, and dismantling structural speciesism will take time and work.

In the urban landscape, explicitly hostile, disciplinary architecture such as pigeon spikes and even deadly weapons, such as rat poison are seen less and less, but only a small number of cities can be identified as the truly inclusive multispecies cities that Darren Chang envisioned in his chapter. Berlin can certainly count itself among these and be referred to as an "animal-friendly city." Focusing on this case is helpful in understanding the politics and practices of multispecies relations at work in urban space. Insect homes have now long been a familiar marker of Berlin streets, and bird shelters allow urban inhabitants to be awakened by the most beautiful songs from outside their windows every day. The Senate of Berlin recently passed a law to regulate the level of noise and lights in order to ensure the birds' good health and reproduction. It has not been difficult for the newly elected representatives for urban animals to promote measures that are also likely to enhance human wellbeing. Conversely, adopting legislation that may go against human interests is a much more difficult task.

For instance, while it has been universally acceptable to place rescued farmed animals in sanctuaries in distant rural areas, the idea of integrating them into the everyday urban landscape created quite a stir among Berliners. Small conservative groups opposed this move, raising the specter of a new zoonosis. However, Berlin was finally declared a solidarity city by the Senate in 2070 and has welcomed large populations of nonhuman asylum seekers ever since. Surveys show popular support for these measures.

Before I make my final remarks, I would like to share my personal experience as an eighty-five-year-old white woman who moved to an Interspecies Intentional Community in the Berlin neighborhood of Neukölln last year. The community in which I live is of medium size, with fifty-four human residents and forty-three nonhuman residents. Its form of governance is democratic; community decisions are made through consensus decision-making at the interspecies council, which represents human and nonhuman residents equally. By recognizing nonhuman animals as active members of our community and by speaking *with* them rather than *for* them, we try to ensure a "multispecies solidarity" (Reggio, this volume). I have volunteered at the Rehabilitation and Care Center hosted by the community, and I spend three evenings per week with residents who suffered from abuse and exploitation by humans. Aided by behavioral specialists and species facilitators, we try to make sure that they flourish in their new home environment and that we best accommodate their species-typical and individual needs. Together with the local activity center, we also organize multispecies encounters, through which neighborhood inhabitants, human and nonhuman, can spend time together and get to know each other. By making sure that cities become increasingly hospitable places for animals, the Interspecies Intentional Community illustrates how the fight against speciesism may be embedded in urban space and how places originally made by humans for humans can allow for thriving multispecies collaboration and cohabitation.

Conclusion

Fifty years after the initial publication of *Vegan Geographies*, it is obvious that the landscape of animal rights has fundamentally transformed. Fifty years ago, none of what I have depicted here would even have been conceivable. Now, more than ever, we are living at a time of possibility and hope. If I could again talk to my younger self, this is what I would tell her:

> As you may see, we have made good progress over the past decades, and while there is still much to be done, I am hopeful that we are heading in the right direction. Our world is more just, our society more empathetic, our environment in a much better state now compared to when you stopped eating animals so long ago. To you, what I have described may sound like a utopia, but we have fought hard to make this dream real. We have raised consciousness; we have mobilized our communities; we have given all our energy in order to change power dynamics and to allow fairer, species-inclusive forms of representation to emerge.
>
> Now that I am in the twilight of my life, there is something I know for sure: change could have happened earlier. We did not need to lose so many human lives to climate change and pandemics; we did not need to let billions and billions of nonhuman animals die during all those years. We should not have listened to those who said that green capitalism and statist politics would save us, that there were no alternatives. We should not have waited to be in a dire situation. We

> should have acted when change was still based on free will, rather than dictated by necessity. We should have listened to those who said that another world was possible. We have always had the potential to transform our society—the key was just to seize it here and now.

So don't lose time—the world won't wait.

ACKNOWLEDGMENTS

The editors would like to acknowledge the outstanding editorial support and enthusiasm of Lantern Publishing & Media, particularly Martin Rowe, Hanh Nguyen, Liza Barkova, Pauline Lafosse, and Emily Lavieri-Scull. We would also like to acknowledge the love and support of our multispecies families and friends: Fee, Charlee, Emily, Lucas, and Poncho (Paul); Karen, Finley, Jarvis, Lucas, Snuffles, Crypto, and Schitzo (Andrew); Marni, Soli, Odin, Tyr, Jovi, Zeppelin, and Teela (Simon); Eric and Nyx (Ophélie); and Rachel, Tilly, Phoebe, and Xanthe (Richard).

BIBLIOGRAPHY

Adams, C. (1990). *The Sexual Politics of Meat: A Feminist-Vegetarian Critical Theory* (London: Polity).

——. (1990). *The Sexual Politics of Meat: A Feminist-Vegetarian Critical Theory* (New York: Continuum).

——. (2003). *The Pornography of Meat* (New York: Continuum).

——. (2010). *The Sexual Politics of Meat: A Feminist-Vegetarian Critical Theory* (20th Anniversary Edition) (New York: Continuum).

——. (2010). Why Feminist-Vegan Now? *Feminism & Psychology* 20(3): 302–317.

——. (2015 [1990]). *The Sexual Politics of Meat: A Feminist-Vegetarian Critical Theory* (New York: Bloomsbury).

Adams, C., & Gruen, L. (2014). Groundwork. In Adams, C. & Gruen, L. (eds.), *Ecofeminism: Feminist Intersections with Other Animals and the Earth* (New York: Bloomsbury), pp. 7–36.

Adams, M. (2018). Towards a Critical Psychology of Human–Animal Relations. *Social and Personality Psychological Compass* 12(4): 1–14.

Agamben, G. (1998). *Homo Sacer: Sovereign Power and Bare Life* (Palo Alto, CA: Stanford University).

——. (2004). *The Open: Man and Animal* (Palo Alto, CA: Stanford University).

——. (2005). *State of Exception* (Chicago: The University of Chicago).

Agripunk (2016). Scilla!!!, October 27, https://agripunkblog.blogspot.com/2016/10/scilla.html.

Ahmed, S. (1998). *Differences that Matter* (New York: Cambridge University).

——. (2000). *Strange Encounters: Embodied Others in Post-Coloniality* (New York: Routledge).

——. (2012). *The Cultural Politics of Emotion* (2nd Edition) (New York: Routledge).

——. (2014). *The Cultural Politics of Emotion* (2nd Edition) (Edinburgh: Edinburgh University).

——. (2016). *Living a Feminist Life* (Durham, NC: Duke University).

Alberts, H. (2010). Using Cocoa and Chocolate to Teach Human Geography. *Journal of Geography* 109(3): 105–112.

Alger, J. & Alger, S. (2003). *Cat Culture: The Social World of a Cat Shelter* (Philadelphia, PA: Temple University).

Allievi, F., Vinnari, M., & Luukkanen, J. (2015). Meat Consumption and Production—Analysis of Efficiency, Sufficiency and Consistency of Global Trends. *Journal of Cleaner Production* 92: 142–151, http://dx.doi.org/10.1016/j.jclepro.2014.12.075.

Alloun, E. (2015). Ecofeminism and Animal Advocacy in Australia: Productive Encounters for an Integrative Ethics and Politics. *Animal Studies Journal* 4(1): 148–173.

Almiron, N., Cole, M., & Freeman, C. (eds.) (2016). *Critical Animal and Media Studies: Communication for Nonhuman Animal Advocacy* (New York: Routledge).

Amnesty International (2012). Exploited Labour: Migrant Workers in Italy's Agricultural Sector, December 18, https://www.amnesty.org/en/documents/EUR30/020/2012/en/.

Andersen, V. (2004). *Creatures of Empire: How Domestic Animals Transformed Early America* (New York: Oxford University).

Anderson, E. (2010). *The Imperative of Integration* (Princeton, NJ: Princeton University).

Anderson, W. (1987). *To Govern Evolution: Further Adventures of the Political Animal* (Boston, MA: Harcourt Brace Jovanovich).

Animal Medicines Australia (2016). Pet Ownership in Australia 2016, https://animalmedicinesaustralia.org.au/wp-content/uploads/2016/12/AMA_Pet-Ownership-in-Australia-2016-Report_sml.pdf.

Anonymous (2019). *Total Liberation* (London: Active Distribution; Signal Fire), https://theanarchistlibrary.org/library/total-liberation-anonymous-english.

Anzaldua, G. (1987). *Borderlands/La Frontera: The New Mestiza* (San Francisco: Aunt Lute).

Arad, K. (2003). Posthumanist Performativity: Toward an Understanding of How Matter Comes to Matter. *Signs: Journal of Women in Culture and Society* 28(3): 801–831.

Arendt, H. (1951). *The Origins of Totalitarianism* (New York: A Harvest Book).

Arima, E., Barreto, P., Araújo, E., et al. (2014). Public Policies Can Reduce Tropical Deforestation: Lessons and Challenges from Brazil. *Laud Use Policy* 41: 465–473.

Asafu-Adjaye, J., Blomqvist, L., Brand, S., et al. (2015). An Ecomodernist Manifesto, https://static1.squarespace.com/static/5515d9f9e4b04d5c3198b7bb/t/552d37bbe4b07a7dd69fcdbb/1429026747046/An+Ecomodernist+Manifesto.pdf.

Asheim, B., Coenen, L., & Vang, L. (2007). Face-to-Face, Buzz, and Knowledge Spaces: Sociospatial Implications for Learning, Innovation, and Innovation Policy. *Environment and Planning C* 25(5): 655–670.

Atalay, S. (2006). No Sense of the Struggle: Creating a Context for Survivance at the NMAI. *American Indian Quarterly* 30(3–4): 597–618.

Atterton, P. (2012). Facing Animals. In Edelglass, W., Hatley, J., & Diehm C. (eds.), *Facing Nature: Levinas and Environmental Thought* (Pittsburgh, PA: Duquesne University), pp. 25–40.

ACLUMP [Australian Collaborative Land Use Mapping Programme] (2006). Land Use in Australia: At a Glance, https://www.agriculture.gov.au/sites/default/files/abares/aclump/documents/Land_use_in_Australia_at_a_glance_2006.pdf.

Autin, G. (2016). Ouverture des Possibles: Utopies Concrètes et Pratiques Préfiguratives. *Possibles* 40(2): 90–101.

Bagelman, J. (2016). *Sanctuary City: A Suspended State* (New York: Palgrave).

Bahna-James, T. (2011). The Art of Truth-Telling: Theatre as Compassionate Action and Social Chance. In Kemmerer, L. (ed.), *Sister Species: Women, Animals, and Social Justice* (Chicago: University of Illinois), pp. 117–126.

Baker, A. (2009). Grow Vegan! *American Vegan* 9(1): 22–23.

Bakker, K. & Bridge, G. (2006). Material Worlds? Resource Geographies and the "Matter of Nature." *Progress in Human Geography* 30: 5–27.

Balcomb, R. (1986). Songbird Carcasses Disappear Rapidly from Agricultural Fields. *The Auk* 103(4): 817–820.

Ball, C. (1858). *The History of the Indian Mutiny* (London: London Printing and Publishing Company).

Banks, R. & Ford, R. (2008). (How) Does Unconscious Bias Matter: Law, Politics and Racial Inequality. *Emory Law Journal* (58): 1053.

Barad, K. (2003). Posthumanist Performativity: Toward an Understanding of How Matter Comes to Matter. *Signs* 28(3): 801–831, https://doi.org/10.1086/345321.

——. (2007). *Meeting the Universe Halfway: Quantum Physics and the Entanglement of Matter and Meaning* (Durham, NC: Duke University).

Barlow, J. (2015). Tiger, Tiger, Burning Rubber: Meet Tony, the Truck Stop Mascot Dividing Louisiana. *The Guardian*, February 4, https://www.theguardian.com/world/2015/feb/04/tiger-tiger-burning-rubber-meet-tony-truck-stop-mascot-louisiana.

Barona, E., Ramankutty, N., Hyman, G., et al. (2010). The Role of Pasture and Soybean in Deforestation of the Brazilian Amazon. *Environmental Research Letters* 5(2), https://doi.org/10.1088/1748-9326/5/2/024002.

Bastian, B., Loughnan, S., Haslam, N., et al. (2012). Don't Mind Meat? The Denial of Mind to Animals Used for Human Consumption. *Personality and Social Psychology Bulletin* 38(2): 247–256.

Bathelt, H., Malmberg, A., & Maskell, P. (2004). Clusters and Knowledge: Local Buzz, Global Pipelines and the Process of Knowledge Creation. *Progress in Human Geography* 28(1): 31–56.

Bauman, Z. (1990). Modernity and Ambivalence. *Theory, Culture and Society* 7(2): 143–169.

Bawaka Country Collective (2013). Caring as Country: Towards an Ontology of Co-Becoming in Natural Resource Management. *Asia Pacific Viewpoint* (54): 185–197, (See: https://bawakacollective.com/books/).

——. (2016). Co-Becoming Bawaka: Towards an Emergent Understanding of Place/Space. *Progress in Human Geography* 40(4): 455–475, https://doi.org/10.1177/0309132515589437.

——. (2018). Goŋ Gurtha: Enacting Response-Abilities as Situated Co-Becoming. *Environment and Planning D: Society and Space* 37(4): 682–702, https://doi.org/10.1177/0263775818799749.

BBC News (2018). Mamoudou Gassama: Mali "Spiderman" Becomes French Citizen, September 13, https://www.bbc.com/news/world-europe-45507663.

Beauregard, R. (1993). *Voices of Decline: The Postwar Fate of US Cities* (Hoboken, NJ: Wiley-Blackwell).

Bekoff, M. (2013). *Les Émotions des Animaux* (Paris: Rivages Poche).

Belcourt, B. (2015). Animal Bodies, Colonial Subjects: (Re)Locating Animality in Decolonial Thought. *Societies* 5(1): 1–11.

Bennett, C., Thomas, R., Williams, M., et al. (2018). The Broiler Chicken as a Signal of a Human Reconfigured Biosphere. *Royal Society Open Science* 5(12): 180325, https://doi.org/10.1098/rsos.180325.

Bergstrom, B., Arias, L., Davidson, A., et al. (2014). License to Kill: Reforming Federal Wildlife Control to Restore Biodiversity and Ecosystem Function. *Conservation Letters* 7(2): 131–142.

Berlant, L. (2011). *Cruel Optimism* (Durham, NC: Duke University).

Best, S. (2007). Introduction. *Journal for Critical Animal Studies* 5(1): 2–3.

——. (2009). The Rise of Critical Animal Studies: Putting Theory into Action and Animal Liberation into Higher Education. *Journal for Critical Animal Studies* 7(1): 9–52.

Best, S., Nocella II, A., Kahn, R., et al. (2007). Introducing Critical Animal Studies. *Journal for Critical Animal Studies* 5(1): 4–5.

Bhopal, K. (2018). *White Privilege: The Myth of a Post-Racial Society* (Bristol, U.K.: Policy).

Bingham, N. (2006). Bees, Butterflies, and Bacteria: Biotechnology and the Politics of Nonhuman Friendship. *Environment and Planning A* 38(3): 483–498, https://doi.org/10.1068/a38436.

Birke, L. (2014). Listening to Voices: On the Pleasures and Problems of Studying Human–Animal Relationships. In Taylor, N. & Twine, R. (eds.), *The Rise of Critical Animal Studies: From the Margins to the Centre* (New York: Routledge), pp. 71–87.

Bittman, M. (2011). Who Protects the Animals? *The New York Times,* April 26, https://opinionator.blogs.nytimes.com/2011/04/26/who-protects-the-animals/.

Blue, G. & Rock, M. (2014). Animal Publics: Accounting for Heterogeneity in Political Life. *Society & Animals* 22(5): 503–519, https://doi.org/10.1163/15685306-12341350.

Blum, L. (2008). White Privilege: A Mild Critique. *Theory and Research in Education* 6(3): 309–321.

BNS Biocyclic Network Services Ltd. (2017). Biocyclic-Vegan Standards V.1.02, http://www.biocyclic-vegan.org/wp-content/uploads/2019/01/BIOCYCLIC-VEGAN-STANDARDS-2017.pdf.

Bomberg, E. & Schlosberg, D. (2013). *Environmentalism in the United States: Changing Conceptions of Activism* (New York: Routledge).

Bondi, L. (2003). Empathy and Identification: Conceptual Resources for Feminist Fieldwork. *ACME* 2(1): 64–76.

Bonsall, W. (2015). *Will Bonsall's Essential Guide to Radical, Self-Reliant Gardening* (White River Junction, VT: Chelsea Green).

Bookchin, M. (1993). The Ghost of Anarcho-Syndicalism. *Anarchist Studies* 1(1): 3–24.

Bordo, S. (2004). *Unbearable Weight: Feminism, Western Culture, and the Body* (Berkeley, CA: University of California).

Borsellino, L. (2015). Animales Liminales en la Urbe: Espacios, Resistencia y Convivencia. *Revista Latinoamericana de Estudios Críticos Animales* 2(1): 74–95.

Braakman, M., von Bon, S., Walz, G., et al. (2014). Severe Forms of Labour Exploitation: Supporting Victims of Severe Forms of Labour Exploitation in Having Access to Justice in EU Member States – The Netherlands, https://fra.europa.eu/sites/default/files/fra_uploads/severe-labour-exploitation-country_nl.pdf.

Braidotti, R. (1994). *Nomadic Subjects: Embodiment and Difference in Contemporary Feminist Theory* (New York: Columbia University).

——. (2014). Writing as a Nomadic Subject. *Comparative Critical Studies* 11(2–3): 163–184.

Bratanova, B., Loughnan, S., & Bastian, B. (2011). The Effect of Categorization as Food on the Perceived Moral Standing of Animals. *Appetite* 57(1): 193–196.

Braun, B. (2004). Modalities of Posthumanism. *Environment and Planning A* 36: 1352–1355.

Braun, B. (2008). Environmental Issues: Inventive Life. *Progress in Human Geography* 32(5): 667–679, https://doi.org/10.1177/0309132507088030.

Braun, B. & Whatmore, S. (2010). The Stuff of Politics: An Introduction. In Braun, B., Whatmore, S., & Stengers I. (eds.), *Political Matter: Technoscience, Democracy, and Public Life* (Minneapolis, MN: University of Minnesota).

Braverman, I. (2013). Animal Mobilegalities: The Regulation of Animal Movement in the American City. *Humaniamlia* 5(1): 104–135, https://doi.org/10.52537/humanimalia.9969.

Breeden A. & Cowell, A. (2018). Paris "Spider-Man" Saves Young Boy. Cue Debate on Migrants. *The New York Times*, May 28, https://www.nytimes.com/2018/05/28/world/europe/paris-migrant-hero-spiderman.html.

Brion, R. (2011). New Dining Trends: Foodie Kids, No Dress Code, and Hay. *Eater*, April 11, https://www.eater.com/2011/4/11/6687483/new-dining-trends-foodie-kids-no-dress-code-and-hay.

Browne, K. (2008). Power and Privilege: (Re)Making Feminist Geographies. In Moss, P. & Falconer Al-Hindi, K. (eds.), *Feminisms in Geography: Rethinking Space, Place, and Knowledges* (Lanham, MD: Rowman & Littlefield), pp. 140–149.

Bruers S. (2015). The Core Argument for Veganism. *Philosophia* 43: 271–290, https://doi.org/10.1007/s11406-015-9595-5.

Bucalo, G. (2016). *Antipsichiatria e Resistenza Animale – con Giuseppe Bucalo. Resistenza Animale*, July 18, https://resistenzanimale.noblogs.org/post/2016/07/18/antipsichiatria-e-resistenza-animale-con-giuseppe-bucalo/.

Bullard, R. (1994). The Legacy of American Apartheid and Environmental Racism. *Journal of Civil Rights and Economic Development* 9(2): 445–474.

Buller, H. (2016). Animal Geographies III: Ethics. *Progress in Human Geography* 40(3): 422–430.

Burarrwanga, L., Ganambarr, R., Ganambarr-Stubbs, M., et al. (2012). They Are Not Voiceless. In *2013 Voiceless Anthology* (Crows Nest, NSW: Allen and Unwin), pp. 22–39.

Burgat, F. (2001). Les Revendications des Associations de Protection des Animaux d'Élevage. In Burgat, F. (ed.), *Les Animaux d'Élevage Ont-Ils Droit au Bien-Être?* (Paris: INRA), pp. 65–89.

Burnett, G. (2014). *The Vegan Book of Permaculture* (East Meon, Hampshire: Permanent).

Büschel, I., & Azcárraga, J. (2013). Quelle Protection Juridique des Animaux en Europe?—L'Apport du Traité de Lisbonne à la Lumière du Droit Comparé. *Trajectoires* (7), http://journals.openedition.org/trajectoires/1162.

Butler, J. (1990). *Gender Trouble* (New York: Routledge).

——. (1993). *Bodies that Matter* (New York: Routledge).

——. (2015). *Notes Toward a Performative Theory of Assembly* (Cambridge, MA: Harvard University).

Calarco, M. (2008). *Zoographies: The Question of the Animal from Heidegger to Derrida* (New York: Columbia University).

Callon, M. (1998). *The Laws of the Markets* (Hoboken, NJ: Wiley–Blackwell).

Cappellini, S. & Reggio, M. (2014). Quando i Maialifanno la Rivoluzione: Proposte per un Movimento Antispecista Non Paternalista. *Liberazioni* 16: 43–61.

Carle, Z. (2017). Contre-Révolutions Écologiques. *Revue du Crieur* 8(3): 44–61.

Carson, R. (1962). *Silent Spring* (New York: Houghton Miffin).

Case, K., Hensley, R., & Anderson, A. (2014). Reflecting on Heterosexual and Male Privilege: Interventions to Raise Awareness. *Journal of Social Issues* 70(4): 722–740.

Case, K., Iuzzini, J., & Hopkins, M. (2012). Systems of Privilege: Intersections, Awareness, and Applications. *Journal of Social Issues* 68(1): 1–10.

Casey, E. (1997). *The Fate of Place: A Philosophical History* (Berkeley: University of California).

Castree, N. (2005). *Nature* (New York: Routledge).

——. (2014). The Anthropocene and Geography I: The Back Story. *Geography Compass* 8(7): 436–449.

——. (2014). The Anthropocene and the Environmental Humanities: Extending the Conversation. *Environmental Humanities* 5(1): 233–260.

——. (2015). Geography and Global Change Science: Relationships Necessary, Absent, and Possible. *Geographical Research* 53: 1–15.

Castricano, C. & Corman, L. (2016b). Introduction. In Castricano, C. & Corman, L. (eds.), *Animal Subjects 2.0* (Waterloo, ON: Wilfrid Laurier University), pp. 1–25.

Castricano, C. & Corman, L. (eds.). (2016a). *Animal Subjects 2.0* (Waterloo, ON: Wilfrid Laurier University).

Cavalieri, P. (2011). Cetaceans: From Bare Life to Nonhuman Others. *Logos: A Journal of Modern Society and Culture* 10(1), http://www.logosjournal.com/cetaceans-bare-life-nonhuman-others.php.

CBC News (2015). Victoria Pig Lover Refuses to Part with Pot-Bellied Pigs, October 24, http://www.cbc.ca/news/canada/british-columbia/victoria-pig-lover-refuses-to-part-with-pot-bellied-babies-1.3286893.

——. (2013). New Yorkers Boldly Flout Law to Keep Pigs. March 25, http://www.cbsnews.com/news/new-yorkers-boldly-flout-law-to-keep-pigs/.

Chakrabarty, D. (2000). *Provincializing Europe: Postcolonial Thought and Historical Difference* (Princeton, NJ: Princeton University).

Champlin, D. & Hake, E. (2006). Immigration as Industrial Strategy in American Meatpacking. *Review of Political Economy* 18(1): 49–70.

Charlebois, S. (2019). How Restaurants Are Wooing "Flexitarians." *The Conversation*, January 10, https://theconversation.com/how-restaurants-are-wooing-flexitarians-109542.

Charney, M. (2004). *Southeast Asian Warfare, 1300–1900* (New York: Brill).

Chavez, C. (2002). *The Words of César Chávez* (College Station, TX: Texas A&M University).

Chemnitz, C. & Becheva, S. (eds.) (2014). Meat Atlas: Facts and Figures about the Animals We Eat. Heinrich Böll Stiftung; Friends of the Earth Europe.

Cherry, E. (2016). *Culture and Activism: Animal Rights in France and the United States* (New York: Routledge).

Clay, M. & Albers, J. (2016). Decision Making and Sustainability in Built Environments. In Gatrell, J., Jensen, R., Patterson, M., et al. (eds.), *Urban Sustainability: Policy and Praxis – Geotechnologies and the Environment* (New York: Springer International), Vol. 14.

Cogger, H., Ford, H., Johnson, C., et al. (2003). Impacts of Land Clearing on Australian Wildlife in Queensland. World Wildlife Fund Australia.

Cohen, A. (2016). From Mute Objects to Militant Subjects: The Politics of Rebellious Animals. In Oberprantacher, A. & Siclodi, A. (eds.), *Subjectivation in Political Theory and Contemporary Practices* (New York: Palgrave), pp. 237–263.

Cole, M. (2014). "The Greatest Cause on Earth": The Historical Formation of Veganism as an Ethical Practice. In Taylor, N. & Twine, R. (eds.), *The Rise of Critical Animal Studies: From the Margins to the Centre* (New York: Routledge), pp. 203–224.

——. (2016). Getting (Green) Beef: Anti-Vegan Rhetoric and the Legitimizing of Eco-

Friendly Oppression. In Almiron, N., Cole, M., & Freeman C. (eds.), *Critical Animal and Media Studies* (New York: Routledge), pp. 107–123.

Cole, M. & Morgan, K. (2011). Veganism Contra Speciesism: Beyond Debate. *The Brock Review* 12(1): 144–163.

Cole, M. & Stewart, K. (2014). *Our Children and Other Animals: The Cultural Construction of Human–Animal Relations in Childhood* (New York: Routledge).

——. & ——. (2016). *Our Children and Other Animals: The Cultural Construction of Human–Animal Relations in Childhood* (New York: Routledge).

Collard, R. (2013). Panda Politics. *The Canadian Geographer/Le Géographe Canadien* 57(2): 226–232.

——. (2014). Putting Animals Back Together, Taking Commodities Apart. *Annals of the Association of American Geographers* 104(1): 151–165.

Collard, R. & Dempsey, J. (2013). Life for Sale? The Politics of Lively Commodities. *Environment and Planning A* 45(11): 2682–2699.

Collard, R. & Gillespie, K. (2015). Introduction. In Gillespie K. & Collard R. (eds.), *Critical Animal Geographies: Politics, Intersections, and Hierarchies in a Multispecies World* (New York: Routledge), pp. 1–16.

——. & ——. (2015). Doing Critical Animal Geographies: Future Directions. In Gillespie, K. & Collard, R. (eds.), *Critical Animal Geographies: Politics, Intersections, and Hierarchies in a Multispecies World* (New York: Routledge), pp. 203–212.

——. & ——. (2017). Introduction. In Gillespie, K. & Collard, R. (eds.), *Critical Animal Geographies: Politics, Intersections, and Hierarchies in a Multispecies World* (New York: Routledge), pp. 1–16.

Colling, S. (2013). *Animals Without Borders: Farmed Animal Resistance in New York* (Master's Thesis, Brock University).

——. (2021). *Animal Resistance in the Global Capitalist Era* (East Lansing: Michigan State University).

Colling, S., Parson, S., & Arrigoni, A. (2014). Until All Are Free: Total Liberation Through Revolutionary Decolonization, Groundless Solidarity, and a Relationship Framework. *Counterpoints* 448: 51–73.

Colombino, A. & Giaccaria, P. (2016). Dead Liveness/Living Deadness: Thresholds of Non-Human Life and Death in Biocapitalism. *Environment and Planning D: Society and Space* 34: 1044–1062.

Conejo, M. (2013). At the Intersection of Feminist and Disability Rights Movements: From Equality in Difference to Human Diversity Claims. *Disability and Intersecting Statuses* 7: 23–45.

Connaughton, T. (2012). Clybucca's Golden Secret. *The Macleay Argus*, July 16, https://www.macleayargus.com.au/story/200846/clybuccas-golden-secret/.

Coren, S. (2005). *How to Speak Dog* (New York: Simon & Schuster).

Corman, L. (2012). *The Ventriloquist's Burden? Animals, Voice, and Politics* (Doctoral Dissertation, York University).

——. (2016). The Ventriloquist's Burden: Animal Advocacy and the Problem of Speaking for Others. In Castricano J. & Corman L. (eds.), *Animal Subjects 2.0* (Waterloo, ON: Wilfrid Laurier University), pp. 473–512.

Corriere, I. (2014). La Mucca Camilla è Tornata a Casa, August 20, https://corrierefiorentino.

corriere.it/firenze/notizie/cronaca/2014/20-agosto-2014/mucca-camilla-tornata-casa-223767438659.shtml.

Coston, B. & Kimmel, M. (2012). Seeing Privilege Where It Isn't: Marginalized Masculinities and the Intersectionality of Privilege. *Journal of Social Issues* 68(1): 97–111.

Coulthard, G. (2014). *Red Skins, White Masks: Rejecting the Colonial Politics of Recognition* (Minneapolis, MN: University of Minnesota).

Country, B., Suchet-Pearson, S., Wright, S., et al. (2013). Caringas Country: Towards an Ontology of Co-Becoming in Natural Resource Management. *Asia Pacific Viewpoint* 54: 185–197.

Cowen, T. (2012). *An Economist Gets Lunch: New Rules for Everyday Foodies* (New York: Dutton).

Craggs, S. (2017). Pig Trial: Anita Krajnc Found Not Guilty of Mischief Charge for Giving Water to Pigs. *CBC News*, May 4, https://www.cbc.ca/news/canada/hamilton/pig-trial-verdict-1.4098046.

Cramer, J., Green, C., & Walters, L. (2011). *Food as Communication: Communication as Food* (New York: Peter Lang).

Craviotti, C. (2016). Which Territorial Embeddedness? Territorial Relationships of Recently Internationalized Firms of the Soybean Chain. *The Journal of Peasant Studies* 43(2): 331–347, https://doi.org/10.1080/03066150.2015.1119121.

Cronon, W. (1996). The Trouble with Wilderness; or, Getting Back to Wrong Nature. In Cronon, W. (ed.), *Uncommon Ground: Rethinking the Human Place in Nature*. (New York: W. W. Norton), pp. 23–56.

Cross, L. (1949). In Search of Veganism. *The Vegan: Advocating Living without Exploitation* 5(2): 13–15.

——. (1954). The Surge of Freedom. *The Vegan: Advocating Living without Exploitation* 9(3): 9–12.

Cudworth, E. (2005). *Developing Ecofeminist Theory: The Complexity of Difference* (New York: Palgrave).

——. (2007). Complexity Theory and the Sociology of Natures. *International Journal of Interdisciplinary Social Sciences* 2(3): 351–358.

——. (2008). "Most Farmers Prefer Blondes": The Dynamics of Anthroparchy in Animals' Becoming Meat. *Journal for Critical Animal Studies* 6(1): 32–45.

——. (2011). *Social Lives with Other Animals: Tales of Sex, Death and Love* (New York: Palgrave).

——. (2015). Intersectionality, Species and Social Domination. In Nocella II, A., White, R., & Cudworth, E. (eds.), *Anarchism and Animal Liberation: Essays on Complementary Elements of Total Liberation* (Jefferson, NC: McFarland).

Cuomo, C. & Gruen, L. (1998). On Puppies and Pussies: Animals, Intimacy and Moral Distance. In Bar On, B. & Ferguson, A. (eds.), *Daring to Be Good: Essays in Feminist Ethico-Politics* (New York: Routledge), pp. 129–142.

Curtin, D. (2014). Compassion and Being Human. In Adams, C. & Gruen, L. (eds.), *Ecofeminism: Feminist Intersections with Other Animals and the Earth* (New York: Bloomsbury), pp. 39–58.

Cyrus, N. (2005). *Trafficking for Labour and Sexual Exploitation in Germany* (Geneva: International Labour Office).

Dalziell, J. & Wadiwel, D. (2016). Live Exports, Animal Advocacy, Race and "Animal Nationalism." In Potts, A. (ed.), *Meat Culture* (New York: Brill), pp. 73–89.

David, S. (2003). *The Indian Mutiny: 1857* (New York: Penguin).

Davis, S. (2003). The Least Harm Principle May Require that Humans Consume a Diet Containing Large Herbivores and Not a Vegan Diet. *Journal of Agriculture and Environmental Ethics* 16: 387–394.

Davison, A. (2008). The Trouble with Nature: Ambivalence in the Lives of Urban Australian Environmentalists. *Geoforum* 39: 1284–1295.

Deckers, J. (2013). In Defence of the Vegan Project. *Journal of Bioethical Inquiry* 10(2): 187–195.

Dell'Aversano, C. (2010). The Love Whose Name Cannot Be Spoken: Queering the Human–Animal Bond. *Journal for Critical Animal Studies* 7(1/2): 73–125.

Dempsey, J. (2010). Tracking Grizzly Bears in British Columbia's Environmental Politics. *Environment and Planning A* 42(5): 1138–1156.

Déplaude, M. (2018). Pour une Histoire de la Modernisation de l'Élevage en France (Années 1960-2010). *Transhumances: Enquêter sur les Risques et les Mondes Économiques*, https://ritme.hypotheses.org/1416.

Derrida, J. (1978). Structure, Sign and Play in the Discourse of the Human Sciences. In Derrida, J., *Writing and Difference* (New York: Routledge), pp. 351–370.

——. (1996). *Archive Fever: A Freudian Impression* (Chicago: University of Chicago).

——. (2005). *The Politics of Friendship* (New York: Verso).

——. (2006). *The Animal That Therefore I Am* (New York: Fordham University).

——. (2008). *The Animal That Therefore I Am* (New York: Fordham University).

De Souza, M., White, R., & Springer, S. (eds.). (2016). *Theories of Resistance: Anarchism, Geography and the Spirit of Revolt* (Lanham, MD: Rowman & Littlefield).

Despret, V. & Meuret, M. (2016). Cosmoecological Sheep and the Arts of Living on a Damaged Planet. *Environmental Humanities* 8: 24–36.

Desriers, M. (2007). L'Agriculture Française Depuis Cinquante Ans: Des Petites Exploitations Familiales aux Droits à Paiement Unique. *Agreste Cahiers* (2): 3–14, http://sg-proxy02.maaf.ate.info/IMG/pdf/AGRIFRA07c-2.pdf.

Deutsch, B. (2004). The Male Privilege Checklist. *Alas! A Blog*, http://www.houseofalkebulan.com/The_Male_Privilege_Checklist_Peggy_McIntosh.pdf.

De Vries, M. & De Boer, I. (2010). Comparing Environmental Impacts for Livestock Products: A Review of Life Cycle Assessments. *Livestock Science* 128(1–3): 1–11, https://doi.org/10.1016/j.livsci.2009.11.007.

De Waal, F. (2018). *La Dernière Étreinte: Le Monde Fabuleux des Émotions Animales . . . et ce qu'Il Révèle de Nous* (Lonrai: Éditions Les Liens qui Libèrent).

DiAngelo, R. (2018). *White Fragility: Why It's So Hard for White People to Talk About Racism* (Boston, MA: Beacon).

Dickens, S. (2017). Reading a Cultural Landscape: Fieldwork Exercise for Cultural Geography or Advanced Placement Human Geography Students. *The Geography Teacher* 14(4): 173–181.

Dillard, J. (2008). A Slaughterhouse Nightmare: Psychological Harm Suffered by Slaughterhouse Employees and the Possibility of Redress Through Legal Reform. *Georgetown Journal on Poverty Law and Policy* 15(2): 1–18, http://img2.timg.co.il/forums/1/badfa52a-4115-491a-aba1-a9376ea2e193.pdf.

Dominick, B. (1997). *Animal Liberation and Social Revolution* (Syracuse, NY: Critical Mess Media).

——. (2015). Anarcho-Veganism Revisited. In Nocella II, A., White, R., & Cudworth, E. (eds.), *Anarchism and Animal Liberation: Essays on Complementary Elements of Total Liberation* (Jefferson, NC: McFarland), pp. 23–29.

Donaldson, S. & Kymlicka, W. (2011). *Zoopolis: A Political Theory of Animal Rights* (New York: Oxford University).

——. & ——. (2015). Farmed Animal Sanctuaries: The Heart of the Movement? *Politics & Animals* 1(1): 50–74.

——. & ——. (2016). Making It So: Envisioning a Zoopolitical Revolution. In P. Cavalieri (ed.), *Philosophy and the Politics of Animal Liberation* (New York: Palgrave), pp. 71–116.

Donovan, J. & Adams, C. (eds.) (2007). *The Feminist Care Tradition in Animal Ethics: A Reader* (New York: Columbia University).

Dorthe, G. & Roduit, J. (2014). Modifier l'Espèce Humaine ou l'Environnement? Les Transhumanistes Face à la Crise Écologique. *Bioethica Forum* 7: 79–86.

Douglas, M. (2003). *Purity and Danger: An Analysis of Concepts of Pollution and Taboo* (New York: Routledge).

Drew, L. (2017). Capitalism and Masculinity: Kangaroo Killing in Australia. In Nibert, D. (ed.), *Animal Oppression and Capitalism: The Oppressive and Destructive Role of Capitalism* (Santa Barbara, CA: Praeger), Vol. 2, pp. 151–166.

Drew, L. & Socha, K. (2015). Anarchy for Educational Praxis in the Animal Liberation Movements in an Era of Capitalist Triumphalism. In Nocella II, A., White, R., & Cudworth, E. (eds.), *Anarchism and Animal Liberation: Essays on Complementary Elements of Total Liberation* (Jefferson, NC: McFarland).

Du Bois, W. (2007 [1903]). *The Souls of Black Folk* (New York: Oxford University).

Duberly, H. (2009 [1859]). Campaigning Experiences in Rajpootana and Central India During the Suppression of the Mutiny 1857–1858 (Uckfield, U.K.: Naval and Military).

Ducey, K. (2017). The Chicken–Industrial Complex and Elite White Men: Connecting the Oppression of Humans and Other Animals. In Nibert, D. (ed.), *Animal Oppression and Capitalism: The Oppression of Nonhuman Animals as Sources of Food* (Santa Barbara, CA: Praeger), Vol. 1, pp. 1–17.

Dunham, D. (2010). On Being Black and Vegan. In Harper, A. (ed.), *Sistah Vegan: Black Female Vegans Speak on Food, Identity, Health, and Society* (Brooklyn, NY: Lantern), pp. 42–46.

Dutta, M. (2020). Focus on Rising Demand for Vegan Meat with These 4 Stocks. *Nasdaq*, June 23, https://www.nasdaq.com/articles/focus-on-rising-demand-for-vegan-meat-with-these-4-stocks-2020-06-23.

Elder, M. (2019). The Moral Poverty of Pescetarianism. In Linzey, A. & Linzey, C. (eds.), *Ethical Vegetarianism and Veganism* (New York: Routledge).

Emel, J., Johnston, C., & Stoddard, E. (2015). Livelier Livelihoods: Animal and Human Collaboration on the Farm. In Gillespie, K. & Collard, R. (eds.), *Critical Animal Geographies: Politics, Intersections and Hierarchies in a Multispecies World* (New York: Routledge), pp. 164–183.

Emel, J., Wilbert, C., & Wolch, J. (2002). Animal Geographies. *Society and Animals* 10(4): 407–412.

Engster, D. (2006). Care Ethics and Animal Welfare. *Journal of Social Philosophy* 37: 521–536.

Erb, K., Lauk, C., Kastner, T., et al. (2016). Exploring the Biophysical Option Space for Feeding the World Without Deforestation. *Nature Communications* 7: 11382, https://doi.org/10.1038/ncomms11382.

Errett, J. (2016). No Meat? Yes Please: Vegan Restaurants Get More Aggressive, and More Popular. *CBC News*, May 28, http://www.cbc.ca/news/canada/toronto/vegan-doomies-toronto-1.3589687.

Escobar, A. (2011). *Encountering Development: The Making and Unmaking of the Third World* (Princeton, NJ: Princeton University).

Espinosa, R., Tago, D., & Treich, N. (2020). Infectious Diseases and Meat Production. *Environmental and Resource Economics* 76: 1019–1044.

Estebanez, J., Gouabault, E., & Michalon, J. (2013). Où Sont les Animaux? Vers une Géographie Humanimale. *Carnets de Géographes* (5), https://journals.openedition.org/cdg/1046.

Ethical Consumer (2021). Vegan Food Brands Whose Owners Sell Meat or Dairy, August 31, https://www.ethicalconsumer.org/food-drink/vegan-food-brands-whose-owners-sell-meat-or-dairy.

European Union Agency for Fundamental Rights (FRA) (2018). Protecting Migrant Workers from Exploitation in the EU: Boosting Workplace Inspections, https://fra.europa.eu/sites/default/files/fra_uploads/fra-2018-protecting-migrant-workers-boosting-inspections_en.pdf.

ExEn [The Expanded Environment] (n.d.), http://www.expandedenvironment.org/category/about-an_arch/.

Fairlie, S. (2010). *Meat: A Benign Extravagance* (White River Junction, VT: Chelsea Green).

FAO (2021). Food Balances (2014–). https://www.fao.org/faostat/en/#data/FBS.

Farge, A. (2013). *The Allure of the Archives* (New Haven, CT: Yale University).

Faunalytics (2020). Global Animal Slaughter Statistics & Charts: 2020 Update, https://faunalytics.org/global-animal-slaughter-statistics-and-charts-2020-update.

Fazzino, D. (2012). The Will to End Hunger in the Age of Security: Food Security, National Security and Community-Based Food Security in the United States. In Coulter, K. & Schumann, W. (eds.), *Governing Cultures: Anthropological Perspectives on Political Labor, Power and Government* (New York: Palgrave), pp. 183–205.

Feliz Brueck, J. (ed.) (2019). *Veganism of Color: Decentering Whiteness in Human and Nonhuman Liberation* (Sanctuary Publishers).

Felman, S. & Laub, D. (1991). *Testimony:* Crises of Witnessing in Literature, Psychoanalysis, and History (New York: Routledge).

feminoska. (2017). Intersezionalità: Di Oppressioni e Privilegi. In Colling, S., *Animali in Rivolta: Confini, Resistenza e Solidarietà Umana* (Milano: Mimesis), pp. 37–45.

Fernandez, J. (2015). Spécisme, Sexisme et Racisme: Idéologie Naturaliste et Mécanismes Discriminatoires. *Nouvelles Questions Féministes* 34: 51–69, https://www.cairn.info/revue-nouvelles-questions-feministes-2015-1-page-51.htm.

Fiege, M. (2005). The Weedy West: Mobile Nature, Boundaries, and Common Space in the Montana Landscape. *Western Historical Quarterly* 36(1): 22–47, https://doi.org/10.2307/25443100.

Filippi, M. (2016). Not in Your Name: Interview with Michael Hardt, http://www.liberazioni.eu/wp-content/uploads/2019/10/Hardt-lib20.pdf.

Fisher, G. (2015). Burnaby Pygmy Goats: Woman Gets Reprieve in Fight to Keep

Them as Pets. *CBC News*, February 24, http://www.cbc.ca/news/canada/british-columbia/burnaby-pygmy-goats-woman-gets-reprieve-in-fight-to-keep-them-as-pets-1.2966950.

Fitzgerald, A. (2010). A Social History of the Slaughterhouse: From Inception to Contemporary Implications. *Human Ecology Review* 17(1): 58–69.

Fitzgerald, A., Kalof, L., & Dietz, T. (2009). Slaughterhouses and Increased Crime Rates: An Empirical Analysis of the Spillover from "The Jungle" into the Surrounding Community. *Organization & Environment* 22(2): 158–184.

Flanagan, R. (2018). More than 3 Million Canadians Vegetarian or Vegan: Study. *CTV News*, July 25, https://www.ctvnews.ca/canada/more-than-3-million-canadians-vegetarian-or-vegan-study-1.4027606.

Flint, C. (2003). Dying for a "P"? Some Questions Facing Contemporary Political Geography. *Political Geography* 22: 617–620.

Food and Agriculture Organization (FAO) of the United Nations (see Steinfeld, H. et al.).

——. (2018). Livestock and the Environment, http://www.fao.org/livestock-environment/en/.

Food Empowerment Project (n.d.). Child Labor and Slavery in the Chocolate Industry, http://www.foodispower.org/slavery-chocolate/.

——. (n.d.). Peeling Back the Truth on Bananas, http://www.foodispower.org/bananas/.

——. (n.d.). Produce Workers, http://www.foodispower.org/produce-workers/.

Food Not Bombs. (n.d.). The First Thirty Years of the Food Not Bombs Movement, https://foodnotbombs.net/new_site/story.php.

Forgrieve, J. (2018). The Growing Acceptance of Veganism. *Forbes*, November 2, https://www.forbes.com/sites/janetforgrieve/2018/11/02/picturing-a-kindler-gentler-world-vegan-month/.

Foucault, M. (1972). Les Intellectuels et le Pouvoir. *L'Arc* 49: 3–10.

——. (1972). *The Archaeology of Knowledge* (New York: Routledge).

——. (1976). *Histoire de la Sexualité: La Volonté de Savoir* (Paris: Gallimard), Vol. 1.

——. (1977). Intellectuals and Power. In Bouchard, D. (ed.), *Language, Counter-memory, Practice: Selected Essays and Interviews by Michel Foucault* (Itaca, NY: Cornell University), pp. 205–217.

——. (1980). *Power/Knowledge: Selected Interviews and Other Writings, 1972-1977* (New York: Random House).

Fox, R. (2017). Intimate Cartographies: Creating Place with Companion Animals. In Bull, J., Holmberg, T., & Åsberg, C. (eds.), *Animal Places: Lively Cartographies of Human–Animal Relations* (New York: Routledge), pp. 67–85.

Francione, G. (2010). Animal Welfare and the Moral Value of Nonhuman Animals. *Law, Culture and the Humanities* 6(1): 24–36, https://doi.org/10.1177/1743872109348989.

Franklin, A. (2006). *Animal Nation* (Randwick, NSW: University of New South Wales).

Fudge, E. (2008). *Pets* (New York: Routledge).

Gaard, G. (1997). Toward a Queer Ecofeminism. *Hypatia* 12: 114–137.

Gaigne, C. & Ben Arfa, N. (2011). Environnement et Concentration Géographique des Productions Animales: Quels Effets sur la Compétitivité de l'Ouest de la France? (Projet PSDR CLAP, Grand Ouest). *Les Focus PSDR3: Focus CLAP* (2), https://www.psdrgo.org/content/download/3289/33634/version/1/file/FOCUS2_CLAP.pdf.

Gaillard, S. (2019). Le Droit Protège-t-Il les Animaux? (Presentation). *Semaine de Réflexions Autour du Spécisme*, January 23.

Garlick, B. (2015). Not All Dogs Go to Heaven, Some Go to Battersea: Sharing Suffering and the "Brown Dog Affair." *Social and Cultural Geography* 16(7): 798–820.

Garrett, R. & Rausch, L. (2016). Green for Gold: Social and Ecological Tradeoffs Influencing the Sustainability of the Brazilian Soy Industry. *The Journal of Peasant Studies* 43: 461–493, https://doi.org/10.1080/03066150.2015.1010077.

Gayle, D. (2020). Ethical Veganism Is a Belief Protected by Law, Tribunal Rules. *The Guardian*, January 3, https://www.theguardian.com/lifeandstyle/2020/jan/03/ethical-veganism-is-a-belief-protected-by-law-tribunal-rules.

Gaynor, K., Hojnowski, C., Carter, N., et al. (2018). The Influence of Human Disturbance on Wildlife Nocturnality. *Science* 360(6394): 1232–1235.

Geertz, C. (1973). *The Interpretation of Cultures* (New York: Basic Books).

Gelderloos, P. (2008). Veganism Is a Consumer Activity. *The Anarchist Library*, https://theanarchistlibrary.org/library/peter-gelderloos-veganism-is-a-consumer-activity.

Gemme, A. (2019). Autista Dirotta Autobus con Ragazzini e Poi Gli dà Fuoco: "Da qui Non Esce Vivo Nessuno." *Milano Today*, March 20, http://www.milanotoday.it/cronaca/dirotta-autobus-crema.html.

Gerber, P., Chilonda, P., Franceschini, G., et al. (2005). Geographical Determinants and Environmental Implications of Livestock Production Intensification in Asia. *Bioresource Technology* 96: 263–276, https://doi.org/10.1016/j.biortech.2004.05.016.

Gerber, P., Steinfeld, H., Henderson, B., et al. (2013). Tackling Climate Change Through Livestock: A Global Assessment of Emissions and Mitigation Opportunities. *Food and Agriculture Organization of the United Nations*, http://www.fao.org/3/i3437e/i3437e08.pdf.

Gerber, P., Vellinga, T., & Steinfeld, H. (2010). Issues and Options in Addressing the Environmental Consequences of Livestock Sector's Growth. *Meat Science* 84: 244–247, https://doi.org/10.1016/j.meatsci.2009.10.016.

Gilbert, N. (2012). Palm-Oil Boom Raises Conservation Concerns: Industry Urged Towards Sustainable Farming Practices as Rising Demand Drives Deforestation. *Nature* 487 (7405): 14.

Gill, N. (2005). Aboriginal Pastoralism, Social Embeddedness, and Cultural Continuity in Central Australia. *Society and Natural Resources* 18: 699–714.

Gillespie, K. & Collard, R. (eds.) (2015). *Critical Animal Geographies: Politics, Intersections and Hierarchies in a Multispecies World* (New York: Routledge).

Gilley, J. (2010). Geographical Imagination. In B. Warf (ed.), *Encyclopedia of Geography* (Thousand Oaks, CA: SAGE), pp. 1222–1226.

Ginn, F. (2008). Extension, Subversion, Containment: Eco-Nationalism and (Post) Colonial Nature in Aotearoa New Zealand. *Transactions Institute of British Geography* 33: 335–353.

Giraud, E. (2015). Practice as Theory: Learning from Food Activism and Performative Protest. In Gillespie, K. & Collard, R. (eds.), *Critical Animal Geographies: Politics, Intersections, and Hierarchies in a Multispecies World* (New York: Routledge), pp. 36–53.

——. (2019). *What Comes after Entanglement? Activism, Anthropocentrism and an Ethics of Exclusion* (Durham, NC: Duke University).

Glancy, D. (2008). The Naked Spot: A Journey toward Survivance. In Vizenor, G. (ed.), *Survivance: Narratives of Native Presence* (Lincoln, NE: Nebraska).

Glasser, C. (2015). Beyond Intersectionality to Total Liberation. In Kemmerer, L. (ed.), *Animals and the Environment: Advocacy, Activism, and the Quest for Common Ground* (New York: Routledge), pp. 41–49.

Goad, M. (2014). The Ultimate Farm-to-Table Restaurants: Six in Maine You Need to Know About (and Experience). *Portland Press Herald*, July 14, http://www.pressherald.com/2014/07/06/the-ultimate-farm-to-table-restaurants/.

Godar, J., Tizado, E., & Pokorny, B. (2012). Who Is Responsible for Deforestation in the Amazon? A Spatially Explicit Analysis along the Transamazon Highway in Brazil. *Forest Ecology and Management* 267: 58–73, https://www.sciencedirect.com/science/article/abs/pii/S0378112711007316.

Godlovitch, S., Godlovitch, R., & Harris, J. (1971). *Animals, Men and Morals* (New York: Grove).

Goffman, E. (1956). *The Presentation of Self in Everyday Life* (New York: Random House).

——. (1974). *Frame Analysis: An Essay on the Organization of Experience* (Boston, MA: Northeastern University).

Graham, D. (2014). Mind Your Language, and Know Your Terminology. *Growing Green International* (33): 9–10.

Greenwald, J., Hoover, C., & Lefevre, N. (2013). Ethical Traveler: Best Ethical Destinations for 2013. *Earth Island Journal* 28(1): 16–17.

Gregory, A., Wang, Y., & DiPietro, R. (2010). Towards a Functional Model of Website Evaluation: A Case Study of Casual Dining Restaurants. *Worldwide Hospitality and Tourism Themes* 2(1): 66–85.

Gregory, D. (2004). *The Colonial Present: Afghanistan, Palestine, Iraq* (Malden, MA: Wiley-Blackwell).

Griffiths, H., Poulter, I., & Sibley, D. (2000). Feral Cats in the City. In Philol, C. & Wilbert, C. (eds.), *Animal Spaces, Beastly Places: New Geographies of Human–Animal Relations* (New York: Routledge), pp. 56–70.

Grosz, E. (1994). *Volatile Bodies: Toward a Corporeal Feminism* (Bloomington, IN: Indiana University).

Gruen, L. (2013). Entangled Empathy: An Alternative Approach to Animal Ethics. In Corbey, R. & Lanjouw, A. (eds.), *The Politics of Species: Reshaping Our Relationships with Other Animals* (New York: Lexington Books).

——. (2015). *Entangled Empathy: An Alternative Ethics for Our Relationships with Animals* (Brooklyn, NY: Lantern).

Gruen, L. & Jones, R. (2015). Veganism as an Aspiration. In Bramble, B. & Fischer, B. (eds.), *The Moral Complexities of Eating Meat* (New York: Oxford University), pp. 153–171.

Guardian, The (2019). Scott Morrison Denounces "Green Criminals" as Vegan Protests Block Melbourne CBD, April 8, https://www.theguardian.com/world/2019/apr/08/animal-rights-activists-block-melbourne-cbd-amid-protests-at-abattoirs-around-australia.

Guillaumin, C. (1972). Caractères Spécifiques de l'Idéologie Raciste. *Cahiers Internationaux de Sociologie* 54: 247–274.

Gunderman, H. & White, R. (2021). Critical Posthumanism for All: A Call to Reject Insect Speciesism. *International Journal of Sociology and Social Policy* 41(3/4): 489–505, https://doi.org/10.1108/IJSSP-09-2019-0196.

Guthman, J. (2008). "If They Only Knew": Color Blindness and Universalism in California Alternative Food Institutions. *The Professional Geographer* 60(3): 387–397.

Hajer, M. (1989). The Discursive Paradox of the New Environmentalism. *Industrial Crisis Quarterly* 4: 307–310.

Hall, J. (2018). Personal Communication with Author, January 11.

Hall, J. & Tolhurst, I. (2007). *Growing Green* (White River Junction, VT: Chelsea Green).

Hall, M. (2009). Plant Autonomy and Human Plant Ethics. *Environment Ethics* 31(2): 169–181.

Hall, S. (2001). Constituting an Archive. *Third Text* 15(54): 89–92.

Halls, D. (2012). Agency, Vulnerability, and Societas: Toward a Levinasian Politics of the Animal. In Edelglass, W., Hatley, J., & Diehm, C. (eds.), *Facing Nature: Levinas and Environmental Thought* (Pittsburgh, PA: Duquesne University), pp. 41–66.

Hamilton, L. & Taylor, N. (2017). *Ethnography after Humanism: Power, Politics and Method in Multi-Species Research* (New York: Palgrave).

Hancox, D. (2018). The Unstoppable Rise of Veganism: How a Fringe Movement Went Mainstream. *The Guardian*, April 1, https://www.theguardian.com/lifeandstyle/2018/apr/01/vegans-are-coming-millennials-health-climate-change-animal-welfare.

Hanson, H. (2017). Tiger Kept at Truck Stop for 17 Years Dies, but the Legal Battle Isn't Over. *Huffington Post*, (November 20), https://www.huffpost.com/entry/tony-truck-stop-tiger-dead_n_59ea6835e4b0958c468217df.

Haraway, D. (1984). *A Cyborg Manifesto, Simians, Cyborgs and Women: The Reinvention of Nature* (New York: Routledge).

——. (1988). Situated Knowledges: The Science Question in Feminism and the Privilege of Partial Perspective. *Feminist Studies* 14(3): 575–599.

——. (1992). The Promise of Monsters: A Regenerative Politics for Inappropriate/d Others. In Grossberg, L., Nelson, C., & Treichler, P. (eds.), *Cultural Studies* (New York: Routledge), pp. 298–336.

——. (2003). *The Companion Species Manifesto: Dogs, People and Significant Otherness* (Chicago: University of Chicago).

——. (2008). *When Species Meet* (Minneapolis, MN: University of Minnesota).

——. (2015). Anthropocene, Capitalocene, Plantationocene, Chthulucene: Making Kin. *Environmental Humanities* 6: 159–165.

——. (2016). *Staying with the Trouble: Making Kin in the Chthulucene* (Durham, NC: Duke University).

Hardt, M. (2016). Non Parlare a Nome d'Altri: Intervista di Massimo Filippi. In Filippi, M., Hardt, M., & Maurizi, M., *Altre*specie *di Politica* (Milano: Mimesis), pp. 31–45.

Harnad, S. (2019). L'Agonie Animale: Comment Inspirer l'Action? (Presentation). *Semaine de Réflexions Autour du Spécisme*, January 24.

Harper, A. (2010a). *Sistah Vegan: Black Female Vegans Speak on Food, Identity, Health, and Society* (Brooklyn, NY: Lantern).

——. (2010b). Race as "Feeble Matter" in Veganism: Interrogating Whiteness, Geopolitical Privilege, and Consumption Philosophy of "Cruelty-Free" Products. *Journal for Critical Animal Studies* 8(3): 5–27.

——. (2011). Vegans of Color, Racialized Embodiment, and Problematics of the "Exotic." In Alkon, A. & Agyeman, J. (eds.), *Cultivating Food Justice: Race, Class, and Sustainability* (Cambridge, MA: MIT), pp. 221–238.

Harrison, R. (1966). *Animal Machines: The New Factory Farming Industry* (New York: Ballantine).

Haslam, N. (2006). Dehumanization: An Integrative Review. *Personality and Social Psychology Review* 10(3): 252–264.

Hathaway, M. (2016). Animals as Historical Actors? In Thorpe, J., Rutherford, S., & Sandberg, L. (eds.), *Methodological Challenges in Nature–Culture and Environmental History Research* (New York: Routledge).

Hatley, J. (2000). *Suffering Witness: The Quandary of Responsibility after the Irreparable* (New York: SUNY).

Hawthorne, M. (2016). *A Vegan Ethic: Embracing a Life of Compassion Toward All* (Washington DC: Changemakers).

Hayes-Conroy, A. & Hayes-Conroy, J. (eds.). (2013). *Doing Nutrition Differently: Critical Approaches to Diet and Dietary Intervention* (Farnham, Surrey: Ashgate).

——. & ——. (eds.). (2016). *Doing Nutrition Differently: Critical Approaches to Diet and Dietary Intervention* (New York: Routledge).

Head, L. (2012). Decentring 1788: Beyond Biotic Nativeness. *Geographical Research* 50: 166–178.

——. (2016). *Hope and Grief in the Anthropocene: Re-Conceptualising Human–Nature Relations* (New York: Routledge).

Hels, T. & Buchwald, E. (2001). The Effect of Road Kills on Amphibian Populations. *Biological Conservation* 99(3): 331–340.

Henchion, M., McCarthy, M., Resconi, V., et al. (2014). Meat Consumption: Trends and Quality Matters. *Meat Science* 98(3): 561–568, http://dx.doi.org/10.1016/j.meatsci.2014.06.007.

Henderman, R. (2019). The Cost of Cruelty. In Linzey, A. & Linzey, C. (eds.), *Ethical Vegetarianism and Veganism* (New York: Routledge).

Hervé-Gruyer, P. & Hervé-Gruyer, C. (2016). *Miraculous Abundance: One Quarter Acre, Two French Farmers, and Enough Food to Feed the World* (White River Junction, VT: Chelsea Green).

Hetherington, K. (2004). Secondhandedness: Consumption, Disposal, and Absent Presence. *Environment and Planning D* 22(1): 157–173.

Heynen, N. (2010). Cooking Up Non-Violent Civil-Disobedient Direct Action for the Hungry: "Food Not Bombs" and the Resurgence of Radical Democracy in the US. *Urban Studies* 47(6): 1225–1240.

Hibbert, C. (1978). *The Great Mutiny: India 1857* (New York: Viking).

Hobson, K. (2007). Political Animals? On Animals as Subjects in an Enlarged Political Geography. *Political Geography* 26(3): 250–267.

Holden, E. (2019). Pesticide Residues Found in 70% of Produce Sold in US Even after Washing. *The Guardian*, March 20, https://www.theguardian.com/environment/2019/mar/20/pesticide-residues-produce-even-after-washing-us.

Holmes, J. (2002). Diversity and Change in Australia's Rangelands: A Post-Productivist Transition with a Difference? *Transactions Institute of British Geography* 27: 362–384.

Holmes, M. (2004). The Importance of Being Angry: Anger in Political Life. *European Journal of Social Theory* 7(2): 123–132.

Holmes, S. (2013). *Fresh Fruit, Broken Bodies: Migrant Farmworkers in the United States* (Berkeley, CA: University of California), Vol. 27.

Holt-Giménez, E. (2017). *A Foodie's Guide to Capitalism: Understanding the Political Economy of What We Eat* (New York: Monthly Review).

hooks, b. (2015). *Yearning: Race, Gender, and Cultural Politics* (New York: Routledge).

Hooley, D. & Nobis, N. (2015). A Moral Argument for Veganism. In Halteman, M., Chignell, A., & Cuneo, T. (eds.), *Philosophy Comes to Dinner: Arguments about the Ethics of Eating* (New York: Routledge), pp. 92–108.

Hornborg, A. (2007). Learning from the Tiv: Why a Sustainable Economy Would Have to Be Multicentric. *Culture, Agriculture, Food and Environment* 29(2): 63–69.

Horowitz, A. (2010). *Inside of a Dog: What Dogs See, Smell, and Know* (New York: Scribner).

Horta, O. (2010). What is Speciesism? *Journal of Agricultural and Environmental Ethics* 23(3): 243–266.

Hostetter, E. (2016). Reading Place, Reading Landscape: A Consideration of City as Text and Geography. *Journal of the National Collegiate Honors Council* 17(2): 63–81.

Houston, D. (2012). Greening Geography. In Fassbinder, S., Nocella II, A., & Kahn, R. (eds.), *Greening the Academy: Ecopedagogy Through the Liberal Arts* (Boston, MA: Sense), pp. 107–120.

Hovorka, A. (2008). Transspecies Urban Theory: Chickens in an African City. *Cultural Geographies* 15(1): 95–117.

Howells, L. (2018). Esther the Wonder Pig Is Now Cancer-Free after Surgery. *CBC News*, September 15, https://www.cbc.ca/news/canada/hamilton/esther-pig-cancer-free-1.4824623.

Howitt, M. (1864 [1873]). *M. Howitt's Sketches of Natural History* (New York: T. Nelson and Sons).

Hribal, J. (2003). Animals Are Part of the Working Class: A Challenge to Labor History. *Labor History* 44(4): 435–453.

——. (2007). Animals, Agency, and Class: Writing the History of Animals from Below. *Human Ecology Review* 14(1): 101–113.

——. (2010). *Fear of the Animal Planet: The Hidden History of Animal Resistance* (Chico, CA: AK Press/CounterPunch).

——. (2017). Tilikum and the Fall of SeaWorld. *CounterPunch*, January 6, https://www.counterpunch.org/2017/01/06/tilikum-and-the-fall-of-sea-world/.

Hsu, M., Howitt, R., & Chi, C. (2014). The Idea of "Country" and Post-Disaster Recovery in Indigenous Settings: Reframing Research in Taiwan and Australia. *Asia Pacific Viewpoint* 55(3): 370–380.

Hubbard, P. (2005). Accommodating Otherness: Anti-Asylum Centre Protest and the Maintenance of White Privilege. *Transactions of the Institute of British Geographers* 30(1): 52–65.

Humanity Plus. (2009). Transhumanist Declaration, https://humanityplus.org/philosophy/transhumanist-declaration/.

Hunn, E. (1999). The Value of Subsistence for the Future of the World. In Nazarea, V. (ed.), *Ethnoecology: Situated Knowledge/Located Lives* (Tucson, AZ: University of Arizona), pp. 23–36.

Hutton, D. & Connors, L. (1999). *A History of the Australian Environment Movement* (New York: Cambridge University).

Ince, A. (2010). Whither Anarchist Geography? In Jun, N. & Wahl, S. (eds.), *New Perspectives on Anarchism* (Lanham, MD: Lexington Books), pp. 281–302.

Indigenous Action Media (2014). Accomplices Not Allies: Abolishing the Ally Industrial Complex, May 2, http://www.indigenousaction.org/wp-content/uploads/Accomplices-Not-Allies-print.pdf.

Ingold, T. (2011). *Being Alive: Essays on Movement, Knowledge and Description* (New York: Routledge).

International Agency for Research on Cancer (IARC) (2017). Some Organophosphate Insecticides and Herbicides. *IARC Monographs on the Evaluation of Carcinogenic Risks to Humans* (112), https://monographs.iarc.who.int/wp-content/uploads/2018/07/mono112.pdf.

Irigaray, L. (1996). *I Love to You: Sketch of a Possible Felicity in History* (New York: Routledge).

Irvine, L. (2004). *If You Tame Me: Understanding Our Connection with Animals* (Philadelphia, PA: Temple University).

Irvine, R. (2013). Food Ethics: Issues of Consumption and Production: Self-Restraint and Voluntaristic Measures Are Not Enough. *Journal of Bioethical Inquiry* 10(2): 145–148.

Jaeger, J. & Fahrig, L. (2004). Effects of Road Fencing on Population Persistence. *Conservation Biology* 18(6): 1651–1657.

Jagerskog, A. & Jonch-Clausen, T. (2012). Feeding a Thirsty World: Challenges and Opportunities for a Water and Food Secure Future. *Stockholm International Water Institute*.

Jenkins, S. & Stănescu, V. (2014). One Struggle. In Nocella II, A., Sorenson, J., Socha, K., et al. (eds.), *Defining Critical Animal Studies: An Intersectional Social Justice Approach for Liberation* (New York: Peter Lang), pp. 74–85.

Jenni, K. (2018). Bearing Witness to the Animal Dead. *Proceedings of the XXII World Congress of Philosophy* 12: 167–181.

Jeunes Agriculteurs (2018). Lettre Ouverte au Président de la République. October 11, https://www.jeunes-agriculteurs.fr/lettre-ouverte-president-de-republique/.

Johnson, E., Metayer, C., & Rice, J. (1998). Nested Case-Control Study of Tumors of the Hemopoietic and Lymphatic Systems Among Workers in the Meat Industry. *Am J Epidemiol* 147(8): 727–738, https://doi.org/10.1093/oxfordjournals.aje.a009517.

Johnson, E., Ndetan, H., Felini, M., et al. (2011). Mortality in Workers Employed in Pig Abattoirs. *Environmental Research* 111: 871–876.

Johnston, C. (2008). Beyond the Clearing: Towards a Dwelt Animal Geography. *Progress in Human Geography* 32(5): 633–649, http://dx.doi.org/10.1177/0309132508089825.

Johnston, J. & Baumann, S. (2015). *Foodies: Democracy and Distinction in the Gourmet Foodscape* (2nd Edition) (New York: Routledge).

Jones, M. (2002). Bean by Bean—Supporting Indigenous Rights: He Runs His Coffee Business to Improve Life in Chiapas. *National Catholic Reporter* 39(9).

Jones, O. (2000). (Un)Ethical Geographies of Human–Non-Human Relations: Encounters, Collectives and Spaces. In Philol, C. & Wilbert, C. (eds.), *Animal Spaces, Beastly Places* (New York: Routledge), pp. 267–290.

jones, p. (2009). Free as a Bird: Natural Anarchism in Action. In Amster, R., DeLeon, A., Fernandez, L., et al. (eds.), *Contemporary Anarchist Studies: An Introductory Anthology of Anarchy in the Academy* (New York: Routledge), pp. 236–246.

——. (2010). Liberation as Connection and the Decolonization of Desire. In Harper, A. (ed.), *Sistah Vegan: Black Female Vegans Speak on Food, Identity, Health, and Society* (Brooklyn, NY: Lantern), pp. 187–201.

Jones, R. (2016). Veganisms. In Castricano, J. & Simonsen, R. (eds.), *Critical Perspectives on Veganism* (New York: Palgrave), pp. 15–39.

Jones, T. (2017). Truck Stop Owner Plans to Pursue Another Tiger, Stuff Tony for Display; Critic Calls that "Disrespectful." *The Advocate*, October 17, https://www.theadvocate.com/baton_rouge/news/communities/westside/article_46251bf8-b357-11e7-b2b6-afcbb7a5925b.html.

——. (2018). Tiger Truck Stop's Two New Animals Frustrate Activists, but Local, State Officials Staying out of Fight. *The Advocate*, July 29, https://www.theadvocate.com/baton_rouge/news/communities/westside/article_8ac4a3a0-910a-11e8-8c22-5be8072ae1dd.html.

Joy, M. (2001). From Carnivore to Carnist: Liberating the Language of Meat. *Satya*, http://www.satyamag.com/sept01/joy.html.

——. (2010/2011). *Why We Love Dogs, Eat Pigs, and Wear Cows: An Introduction to Carnism* (San Francisco: Conari).

Joy, M. & Tuider, J. (2016). Foreword. In Castricano, J. & Simonsen, R. (eds.), *Critical Perspectives on Veganism* (New York: Palgrave), pp. v–xv.

Joyce, J., Nevins, J., & Schneiderman, J. (2017). Commodification, Violence, and the Making of Workers and Ducks at Hudson Valley Foie Gras. In Gillespie, K. & Collard, R. (eds.), *Critical Animal Geographies: Politics, Intersections, and Hierarchies in a Multispecies World* (London: Routledge), pp. 93–107.

Judd, A. (2018). Pet Pig Adopted from BC SPCA Killed and Eaten by New Owners. *Global News*, February 22, https://globalnews.ca/news/4042125/pig-adopted-bc-spca-killed-eaten-owners/.

Kamp, D. (2006). *The United States of Arugula: How We Became a Gourmet Nation* (New York: Broadway Books).

Karasiak, N. (2015). *Elevage et Pollution: Projet de Webmapping et de Visualisation de Données* (Master's Thesis, Université de Toulouse – Jean-Jaurès).

Kareiva, P., Watts, S., McDonald, R., et al. (2007). Domesticated Nature: Shaping Landscapes and Ecosystems for Human Welfare. *Science* 316: 1866–1869.

Kauffman, L. (2017). *Direct Action: Protest and the Reinvention of American Radicalism* (New York: Verso).

Kean, H. (1998). *Animal Rights: Political and Social Change in Britain Since 1800* (London: Reaktion).

Kemmerer, L. (2011). *Sister Species: Women, Animals, and Social Justice*. (Champaign, IL. University of Illinois).

Kemmerer, L. & Kirjner, D. (2015). Conflict and Accord: A Critical Review of Theory and Methods for Earth and Animal Advocacy. In Kemmerer, L. (ed.), *Animals and the Environment: Advocacy, Activism, and the Quest for Common Ground* (London: Routledge), pp. 15–38.

Keul, A. (2013). Embodied Encounters Between Humans and Gators. *Social & Cultural Geography* 14(8): 930–953, https://doi.org/10.1080/14649365.2013.837190.

Killerman, S. (2012). Heterosexual Privilege Checklist. *Project Humanities*, https://projecthumanities.asu.edu/content/heterosexual-privilege-checklist.

Kimell, M. (2017). Introduction: Toward a Sociology of the Subordinate. In Kimell, M. & Ferber, A. (eds.), *Privilege: A Reader* (Boulder, CO: Westview), pp. 1–12.

Kittay, E. (2001). When Caring Is Just and Justice Is Caring: Justice and Mental Retardation. *Public Culture* 13(3): 557–579.

Kittay, E. & Carlson, L. (eds.) (2010). *Cognitive Disability and Its Challenge to Moral Philosophy* (Malden, MA: Wiley-Blackwell).

Ko, A. & Ko, S. (2017). *Aphro-ism: Essays on Pop Culture, Feminism, and Black Veganism from Two Sisters* (Brooklyn, NY: Lantern).

Kobayashi, A. (2009). Situated Knowledge, Reflexivity. In Kitchin, R. & Thrift, N. (eds.), *International Encyclopedia of Human Geography* (Boston, MA: Elsevier), pp. 138–143.

Koneswaran, G. & Nierenberg, D. (2008). Global Farm Animal Production and Global Warming: Impacting and Mitigating Climate Change. *Environmental Health Perspectives* 116(5): 578–582.

Konju (2010). Letter to a Brotha, https://vegansofcolor.wordpress.com/tag/revolution.

Koopman, J. (2008). Sculpture of Tatiana the Tiger Unveiled. *SFGATE*, December 26, https://www.sfgate.com/bayarea/article/Sculpture-of-Tatiana-the-tiger-unveiled-3178715.php.

Kowalczyk, A. (2014). Mapping Non-Human Resistance in the Age of Biocapital. In Taylor, N. & Twine, R. (eds.), *The Rise of Critical Animal Studies: From the Margins to the Centre* (New York: Routledge), pp. 183–200.

Kunst, J. & Haugestad, C. (2018). The Effects of Dissociation on Willingness to Eat Meat Are Moderated by Exposure to Unprocessed Meat: A Cross-Cultural Demonstration. *Appetite* (120): 356–366.

Kwaymullina, B. (2012). *Stories and Ngurra (Country): Creative Writing and Aboriginal Knowledge Systems* (Unpublished Doctoral Thesis, University of Western Australia).

Labchuk, C. (2016). Canada's Animal Cruelty Laws Outdates, Full of Loopholes. *The Hill Times*, May 16, https://www.hilltimes.com/wp-content/uploads/2016/05/051616_ht.pdf.

Laird, C. (dir.) (2003). *Through These Eyes*. Documentary Education Resources.

Lambert, L. (2012). *Weaponized Architecture: The Impossibility of Innocence* (New York: dpr-barcelona).

——. (2016). *Topie Impitoyable: The Corporeal Politics of the Cloth, the Wall, and the Street* (A. Klosowska, trans.) (Santa Barbara, CA: Punctum).

Lambin, E., Turner, B., Geist, H., et al. (2001). The Causes of Land-Use and Land-Cover Change: Moving Beyond the Myths. *Global Environmental Change* 11(4): 261–269.

Lang, J. (2007). *Emerging Food Concept Trends in Food Service* (New York: Packaged Facts).

Langton, M. (1996). What Do We Mean by Wilderness? Wilderness and *Terra Nullius* in Australian Art (Address to The Sydney Institute). *The Sydney Papers* 8: 11–31.

——. (2013). *The Quiet Revolution: Indigenous People and the Resources Boom* (Sydney: ABC).

Larrère, C. & Larrère, R. (2001). L'Animal-Machine à Produire: Rupture du Contrat Domestique. In Burgat, F. (ed.), *Les Animaux d'Élevage Ont-Ils Droit au Bien-Être?* (Paris: INRA), pp. 9–24.

Larrère, C. (2006). Éthiques de l'Environnement. *Multitudes* 24(1): 75–84, https://doi.org/10.3917/mult.024.0075.

Larsen, S. & Johnson, J. (2017). *Being Together in Place: Indigenous Coexistence in a More Than Human World* (Minneapolis, MN: University of Minnesota).

Latour, B. (2004a). *Politics of Nature: How to Bring the Sciences into Democracy* (Cambridge, MA: Harvard University).

——. (2004b). Why Has Critique Run Out of Steam? From Matters of Fact to Matters of Concern. *Critical Inquiry* 30: 225–248.

Leach, E. (1964). Anthropological Aspects of Language: Animal Categories and Verbal Abuse. In Lenneberg, E. (ed.), *New Directions in the Study of Language* (Cambridge, MA: MIT), pp. 23–63.

Leavy, P. (2017). Introduction. In Leavy, P. (ed.), *Privilege Through the Looking-Glass* (Boston, MA: Sense), pp. 1–6.

Lee, J. (2016). Be/Longing in the Archival Body: Eros and the "Endearing" Value of Material Lives. *Archival Science* 16(1): 33–51.

Lees, L. (2004). Urban Geography: Discourse Analysis and Urban Research. *Progress in Human Geography* 28(1): 101–107.

Lefevbre, H. (1991 [1974]). *The Production of Space* (D. Nicholson-Smith, trans.) (Malden, MA: Wiley-Blackwell).

Leneman, L. (1999). No Animal Food: The Road to Veganism in Britain, 1909–1944. *Society & Animals* 7(3): 219–228.

Leopold, A. (1949). *A Sand County Almanac: And sketches Here and There* (New York: Oxford University).

Lestel, D., Brunois, F., & Gaunet, F. (2006). Towards an Etho-Ethnology and an Ethno-Ethology. *Social Sciences Information* 45: 155–177.

Lévi-Strauss, C. (2001). La Leçon de Sagesse des Vaches Folles. *Études Rurales* (157–158): 9–14.

Levinas, E. (1969 [1961]). *Totality and Infinity: An Essay on Exteriority* (A. Lingis, trans.) (Pittsburgh, PA: Duquesne University).

Lind-af-Hageby, L. & Schartau, L. (2012). *The Shambles of Science: Extracts from the Diary of Two Students of Physiology* (Charleston, SC: Nabu).

Lines, W. (2006). *Patriots: Defending Australia's Natural Heritage* (St Lucia, Queensland: University of Queensland).

Linzey, A. & Linzey, C. (2019). Introduction: Vegetarianism as Ethical Protest. In Linzey, A. & Linzey, C. (eds.), *Ethical Vegetarianism and Veganism* (London: Routledge).

Lipsitz, G. (2006). Learning from New Orleans: The Social Warrant of Hostile Privatism and Competitive Consumer Citizenship. *Cultural Anthropology* 21(3): 451–468.

Litvaitis, J. & Tash, J. (2008). An Approach Toward Understanding Wildlife–Vehicle Collisions. *Environmental Management* 42(4): 688–697.

Livingstone Smith, D. (2011). *Less than Human: Why We Demean, Enslave, and Exterminate Others* (New York: St. Martin's).

Lock, M. (2002). Alienation of Body Tissue and the Biopolitics of Immortalized Cell Lines. In Scheper-Hughes, N. & Wacwuant, L. (eds.), *Commodifying Bodies* (Thousand Oaks, CA: SAGE), pp. 63–91.

Lockwood, A. (2016). *The Pig in Thin Air: An Identification* (Brooklyn, NY: Lantern).

——. (2018). Bodily Encounter, Bearing Witness and the Engaged Activism of the Global Save Movement. *Animal Studies Journal* 7(1): 104–126.

Lopez, E., Simpson, C., & Valiente, A. (2014). Potbellied Pigs Spark Clashes with Neighbors. *ABC News*, December 30, http://abcnews.go.com/US/potbellied-pigs-spark-clashes-neighbors/story?id=27879921.

Lorimer, J. (2015). *Wildlife in the Anthropocene* (Minneapolis, MN: University of Minnesota).

Lorimer, J. & Srinivasan, K. (2013). Animal Geographies. In Johnson, N., Schein, R., & Winders, J. (eds.), *The Wiley-Blackwell Companion to Cultural Geography* (Chichester, U.K.: Wiley-Blackwell), pp. 332–342.

Luke, B. (1995). Solidarity Across Diversity: A Pluralistic Rapprochement of Environmentalism and Animal Liberation. *Social Theory and Practice* 21: 177–206.

Lussault, M. (1997). Espace, Société, Nature. In Knafou, R., *L'état de la Géographie: Autoscopie d'une Science* (Paris: Belin), pp. 408–419.

Lykke, N. (2010). *Feminist Studies: Guide to Intersectional Theory, Methodology and Writing* (New York: Routledge).

Lyons, D. (2013). *The Politics of Animal Experimentation* (New York: Palgrave).

MacLaughlin, J. (2016). *Kropotkin and the Anarchist Intellectual Tradition* (London: Pluto).

Main, D. (2019). Why Insect Populations Are Plummeting—and Why It Matters. *National Geographic,* February 18, https://www.nationalgeographic.co.uk/environment/2019/02/why-insect-populations-are-plummeting-and-why-it-matters.

Majocchi, D. (2018). Non Agire a Nome d'Altri: Intervista a Giuseppe Bucalo. *Liberazioni: Rivista di Criticaantispecista* 32(8): 77–90.

Malkin, V. (2004). "We Go to Get Ahead": Gender and Status in Two Mexican Migrant Communities. *Latin American Perspectives* 31(5): 75–99.

Malleson, G. (1896). *History of the Indian Mutiny: Commencing from the Close of the Second Volume of Sir John Kaye's History of the Sepoy War* (New York: Longman), Vol. 3.

Mallett, S. (2004). Understanding Home: A Critical Review of the Literature. *The Sociological Review* 52(1): 62–89.

Malm, A. & Hornborg, A. (2014). The Geology of Mankind? A Critique of the Anthropocene Narrative. *The Anthropocene Review* 1: 62–69.

Mancuso, S. & Viola, A. (2015). *Brilliant Green: The Surprising History and Science of Plant Intelligence* (Washington, DC: Island).

Mansfield, B., Biermann, C., McSweeney, K., et al. (2014). Environmental Politics after Nature: Conflicting Socioecological Futures. *Annals of the Association of American Geographers* 105: 284–293.

Mantyla, R. (2019). Rick Wiles: Plant-Based Meat Alternatives Are a Satanic Plot to "Create a Race of Soulless Creatures." *Right Wing Watch,* June 13, https://www.rightwingwatch.org/post/rick-wiles-plant-based-meat-alternatives-are-a-satanic-plot-to-create-a-race-of-soulless-creatures/.

Markus, N. (2009). *On Our Watch: The Race to Save Australia's Environment* (Melbourne: Melbourne University).

Marris, E. (2011). *Rambunctious Garden: Saving Nature in a Post-Wild World* (New York: Bloomsbury).

Marshall, P. (2015). *Nature's Web: Rethinking Our Place on Earth* (Armonk, NY: Routledge).

Massey, D. (2005). *For Space* (Thousand Oaks, CA: SAGE).

Masson, J. (2005). *The Pig Who Sang to the Moon: The Emotional World of Farm Animals* (New York: Vintage).

Massumi, B. (2014). *What Animals Teach Us about Politics* (Durham, NC: Duke University).

Mateer, J. (2018). Rebel Elephants: Resistance Through Human–Elephant Partnerships. In Rutherford, S. & Wilcox, S. (eds.), *Historical Animal Geographies* (London: Routledge).

Matsuoka, A. & Sorenson, J. (2018). Introduction. In Matsuoka, A. & Sorenson, J. (eds.), *Critical Animal Studies: Towards Trans-Species Social Justice* (New York: Rowman & Littlefield), pp. 1–17.

May, T. (2010). Introduction. In Jun, N. & Wahl, S. (eds.), *New Perspectives on Anarchism* (Plymouth, MA: Lexington Books), pp. 1–5.

McCann, E. J. (2004). "Best Places": Inter-Urban Competition, Quality of Life, and Popular Media Discourses. *Urban Studies* 41(10): 1909–1929.

McDonald, B. (2000). "Once You Know Something, You Can't Not Know It": An Empirical Look at Becoming Vegan. *Society & Animals* 8(1): 1–23.

McDonald, G. (2017). How Edinburgh Is Becoming Scotland's Vegan Capital. *iNews*, July 24, https://inews.co.uk/inews-lifestyle/food-and-drink/edinburgh-becoming-scotlands-vegan-capital/.

McGregor, A. (2004). Sustainable Development and "Warm Fuzzy Feelings": Discourse and Nature within Australian Environmental Imaginaries. *Geoforum* 35: 593–606.

McGregor, A. & Houston, D. (2018). Cattle in the Anthropocene: Four Propositions. *Transactions Institute of British Geography* 43: 3–16.

McIntosh, P. (1989). White Privilege: Unpacking the Invisible Knapsack. *Peace & Freedom* 10–12.

——. (2012). Reflections and Future Directions for Privilege Studies. *Journal of Social Issues* 68(1): 194–206.

McKibben, M. (2003). *The End of Nature: Humanity, Climate Change and the Natural World* (Revised Edition) (New York: Bloomsbury).

McNichol, S. (1992). *Law of Privilege* (Sydney: Law Book Company Ltd).

Mealey, L. (2019). Dealing with High Food Costs at Your Restaurant. *The Balance*, January 21, https://www.thebalance.com/food-cost-problems-2888405.

Meijer, E. (2013). Political Communication with Animals. *Humanimalia: Journal of Human/Animal Interface Studies* 5(1): 28–52.

Meinig, D. W. (1979). Symbolic Landscapes: Some Idealizations of American Communities. In Meinig, D. W. (ed.), *The Interpretation of Ordinary Landscapes: Geographical Essays* (New York: Oxford University), pp. 164–192.

Melican, B. & Maxwell, E. (2007). The Ethics of Food and Environmental Challenges. In Friedland, S. (ed.), *Food and Morality: Proceedings of the Oxford Symposium on Food and Cookery 2007* (London: Prospect Books), pp. 207–219.

Merchant, C. (1980). *The Death of Nature: Women, Ecology and the Scientific Revolution* (New York: Harper & Row).

Merry, M. (2013). *Equality, Citizenship, and Segregation: A Defense of Separation* (New York: Palgrave).

Merskin, D. (2011). Hearing Voices: The Promise of Participatory Action Research for Animals. *Action Research* 9(2): 144–161.

Microsanctuary Movement, The (n.d.). http://www.microsanctuarymovement.org/.

Mitchell, D. (1996). *The Lie of the Land: Migrant Workers and the California Landscape* (Minneapolis, MN: University of Minnesota).

Mitchell, K. (1996). Visions of Vancouver: Ideology, Democracy, and the Future of Urban Development. *Urban Geography* 17(6): 478–501.

Mitchell, T. (2002). *Rule of Experts: Egypt, Techno-Politics, Modernity* (Berkeley, CA: University of California).

Mohai, P., Pellow, D., & Roberts, J. (2009). Environmental Justice. *Annual Review of Environment and Resources* 34: 405–430.

Mohanty, C. (2003). *Feminism without Borders: Decolonizing Theory, Practicing Solidarity* (Durham, NC: Duke University).

Mollison, B. (1990). *Permaculture: A Practical Guide for a Sustainable Future* (Washington, DC: Island).

Mooallem, J. (2013). *Wild Ones: A Sometimes Dismaying, Weirdly Reassuring Story About Looking at People Looking at Animals in America* (New York: Penguin).

Mood, A. (2010). Worse Things Happen at Sea: The Welfare of Wild-Caught Fish. *Fish Count*, http://www.fishcount.org.uk/published/standard/fishcountfullrptSR.pdf.

Moore Lappé, F. (1971). *Diet for a Small Planet* (New York: Ballantine).

Moore, A. & Swanson, E. (eds.) (2018). *Witnessing Torture: Perspectives of Torture Survivors and Human Rights Workers* (New York: Palgrave).

Moore, J. (2016). Anthropocene or Capitalocene? Nature, History, and the Crisis of Capitalism. In Moore, J. (ed.), *Anthropocene or Capitalocene? Nature, History, and the Crisis of Capitalism* (Oakland, CA: PM).

——. (2017). The Capitalocene I: On the Nature and Origins of Our Ecological Crisis. *The Journal of Peasant Studies* 44(3): 594–630, http://dx.doi.org/10.1080/03066150.2016.1235036.

Moore, L. (2013). Speciesism. *Contexts* 12: 12–13.

Moreton-Robinson, A (2015). *The White Possessive: Property, Power, and Indigenous Sovereignty* (Minneapolis and London: University of Minnesota).

Morin, K. (2015). Wildspace: The Cage, the Supermax and the Zoo. In Gillespie, K. & Collard, R. (eds.), *Critical Animal Geographies: Politics, Intersections, and Hierarchies in a Multispecies World* (London: Routledge).

——. (2018). *Carceral Space, Prisoners and Animals* (London: Routledge).

Morris, D. (1999). McLibel: Do-It-Yourself Justice. *Alternative Law Journal* 24(1): 269–273.

Mosley, G. (1999). *Battle for the Bush: The Blue Mountains, the Australian Alps and the Origins of the Wilderness Movement* (Sydney: Envirobook).

Mouffe, C. (2005a). For an Agonist Public Sphere. In Tønder, L. & Thomassen, L. (eds.), *Radical Democracy: Politics Between Abundance and Lack* (Manchester: Manchester University), pp. 123–132.

——. (2005b). *On the Political* (New York: Routledge).

Moule, J. (2009). Understanding Unconscious Bias and Unintentional Racism. *Phi Delta Kappan* 90(5): 320–326.

Moyer, J. (2015). The Murky Ethics of Making Monkeys Pick Our Coconuts. *The Washington Post*, October 20, https://www.washingtonpost.com/news/morning-mix/wp/2015/10/20/the-murky-ethics-of-making-monkeys-pick-our-coconuts.

Mummery, J. & Rodan, D. (2017). Mediation for Affect: Coming to Care About Factory-Farmed Animals. *Media International Australia* 165: 37–50.

Nagy, K. & Johnson II, P. (2013). *Trash Animals: How We Live with Nature's Filthy, Feral, Invasive, and Unwanted Species* (Minneapolis, MN: University of Minnesota).

Nakata, M. (2002). Indigenous Knowledge and the Cultural Interface: Underlying Issues at the Intersection of Knowledge and Information Systems. *IFLA* 28(5/6): 281–291.

——. (2007). Cultural Interface. *The Australian Journal of Indigenous Education* (36): 7–14.

Narayanan, Y. (2017). Street Dogs at the Intersection of Colonialism and Informality: "Subaltern Animism" as a Posthuman Critique of Indian Cities. *Environment and Planning* 35(3): 475–494.

Nazione, La (2014). Camilla, la Mucca in Fugatorna a Casa, August 20, https://www.lanazione.it/empoli/cronaca/camilla-la-mucca-in-fuga-torna-a-casa-1.136228.

Nelson, T. (2009). *Handbook of Prejudice, Stereotyping, and Discrimination* (Hove, East Sussex: Psychology).

Nepstad, D., McGrath, D., Stickler, C., et al. (2014). Slowing Amazon Deforestation Through Public Policy and Interventions in Beef and Soy Supply Chains. *Science* 344(6): 1118–1123, https://doi.org/10.1126/science.1248525.

Nestlé (2017). Nestlé USA Agrees to Acquire Sweet Earth, September 7, https://www.nestleusa.com/media/pressreleases/nestle-sweet-earth-foods.

Netz, R. (2004). *Barbed Wire: An Ecology of Modernity* (Middletown, CT: Wesleyan University).

Newman, A. (2017). Pet Pigs of New York: Illegal, Embattled, Beloved. *The New York Times*, January 19, https://www.nytimes.com/2017/01/19/nyregion/illegal-but-still-around-new-yorks-hidden-network-of-pet-pigs.html.

Nibert, D. (2013). *Animal Oppression and Human Violence: Domesecration, Capitalism, and Global Conflict* (New York: Columbia University).

——. (2017). *Animal Oppression and Capitalism: The Oppression of Nonhuman Animals as Sources of Food* (Santa Barbara, CA: Praeger), Vol. 1.

——. (2017). Introduction. In Nibert, D. (ed.), *Animal Oppression and Capitalism: The Oppression of Nonhuman Animals as Sources of Food* (Santa Barbara, CA: Praeger), Vol. 1, pp. xi–xxv.

NLWRA [National Land and Water Resources] Audit (2001). Rangelands: Tracking changes.

Nocella II, A., Sorenson, J., Socha, K., et al. (2014). The Emergence of Critical Animal Studies: The Rise of Intersectional Animal Liberation. In Nocella II, A., Sorenson, J., Socha, K., et al. (eds.), *Defining Critical Animal Studies: An Intersectional Social Justice Approach for Liberation* (New York: Peter Lang), pp. xix–xxxvi.

Nocella II, A., White, R., & Cudworth, E. (2015). *Anarchism and Animal Liberation: Essays on Complementary Elements of Total Liberation* (Jefferson, NC: McFarland).

——., ——., & ——. (2015). Introduction. In Nocella II, A., White, R., & Cudworth, E. (eds.), *Anarchism and Animal Liberation: Essays on Complementary Elements of Total Liberation* (Jefferson, NC: McFarland), pp. 7–19.

Nye, C. (2018). Farming Out the Field Work Won't Stop Migrant Worker Exploitation Post-Brexit. *Huffington Post*, January 21, https://www.huffingtonpost.co.uk/caroline-nye/farming-out-the-field-wor_b_14281946.html.

O'Brien, K. (1986). *Veganic Gardening: The Alternative System for Healthier Crops* (New York: HarperCollins).

O'Neil, L. (2017). Toronto Is Having Its Vegan Movement. *BlogTO*, September 19, https://www.blogto.com/eat_drink/2017/09/toronto-vegan-restaurants/.

Obidzinski, K., Andriani, R., Komarudin, H., et al. (2012). Environmental and Social Impacts of Oil Palm Plantations and Their Implications for Biofuel Production in Indonesia. *Ecology & Society* 17(1): 25.

Ocejo, R. (2014). Show the Animal: Constructing and Communicating New Elite Food Tastes at Upscale Butcher Shops. *Poetics* 47: 106–121.

Ogden, L. (2011). *Swamplife: People, Gators, and Mangroves Entangled in the Everglades* (Minneapolis, MN: University of Minnesota).

Okur-Berberoglu, E. (2014). Exploitation of Environmental Resources and Rural Communities by Global Food Companies. *Geography, Environment, Sustainability* 7(4): 54–67.

Oleksiak, T. (2018). Composing in a Sling: BDSM, Power, and Non-Identification. *Pre/Text* 24: 9–24.

Oliver, K. (2001). *Witnessing: Beyond Recognition* (Minneapolis, MN: University of Minnesota).

——. (2015). *Animal Lessons: How They Teach Us to Be Human* (New York: Columbia University).

Ornelas, l. (2014). A Hunger for Justice. In Tuttle, W. (ed.), *Circles of Compassion* (Danvers, MN: Vegan Publishers), pp. 182–197.

Pachirat, T. (2011). *Every Twelve Seconds: Industrialized Slaughter and the Politics of Sight* (New Haven, CT: Yale University).

Pai, H. (2019). "You're Lucky to Get Paid at All": How African Migrants Are Exploited in Italy. *The Guardian*, February 9, https://www.theguardian.com/commentisfree/2019/feb/09/african-migrants-italy-hard-right-authorities.

Pan, W., Lin, L., Luo, A., et al. (2009). Corridor Use by Asian Elephants. *Integrative Zoology* 4(2): 220–231.

Parmentier, B. (2014). *Faim Zéro en Finir avec la Faim dans le Monde* (Paris: La Découverte).

Pascoe, B. (2014). *Dark Emu: Aboriginal Australia and the Birth of Agriculture* (Broome, Western Australia: Magabala Books).

Patterson, C. (2002). *Eternal Treblinka: Our Treatment of Animals and the Holocaust* (Lantern: New York).

Pearson, M., Albon, S., & Hubball, H. (2015). Case Study Methodology: Flexibility, Rigour, and Ethical Considerations for the Scholarship of Teaching and Learning. *The Canadian Journal for the Scholarship of Teaching and Learning* 6(3): 1–8.

Pedersen, H. & Stănescu, V. (2014). Conclusion: Future Directions for Critical Animal Studies. In Taylor, N. & Twine, R. (eds). *The Rise of Critical Animal Studies: From the Margins to the Centre* (New York: Routledge), pp. 262–276.

Peggs, K. (2014). From Centre to Margin and Back Again: Critical Animal Studies and the Reflexive Human Self. In Taylor, N. & Twine, R. (eds.), *The Rise of Critical Animal Studies: From the Margins to the Centre* (New York: Routledge), pp. 36–51.

Pellow, D. (2014). *Total Liberation: The Power and Promise of Animal Rights and the Radical Earth Movement* (Minneapolis, MN: University of Minnesota).

——. (2015). Foreword. In Nocella II, A., White, R., & Cudworth, E. (eds.), *Anarchism and Animal Liberation: Essays on Complementary Elements of Total Liberation* (Jefferson, NC: McFarland), pp. 1–3.

Perlman, F. (2018). *The Machine and Its Discontents: A Fredy Perlman Anthology* (Bristol: Active Distribution).

Phillips, L. (2010). Veganism as Ecowomanism. In Harper, A. (ed.), *Sistah Vegan: Black Female Vegans Speak on Food, Identity, Health, and Society* (Brooklyn, NY: Lantern), pp. 8–19.

Philol, C. (1995). Animals, Geography and the City: Notes on Inclusions and Exclusions. *Environment and Planning D: Society and Space* 13: 655–681.

Philol, C. & Wilbert, C. (eds.) (2000). *Animal Spaces, Beastly Places: New Geographies of Human–Animal Relations* (New York: Routledge).

Philol, C. & Wolch, J. (1998). Through the Geographical Looking Glass: Space, Place, and Society–Animal Relations. *Society and Animals* 6(2): 103–118, https://doi.org/10.1163/156853098x00096.

Piazzesi, B. (2015). *Così Perfetti e Utili: Genealogia dello Sfruttamento Animale* (Milano: Mimesis).

Picard, B. (2013). Le Protocole du Jabiru: Agentivités Animales et Animalières au Zoo de Barcelone. *Carnets de Géographes* (5), http://dx.doi.org/10.4000/cdg.1072.

Pierce, J. (2016). *Run, Spot, Run: The Ethics of Keeping Pets* (Chicago: The University of Chicago).

Pimentel, D. & Burgess, M. (2005). Environmental and Economic Costs of the Application of Pesticides Primarily in the United States. *Environment, Development and Sustainability* 7(2): 229–252.

Pimm, S. & Aarde, R. (2001). African Elephants and Contraception. *Nature* 411(6839): 766–766.

Plumwood, V. (1992). Feminism and Ecofeminism: Beyond the Dualistic Assumptions of Women, Men and Nature. *The Ecologist* 22: 8–13.

——. (1993). *Feminism and the Mastery of Nature* (New York: Routledge).

——. (2000). Integrating Ethical Frameworks for Animals, Humans, and Nature: A Critical Femiist Eco-Socialist Analysis. *Ethics & the Environment* 5(2): 285–322.

——. (2004). Gender, Eco-Feminism and the Environment. In White, R. (ed.), *Controversies in Environmental Sociology* (New York: Cambridge University), pp. 43–60.

——. (2012). Animals and Ecology: Towards Better Integration. In Shannon, L. (ed.), *The Eye of the Crocodile* (Canberra: ANU), pp. 77–90.

Polish, J. (2016). Decolonizing Veganism: On Resisting Vegan Whiteness and Racism. In Castricano, J. & Simonsen, R. (eds.), *Critical Perspectives on Veganism* (New York: Palgrave), pp. 373–391.

Porcher, J. (2001). Le Travail dans l'Élevage Industriel des Porcs: Souffrance des Animaux, Souffrance des Hommes. In Burgat, F. (ed.), *Les Animaux d'Élevage Ont-Ils Droit au Bien-Être?* (Paris: INRA), pp. 23–64.

——. (2005). Élevage/Industriel: Penser l'Impensable? *Travailler* 14(2): 9–20.

——. (2010). The Relationship Between Workers and Animals in the Pork Industry: A Shared Suffering. *Journal of Agricultural and Environmental Ethics* 24: 3–17.

——. (2014). *Vivre avec les Animaux: Une Utopie pour le XXIe Siècle* (Paris: La Découverte).

Power, E. (2008). Furry Families: Making a Human–Dog Family Through Home. *Social & Cultural Geography* 9(5): 535–555.

Pratt, G. (2005). Abandoned Women and Spaces of the Exception. *Antipode* 37(5): 1052–1078.

Pretty, J. (2002). *Agri-Culture: Reconnecting People, Land, and Nature* (New York: Routledge).

Probyn-Rapsey, F. (2016). Fiona Probyn-Rapsey on Australia's War on Feral Cats. *Australian Animal Studies Association*, September 6, http://animalstudies.org.au/archives/5555.

Proudhon, P. (1876). *What Is Property?* (Princeton, MA: Benjamin R. Tucker).

Proulx, D. (2007). Un Portrait de la Situation Porcine au Québec. In Proulx, D. & Sauvé, L. (eds.), *Porcheries! La Porciculture Intempestive au Québec* (Montréal: Écosociété), pp. 23–163.

Proulx, D. & Sauvé, L. (eds.) (2007). *Porcheries! La Porciculture Intempestive au Québec* (Montréal: Écosociété).

Pui-Lan, K. (2009). Elisabeth Schüsslet Fiorenza and Postcolonial Studies. *Journal of Feminist* Studies 25(1): 191–197.

Puig de la Bellacasa, M. (2011). Matters of Care in Technoscience: Assembling Neglected Things. *Social Studies of Science* 41: 85–106.

——. (2017). *Matters of Care: Speculative Ethics in More Than Human Worlds* (Minneapolis, MN: University of Minnesota).

Pulido, L. (2000). Rethinking Environmental Racism: White Privilege and Urban Development in Southern California. *Annals of the Association of American Geographers* 90(1): 12–40.

——. (2015). Geographies of Race and Ethnicity 1: White Supremacy vs. White Privilege in Environmental Racism Research. *Progress in Human Geography* 39(6): 809–817.

Putfarken, D., Dengler, J., Lehmann, S., et al. (2008). Site Use of Grazing Cattle and Sheep in a Large-Scale Pasture Landscape: A GPS/GIS Assessment. *Applied Animal Behaviour Science* 111(1–2): 54–67, https://doi.org/10.1016/j.applanim.2007.05.012.

Puwar, N. (2004). *Space Invaders: Race, Gender and Bodies Out of Place* (New York: Berg).

Quinn, D. (1992). *Ishmael* (New York: Penguin Random House).

Rancière, J. (1999). *Disagreement: Politics and Philosophy* (Minneapolis, MN: University of Minnesota).

Rawlinson, M. & Ward, C. (eds.). (2015). *Global Food, Global Justice: Essays on Eating under Globalization* (Newcastle-upon-Tyne: Cambridge Scholars).

Reclus, E. (1901). On Vegetarianism. *The Anarchist Library*, https://theanarchistlibrary.org/library/elisee-reclus-on-vegetarianism.

Regan, T. (1983). *The Case for Animal Rights* (Berkeley, CA: University of California).

——. (1986). The Case for Animal Rights. In Fox, M. & Mickley, L. (eds.), *Advances in Animal Welfare Science 1986/87* (Washington, DC: The Humane Society of the United States), pp. 179–189.

Reggio, M. (2017). Per un Antispecismo Decoloniale. In Colling, S., *Animali in Rivolta: Confini, Resistenza e Solidarietà Umana* (Milano: Mimesis), pp. 9–36.

——. (2018). Performare la Specie. *Whatever: A Transdisciplinary Journal of Queer Theories and Studies* 1(1): 233–263.

Regulations Amending the Health of Animals Regulations (2016). *Canada Gazette* 150(49), December 3, http://gazette.gc.ca/rp-pr/p1/2016/2016-12-03/html/reg2-eng.html.

Reindal, S. (1999). Independence, Dependence, Interdependence: Some Reflections on the Subject and Personal Autonomy. *Disability & Society* 14(3): 353–367.

Resistenza Animale (2014). Camilla, Dove Ti Portano? December 15, https://resistenzanimale.noblogs.org/post/2014/12/15/camilla-dove-ti-portano/.

——. (2016). Non Lasciamo Solo Scilla, Il Vitello Fuggito a Messina. April 13, https://resistenzanimale.noblogs.org/post/2016/04/13/non-lasciamo-solo-scilla-il-vitello-fuggito-a-messina-scriviamo-alle-autorita-aggiornamento-importante/.

——. (2019). Corpi Fuori Luogo: Gli Animali Ribelli. In Bertuzzi, N. & Reggio, M. (eds.), *Smontare la Gabbia: Anticapitalismo e Movimento di Liberazione Animale* (Milano: Mimesis), pp. 83–94.

Reus, E. (2018a). Les Cahiers Antispécistes N°40—Réduire la Souffrance des Animaux Sauvages (Online Publication). *Plouarzel*, https://www.cahiers-antispecistes.org/numero/40/.

——. (2018b). Les Cahiers Antispécistes N°41—Éliminer les Animaux pour Leur Bien: Promenade chez les Réducteurs de la Souffrance dans la Nature (Online Publication). *Plouarzel*, https://www.cahiers-antispecistes.org/numero/41/.

Rich, A. (1984). Notes Toward a Politics of Location. In Rich, A. (ed.), *Blood, Bread and Poetry: Selected Prose 1979–1985* (Boston, MA: Little, Brown), pp. 210–231.

——. (1986). Notes Toward a Politics of Location. In Rich, A. (ed.), *Blood, Bread, and Poetry: Selected Prose, 1979–1985* (New York: Norton), pp. 210–231.

Richards, E., Signal, T., & Taylor, N. (2013). A Different Cut? Comparing Attitudes Toward Animals and Propensity for Aggression Within Two Primary Industry Cohorts—Farmers and Meatworkers. *Society & Animals* 21: 395–413.

Ridler, J. (2020). Coronavirus Sparks Plant-Based Sales Explosion. *Food Manufacture*, April 17, https://www.foodmanufacture.co.uk/Article/2020/04/16/Coronavirus-sparks-plant-based-sales-explosion.

Rigney, L-I. (1999). Internationalization of an Indigenous Anticolonial Cultural Critique of Research Methodologies. *Wicazo Sa Review* 14(2): 109–121.

Riley, S., Sauvajot, R., Fuller, T., et al. (2003). Effects of Urbanization and Habitat Fragmentation on Bobcats and Coyotes in Southern California. *Conservation Biology* 17(2): 566–576.

Rivera L. (2016). Veganism Grows by 360 Per Cent in Britain, *Independent*, May 18, https://www.independent.co.uk/life-style/veganism-grows-360-cent-britain-david-haye-novak-djokovic-and-venus-williams-among-athletes-choosing-go-meat-free-a7034031.html.

Robbins, P. (2005). The Last Enclosure: Resisting Privatization of Wildlife in the Western United States. *Capitalism, Nature, Socialism* 16(1): 45–61, https://doi.org/10.1080/10455750520003353 66.

Robertson, C. (2013). A Tiger, a Truck Stop and a Pitched Legal Battle. *The New York Times*, March 27, https://www.nytimes.com/2013/03/28/us/truck-stop-tiger-in-louisiana-stirs-legal-battle.html.

Robinson, T., Wint, G., Conchedda, G., et al. (2014) Mapping the Global Distribution of Livestock. *PLoS ONE* 9(5): e96084, https://doi.org/10.1371/journal.pone.0096084.

Rollo, T. (2017). Everyday Deeds: Enactive Protest, Exit, and Silence in Deliberative Systems. *Political Theory* 45(5): 587–609.

Rose, D. (1996). *Nourishing Terrains: Australian Aboriginal Views of Landscape and Wilderness* (Canberra: Australian Heritage Commission).

——. (2011). *Wild Dog Dreaming* (Charlottesville, VA: University of Virginia).

——. (2012). Ruined Faces. In Edelglass, W., Hatley, J., & Diehm, C. (eds.), *Facing Nature: Levinas and Environmental Thought* (Pittsburgh, PA: Duquesne University), pp. 95–108.

Rossellini, G. (2016). Messina, Mucca in Mare: Salvata. *Corriere del Mezzogiorno*, April 8, https://corrieredelmezzogiorno.corriere.it/catania/cronaca/16_aprile_08/messina-mucca-mare-salvata-50617580-fda5-11e5-a92e-29a59aeea3d1.shtml.

Rothgerber, H. & Mican, F. (2014). Childhood Pet Ownership, Attachment to Pets, and Subsequent Meat Avoidance: The Mediating Role of Empathy Toward Animals. *Appetite* 79: 11–17.

Rothenberg, D. (2000). *With These Hands: The Hidden World of Migrant Farmworkers Today* (Berkeley, CA: University of California).

Rousset, D. (Host) (2019). L'Animal est l'Avenir de l'Homme: Aimer la Biodiversité ou Partir avec Elle (3/5) (Radio). In *Matières à Penser. France Culture*, June 2, https://www.franceculture.fr/emissions/matieres-a-penser/lanimal-est-lavenir-de-lhomme-35-aimer-la-biodiversite-ou-partir-avec-elle.

Roux, P., Gianettoni, L., & Perrin, C. (2006). Féminisme et Racisme: Une Recherche Exploratoire sur les Fondements des Divergences Relatives au Port du Foulard. *Nouvelles Questions Féministes* 25(1): 84–106, https://doi.org/10.3917/nqf.251.0084.

Royle, N. (2003). *Jacques Derrida* (New York: Routledge).

RSPCA (2017). Stop Live Exports International Awareness Day. *RSPCA Insights: The Official Blog of the RSPCA*, https://www.rspca.org.uk/-/stop-live-exports-international-awareness-day.

Ryder Archive, The (Uncatalogued). Department for Politics and Public Life. The British Library, London.

Ryder, R. (1989). *Animal Revolution: Changing Attitudes Towards Speciesism* (Cambridge, MA: Basil Blackwell Ltd).

——. (1998). Interview Recorded by Melanie Oxley at Interviewee's Home. *Animal Welfare Activists Collection* (Tape 1, Shelfmark C894/02), September 16, The British Library, London.

——. (2000). *Animal Revolution: Changing Attitudes Towards Speciesism* (Revised Edition) (Providence, RI: Berg).

——. (2002 [1983]). *Painism: A Modern Morality* (London: Open Gate).

——. (2010). Speciesism Again: The Original Leaflet. *Critical Society* (2).

——. (2011). *Speciesism, Painism and Happiness: A Morality for the 21st Century* (Exeter, U.K.: Imprint Academic).

Said, E. (1978). *Orientalism* (New York: Penguin).

Salih, S. (2018). Remnants: The Witness and the Animal. In Quinn, E. & Westwood, B. (eds.), *Thinking Veganism in Literature and Culture: Towards a Vegan Theory* (New York: Palgrave), pp. 57–77.

Sanbonmatsu, J. (2017). Capitalism and Speciesism. In Nibert, D. (ed.), *Animal Oppression and Capitalism: The Oppressive and Destructive Role of Capitalism* (Santa Barbara, CA: Praeger), Vol. 2, pp. 1–30.

Sanders, B. (2018). Global Animal Slaughter Statistics and Charts. *Faunalytics*, October 10, https://faunalytics.org/global-animal-slaughter-statistics-and-charts/.

Sanders, C. (1990). Excusing Tactics: Social Responses to the Public Misbehavior of Companion Animals. *Anthrozoös* 4(2): 82–90.

——. (1990). The Animal "Other": Self Definition, Social Identity and Companion Animals. In M. Goldberg, G. Gorn, & R. Pollay (eds.), *NA – Advances in Consumer Research* 17: 662–668.

Sanders, C. & Arluke, A. (1993). If Lions Could Speak: Investigating the Animal–Human Relationship and the Perspectives of Nonhuman Others. *Sociological Quarterly* 34(3): 377–390.

Saunders, A. (2013). Recovering the Street: Relocalising Urban Geography. *Journal of Geography in Higher Education* 37(4): 536–546.

Saunders, T. (2002). *Baiting the Trap: One Man's Secret Battle to Save Our Wildlife* (New York: Pocket).

Scarry, E. (1985). *The Body in Pain: The Making and Unmaking of the World* (New York: Oxford University).

Schmutz, U. & Foresi, L. (2017). Vegan Organic Horticulture – Standards, Challenges, Socio-Economics and Impact on Global Food Security. *Acta Horticulturae* (1164): 475–484.

Schouten, G. & Glasbergen, P. (2011). Creating Legitimacy in Global Private Governance: The Case of the Roundtable on Sustainable Palm Oil. *Ecological Economics* 70(11): 1891–1899.

Scotsman Food and Drink, The (2015). Why Edinburgh Has the Best Restaurant Scene in Scotland, December 11, https://foodanddrink.scotsman.com/food/why-edinburgh-has-the-best-restaurant-scene-in-scotland/.

Scott, J. (2010). *The Art of Not Being Governed: An Anarchist History of Upland Southeast Asia* (New Haven, CT: Yale University).

Searchinger, T., Wirsenius, S., Beringer, T., et al. (2018). Assessing the Efficiency of Changes in Land Use for Mitigating Climate Change. *Nature* 564: 249–253, https://www.nature.com/articles/s41586-018-0757-z.

Sébastia, B. (2017). *Eating Traditional Food: Politics, Identity, and Practices* (New York: Routledge).

Sebastian, M. (2017). Deadly Efficiency: The Impact of Capitalist Production in the "Meat" Industry, Slaughterhouse Workers, and Nonhuman Animals. In Nibert, D. (ed.), *Animal Oppression and Capitalism: The Oppression of Nonhuman Animals as Sources of Food* (Santa Barbara, CA: Praeger), Vol. 1, pp. 167–183.

Seed the Commons (2016). Lazy Millennial Farms. August 25, https://seedthecommons.org/lazy-millennial-farms/.

Sen, C. (2007). Jainism: The World's Most Ethical Religion. In Friedland, S. (ed.), *Food and Morality: Proceedings of the Oxford Symposium on Food and Cookery 2007* (London: Prospect Books), pp. 230–240.

Severson, K. (2017). Black Vegans Step Out, for Their Health and Other Causes. *The New York Times*, November 28, https://www.nytimes.com/2017/11/28/dining/black-vegan-cooking.html.

Seymour, M. (2019). *Map of North American Veganic Farms. ArcGIS*, https://arcg.is/1uOyPD.

Seymour, M. & Utter, A. (n.d.). Growing Veganic: Exploring Plant-Based Agriculture in the United States (Unpublished Data).

Shapiro, K. (2017). Human–Animal Studies: Fertile Ground for Qualitative Analysis (Symposium Presentation). *Society of Qualitative Investigations in Psychology Symposium* (Fordham University, New York).

Sharp, G. (1973). *The Politics of Non-Violent Action* (New York: Porter Sargent).

Sharp, J. (2008). *Geographies of Postcolonialism* (Thousand Oaks, CA: SAGE).

Shaw, V. (2020). Appetite for Vegan Diets Is Growing. *The Ecologist*, June 9, https://theecologist.org/2020/jun/09/appetite-vegan-diets-growing.

Shell, J. (2015). When Roads Cannot Be Used: The Use of Asian Elephants for Emergency Logistics, Off-Road Conveyance and Political Revolt in South and Southeast Asia. *Transfers: Interdisciplinary Journal Of Mobility Studies* 5(2): 62–80.

Shulman, M. (2016). Canada's Livestock Transportation Rules "Worst in the Western World": Advocate. *CTV News*, March 17, https://www.ctvnews.ca/canada/canada-s-livestock-transportation-rules-worst-in-the-western-world-advocate-1.2820563.

Simonsen, R. (2012). A Queer Vegan Manifesto. *Journal for Critical Animal Studies* 10(3): 51–81.

Simpson, M. & Bagelman, J. (2018). Decolonizing Urban Political Ecologies: The Production of Nature in Settler Colonial Cities. *Annals of the American Association of Geographers* 108(2): 558–568.

Singer, I. (1968). The Letter Writer. *The New Yorker*, January 13, https://www.newyorker.com/magazine/1968/01/13/the-letter-writer.

Singer, J. (2016). *Always Too Much and Never Enough: A Memoir* (New York: Berkley Books).

Singer, P. (1975). *Animal Liberation: A New Ethics for Our Treatment of Animals* (New York: HarperCollins).

——. (1975). *Animal Liberation: A New Ethics for Our Treatment of Animals* (London: Jonathon Cape).

——. (1995 [1975]). *Animal Liberation: A New Ethics for Our Treatment of Animals* (New York: Random House).

——. (2009). *The Life You Can Save* (New York: Random House).

——. (2012). *La Libération Animale* (Paris: Éditions Payot & Rivages).

Slicer, J. (2014). Joy. In Adams, C. & Gruen, L. (eds.), *Ecofeminism: Feminist Intersections with Other Animals and the Earth* (New York: Bloomsbury), pp. 59–74.

Smith, J. (2003). Beyond Dominance and Affection: Living with Rabbits in Post-Humanist Households. *Society & Animals* 11(2): 181–197.

Smith, L. (1999). *Decolonizing Methodologies: Research and Indigenous Peoples* (London: Zed).

Smith, N. (2017). *Invitation: Clan Gathering Gaarrawaygam, The Returning, at the Golden Hole, Gumabynggirr Country* (Unpublished Document).

Smith, P., Haberl, H., Popp, A., et al. (2013). How Much Land-Based Greenhouse Gas Mitigation Can Be Achieved Without Compromising Food Security and Environmental Goals? *Global Change Biology* 19(8): 2285–2303, https://doi.org/10.1111/gcb.12160.

Smith, S., Smith, N., Wright, S., et al. (2020). Yandaarra is Protocol. *Social and Cultural Geography* 21(7): 940–961.

Snelgrove, C., Dhamoon, R., & Corntassel, J. (2014). Unsettling Settler Colonialism: The Discourse and Politics of Settlers, and Solidarity with Indigenous Nations. *Decolonization: Indigeneity, Education and Society* 3(2): 1–32.

Sobal, J. (2005). Men, Meat and Marriage: Models of Masculinity. *Food and Foodways* 13(1–2): 135–158.

Socha, K. (2012). *Women, Destruction, and the Avant-Garde: A Paradigm for Animal Liberation* (New York: Rodopi).

Solidarity Across Borders (2013). What Is a Solidarity City? May 11, http://www.solidarityacrossborders.org/en/solidarity-city/solidarity-city-journal/what-is-a-solidarity-city.

Spencer, T. & Whatmore, S. (2001). Bio-Geographies: Putting Life Back into the Discipline. *Transactions of the Institute of British Geographers* 26(2): 139–141.

Spiegel Online (2011a). Yvonne Ist Zurück auf der Weide. September 1, https://www.spiegel.de/panorama/entlaufene-kuh-yvonne-ist-zurueck-auf-der-weide-a-783894.html.

——. (2011b). Yvonne Wankt, Schwankt und Fällt. September 2, https://www.spiegel.de/panorama/eingefangene-kultkuh-yvonne-wankt-schwankt-und-faellt-a-784030.html.

Spiegel, M. (1988). *The Dreaded Comparison: Human and Animal Slavery* (Philadelphia, PA: New Society).

——. (1996). *The Dreaded Comparison: Human and Animal Slavery* (New York: Mirror).

——. (1997). *The Dreaded Comparison: Human and Animal Slavery* (Revised and Expanded Edition) (New York: Mirror).

Spivak, G. (1988). Can the Subaltern Speak? In Morris, R. (ed.), *Can the Subaltern Speak?: Reflections on the History of an Idea* (New York: Columbia University), pp. 21–78.

——. (1999). *A Critique of Postcolonial Reason: Toward a History of the Vanishing Present* (Cambridge, MA: Oxford University).

Springer, S. (2011). Violence Sits in Places? Cultural Practice, Neoliberal Rationalism, and Virulent Imaginative Geographies. *Political Geography* 30(2): 90–98.

——. (2013). Anarchism and Geography: A Brief Genealogy of Anarchist Geographies. *Geography Compass* 7(1): 46–60.

——. (2016). *The Anarchist Roots of Geography: Toward Spatial Emancipation* (Minneapolis, MN: University of Minnesota).

——. (2018). *Pour une Géographie Anarchiste* (Montréal: Lux).

——. (2021). Total Liberation Ecology: Integral Anarchism, Anthroparchy, and the Violence of Indifference. In Springer, S., Mateer, J., Locret-Collet, M., et al. (eds.), *Undoing Human Supremacy: Anarchist Political Ecology and the End of Anthroparchy* (Advance Online Publication).

Springer, S. & Le Billon, P. (2016). Violence and Space: An Introduction to the Geographies of Violence. *Political Geography* 52: 1–3.

Springer, S., White, R., & De Souza, M. (eds.) (2016). *The Radicalization of Pedagogy: Anarchism, Geography and the Spirit of Revolt* (Lanham, MD: Rowman & Littlefield).

Springmann, M., Clark, M., Mason-D'Croz, D., et al. (2018). Options for Keeping the Food System within Environmental Limits. *Nature* 562(7728): 519, https://doi.org/10.1038/s41586-018-0594-0.

Springmann, M., Godfray, H., Raynar, M., et al. (2016). Analysis and Valuation of the Health and Climate Change Cobenefits of Dietary Change. *Proceedings of the National Academy of Sciences* 113(15): 4146–4151.

Stallwood, K. (2014). *Growl: Life Lessons, Hard Truths, and Bold Strategies from an Animal Advocate* (Brooklyn, NY: Lantern).

Starmer, E., Witteman, A., & Wise, T. (2006). Feeding the Factory Farm: Implicit Subsidies to the Broiler Chicken Industry. *Global Development and Environment Institute*, Working Paper 6(3), https://www.researchgate.net/publication/23516226_Feeding_the_Factory_Farm_Implicit_Subsidies_to_the_Broiler_Chicken_Industry.

Steffen, W., Crutzen, P., & McNeill, J. (2007). The Anthropocene: Are Humans Now Overwhelimng the Great Forces of Nature? *Ambio* 36: 614–621.

Steinfeld, H., Gerber, P., Wassenaar, T., et al. (2006). *Livestock's Long Shadow: Environmental Issues and Options*. Food and Agriculture Organization of the United Nations, http://www.fao.org/3/a0701e/a0701e.pdf.

Stewart, K. & Cole, M. (2020). Veganism Has Always Been More about Living an Ethical Life than Just Avoiding Meat and Dairy. *The Open University*, January 7, https://ounews.co/arts-social-sciences/society-politics/veganism-has-always-been-more-about-living-an-ethical-life-than-just-avoiding-meat-and-dairy/.

Stockfree Organic Services (n.d.). Grower-to-Grower Certification, http://stockfreeorganic.net/stockfree-grower-to-grower-certification-facebook-scheme/.

Stoler, A. (2009). *Along the Archival Grain: Epistemic Anxieties and Colonial Common Sense* (Princeton, NJ: Princeton University).

Striffler, S. (2002). Inside a Poultry Processing Plant: An Ethnographic Portrait. *Labor History* 43(3): 305–313.

——. (2007). Neither Here Nor There: Mexican Immigrant Workers and the Search for Home. *American Ethnologist* 34(4): 674–688.

Subramaniam, B. (2001). The Aliens Have Landed! Reflections on the Rhetoric of Biological Invasions. *Medridians* 2(1): 26–40.

Suissa, J. (2019). Education and NonDomination: Reflections from the Radical Tradition. *Studies in Philosophy and Education* 34(4): 359–375.

Sukumar, R. (1993). *The Asian Elephant: Ecology and Management* (New York: Cambridge University).

Sukumar, R. & Gadgil, M. (1988). Male–Female Differences in Foraging on Crops by Asian Elephants. *Animal Behaviour* 36(4): 1233–1235.

Sullivan, S. (2006). *Revealing Whiteness: The Unconscious Habits of Racial Privilege* (Bloomington, IN: Indiana University).

Sundberg, J. (2011). Diabolic Caminos in the Desert and Cat Fights on the Río: A Posthumanist Political Ecology of Boundary Enforcement in the United States–Mexico Borderlands. *Annals of the American Association of Geographers* 101(2): 318–336, https://doi.org/10.1080/00045608.2010.538323.

Sverdrup-Thygeson, A. (2019). *Extraordinary Insects: Weird. Wonderful. Indispensable—The Ones Who Run Our World* (London: Mudlark).

Swain, H., Boughton, E., Bohlen, P. et al. (2013). Trade-offs Among Ecosystem Services and Disservices on a Florida Ranch. *Rangelands* 35(5): 77–87.

Symons, J. (2019). *Ecomodernism: Technology, Politics and the Climate Crisis* (London: Polity).

Tai Le, L. & Sabaté, J. (2014). Beyond Meatless, the Health Effects of Vegan Diets: Findings from the Adventist Cohorts. *Nutrients* 6(6): 2131–2147.

Taylor, N. (2007). "Never an It": Intersubjectivity and the Creation of Animal Personhood in Animal Shelters. *Qualitative Sociological Review* 3(1): 59–73.

Taylor, N. & Twine, R. (2014). Introduction: Locating the "Critical" in Critical Animal Studies. In Taylor, N. & Twine, R. (eds.), *The Rise of Critical Animal Studies: From the Margins to the Centre* (New York: Routledge), pp. 1–15.

Taylor, S. (2011). Beasts of Burden: Disability Studies and Animal Rights. *Qui Parle* 19(2): 191–222.

——. (2017). *Beasts of Burden: Animal and Disability Liberation* (New York: The New Press).

Tekanji/Andrea Rubenstein (2008). "Check My What?" On Privilege and What We Can Do About It. *Official Shrub.com Blog*, June 30, http://blog.shrub.com/check-my-what/.

The Local (2019). Immigrant Children on Hijacked School Bus to Get Italian Citizenship, March 27, https://www.thelocal.it/20190327/immigrant-children-on-hijacked-school-bus-to-get-italian-citizenship.

The London Greenpeace Group (1986). What's Wrong with McDonald's?, http://www.mcspotlight.org/case/pretrial/factsheet.html.

The Vegan Society (1949). *The Vegan: Advocating Living without Exploitation* 5(2), https://issuu.com/vegan_society/docs/the-vegan-summer-1949.

——. (2014). Ripened by Human Determination: 70 Years of the Vegan Society, https://www.vegansociety.com/sites/default/files/uploads/Ripened%20by%20human%20determination.pdf.

——. (n.d.-a). Definition of Veganism, https://www.vegansociety.com/go-vegan/definition-veganism.

——. (n.d.-b). Stock-Free Crop Farming, https://www.vegansociety.com/society/whos-involved/partners/vegan-organic-network.

——. (n.d.). Statistics, https://www.vegansociety.com/news/media/statistics.

Thibodeau, L. (2019). "All Creation Groans": The Lives of Factory Farmed Animals in the United States. In Linzey, A. & Linzey, C. (eds.), *Ethical Vegetarianism and Veganism* (New York: Routledge).

Thien, D. (2005). Affect or Beyond Feeling? A Consideration of Affect and Emotion in Geography. *Area* 37(4): 450–454.

Thierman, S. (2010). Apparatuses of Animality: Foucault Goes to a Slaughterhouse. *Foucault Studies* 9: 89–110.

Thomson, A. (2018). "Mind-Blowing": Survey Finds Most Vegans, Vegetarians in Canada Are Under 35. *The Canadian Press*, March 13, https://www.ctvnews.ca/health/mind-blowing-survey-finds-most-vegans-vegetarians-in-canada-are-under-35-1.3841041.

Thoreau, H. (1854). *Walden; or, Life in the Woods* (Boston, MA: Ticknor & Fields).

Tipper, B. (2011). "A Dog Who I Know Quite Well": Everyday Relationships Between Children and Animals. *Children's Geographies* 9(2): 145–165.

TMR Research. (2020). Plant-Based Snacks Market Poised to Garner Maximum Revenues during COVID-19 Crisis 2018–2028. *Kentucky Journal 24*, July 7, https://www.transparencymarketresearch.com/plantbased-snacks-market.html.

Tolhurst Organic (n.d.). What Is Stockfree Organic?, https://www.tolhurstorganic.co.uk/about-us/what-is-stockfree-organic/.

Torres, B. (2007). *Making a Killing: The Political Economy of Animal Rights* (Oakland, CA: AK Press).

Tovey, H. (2003). Theorising Nature and Society in Sociology: The Invisibility of Animals. *Sociologia Ruralis* 43(3): 196–215, https://doi.org/10.1111/1467-9523.00241.

Trautmann, T. (2015). *Elephants and Kings: An Environmental History* (Chicago: University of Chicago).

Tuan, Y. (1977). *Space and Place: The Perspective of Experience* (Minneapolis, MN: University of Minnesota).

——. (1984). *Dominance and Affection* (Binghamton, NY: Vail-Ballou).

Turner, C. (2020). Shock as Devon Loses Swathe of Vegan Businesses in One Week. *Devon Live*, February 8, https://www.devonlive.com/news/devon-news/shock-devon-loses-swathe-vegan-3818390.

Turrini, D. (2012). Imola, Morta la Giraffafuggita per la Città. Il Sindaco: "Il Circo se ne Vada". *Il Fatto Quotidiano*, September 21, https://www.ilfattoquotidiano.it/2012/09/21/imola-morta-la-giraffa-fuggita-dal-circo/359357/.

Tuttle, W. (2014). Unrecognized Roots of Injustice and the Vegan Transformation. In Tuttle, W. (ed.), *Circles of Compassion* (Danvers, MN: Vegan Publishers), pp. 280–290.

Twine, R. (2013). Addressing the Animal–Industrial Complex. In Lanjouw, A. & Corbey, R. (eds.), *The Politics of Species: Reshaping Our Relationships with Other Animals* (New York: Cambridge University), pp. 77–91.

——. (2014). Ecofeminism and Veganism: Revisiting the Question of Universalism. In Adams, C. & Gruen, L. (eds.), *Ecofeminism: Feminist Intersections with Other Animals and the Earth* (New York: Bloomsbury), pp. 191–208.

——. (2014). Intersectional Disgust? Animals and (Eco)Feminism. *Feminism & Psychology* 20(3): 397–406.

TWS [The Wilderness Society] (2017). The Wilderness Society: Our Purpose.

Tyler, R. (2019). Global Brands Are Riding the Vegan Wave. *Supply Management*, May 10, https://www.cips.org/supply-management/analysis/2019/may/is-meat-the-new-fur/.

Unilever (2018). Unilever Acquires The Vegetarian Butcher. December 12, https://www.unilever.com/news/press-releases/2018/unilever-acquires-the-vegetarian-butcher.html.

UPI (2006). "Humanely Raised" Meat Served for Dinner. *Odd News*, October 24, https://www.upi.com/Odd_News/2006/10/24/Humanely-raised-meat-served-for-dinner/25921161714676/.

United States Department of Agriculture (USDA) Animal and Plant Health Inspection Service (2017). Program Data Report G, https://www.aphis.usda.gov/aphis/ourfocus/wildlifedamage/pdr/?file=PDR-G_Report?p=2017:INDEX.

Urbanik, J. (2012). *Placing Animals: An Introduction to the Geography of Human–Animal Relations* (Lanham, MD: Rowman & Littlefield).

Van Waas, L. & Jaghai, S. (2018). All Citizens Are Created Equal, but Some Are More Equal than Others. *Netherlands International Law Review* 65(3): 413–430.

Vegan Organic Network (n.d.). http://veganorganic.net.

Veganic Agriculture Network (2014). Introduction to Veganics. September 20, https://www.goveganic.net/article19.html.

Vegans of Color (2010). Veganism and the Class War. August 18, https://vegansofcolor.wordpress.com/2010/08/18/veganism-and-the-class-war/.

Velasco, M. (2017). Does Foodie Culture Exclude the Working Class? *Foodable Network*, May 1, https://www.foodabletv.com/blog/2017/5/1/does-foodie-culture-leave-out-the-working-class.

Véron, O. (2016). (Extra)Ordinary Activism: Veganism and the Shaping of Hemeratopias. *International Journal of Sociology and Social Policy* 36(11/12): 756–773.

Véron, O. & White, R. (2021). Anarchism, Feminism and Veganism: A Convergence of Struggles. In Springer, S., Mateer, J., Locret-Collet, M., et al. (eds.), *Undoing Human Supremacy: Anarchist Political Ecology and the End of Anthroparchy* (Oakland, CA: PM Press).

Vilda Magazine (2019). A Conversation on Diversity in Veganism with Writer Aph Ko. January 18, http://www.vildamagazine.com/2019/01/diversity-in-veganism/.

Vincent, E. & Neale, T. (2017). Unstable Relations: A Critical Appraisal of Indigeneity and Environmentalism in Contemporary Australia. *The Australian Journal of Anthropology* 28: 301–323.

Visak, T. (2007). Vegan Agriculture: Animal-Friendly and Sustainable. In Zollitsch, W., Winckler, C., Waiblinger, S., et al. (eds.), *Sustainable Food Production and Ethics* (Wageningen, Netherlands: Wageningen Academic), pp. 193–197.

Vizenor, G. (ed.) (2008). *Survivance: Narratives of Native Presence* (Lincoln, NE: Nebraska University).

Von Uexküll, J. (1992 [1934]). A Stroll Through the Worlds of Animals and Men: A Picture Book of Invisible Worlds. *Semiotica* 89(4): 319–391.

Wadiwel, D. (2015). *The War Against Animals* (Boston, MA: Brill/Rodopi).

——. (2016). Do Fish Resist? *Cultural Studies Review* 22(1): 196–242.

Walia, H. (2013). *Undoing Border Imperialism* (eBook Edition) (Oakland, CA: AK Press).

Walker, A. (1988). Preface. In Spiegel, M., *The Dreaded Comparison: Human and Animal Slavery* (London: Heretic).

Walker, D. (2002). (Interview recorded by Alex White in Oxfordshire). Food: From Source to Salespoint (C821/89/01-10, Tape 6, F12018). The British Library, July 25, http://sounds.bl.uk/Oral-history/Food/021M-C0821X0089XX-0008V0.

Walker, R., Moran, E., & Anselin, L. (2000). Deforestation and Cattle Ranching in the Brazilian Amazon: External Capital and Household Processes. *World Development* 28(4): 683–699, https://doi.org/10.1016/S0305-750X(99)00149-7.

Warren, C. (1990). The Power and Promise of Ecological Feminism. *Environmental Ethics* 12: 125–146.

Wasley, A. & Heal, A. (2018). Revealed: US-Style Industrial Farms Receive Millions in Subsidies. *The Guardian*, December 28, https://www.theguardian.com/environment/2018/dec/28/revealed-industrial-scale-farms-receive-millions-in-subsidies.

Watkinson, K. & O'Driscoll, D. (2014). From Animals to Anarchism: Open Letter #3. *Dysophia*, http://dysophia.org.uk/wp-content/uploads/2015/09/ARzineweb2.pdf.

Watson, A. & Huntington, O. (2008). They're *Here*—I Can *Feel* Them: The Epistemic Spaces of Indigenous and Western Knowledges. *Social and Cultural Geography* (9): 257–281.

Watson, D. (1944). *The Vegan News* (1), https://issuu.com/vegan_society/docs/the_vegan_news_1944.

Watts, V. (2013). Indigenous Place-Thought and Agency Amongst Humans and Non-Humans (First Woman and Sky Woman Go on a European World Tour!). *Decolonization: Indigeneity, Education and Society* 2(1): 20–34.

Wedderburn-Bisshop, G., Longmire, A., & Rickards, L. (2015). Neglected Transformational Responses: Implications of Excluding Short Lived Emissions and Near Term Projections in Greenhouse Gas Accounting. *International Journal of Climate Change: Impacts & Responses* 7: 11–27.

Weis, T. (2013). *The Ecological Hoofprint: The Global Burden of Industrial Livestock* (London: Zed).

Weiss, G. (1999). *Body Images: Embodiment as Intercorporeality* (New York: Routledge).

Weisser, W. & Siemann, E. (eds.) (2008). *Insects and Ecosystem Function* (New York: Springer).

Weitzenfeld, A. & Joy, M. (2014). An Overview of Anthropocentrism, Humanism, and Speciesism in Critical Animal Theory. In Nocella II, A., Sorenson, J., Socha, K., et al. (eds.), *Defining Critical Animal Studies: An Intersectional Social Justice Approach for Liberation* (New York: Peter Lang), pp. 3–27.

Werkheiser, I. (2013). Domination and Consumption: An Examination of Veganism, Anarchism, and Ecofeminism. *PhaenEx* 8(2): 161–184.

Werner, M. & Zimmerman, B. (2006). Beyond Comparison: Histoire Croisée and the Challenge of Reflexivity. *History & Theory* 15(1): 30–50.

Whatmore, S. (1997). Dissecting the Autonomous Self: Hybrid Cartographies for a Relational Ethics. *Environment and Planning D* 15(1): 37–53.

——. (2002). *Hybrid Geographies: Natures, Cultures, Spaces* (Thousand Oaks, CA: SAGE).

——. (2006). Materialist Returns: Practising Cultural Geography in and for a More-than-Human World. *Cultural Geographies* 13(4): 600–609.

Whatmore, S. & Thorne, L. (1998). Wild(er)ness: Reconfiguring the Geographies of Wildlife. *Transactions of the Institute of British Geographers* 23(4): 435–454.

White, R. (2015). Animal Geographies, Anarchist Praxis, and Critical Animal Studies. In Gillespie, K. & Collard, R. (eds.), *Critical Animal Geographies: Politics, Intersections and Hierarchies in a Multispecies World* (New York: Routledge), pp. 19–35.

——. (2015). Following in the Footsteps of Élisée Reclus: Disturbing Places of Inter-Species Violence that Are Hidden in Plain Sight. In Nocella II, A., White, R., & Cudworth, E. (eds.), *Anarchism and Animal Liberation: Essays on Complementary Elements of Total Liberation* (Jefferson, NC: McFarland), pp. 212–231.

——. (2017). Capitalism and the Commodification of Animals: The Need for Critical Vegan Praxis, Animated by Anarchism! In Nibert, D. (ed.), *Animal Oppression and Capitalism: The Oppressive and Destructive Role of Capitalism* (Santa Barbara, CA: Praeger), Vol. 2, pp. 270–293.

——. (2017b). Animal Geographies, Anarchist Praxis, and Critical Animal Studies. In Gillespie, K. & Collard, R. (eds.), *Critical Animal Geographies: Politics, Intersections, and Hierarchies in a Multispecies World* (New York: Routledge), pp. 19–35.

——. (2018). Looking Backward/Moving Forward: Articulating a "Yes, BUT . . . !" Response to Lifestyle Veganism, and Outlining Post-Capitalist Futures in Critical Veganic Agriculture. *EuropeNow* (20).

White, R. & Cudworth, E. (2014). Taking It to the Streets: Challenging Systems of Domination from Below. In Nocella II, A., Sorenson, J., Socha, K., et al. (eds.), *Defining Critical Animal Studies: An Intersectional Social Justice Approach for Liberation* (New York: Peter Lang), pp. 202–220.

White, R. & Springer, S. (2018). For Spatial Emancipation in Critical Animal Studies. In Matsuoka, A. & Sorenson, J. (eds.), *Critical Animal Studies: Towards Trans-Species Social Justice* (Lanham, MD: Rowman & Littlefield), pp. 160–183.

——. & ——. (2018). Making Space for Anarchist Geographies in Critical Animal Studies. In Matsuoka, A. & Sorenson, J. (eds.), *Critical Animal Studies: Towards Trans-Species Social Justice* (Lanham, MD: Rowman & Littlefield).

White, R., Springer, S., & De Souza, M. (eds.) (2016). *The Practice of Freedom: Anarchism, Geography and the Spirit of Revolt* (Lanham, MD: Rowman & Littlefield).

Whitehead, H. & Rendell, L. (2014). *The Cultural Lives of Whales and Dolphins* (Chicago: University of Chicago).

Whiten, A. (2011). The Scope of Culture in Chimpanzees, Humans and Ancestral Apes. *Philosophical Transactions of the Royal Society B: Biological Sciences* 366(1567): 997–1007.

Wilbert, C. (2000). *Anti*-This – *Against-That*: Resistances along a Human–Non-Human Axis. In Sharp, J., Paddison, R., Philol, C., et al. (eds.), *Entanglements of Power: Geographies of Domination/Resistance* (New York: Routledge), pp. 238–255.

Wilcox, S. & Rutherford, S. (eds.) (2018). *Historical Animal Geographies* (New York: Routledge).

Wilkie, R. (2013). Multispecies Scholarship and Encounters: Changing Assumptions at the Human–Animal Nexus. *Sociology* 49(2): 323–339.

Willems-Braun, B. (1997). Buried Epistemologies: The Politics of Nature in (Post)Colonial British Columbia. *Annals of the Association of American Geographers* 87: 3–31.

Willett, W., Rockström, J., Loken, B., et al. (2019). Food in the Anthropocene: The EAT–Lancet Commission on Healthy Diets from Sustainable Food Systems. *The Lancet* 393(10170): 447–492.

Willick, F. (2017). "They Ain't Hurtin' Nobody": Kentville Man Told to Get Rid of Pet Pigs. *CBC News Nova Scotia*, July 27, http://www.cbc.ca/news/canada/nova-scotia/vietnamese-pot-bellied-pigs-kentville-bylaw-1.4217640.

Winter, D. (2015). Doing Liberation: The Story and Strategy of Food Not Bombs. In Nocella II, A., White, R. & Cudworth, E. (eds.), *Anarchism and Animal Liberation: Essays on Complementary Elements of Total Liberation* (Jefferson, NC: McFarland), pp. 59–70.

Wolch, J. & Emel, J. (1996). Preface. In Wolch, J. & Emel, J. (eds.), *Animal Geographies: Place, Politics, and Identity in the Nature–Culture Borderlands* (New York: Verso), pp. ix–xx.

——. & ——. (eds.) (1995). Bringing the Animals Back In. *Environment and Planning D: Society and Space* 13: 631–760.

——. & ——. (eds.) (1998). *Animal Geographies: Place, Politics, and Identity in the Nature–Culture Borderlands* (New York: Verso).

Wolfe, C. (2010). *What Is Posthumanism?* (Minneapolis, MN: University of Minnesota).

Wolfe, P. (2006). Settler Colonialism and the Elimination of the Native. *Journal of Genocide Research* 8(4): 387–409.

Wolfson, D. (1999). McLibel. *Animal Law* 5: 21–60.

World Ocean Review (2010). World Ocean Review 1: Living with the Oceans – A Report on the State of the World's Oceans, https://worldoceanreview.com/en/wor-1/fisheries/.

Wrenn, C. (2013). Resonance of Moral Shocks in Abolitionist Animal Rights Advocacy: Overcoming Contextual Constraints. *Society & Animals* 21(4): 379–394.

——. (2014). Abolition Then and Now. *Journal of Agricultural and Environmental Ethics* 27(2): 177–200.

——. (2016). An Analysis of Diversity in Nonhuman Animal Rights Media. *Journal of Agricultural and Environmental Ethics* 29(2): 143–165.

Xu, Z., Sun, D., Zeng, X., et al. (2015). Research Developments in Methods to Reduce the Carbon Footprint of the Food System: A Review. *Critical Reviews in Food Science and Nutrition* 55(9): 1270–1286, https://doi.org/10.1080/10408398.2013.821593.

Yancy, G. (2005). Whiteness and the Return of the Black Body. *Journal of Speculative Philosophy* 19(4): 215–241.

Yandaarra (2017). What Does the Representation Mean for Us? (Unpublished Document), https://www.jalilgin.com.au/wp content/uploads/Yandaarra-Representation-what-does-it-mean.pdf.

Yarwood, R. & Evans, N. (2000). Taking Stock of Farm Animals and Rurality. In Philol, C. & Wilbert, C. (eds.), *Animal Spaces, Beastly Places* (New York: Routledge), pp. 99–116.

Yates, L. (2015). Rethinking Prefiguration: Alternatives, Micropolitics and Goals in Social Movements. *Social Movement Studies* 14(1): 1–21.

Yates, R. (2017). The Business of Revolution Is Counter-Revolutionary. In Nibert, D. (ed.), *Animal Oppression and Capitalism: The Oppressive and Destructive Role of Capitalism* (Santa Barbara, CA: Praeger), Vol. 2, pp. 295–312.

Zappino, F. (2015). Norma Sacrificale/Norma Eterosessuale. In Filippi, M. & Reggio, M. (eds.), *Corpi Che Non Contano: Judith Butler e Gli Animali* (Milano: Mimesis), pp. 75–90.

Zaraska, M. (2016). This Is Why You Crave Beef: Inside Secrets of Big Meat's Billion-Dollar Ad and Lobbying Campaigns. *The Salon*, April 3, https://www.salon.com/2016/04/03/this_is_why_you_crave_beef_inside_secrets_of_big_meats_billion_dollar_ad_and_lobbying_campaigns/.

CONTRIBUTORS

Darren Chang is a PhD student in the Department of Sociology and Social Policy at the University of Sydney, and a member of the Multispecies Justice collective at the Sydney Environment Institute. His research interests broadly include interspecies relations under colonialism and global capitalism, practices of solidarity and mutual aid across species in challenging oppressive powers, and social movement theories. Darren's current research (co-supervised by Danielle Celermajer and Dinesh Wadiwel) explores how animal sanctuaries could be generative sites for the emergence of solidarity between animal liberation and decolonization, and for prefiguring just multispecies relations.

David Fazzino is an Associate Professor of Anthropology at Bloomsburg University of Pennsylvania. His primary research interests include food, health, and wellbeing. He has an academic background in cultural anthropology, sustainable agriculture, complementary and alternative medicine, and law. His work explores power and agency with an emphasis on human and nonhuman potential and violence. Additional experience includes work in retail, restaurants, factories, cultural and biological preservation management, trauma-informed yoga, massage therapy, Zen Shiatsu, and as a soccer referee. He prefers non-motorized recreational, pursuits including long-distance cycling and short walks with his partner, Ashley, and Amme the Cat.

Dr. Hannah Gunderman (uses any pronouns) is a Data, Gaming, and Popular Culture Librarian at Carnegie Mellon University, Pennsylvania, U.S. She received her PhD in Geography with a concentration in Cultural Geography and Popular Culture from the University of Tennessee-Knoxville in 2018, and also holds a BS and MA in Geography and an MS in Information Sciences. Her research specialties include framing data management techniques for humanities and popular culture research, exploring the impact of science fiction and video game fandom on human mobilities and emotions, vegan geographies, and various broader studies in cultural geography.

Paul Hodge is a non-Indigenous person of the unceded lands now known as Australia. He was born on Kamilaroi Country, Tamworth, and spent most of his early life on Worimi Country, Nelson Bay, just north of Muloobinba, Newcastle, the land of the Awabakal and Worimi Nations. He now lives and works on Awabakal,

Worimi, and Gumbaynggirr Countries. He is Senior Lecturer in Geography & Environmental Studies at the University of Newcastle. His research centers people and place in ways that foreground more-than-human relationality. This involves being led by Country and custodians of this land to nourish and support intergenerational and multi-temporal ways of being, knowing, and doing in highly colonized, semi-urban contexts.

Jérôme Lafitte has a PhD in Education. He is a lecturer at the University of Tours, attached to the research team EA7505 "Education, Ethics, Health" (EES). His teaching is more specifically focused on environmental adult education. From a geographical and formative point of view, he is interested in the place and role played by ecoformative and environmental temporalities in the shared inhabitation of humanimal societies, considering socio-ecological issues. In this perspective, he pays attention to the relationship to environmental knowledge and more specifically to the dialogical dynamics between territorial actors.

Dr. Alex Lockwood is a novelist, creative writer, and scholar working at the intersection of animals, activism, and narrative theory. His 2016 memoir *The Pig in Thin Air* explored paths to connect climate change with the animals we eat. His 2019 novel *The Chernobyl Privileges*, shortlisted for the Rubery International Prize, took on the psychological legacy of environmental disaster. His work has appeared in *The Vegan Studies Handbook, Beyond the Creaturely Divide, Through a Vegan Studies Lens*, as well as articles in *Environmental Communication, Environmental Humanities*, and *Animal Studies Journal*.

Nicolas Maestripieri has a PhD in Environmental Geography (University of Toulouse). He has studied the dynamics of industrial forest plantations and native forests in southern Chile. The use of spatial modeling has enabled him to develop prospective spatialized scenarios. He has also worked in other fields (Ecuador, Laos, Tunisia) to understand the perception of local populations using the PBRM (perception-based regional mapping) method. He is a research engineer in an SME and an independent researcher. His research interest is to understand the relationship between society (from individual behavior to public policies) and the environment.

Andrew McGregor is an Associate Professor of Geography and Director of Research in the School of Social Sciences at Macquarie University. He is author of *Southeast Asian Development* (Routledge, 2008) and lead editor of *The Routledge Handbook of Southeast Asian Development* (2018). His research focuses on just transitions and climate mitigation strategies within food and forestry sectors in Indonesia and Australia. He is a former committee member of the New South Wales Vegan Society.

Dr. Jennifer Mateer is a limited-term Assistant Teaching Professor in the Department of Geography at the University of Victoria, Canada. She is also a SSHRC-funded postdoctoral research fellow at the University of British Columbia, Canada. Her research focuses on the intersections of environmental justice, political ecology, animal geographies, and participatory action research. These projects have allowed Jennifer to live and work across Turtle Island (Canada, the U.S., and Mexico) as well as India and Rwanda.

Dr. Catherine Oliver is a postdoctoral researcher, currently working on the ERC-funded project Urban Ecologies at the University of Cambridge. Her current research with backyard chickens and chicken keepers in London asks how we can rethink the city from beyond-human perspectives. Her first monograph, *Veganism, Animals, and Archives* was published with Routledge in 2021. Catherine is also a Royal Geographical Society Wiley Digital Archives Fellow, exploring their archives for stories of animal collaboration, labor, and conflict. Catherine's wider research in feminist geographies explores "dis-belonging" and the reproduction of neoliberal hierarchies in academia. She can be found on twitter at @katiecmoliver.

Marco Reggio is an activist for animal liberation, member of the collective "Resistenza Animale" (resistenzanimale.noblogs.org) and independent researcher. He is co-editor of the Italian editions of Rasmus Simonsen, *A Queer Vegan Manifesto* (2014); of Sarat Colling, *Animals Without Borders* (2017); of Sunaura Taylor, *Beasts of Burden* (2021); of the anthologies *Corpi che non contano—Bodies that Don't Matter,* with an interview with Judith Butler (2015); and *Smontare la gabbia—Dismantling the Cage* (2019). He is the author of *Antispecismo politico: Pratiche e teorie intersezionali—Political Antispeciesism: Intersectional Practices and Theories* (2022).

Mona Seymour is an Associate Professor of Urban and Environmental Studies at Loyola Marymount University in Los Angeles, CA, U.S. She is broadly interested in the ways in which veganism, animal rights, and anti-speciesism appear in agrifood movements. Her research has more narrowly focused on veganic farming in the United States, particularly in terms of the values, experiences, and farming practices of U.S. veganic growers. She also maintains an online map of North American veganic farms in order to support connections between growers.

Simon Springer is Professor of Human Geography, Head of Discipline for Geography and Environmental Studies, and Director of the Centre for Urban and Regional Studies at the University of Newcastle, Australia. He is editor of *Undoing Human Supremacy, Inhabiting the Earth*, and *Energies Beyond the State*, a recent trilogy of books focusing on anarchist political ecology. Most importantly he is a husband, father, brother, and son to an amazing family.

Zoei Sutton is a sociologist pursuing critical, nonhuman animal-centric research. She is a research fellow in the Climate and Sustainability Policy Research Group at Flinders University where she contributes to evidence-based, multidisciplinary work to support policymakers and practitioners responding to rapid social and environmental change. She is also the co-founder of the International Association for Vegan Sociologists (IAVS), co-created and co-convenes the Australian Sociological Association's (TASA) Sociology & Animals thematic group, and is a member of the Institute for Critical Animal Studies (ICAS) Oceania collective. She currently serves as a Book Review Editor for *Society & Animals* and is an affiliate of the New Zealand Centre for Human Animal Studies (NZCHAS). She can be found on twitter, @zoei_sutton, and more about her work is available here: https://www.flinders.edu.au/people/zoei.sutton.

Dr. Nik Taylor is a critical and public sociologist whose research focuses on mechanisms of power and marginalization expressed in/through human relations with other species and is informed by critical/intersectional feminism. Nik is currently Co-Director of the New Zealand Centre for Human–Animal Studies at the University of Canterbury where she also teaches topics that focus on human–animal violence links; scholar-advocacy; social change; and crime and deviance, particularly domestic violence and animal abuse. Nik's latest books include *Queer Entanglements: Intersections of Gender, Sexuality and Animal Companionship* (Cambridge University Press, with Damien Riggs, Heather Fraser and Shoshana Rosenberg) and *Rescuing Me, Rescuing You: Companion Animals and Domestic Violence* (Palgrave, 2019, with Heather Fraser).

Ophélie Véron is a Leverhulme Early Career Research Fellow in Geography at The University of Sheffield. She is also affiliated with the Marc Bloch Centre, Berlin, and with the Center for Metropolitan Studies (TU Berlin), which she will join as a Marie Skłodowska-Curie fellow in Spring 2022. A former student of the École Normale Supérieure of Paris and the University of Oxford, she obtained her PhD degree in Geography at University College London in 2015. Ophélie's research to date has engaged with a range of interweaving themes, including socio-ecological transformation and social justice, urban social movements, anarchist geographies, and vegan geographies.

Richard J. White is a no-dig allotmenteer, and Reader in Human Geography at Sheffield Hallam University, U.K. Greatly influenced by anarchist praxis, his work explores a range of ethical, economic, and activist landscapes rooted in questions of social and spatial justice. He has contributed to several key edited collections, including *A Research Agenda for Animal Geographies* (2021); *A Historical Scholarly Collection of Writings on the Earth Liberation Front* (2019); and *Education for Total Liberation* (2019); and is the co-editor of *The Radicalization of Pedagogy* (2016); *Theories of Resistance* (2016); *The Practice of Freedom* (2016); and *Anarchism and Animal Liberation* (2015).

Yandaarra with Gumbaynggirr Country includes Aunty Shaa Smith, storyholder for Gumbaynggirr Country; her daughter Neeyan Smith, a Gumbaynggirr woman and future Elder; and three non-Gumbaynggirr academics: Lara Daley, Sarah Wright, and Paul Hodge from the University of Newcastle. We come together as Yandaarra, a research collective guided by Country, the Old Fullas (ancestors), Elders, and Aunty Shaa. *Yandaarra* means to "shift camp together" in Gumbaynggirr language. It is both what we are called and what we are doing as we walk this re-creation story from our different places as Elders, Custodians, and guests of Country, learning to come into proper relationship with Country, each other, and ourselves. Aunty Shaa and Neeyan's website is https://www.gumbaynggirrjagun.org.

INDEX

ABOUT THE PUBLISHER

LANTERN PUBLISHING & MEDIA was founded in 2020 to follow and expand on the legacy of Lantern Books—a publishing company started in 1999 on the principles of living with a greater depth and commitment to the preservation of the natural world. Like its predecessor, Lantern Publishing & Media produces books on animal advocacy, veganism, religion, social justice, humane education, psychology, family therapy, and recovery. Lantern is dedicated to printing in the United States on recycled paper and saving resources in our day-to-day operations. Our titles are also available as e-books and audiobooks.

To catch up on Lantern's publishing program, visit us at www.lanternpm.org.

facebook.com/lanternpm
twitter.com/lanternpm
instagram.com/lanternpm